In his former career Roy Williams was a killer litigator at one of the country's largest law firms. Forced to leave the law as a result of a life-changing illness, he now writes full-time. His books, *God, Actually* and *In God They Trust?*, have won accolades from people as diverse as Annabel Crabb, Kim Beazley and Tim Costello. Roy is a regular writer for *The Australian* and several other publications and a regular guest on ABC Radio and Television. He lives in Sydney.

# POST GOD NATION?

## ROY WILLIAMS

ABC
Books

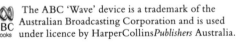 The ABC 'Wave' device is a trademark of the Australian Broadcasting Corporation and is used under licence by HarperCollins*Publishers* Australia.

First published in Australia in 2015
by HarperCollins*Publishers* Australia Pty Limited
ABN 36 009 913 517
harpercollins.com.au

**HarperCollins*Publishers***
Level 13, 201 Elizabeth Street, Sydney, NSW 2000, Australia
Unit D1, 63 Apollo Drive, Rosedale, Auckland 0632, New Zealand
A 53, Sector 57, Noida, UP, India
1 London Bridge Street, London, SE1 9GF, United Kingdom
2 Bloor Street East, 20th floor, Toronto, Ontario M4W 1A8, Canada
195 Broadway, New York, NY 10007, USA

National Library of Australia Cataloguing-in-Publication data:

Williams, Roy Thomas, 1963- author.
  Post-God nation / Roy Williams.
  978 0 7333 3358 3 (paperback)
  978 1 4607 0332 8 (ebook)
  Church renewal – Australia.
  Faith development.
  Religious awakening – Christianity.
  Trust in God – Christianity.
  Christianity – Forecasting.
  Australia – Religious aspects – Christianity.
262.0017

Cover design by Darren Holt, HarperCollins Design Studio
Cover image: Woodcut for 'Die Bibel in Bildern', 1860,
by Julius Schnorr von Carolsfeld
Typeset in Baskerville MT by Kirby Jones
Printed and bound in Australia by Griffin Press
The papers used by HarperCollins in the manufacture of this book are a natural, recyclable product made from wood grown in sustainable plantation forests. The fibre source and manufacturing processes meet recognised international environmental standards, and carry certification.

I suppose what I am increasingly intent on trying to do in my books is to give professed unbelievers glimpses of their own unprofessed faith.

Patrick White

For Sally, with love

# CONTENTS

# Post-God nation?

The Australian has not made up his mind about religion.

Ernest Henry Burgmann
Anglican Bishop of Canberra and Goulburn, 1934-60

Our hearts are restless, until they rest in You.

St Augustine of Hippo

In January 2014 a Victorian senator from the Australian Greens, Richard di Natale, issued a media release that had many people talking. It concerned the saying of the Lord's Prayer at the start of each sitting day in the House of Representatives and the Senate. In Senator di Natale's view, this practice – instituted in the year of Federation, 1901 – was 'jarring'. It had become an anachronism.

In several respects the episode was emblematic of modern-day Australia. Di Natale – a lapsed Catholic – was in deadly earnest. 'We are here to represent everybody,' he explained, 'people of all religious faiths [and] people who don't have a strong religious faith.'[1] So much was incontestable. But his unstated assumption (shared, one presumes, by his Green colleagues in caucus) was that the use of the Lord's Prayer in parliament was an example of religion intruding inappropriately into public life. Australians should be offended by it.

Di Natale's trial balloon fell to earth. Although we live in 'Christophobic times',[2] there are still significant numbers of practising Christians in both the Coalition and Labor caucuses and neither side of politics seemed inclined to rock the boat. The 'Christian vote', though far from monolithic, remains one to be courted. A few conservatives took the chance to denigrate the Greens, and *The Australian* observed in an editorial that the practice of saying the Lord's Prayer was 'not the imposition of a narrow religious code but rather a continuing thread of responsibility and respect for the burden of democratic decision-making'.[3] Christians wrote letters to newspapers along similar lines, roughly balancing out those who wrote in support of Senator di Natale's proposal.

It is often said that Australia – like many prosperous nations across the West – has entered a 'post-Christian' era. Indeed, this is assumed to have happened some decades ago. Historian Ian Turner, writing in 1968, asserted confidently that 'the Australian dream is ... a worldly dream. Its concern has been the natural and social environment rather than the hope of a life to come'.[4] Twenty years later, Manning Clark declared in *The Bulletin*'s Bicentenary issue that we were 'a nation of unbelievers, a people who have liberated themselves from the Judaic-Christian myth'.[5] (The same issue contained a wistful article by a young journalist named Tony Abbott, entitled 'The rise and fall of Anglo-Australia'.)

I suspect that Australia's most famous historian was writing more in sorrow than in anger. The son of an Anglican clergyman, Clark wrestled with faith all his life. He believed that an understanding of religion was crucial to a proper understanding of Australian history. His grand thesis was that Australia was forged in the furnace of an essentially metaphysical conflict between three visions of God and man: Catholicism, (British) Protestantism and the values of the Enlightenment.[6] Implicitly there was a fourth: Aboriginal spirituality. For Clark, irreligion was the end-point of Australian history, but certainly not the starting-point.

A few modern-day secular historians have taken Clark's point. There is a telling passage in Mark Peel and Christina Twomey's *History of Australia* (2011) in which the authors observe that 'among the baggage nineteenth-century migrants carried across the sea, there were few more significant items than their faith'. Why? Because this was 'an age when denomination was not simply about doctrine but shaped belief and behaviour'.[7] A person of faith might well deprecate Peel and Twomey's tone and terminology while agreeing with the thrust of their argument. Religion *mattered* for the simple reason that faith is a key determinant of personal conduct in all fields of life.

Likewise, while disagreeing with his overall thesis, one can respect a commentator such as Warren Bonett, the editor of a book of essays published in 2010 under the title *The Australian Book of Atheism*. Unlike some of his contributors, Bonett was at least beginning from a correct premise. As he put it, the book was an attempt to counter the prevailing opinion among his unbelieving friends and acquaintances that 'Australia was largely uninfluenced by religion in most ways that mattered'.[8] In Bonett's view, Australia *has* been so influenced – for the worse.

Like many Australians of faith, I am sick of being told that religion's influence upon our country has been either minimal or malign. It is a fact of history that Australia would not exist in anything like the form it does but for Judaeo-Christianity. Deep-seated legacies of our religious heritage still endure, and will continue to do so for the foreseeable future: 'we are … secular in a Christian sort of way'.[9] Moreover, there remain signs that a good many people are still involved in a search for meaning. They yearn for that indescribable something beyond the here and now, the spiritual essence that informs authenticity, creativity, vitality and love.

Any non-Indigenous Australian who would wish away our religious heritage is either insufficiently informed or plain dishonest. That is not to deny that some aspects of our history are regrettable, even shameful. But let us all base our opinions on true facts.

At the outset I had better face up squarely to one incontrovertible fact. At first glance it might seem to contradict my thesis.

New South Wales was founded as a dumping ground for convicts. After the loss of the North American colonies in 1776, England's gaols and hulks – old ships, used after 1777 to house convicted criminals – had become hopelessly overcrowded and the powers that be needed somewhere to put the 'dregs' of society. Other factors might have been in the mix – a new colony in the South Seas would bolster Britain's empire after the loss of North America, and it was hoped that Norfolk Island might be a source of flax for sails and cordage on naval ships.[10] But the main reason was sheer convenience. Transportation of unwanted convicts to the other side of world would relieve a pressing political problem at relatively low cost. The choice of Botany Bay was made in August 1786 by the Colonial Secretary, Viscount Sydney (Thomas Townshend), with the approval of the Prime Minister of the day, William Pitt the Younger.[11]

So much is notorious. It is far less well known that prominent Christians in England were agitating for a much more humane and far-reaching solution – prison reform. If they had won the argument, we would not be here.

It follows that all Australians must be thankful Christianity was not an even stronger force than it was in late eighteenth-century Britain. In one vital respect, our collective debt to Judaeo-Christianity is a debt to the *failure* – at a particular juncture in history – of some of its most noble adherents. I mention this partly in the interests of balance, but also to challenge a prevalent modern myth: that Enlightenment values or free-market values are inherently superior to religious values.

The stress on Britain's criminal justice system by 1786 had been brought about by a perfect storm of interrelated factors. Over many generations, technological advances in farming and ruthless conduct by wealthy landowners had forced agrarian workers and their families off feudal lands. The result of this process – 'enclosure', the fencing off of private property previously occupied by poor tenants* – was urban overcrowding, unemployment, and hunger and want on a massive scale. Inevitably, crime rates soared. Indeed, crimes against property – mainly petty theft – became 'a cottage industry, a jumble of individual acts of desperation'.[12] In London, by the late eighteenth century, perhaps as many as one person in eight was living off the proceeds of crime.[13] There was as yet no proper police force, so most crime went unpunished, and the response of the British Parliament was to make cruel examples of the relatively few offenders who were caught. It legislated a huge increase in the number of offences punishable by death. By 1780 around 200 such offences were on the books, and the poor were disproportionately prosecuted and convicted. Many were women and children.[14]

To their eternal credit, Christian judges and juries had become increasingly reluctant to impose the death penalty. And even when it had been imposed, local authorities were reluctant to enforce it. (It is sobering to recall that around a third of the convicts on the First Fleet had originally been sentenced to death, some for extraordinarily minor crimes, such as stealing clothing or a meal of bacon and bread.) But this meant that increasing numbers of convicts needed to be put somewhere. What was to be done? The choices boiled down to two.

For three decades or more there had been calls in Britain for wholesale improvement of the prison system. The existing arrangements

---

* The process had begun in the fifteenth century. Very generally speaking, at least in the early stages, the Crown and the aristocracy supported enclosure (on the grounds of economic efficiency and respect for rights of private property) while the Church and the common people opposed it (on the grounds of social dislocation and injustice). The first recorded written complaint against enclosure was made by a Warwickshire priest, John Rous, in his *History of the Kings of England* (1459–86). Thomas More, Henry VIII's martyred Lord Chancellor, addressed the issue squarely in *Utopia* (1516). Money and secular power ultimately won out.

were a disgrace. There were too few gaols and those that existed were managed by private concerns, interested only in profit and largely unregulated by the State. The facilities were ramshackle and insecure, the staff badly trained, the diet and hygiene of prisoners atrocious. What is more, prisoners were expected to pay for the privilege of being gaoled. Many were denied release at the end of their terms if they could not pay the fees.

Then – as now – there were few votes to be won by showing mercy to criminals. It is therefore very important to remember that the first – and greatest – proponent of prison reform in Britain was an Evangelical Christian, John Howard (1726–90). The son of a wealthy upholsterer, Howard had been briefly incarcerated in France in 1755 and later became the High Sheriff of Bedfordshire. Appalled by the conditions he found in the local gaol, he undertook a general study of the prison system and in 1777 published a monumental book, *The State of Prisons in England and Wales*.[15] Howard made recommendations for wholesale change along lines which now seem remarkably modern: properly constructed and ventilated buildings; segregation of the sexes; reasonable food and clothing; medical resources; a chaplaincy service; work and leisure activities to combat the sin of idleness.[16] In 1779 parliament passed the Penitentiary Act, but it became a dead letter.

Unlike utilitarians such as Jeremy Bentham, who came later to the cause and whose primary focus was efficiency, John Howard and his supporters were actuated by *morality*. Howard was a Calvinist who drew strength from the life and teachings of John Wesley, the great Methodist reformer. There are statues of both men (Howard and Wesley) in the grounds of London's St Paul's Cathedral.

For Wesley, prison reform had been an important cause since 1759. In that year he had walked to the town of Knowle, near Bristol, to visit a company of French prisoners of the Seven Years' War. 'About 1,100 of them,' he later wrote,[17] 'were confined in that little place, without anything to lie on but a little dirty straw, or anything to cover them but a few foul, thin rags, either by day or night ... I was much affected and preached in the evening on "Thou shalt not oppress a stranger; for ye know the heart of a stranger, seeing ye were strangers in the land of Egypt"' (Exodus 23:9 (KJV)).

Another Christian champion of prison reform was William Wilberforce (1759–1833). Many Australians have heard of him in connection with the abolition of slavery, but few, I suspect, know much else about him. In fact he played a vital behind-the-scenes role in our history. Of a wealthy Yorkshire family, he was elected to the House of Commons at the age of twenty-one and gained a reputation as a dandy. But in 1784–85 he spent several months in Europe in the company of a man named Isaac Milner. Milner had been a fellow of Queens' College at Cambridge in Wilberforce's first year at the university. He was an Evangelical Anglican of exceptional charisma, and, partly as result of his influence, Wilberforce underwent a profound conversion experience. He moved from nominal Anglicanism to 'serious religion' and undertook to dedicate the rest of his political career to worthy Christian causes.[18]

Prison reform was one of them. Wilberforce was a friend of the Prime Minister, William Pitt the Younger, and in the first half of 1786 he pressed his friend repeatedly on this issue. But Pitt obfuscated. A nominal Christian, he was in the more pragmatic High Anglican tradition.* He was also a canny politician. Ultimately he fobbed Wilberforce off in a letter ('the multitude of things depending, has made the Penitentiary House long in deciding upon. But I still think a beginning will be made on it [soon]'[19]) and opted to endorse Viscount Sydney's plan for New South Wales.

So – does this sound familiar? – practical politics and penny-pinching won out. As for prison reform, the visionary Christian idealism of Wilberforce, Wesley and Howard eventually held sway. But that did not happen for decades. By then, the Australian penal colonies were up and running.

In the nineteenth-century Australian colonies no one needed to defend the proposition that religion mattered. It was a given. There were plenty of critics of the Churches and of individual clerics – leading public figures such as the great explorer, author and statesman William Charles Wentworth, were often scathing in their commentary. But matters spiritual and ecclesiastical were never far from the top of the agenda. Virtually all the key chroniclers and historians of the period were practising Christians, giants of their day such as James Bonwick, George William Rusden and Charles Pearson; many, indeed, were office-holders in their churches. So too were most of the early newspaper proprietors and journalists.

The founder of the *Sydney Morning Herald*, John Fairfax (1804–77), was a deacon of the Congregationalist church in Pitt Street who attended up

---

* For a full explanation of the differences between the 'High Anglicans' and the 'Evangelicals', see Chapter 3.

to four services on a Sunday. His personal motto was 'Let him be a true servant of Christ and God will not suffer his life to be a failure.'[20] Four of the *Herald*'s first five editors were ministers of religion: John McGarvie (Presbyterian, 1831–40), Ralph Mansfield (Methodist, 1840–54), John West (Congregationalist, 1854–73), and William Curnow (Methodist, 1886–1903).[21] This was not, at the time, especially unusual.

To put it mildly, things have changed. The Fairfax media group – with honourable individual exceptions – is now one of the leading voices of Christophobia in Australia. Look on any given day at the opinion and letters pages of the *Sydney Morning Herald* or *The Age* in Melbourne. If religion is not ignored altogether, it is frequently treated with contempt. This annoys me more than it does most Fairfax readers, I suspect, because on issues other than religion I am often in agreement with its editorialists and leader-writers. On the other hand, while I often disagree with the slant of the Murdoch press, *The Australian* continues to display at least a formal respect for religion and the Churches.

A decade ago the legal historian Helen Irving wrote a piece for the *Sydney Morning Herald* that has stayed with me for its sheer dismissiveness. Basing her case on arguments about the drafting of the Constitution, she rejected the idea that our highest values are rooted in the Christian faith and that our founding fathers were conscious of the fact. For her, that idea was not merely wrong – Australia, she asserted, has a 'secular heritage' – but offensive.[22] Few historians and social commentators have gone as far as that. Among opinion-leaders in this country, the drift away from religion has been a slow, subtle process. Increasingly there has been a tendency to ignore, or at least downplay, the influence of religion on wider Australian life. Eloquent secular-humanist voices began to make themselves heard way back in the nineteenth century but, among what might be called the mainstream, the pattern was set by two prominent historians of the first half of the twentieth century: Ernest Scott and W.K. (Keith) Hancock. Scott was an unbeliever and Hancock, though the son of an archdeacon, emphasised economic themes.

As time went on, more historians began to nail their anti-religious colours to the mast. They have come mainly, but not exclusively, from the Left. Some have revelled in typecasting religious figures as irredeemable villains – the Reverend Samuel Marsden, for example, or B.A. Santamaria, or many of the Christian missionaries. They have also tried valiantly to make secular heroes of people like James Cook and Arthur Phillip and John Curtin. In *Australia Since the Coming of Man* (1982), the redoubtable Marxist historian Russel Ward was at least honest about his biases: 'I believe that reason has done more for mankind than religion.'[23]

Even some overtly Christian thinkers have argued that the influence of their faith on their country has been, if not totally marginal, then relatively insignificant. Patrick O'Farrell, an eminent chronicler of Catholicism in Australia, lamented the 'decline and disarray' of Christianity from the very start of colonisation.[24] Psychologist Ronald Conway, in *The Great Australian Stupor* (1971), contended that 'there is no evidence that religious faith has ever been deeply and practically professed by more than a small minority of Australians'.[25] More recently, the former Anglican bishop Tom Frame published an entire book on the subject, *Losing My Religion: Unbelief in Australia* (2009).[26] His broad conclusions were in line with those of O'Farrell and Conway. Dolefully, it seemed to me, he downplayed the influence of Christianity, not only in the modern era but at all times since 1788. He doubted its chances of flourishing here in the future.

In my opinion, Frame and others like him[27] are too pessimistic. But there is no doubting the stiff challenge that religion faces. Among a growing and influential section of the community, various factors are often put forward as self-evidently disqualifying Christianity (and Islam) from serious consideration – not merely as a personal belief system but even as a positive influence in our history. While these factors are not, in my view, the most important in secularisation, they appear to resonate with many people. Consider the following passage from an article in the *Sydney Morning Herald* in November 2013 by journalist Elizabeth Farrelly:

> I do understand my friends' dislike. For many, Christianity has over the centuries – arguably since Paul – come to represent the very worst aspects of white patriarchal Western culture. Arrogant, sexist, racist and monomaniacal, even while preaching humility, tolerance and love, it seems to compound all these sins with hypocrisy. It represents every aspect of establishment the boomers want to shed.[28]

Although Farrelly is a feminist progressive, she has found herself irresistibly drawn to the Anglican Church by a 'hunger for spiritual meaning'. She attributed her friends' hostility to two misconceptions: 'that fundamentalism and religion are identical and that history presupposes conservatism'. In essence, her friends equated Christianity with sexism, racism and all things Neanderthal. They are ingrained preconceptions that I shall challenge in this book.

*

Of one thing there can be little doubt: religious belief in Australia is at its lowest ever level. In a census conducted in 1828 – the first in New South Wales – not a single person out of a population of 36,598 identified as an atheist.[29] Of course, many people in 1828 were not regular churchgoers and, for some, faith probably played little part in their lives. But there is plenty of revealing evidence about individual believers in all of the three main 'classes' of colonial society – the military, convicts and free settlers. The census result of 1828 shows, if nothing else, that religious belief was the accepted norm.

It was the same in 1901, the year of Federation. In the census of that year, some 96 per cent of respondents identified as Christian. Moreover, around half of all adult citizens attended church services on a regular basis; in two States (Victoria and South Australia) it was closer to three-quarters.[30] By comparison, in the 2011 census, only 61 per cent of respondents identified as even nominally Christian. Some 22 per cent (a record high) specified that they had 'no religion', and another 8.6 per cent left the question about religion unanswered. Other market research paints an even grimmer picture: in responses to one survey in late 2013, only 53 per cent described themselves as Christian and a full 38 per cent as having no religion.[31] Only about 8 per cent of Australians regularly attend services of worship – more than in Scandinavia, and about the same as in Britain and France, but considerably less than in Canada or the United States.[32]

Religion in Australia is no longer *socially* significant. True, the Churches remain weighty institutions: they own a great deal of property and continue to enjoy substantial monetary support from governments in the form of exemptions from taxation and funding of their schools (the so-called 'purple economy', castigated by secularist Max Wallace in his 2007 book of that title). But most Australians show scant interest in the Churches' opinions and activities. There is now little or no stigma attached to being known, publicly, as an unbeliever – let alone as someone who does not regularly attend church. For some contemporary theorists of secularisation, this is the key test of a nation's religious health. It matters even more than the proportion of people in the population who take religion seriously, or how seriously they take it. Religious communities must be self-reinforcing and self-reproducing.[33]

On the measure of social significance, it must be said that Australia is no longer a Judaeo-Christian country. Baptisms are the exception rather than the rule. The majority of weddings and funerals do not take place in church.[34] Few people attend services of worship even on occasions such as Easter and Christmas. Many church buildings are being sold because the congregations who used to occupy them are literally dying out. The buildings themselves, when not demolished by their new owners, are being converted to housing and other uses: bars, cafes, offices, design studios, theatres, art galleries, antiques markets and the like.[35]

Christianity seems to be perceived by more Australians than ever as implausible, undesirable or irrelevant. Religious literacy – working knowledge of the Bible, of the function of the Churches, even of basic ethics – is exceedingly shallow. It is difficult to imagine a repeat of the Billy Graham Crusade of February–May 1959, when around 3 million Australians attended events across the nation. And this was at a time when the total population of Australia was just 10 million, of which about a quarter was Catholic. (Billy Graham, of course, was a Protestant.) In Sydney alone, over the course of four weeks, some 57,000 souls converted to Christianity, or claimed they had. On Graham's last day in Sydney, in bad weather, 150,000 people crammed into the Sydney Showground at Moore Park and spilled over into the adjacent Sydney Cricket Ground.[36] Many now-elderly Australian Christians recall the day clearly (including my father-in-law). One prominent citizen who went along was a future prime minister, Gough Whitlam, then an up-and-coming federal Labor MP. Though a lapsed Anglican himself, he took his three sons to the showground to witness and participate in the grand event. His youngest son took home a free Gospel.[37] My own father reported the event for the *Sydney Morning Herald*.

Since 1959 the number of outspoken atheists has risen exponentially. One of the most prominent, Phillip Adams, published his first book on the subject in 1985, a collection of essays entitled *Adams versus God*. In the 2007 edition, Adams remarked on the change he had noticed in Australian society since the 1960s. Then, 'the atheist was as lonely a figure as the Biblical leper'. In 2007, 'all of a sudden atheism is fashionable'.[38]

Like Manning Clark, Adams is the son of a Protestant minister (in Adams' case, a Congregationalist). Perhaps partly for that reason, his brand of public atheism is unusual. He is well educated in theology, and, deep down, despite a propensity to indulge in clever satire, is respectful of the religious impulse. Too many atheists in the public square display neither trait. (Peter FitzSimons is an obvious local example, but there are plenty of others.) Their rhetoric is unfocused, uninformed and ungracious. Not a few of them seem almost hysterical. One can empathise with, if not endorse, the attitude of atheists like Thomas Wells: 'I don't see why I should care about the non-existence of gods ... Of course god doesn't exist. So what?'[39]

But atheism, passionate or dispassionate, remains a small minority creed in Australia. Far more prevalent is agnosticism, or – the term preferred by Tom Frame – 'unbelief'.[40] These are people who do not have a belief about God one way or the other. Few of them have agonised over the question of His existence, only to remain in genuine doubt. Most have never seriously turned their minds to the relevant issues; they have never been taught what the relevant issues are. As a result they are religiously tone-deaf. They lack any sense of the numinous and try to ignore their mortality. They struggle hopelessly with the language of grief. They could not care one way or the other whether the Lord's Prayer is recited in parliament.

Of course, religious faith is not solely, or even mainly, an external thing. It is possible to worship God without joining a church or otherwise displaying one's beliefs in public. An English sociologist of the 1940s coined the term 'believing but not belonging' to describe this phenomenon, and it is probable that, at least until the 1970s, the term was applicable to large numbers of Australians. The sociologist Hans Mol, one of Australia's most important twentieth-century writers on religion, called such people 'private believers' or 'believing secularists'.[41]

Are there still such people in Australia? As I have noted, in the 2011 census some 61 per cent of respondents identified as Christian. Another 0.5 per cent identified as Jewish. But there are sound reasons for believing that the figure for Christianity, while the lowest on record, may in fact be even lower. It is likely that many people's 'conforming side' prompted to them to respond as they did. Some may have harboured a vague notion that religion is 'a good thing', even if it is not for them.[42] Among older generations, nostalgia may also have played a part: for many of them, 'Christian' is little more than a respectable cultural label. For such people, in Hans Mol's assessment, 'belief in God is residual and certainly not strong enough to consistently make for self-denial and for altruism'.[43]

Among the shrinking cohort of nominal believers, another question looms large. In what, exactly, do they believe? In my observation, even among people who attend Christian churches on a regular basis, there is a reluctance to accept any one 'package' of Christian views as set out in the various Churches' creeds and statements of doctrine. (I have in mind the myriad issues surrounding Creation, Original Sin, Old Testament prophecy, the Virgin Birth, Christ's miracles, the Atonement, the Resurrection, the Trinity, the place of non-Christian religions, the 'test' of salvation, and the nature of Heaven and Hell.) Yet one must resist being too dogmatic. In the evocative words of Patrick O'Farrell, real history is often 'hidden away in the minds and hearts of ordinary men and women'.[44] It goes unrecorded. This is certainly true of much religious history. Many have made the point that little survives of the thoughts and beliefs of the people to whom all clerical activity is directed.[45] The point applies with extra force to laywomen, who often worship humbly and anonymously.

Making all possible allowances, and taking into account the limited survey evidence,[46] I would guess that of the 61 per cent of self-designated Christians in the 2011 census, only about a third hold an essentially Christian view of the world. By that I mean, at a minimum, belief in the following:

- An all-knowing God who created and sustains the Universe, and who is vitally interested in the thoughts and conduct of each individual human being
- An afterlife, in which each of us will be judged by God
- The divinity of Jesus of Nazareth.

Alert Christian purists may instantly object: this formulation is inadequate, even as a brief summary of Christianity. Indeed, it would encompass various heresies rejected in the fourth and fifth centuries.[47] This I concede. And at this stage I have not even attempted to grapple with the differences between, say, Protestantism and Catholicism. But 'Christian orthodoxy is a strange and wondrous thing, unknown to many scholars and to many conventional Christians'.[48] To require belief in any one package of orthodoxy, as a precondition to 'an essentially Christian view of the world', would disqualify, in my judgment, all but about 0.1 per cent of the Australian population – now or in any era. (For the record, my personal positions on most theological issues were laid out in *God, Actually*, a book of Christian apologetics published in 2008. As regards a few issues, I am now a somewhat more conventional Protestant than I was then.)

Some Christians would regard even my three criteria as excessively narrow. Take the second. There is sound evidence that, since the mid-twentieth century, a good many *churchgoers* in Australia have not believed in life after death, let alone in divine judgment.[49] This accords with similar evidence from Britain, both sociological and anecdotal. George Orwell once wrote that 'never, literally never in recent years, have I met anyone who gave me the impression of believing in the next world as firmly as he believed in the existence of, for instance, Australia'.[50]

Innermost beliefs are one thing. What of religious *knowledge*? It is in this respect that the comparison is starkest between contemporary Australia and, say, the Australia of 1901. Or even 1961. Across the community, from otherwise well-educated sophisticates to the ordinary man or woman in the street, there is widespread ignorance of religious history and religious concepts. The level of ignorance increases with each generation. For me, the most incisive sentence in Tom Frame's *Losing My Religion* was this one: 'The majority [of Australians] have either no idea what the Christian religion is offering or they have rejected what they mistakenly think it is offering.'[51] That was me until the age of thirty-five.

Some readers may well be thinking: *So what?* Why should this level of ignorance and unbelief be a cause for concern? Why, indeed, should it even be a matter of interest to anyone but practising Christians with a duty to evangelise?

Of course, if Christianity is true, such trends are tragic. But this is *not* a book of Christian apologetics. It is intended primarily as a work of historical and social observation. My personal beliefs will become clear, but the argument I will advance does not require the reader to assume that Christianity is true. It does assume, however, that 'the *story* of Christianity is undeniably true, in that it is a part of human history'.[52] It is also, as I will endeavour to show, an integral part of *Australian* history.

My thesis is threefold:

## 1. Since 1788, the influence of religion on Australian life has been vital and largely favourable

Assessing the place of religion in Australia, now and in the past, is far more than a matter of head-counting. It requires an analysis of the impact of the Churches, and of individual believers, upon the course of Australian history and the character of our society. My core argument in Part One is that this impact has been profound. Before embarking on the research for this book, I did not fully realise myself just how great that impact has been. I now share the view of Geoffrey Blainey that the Christian Churches did 'more than any other institution, public or private, to civilise Australians'.[53]

Even as I write that last sentence I can anticipate the cries of dissent. What about the Graeco-Romans? Or the Enlightenment? What about science? Or liberal capitalism – Adam Smith's benevolent 'invisible hand'? Or the ALP? I acknowledge the roles played by all these forces and institutions, but I will stick to my thesis. Almost everything goes back to Judaeo-Christianity.

One theme will, I hope, emerge clearly: the key role played in Australian history by outstanding individuals of religious faith. I refer not merely to men and women of the Churches (priests, nuns, ministers and so on), but to lay citizens in almost every field of endeavour. Although it is unfashionable to say so, I admit to being attracted by the Great Man (or Great Woman) theory of history. In the words of Thomas Carlyle, the main populariser of this theory in the mid-nineteenth century: 'There needs not a great soul to make a hero; there needs a god-created soul which will be true to its origin.'[54]

An astonishing number of distinguished figures in Australian history since 1788 have been people for whom faith was a major motivating force. They have had a sense of mission, and they have acted on it, in such disparate fields as politics, law, exploration, business, science, journalism, trade unionism, the arts, architecture, engineering and education. The point applies equally to Christians and Jews.[55] And – a significant fact – they have come disproportionately from the upper levels of society. As I will show in Chapter 2, this was also the position in the first century: Christianity was started from the top down. In my researching, I found it remarkable how often a famous *lay* Australian turned out to have been the son of a clergyman.

Here I should make a confession. I have said that this book is not one of Christian apologetics. So it is not – except in one incidental respect. In detailing the achievements of religious believers throughout Australian history, I am employing a variant of one of the lesser-known arguments for the existence of God: the argument *e consensu gentium*.[56] Broadly, this is the notion that, because religious belief has been so ubiquitous a phenomenon throughout human history, especially among people who changed the world for the better, there must be something in it.

For those interested in knowing more about particular Great Men or Great Women who are mentioned in the text, especially regarding their religious lives, I have included further biographical detail about many of them in Appendix A at the back of the book.

## 2. The decline of religious belief in Australia has been partly the Churches' own fault, and partly the result of forces beyond their control

Please do not think that this book will be a glowing, unqualified tribute to the Australian Churches. As institutions, they have a lot to answer for.

In at least one instance in the late twentieth century – some readers may think this is the elephant in the room – they behaved quite indefensibly. I refer to the dire history of sexual abuse of children by clergymen and the cover-up of their crimes by men in authority. This horror has not been confined to the Churches; it happened in secular institutions too. But it has been most prevalent in the Catholic Church, and it has affected many Protestant denominations as well.

The scandal is impossible to ignore and hard to explain. It has provided secularists with powerful ammunition, but I will argue that it does *not* account for secularisation. And while it is relevant to some of the ultimate metaphysical issues (how could a loving God allow such evil?), it is not ultimately determinative of them. (Those questions belong to a field of intellectual discourse called theodicy.)

In Part Two I will look at the major mistakes and misdeeds of which the Churches have been accused down the years – including those identified by Elizabeth Farrelly's baby-boomer friends ('arrogant, sexist, racist and monomaniacal'). In certain cases the allegations are unjust or misconceived; Indigenous relations is a striking example. I will try to explain, if not always defend, the Churches' stances down the years on now-unfashionable issues: abortion, temperance, Sabbath-keeping, divorce, drug use and gambling, among others. While these stances have often been unpopular, even in the nineteenth and early twentieth centuries, they were largely well motivated. In several respects, the churches' worst fears have been realised in ways that most fair-minded Australians today would, or should, be prepared to acknowledge. There was good sense in much of the Churches' social conservatism.

The Churches' most calamitous mistakes, I shall argue, were in the fields of education policy (schools) and foreign policy (war). They have also, at times, overdone wowserism. But it is necessary to distinguish between mistakes and misdeeds that have been operating causes of secularisation, and those that have had a neutral (or even positive) effect on levels of religious belief. Of course, to some extent these will be value judgments; I do not expect all readers to agree with me.

My other argument in Part Two is that two of the key factors in the decline of religion – the rise of scientism, and unprecedented material prosperity – cannot be sheeted home to the Churches. Nevertheless, they are factors that the Churches must find a way of overcoming.

## 3. Religion is worth saving, and there are ways that this might be done

It is difficult to imagine an entirely secular Australia. I agree with Tom Frame that 'those without religious belief do not have a clearly articulated vision of what a godless world will be like'.[57] Most of them, I expect, imagine an Australia much as it is now, but without the pesky presence of Churches and God-botherers. Holidays such as Christmas and Easter would be abolished or renamed. The Churches would be disbanded. All remaining Church property would be sold off, and all schools, hospitals and charities currently administered by the Churches would be taken over by the government, or privatised.[58]

But beyond that, what? If a rampant free market is not the answer, other historical precedents – the Soviet Union, Communist China – are incomparably worse. Of course, most secularists are not advocating political dictatorship. But they seem unable to acknowledge that liberal democracy and the rule of law (among many other things) are products of Judaeo-Christianity. If that historical foundation were taken away, what would be left to underpin our institutions and motivate many of our most idealistic citizens?

Some would point to such quasi-religious alternatives as New Age spiritualism and celebratory atheism. Rodney Hall's declaration in 1996 is a good example of the latter: 'The exciting fact is that we are adrift in a Universe which is timeless and utterly meaningless.'[59] But these seem unlikely to take hold on any wide scale, and it would be a disaster if they did. They would take us further down the path of moral relativism and unchecked consumerism.

Then there are non-religious alternatives such as 'secular ethics'. But this is a slippery term that means different things to different people. Many of us attempt to 'lose ourselves' in work, or sport, or hobbies, or romantic love. Others become involved in clubs or other community organisations, or global causes such as environmentalism or the relief of poverty. These are good and worthy things. But none, it seems to me, is an adequate substitute for religious belief.

Even granted the failings of the institutional Churches, both here in Australia and overseas, it would be a grave mistake to throw out the baby with the bathwater. We risk losing the things that religion can bring to our lives, not least serious answers to the deepest questions of existence – questions that each individual Australian should be equipped to answer in an informed way. (I offer a selected list of such questions in Chapter 6.) At a purely temporal level, we also risk losing an ideological framework that is neither 'right-wing' nor 'left-wing'; a potentially precious source of emotional sustenance and ambition; and a form of community attachment that, at least in my own personal experience, is unique and valuable. I refer to membership of a thriving, loving church congregation.

Let me be clear: this book will contain no attacks on non-Christian religions. Quite the reverse. According to the 2011 census, people of non-Christian religions now account for some 7.2 per cent of the Australian population. The three largest groups are Buddhists (2.5 per cent), Muslims (2.2 per cent) and Hindus (1.3 per cent).[60] As previously mentioned, Jews account for another 0.5 per cent. For those concerned about the future of Christianity, this ought not to be a cause for concern. It is a good thing that all Australians have the opportunity to interact with people of other faiths. Christians have far more in common with fellow religionists than they do with the broad mass of apathetic unbelievers who now dominate Australian society. The causes of what I call the Secular Juggernaut do not lie here.

My focus will be on Christianity, because that is my area of expertise – and, by far, the religion of most relevance to Australia. But I mean no disrespect to adherents of other faiths. Some of what I will say about Christianity is also applicable to Judaism and Islam – after all, adherents of all three of the great monotheistic religions purport to worship the God of Abraham. As I understand it, most Muslims believe in the first two limbs of my definition of an 'essentially Christian view of the world', and they also believe that Jesus has special status as a prophet. Jews certainly believe in the first limb, and hold a variety of views about the afterlife. That still leaves very big theological differences between adherents of each of these faiths – but the gulf is not as great as that between unbelievers and believers.

In the article by Elizabeth Farrelly that I have earlier quoted, she observed that her friends were 'happy to extol Vietnamese sing-alongs, Buddhist chants and Judaic ritual, but Christian ceremony? Hissss!'[61] I ask only that they and their kind extend respect to Australia's majority religion. Likewise, I ask that conservative Christians try to suspend their own prejudices. Among some of them there is a concomitant view – the nasty flipside of the secular Left's absurd political correctness – that multiculturalism is a central cause of secularism. For reasons I will seek to explain, the opposite is closer to the truth.

Restoring and reinvigorating our religious heritage would be a massive task for our legislators, our educationalists, our opinion-leaders, and our Churches. In the final chapter I make some modest suggestions as to how it might be done.

PART ONE

# OUR RELIGIOUS HERITAGE

# CHAPTER 1

# The survival of colonial Australia

On these wild shores, Repentance' saviour hand
Shall probe my secret soul, shall cleanse its wounds –
And fit the faithful Penitent for Heav'n.

Robert Southey, Botany Bay Eclogue (1794)

We are a Christian people – followers of a Faith which we believe
to be not only of Divine origin, but conducive to both a worldly and
eternal point of view to our welfare.

The Australian newspaper, 21 June 1836

Unlike the first North American colonies, New South Wales was not founded for religious reasons. Indeed, as we have seen, it would not have been founded at all if Evangelical Christian opinion in Britain had held sway in the 1780s. The short-term aims of those involved in the decision to establish a penal colony at Botany Bay were tawdry and secular. However, in the words of Catholic historian Michael Hogan, that 'is not to deny a religious context'.[1] Once the decision to colonise was made, Christians of all kinds looked ahead to the religious possibilities opened up by the new settlement.

From 1788 onward the Christian Churches, and individual Christians, played a massively important role in shaping the nascent Australian society – first in New South Wales, and subsequently in the other colonies. Without a religious foundation, the colonies would not have survived, let alone flourished. But it is not enough to talk in rhetorical generalities; too many Australian Christians, and politicians seeking to curry favour with them, have done that in the past. It is necessary to put flesh on the bones, and at the outset, to rebut an oft-repeated falsehood.

## Colonial Australia was not 'godless'

A common theme of many historians – including some Christian historians – is that religion got off to such a bad start in 1788 that it never truly recovered. According to Michael Duffy, 'New South Wales comprised the two least religious types of Britain: criminals and soldiers. This was the beginning of the failure of religion to take deep roots in Australia.'[2] While I am in qualified agreement with the first sentence, I disagree with the thrust of the second. The Christian religion *did* take deep roots in Australia. To the extent that the start was slow, the major handicaps had been overcome by the mid-nineteenth century.

Even the slowness of the start has been exaggerated. New South Wales was never 'the most godless place under heaven', as one Scottish clergyman, James Denney, famously lamented in 1824. Denney was not even in New South Wales at the time, but his comment has become notorious.[3] It is a shame. Not only did Denney overrate the depravity of the convicts; he underrated the religious passion of some soldiers and many free settlers. And he was oblivious to the profound spirituality of the Indigenous peoples. In 1824 they still comprised the vast majority of the Australian population.

### The Indigenous inhabitants

It is, or should be, a sobering fact that 'by far the greatest number of Australians who have ever lived on this continent have been Aboriginals'.[4] The cumulative population of Australia in the 70,000 years before 1788 has been estimated at 1.6 billion.[5] In assessing the godlessness or otherwise of the Australian people – now and in the past – the beliefs of the original inhabitants must be taken fully into account.

To most of the British colonists, the 'natives' showed few signs of religious belief.[6] Yet we now know that theirs were deeply religious societies. Indeed, in a profound sense, they were much more religious than the inhabitants of eighteenth-century Britain – let alone 21st-century Australia. There was no clear demarcation between religion and the rest of life. Indeed, there were no equivalents of the words 'religion' or 'believe' in any Indigenous language. The existence of the supernatural was taken for granted.[7] A typical Indigenous society was 'one where law and religion inter-twine[d] to such an extent that it [was] not possible to differentiate between them'.[8]

There are obvious dangers in generalising across hundreds of tribes, but some generalisations are possible. In essence, pre-1788 Indigenous peoples were concerned with developing 'a theory of how the Universe became a moral system'.[9] According to a modern expert, Christine Nicholls of Flinders University, they conceptualised a 'process involving the maintenance of life forces, embodied or symbolised as people, spirits, other natural species, or natural phenomena such as rocks, waterholes or constellations'.[10] This belief system was not polytheistic, nor was it pantheistic. Describing it adequately in English words has proved difficult, to say the least. To this day opinion is divided as to whether it encompassed belief in one God in the monotheistic sense of *a* supreme Being; it did encompass belief in life after death.[11]

Understandably, virtually none of these things was appreciated by the earliest generations of British colonists. Yet it would be wrong to conclude that *no one* took an interest in Indigenous spirituality, or, more broadly, in Indigenous language and culture. This kind of interest was a rare phenomenon, to be sure – but not unheard of. Overwhelmingly, the people who did take an interest were dedicated Christians or people raised in that tradition. They had the requisite courage, compassion and curiosity – and the moral and intellectual tools to ask the relevant questions. Crucially for us, they also had the diligence to record, for posterity, the answers they received.

The first to do the latter were Watkin Tench (1758–1833) and William Dawes (1762–1836), two naval officers who arrived on the First Fleet. Tench was a man of remarkable sensibility, perhaps 'the most cultivated mind in the colony',[12] a thoughtful Christian capable of quoting Milton off the cuff. Of all the early chronicles of New South Wales, his is the fairest and most readable. Dawes was just as admirable a figure. By most accounts studious, kind and esteemed, he was 'a very religious man of immovable principles'.[13] He was also a doer. Apart from his exploits with Tench, Dawes built Sydney's first observatory. A young man when he served in New South Wales, he later became acquainted with William Wilberforce, joined the Clapham Sect – a group of prominent Evangelical Christians in London who campaigned for social reform – and was twice governor of Sierra Leone. He died in Antigua while engaged in the anti-slavery cause.

Tench and Dawes became friends, and, often in each other's company, carried out important exploration of the Sydney Plain. In the process they made friendly contact with the local Indigenous people. Tench stated expressly in his journal that he regarded Indigenous religion as 'an important subject'. He posed the rhetorical question: 'Have these people any religion: any knowledge of, or belief in a deity? – any conception of the immortality of the soul?'[14]

After he and Dawes had quizzed the local people at length – exactly how they communicated remains unclear to me, though Dawes kept a priceless record of many Indigenous words – Tench formed the view they had 'consciousness of a higher power'. This power, he believed, amounted to 'a living intellectual principle ... capable of comprehending their petition and of either granting or denying it'. He also ascertained that they believed in the immortality of the soul. 'When asked where their deceased friends are they always point to the skies.'[15] Ultimately Tench concluded that Indigenous beliefs were part of the same golden chain that linked all religions, including Christianity. 'However involved in darkness and disfigured by error,' he wrote, 'no one will, I presume, deny that it conveys a direct implication of superior agency.'[16] These preliminary findings have since been confirmed by modern anthropologists. Although most Christians – including some Indigenous Christians – would agree with Tench's sentiments as to 'darkness' and 'error', very few would attribute any blame to Indigenous peoples. Until British colonisation, none had been exposed to the Gospel.

### The British colonists

So, the Indigenous inhabitants of New South Wales were certainly not godless. And neither – ever – were the British colonists. Too much emphasis has been placed on the outward forms of worship in early New South Wales and not enough on underlying beliefs.

Governor Arthur Phillip's official commission contained a directive to 'enforce a due observance of religion and good order among the inhabitants, and [to] take such steps for the due celebration of public worship as circumstances would permit'. The first Christian service was held on 3 February 1788, a week after the First Fleet's arrival. Though it necessarily took place outdoors – in the shade of a large tree – it was an occasion of some solemnity. 'No Man to be Absent On Any Account Whatever' was the official order, and that meant convicts and Marines.[17] The Fleet's official chaplain, Richard Johnson, took as his theme Psalm 116:12: 'What shall I render unto the Lord for all His benefits towards me?'[18] There was also a reading from the Sermon on the Mount (Matthew 6:24–34)[19] and a baptism (of one Samuel Thomas, the infant son of a marine).[20] According to Watkin Tench, the behaviour of all present 'was equally regular and attentive'.[21] O for a time machine! The pristine setting, near present-day Circular Quay, would have looked both uncannily familiar and wondrously strange. Two of those present were a marine, William Nash RN, and his (then) common-law wife, Maria Haynes. They married in Sydney on 2 February 1789, and were the author's great-great-great-great-great grandparents.

But this service was a one-off. Undeniably, formal worship in the infant colony was sporadic. Formalities were observed as regards marriage, baptism and burial, but the evidence shows that the conventions of regular Sunday worship were followed by a small minority only. Voluntary churchgoing was the exception rather than the rule, and, at least among Protestants, anti-clericism was rife.[22] Put bluntly, most of the convicts and soldiers did not have pious habits. Back in Britain, some in the lower classes had become disenchanted with the Church of England and most had grown 'unaccustomed to the *observance* of religion in their previous lives' (emphasis mine).[23]

More than five years passed before the first church building was constructed in Sydney. Foundations for one were laid in the spring of 1791, but the building, once completed, became a lock-up (and later a granary). Eventually Richard Johnson built a church himself, using convict labour and his own funds.[24] The large wattle and daub structure was located near what is now the junction of Hunter and Castlereagh Streets in the Sydney CBD.[25]

It would have been within Governor Phillip's power to expedite the building of a church, at least of a rustic sort. But he gave priority to storehouses, barracks, dwellings and hospital landing-places.[26] This was understandable on utilitarian grounds, if less so on Christian grounds. In March 1793, when two Spanish ships arrived at Sydney, a Catholic priest was shocked that there was as yet no church in the colony; his own countrymen, he said, would have built a church first of all.[27] It is reasonable to infer that, for Phillip personally, 'religion was not a high priority'.[28] Although he was *not* an unbeliever, he was a phlegmatic High Anglican rather than a passionate Evangelical.* With the stark exception of Governor John Hunter (1795–1800) – a genuinely pious man who had once trained for the ministry of the Church of Scotland – the same was true of all Phillip's successors[29] until the arrival of Lachlan Macquarie in 1810. Nevertheless, there were some notably religious men among the

---

*   For more on Phillip's religious views, and John Hunter's, see Appendix A.

Marine Corps – including high achievers such as Dawes and Tench. (The Marine Corps, incidentally, was a far superior body of men to the New South Wales Corps, which replaced the Marines in 1791. According to historian John Moore, the Marines 'attended church parades without demur and showed a respect for religion which [Reverend Samuel] Marsden was later to find wanting in their successors'.[30])

This patchy start was unfortunate. But it was scarcely fatal. The Anglican chaplains were there from the start, slaving away – Richard Johnson from 1789 until 1800, Samuel Marsden from 1794, Henry Fulton (who arrived as a convict) from 1799. William Cowper, a quiet but towering figure, arrived in 1809. Non-conformist (i.e., non-Anglican) preachers had a substantial presence after 1798 – the first of them to come to Sydney had been missionaries to the South Seas[31] – and Presbyterian services were being conducted from about 1800.[32] In 1809 a group of Presbyterian settlers completed construction of a church in the Hawkesbury district. (The Ebenezer Church still stands; it is Australia's oldest surviving church building.) The Reverend John Dunmore Lang arrived in 1823 – a monumental figure not only in the history of the Presbyterian Church, but in nineteenth-century Australia.

Catholic priests were not permitted in the colony until 1820. To the modern lay reader this might seem remarkable, but there were deep-seated historical reasons for it, to which I will come. In any event, there is clear evidence that many Irish-Catholic convicts and emancipists practised their faith from the beginning, as best they could. Likewise, from the First Fleet onwards, there was a small but significant Jewish presence.[33] And throughout those first few decades, many of the movers and shakers in the colony were deeply pious laymen and laywomen.

There can be no question that the most religiously inclined members of colonial society were the free settlers. Even in the years before 1820, when their numbers were tiny, their influence was significant. The majority were professionals or property owners: pioneers in medicine, agriculture, commerce, journalism, banking and the law. Along with the many fervently Christian governors and lieutenant-governors, the free settlers brought with them to Australia not only their skills and capital but their religious beliefs, their philanthropic instincts, and their churchgoing habits.

New South Wales was never a godless place, but from the mid-1820s onwards the charge is demonstrably untrue. The clinching contrary evidence is to be found in the many newspapers of the period. As Brian

H. Fletcher has observed, there was 'a belief, running across newspapers of all political persuasions, that religion was an essential ingredient of society'.[34]

The colony's first newspaper, the *Sydney Gazette*, was founded in March 1803. From the start it was a source of information about church services and other church activities. After 1821, when Robert Howe, an ardent Methodist, assumed the editorship, it became 'a vehicle for the spread of the Christian message'.[35] The *Australian Magazine*, the first religious journal issued in Australasia, was published by Wesleyan missionaries from 1821. But the Sydney press was not truly free until 1824, when Government House ceased to censor the *Gazette* and *The Australian* was first published.[36] *The Monitor* followed in 1826, and, from that point on, the citizens of Sydney could read lively debate on all matters religious. *The Australian* had an anti-clerical streak, while still acknowledging 'the grand truths of religion [and] the established maxims of morality'.[37] *The Monitor* was likewise anti-establishment, yet 'infused with evangelical principles',[38] having been founded by a former Anglican lay preacher, Edward Smith Hall.[39] The *Sydney Herald*, which started in 1831 and was later renamed the *Sydney Morning Herald*, was a voice of respectable Protestantism. (As we saw in the Introduction, most of its editors in the nineteenth century were ministers of religion.) *The Colonist* was founded by J.D. Lang in 1835 as a voice of radical Presbyterianism and the *Australasian Chronicle* in 1839 as a voice for Catholicism.[40]

In the main, the reputation for godlessness of early New South Wales and Van Diemen's Land has rested on questionable assumptions about both convicts and emancipists. For a start, it is crucial to separate the Catholic minority from the Protestant majority. (Because these matters are no longer common knowledge, I have included an outline of the major differences between formal Catholicism and Protestantism in Appendix B.)

Catholicism was present from the beginning in the hearts of many Irish convicts. The evidence is clear. Some had tattoos of the Cross on their bodies.[41] Naval surgeon Peter Cunningham made five trips on convict ships and observed the Irish convicts on all of them 'counting their [rosary] beads and fervently crossing themselves and repeating their prayers'.[42] True, exactly what they believed is hard to define. According to Edmund Campion, it was 'a bewildering mixture of formal Catholicism, debased Catholic practices, family piety, superstition, magic and Celtic mythology ... a poem that gave life meaning or respite'.[43] I would add a nationalist-ethnic element: resentment of centuries of English political oppression, the roots of which are explained in Chapter 3. Catholics did not obtain full citizenship rights in Britain until 1829.[44]

In early 1787, Viscount Sydney was informed by letter that the 300 or so Irish convicts scheduled to leave on the First Fleet had 'an earnest desire some Catholic clergymen may go with them'. The priest who wrote this letter, Father Thomas Walshe, offered to go to New South Wales without pay. But Sydney was unmoved and the request denied.[45] Given the vital role of priests in the Catholic belief system, this must for many have been the cruellest of blows. And salt was rubbed into their wounds on 13 February 1788, when Phillip took his official oath as governor and swore 'allegiance to the King and to the Protestant succession, while repudiating Romish beliefs in the transubstantiation of the Eucharist'.[46] Subsequent governors did likewise.

Religious resentments simmered among the Catholic convicts for the next four years. By early 1792 transports had started arriving from Ireland itself, and there was a sprinkling of Catholic free settlers and soldiers in the colony. Shortly before Phillip's departure he was presented with a remarkable letter, seeking his help in petitioning the authorities back in England:

> May it please Your Excellency –
> We, the undernamed, with most humble respect, take the liberty
> of representing to Your Excellency the inconvenience we find
> in not being indulged heretofore with a pastor of our religion.
> Notwithstanding the violation of the laws of our country, we still wish
> to inherit the laws of our Creator in the form we have been instructed
> in our youth. We therefore humbly implore Your Excellency's
> assistance, on your return to England, to represent it to Her Majesty's
> Ministry ... that nothing else could induce us to depart from His
> Majesty's Colony here unless the idea of going into eternity without
> the assistance of a Catholick priest.[47]

The request fell on deaf ears, just as Father Walshe's letter to Sydney had done in 1787. This was despite the enactment in Britain in 1791 of the Roman Catholic Relief Act, which admitted Catholics to the practice of law and formally permitted the exercise of their religion.

There was no Catholic priest in New South Wales until January 1800, when two arrived as convicts, Fathers James Dixon and James

Harold. A third, Father Peter O'Neill, arrived in the same manner in early 1801. All three had been transported for alleged complicity in the Irish Rebellion of 1798, though the evidence against each was dubious.[48] It was an opportunity for the exercise of mercy, but none was forthcoming until April 1803, when Governor Philip Gidley King granted Dixon a conditional pardon and permitted him to minister as a priest. The first public Mass was celebrated in Sydney on 15 May 1803, and others followed in Parramatta and the Hawkesbury district. But Dixon's privileges were revoked within twelve months, after a failed rebellion by Irish convicts at Castle Hill in early 1804, and thereafter no priests could officiate legally for another sixteen years.[49] When Father Jeremiah O'Flynn, an Irish Cistercian monk, arrived in the colony in November 1817 without appropriate accreditation from the Colonial Office, he was swiftly deported.[50]

Throughout much of this period, and up until 1820, Catholic convicts were often forced to attend Anglican services. Catholic free settlers and emancipists did not suffer that indignity, and many refused to engage in Anglican rites of marriage or baptism or to send their children to Anglican schools. All used the rosary, and some formed groups who conducted prayer meetings at private homes.[51]

Surprisingly, in these years of adversity and persecution – which some have dubbed 'the Catacomb Era' – Catholicism survived and even prospered. By 1820, some 6,000 or 7,000 people in New South Wales were at least nominally Catholic.[52] More significantly, by 1828, there were some 374 adults *born in New South Wales* who described themselves as Catholic. As Catholic historian Edmund Campion has pointed out, 'this small group [was] … the product of settled family life and lay religious networks stretching back to the beginnings of the colony'.[53]

Eventually, the Colonial Office in Britain relented and appointed two official Catholic chaplains. In May 1820, Fathers Philip Conolly and John Joseph Therry arrived in the colony.[54] It has been suggested this was done more in the hope of better controlling the Irish-Catholic convicts than from pressure of radical opinion in Britain or respect for religious liberty.[55] Probably all three motives were involved – in roughly equal proportion – but in any case, it was a genuine watershed.

So, the charge that most of the convicts were godless is quite inaccurate as regards the Catholics among them. But what of the rest – the majority – most of whom were at least notionally Anglican?

Allan Grocott grappled with this question in his 1980 book *Convicts, Clergymen and Churches*, concluding that they 'were generally irreligious, profane and anti-clerical'.[56] That was broadly in accordance with opinions expressed contemporaneously, from 1788 onwards, by Protestant clergymen in New South Wales. The Reverend William Cowper, for instance, thought the convicts 'generally without any religious feeling, moral habits, character or principles'.[57] The Reverend Robert Cartwright allowed that 'there were particular convicts with religious feelings but, failing the necessary support, [they] reverted to the lowest common denominator'.[58]

These clergymen, and others like them, were too hard on both themselves and the convicts. They tended to focus on the convicts' profanity, irreverence and poor churchgoing habits. Critic and author Robert Hughes noted in *The Fatal Shore* how, on a voyage out to Sydney in 1819, one clergyman was outraged by the sight of convicts tearing up Bibles and prayer books to make playing cards.[59] But too much can be made of these kinds of episodes, which tend to obscure a deeper truth. Modern-day theorists of secularisation have explained the traps involved.

One is over-reliance on the views of highly religious people, who tend to set lofty standards. Another is to focus too much on overtly religious behaviour. The fact is that 'genuine popular devotion of a humble kind leaves very little trace upon the records of any given time'.[60]

What secularisation theorists have found is that, until the mid-nineteenth century, people everywhere, *and among all classes of society*, were much more religiously minded than we may suppose.[61] In colonial New South Wales and Van Diemen's Land, virtually everyone believed in the first two limbs of my definition of an essentially Christian view of the world, and a substantial majority also believed in the third:

- An all-knowing God who created and sustains the Universe, and who is vitally interested in the thoughts and conduct of each individual human being
- An afterlife, in which each of us will be judged by God
- The divinity of Jesus of Nazareth.

A significant minority of Protestant Evangelicals believed that Jesus' death on the Cross had ensured their favourable judgment by God in the afterlife, because (and for so long as) they placed their trust in Jesus.

Drilling down into Grocott's study, we see that what he found among the convicts was not so much 'irreligion' – the absence of any religious belief – as estrangement from organised Christianity and especially from the Church of England. This was part of a broader trend in eighteenth-century Britain among the lower classes of society.[62] But it is far too sweeping to write most of them off as godless and depraved. An emancipist, David Mann, made this very point in 1811: the morals of the colony were 'by no means so debauched as the tongue of prejudice has too frequently asserted'.[63] If it had been so, the colony would not have survived.

Even Grocott adjudged that one in four Catholic convicts was 'sincerely religious',[64] though I suspect that is an understatement. Only one in four, perhaps, was overtly religious. A much greater proportion of convicts – Catholic and Protestant – would have known the basics of their religion. As Robert Hughes observed, 'religious instruction was … basic to the rearing of many convicts, especially the Irish'.[65] Hughes, like Grocott, was inclined to dismiss many of the English Protestant convicts as 'irreligious', but, again, I question that notion. To be sure, most were not churchgoers. But there is suggestive evidence that sincere religious belief touched many who did not worship in public.[66] At a minimum, the vast majority still believed in a Creator God who would dispense justice in the afterlife. In some cases their beliefs may have been vague – even incoherent.[67] But those beliefs were strongly felt, and 'reinforced by state, church and tradition'.[68] This applied even to the vilest of the vile.[69]

The documentary record is sparse, but it is also touching and compelling. It bears out historian John Moore's contention that 'there existed, probably throughout the fleet[s] generally, an adherence to the churches' liturgy'.[70] For instance, during the First Fleet's voyage out, the female convicts on the *Friendship* became frightened during a storm. Of their own accord, they read the collect and lessons for the day from the Book of Common Prayer and sang psalms.[71] On another occasion, when one of the convict women's children died, a male convict, Henry Lovall, took it upon himself to read prayers.[72] At least one of the convict women, Frances Carty, possessed her own much-read copy of the Book of Common Prayer. (It seems she accidentally dropped it overboard; amazingly, it was found in the belly of a shark caught on 1 May 1792 by sailors on the *Gorgon*, a Third Fleet ship returning to England.[73])

One Samuel Peyton wrote an extraordinary letter to his mother on 24 June 1788. He was facing a sentence of death the next day. It was a friend who actually put pen to paper, but the sentiments were Peyton's own. He admitted to 'agony of soul' and confessed his sins. 'For these and all my other transgressions however great,' he wrote, 'I supplicate the Divine forgiveness; and encouraged by the promises of the Saviour who died for us all, I trust to receive that mercy in the world to come.' He then professed himself 'at peace'. Finally, he thought of his mother: 'The affliction which this [his death] will cost you, I hope the Almighty will enable you to bear.'[74]

A surviving letter from an unknown female convict, written in about 1790, referred to 'our disconsolate situation in this solitary waste of the Creation'.[75] A Scots woman on the *Lady Juliana*, shortly before its departure from England, was observed kissing a Bible and weeping.[76] Particularly instructive is Watkin Tench's account of the death of Governor Phillip's gamekeeper, a convict named McIntyre, in December 1790. Having been mortally wounded by an Aboriginal spear, McIntyre was told by a doctor he had no hope of survival. According to Tench, 'the poor wretch now began ... to accuse himself of the commission of crimes of the deepest dye, accompanied with such expressions of his despair of God's mercy as are too terrible to repeat'.[77] There is similar evidence from the early nineteenth century. Not many personal letters from convicts survive, but those that do often mention God. One Thomas Holden, a Lancashire weaver transported in 1812, wrote to both his wife and his mother in explicitly Christian terms ('O my hard fate, may God have mercy on me'; 'Dear mother I do not think of seeing you in this world any more').[78]

By the 1820s, surgeons on the transport ships were instructed to 'use every possible means to promote a religious and moral disposition in the convicts'.[79] They reported limited success, but evidence of belief still peeps into the record – even among some of roughest rogues imaginable. In 1822, a party of escaped convicts in Van Diemen's Land resorted to cannibalism. One of the recaptured survivors, Alexander Pearce, wrote a narrative of the grisly events. He related how, before killing one of their number, John Mather, for the purpose, 'they told him they would give him half an hour to pray for himself, which was agreed to; he then gave the Prayer-book to me, and laid down his head, and Greenhill took the axe and killed him'.[80]

Laurence Frayne was an Irishman who arrived on Norfolk Island in 1830 with his back in a state of maggot-ridden decomposition. Writing a few years later to a clergyman, he admitted having begun 'to question in my own then-perverted mind the infinite mercy, nay the justice, of Deity itself'. Yet he never renounced his faith; instead he sought solace in the Bible, especially the eighty-eighth psalm, and survived his torments.[81]

Similarly, in 1831, in a letter to his wife, an English convict named Peter Withers confided his hope that God might 'be Mersyful to me'. As it happened he was assigned to a beneficent master in Van Diemen's Land, and, feeling immense gratitude to the Almighty, began going to church every Sunday.[82] In 1840 one Richard Boothman promised in a letter to his parents that he would reform his behaviour 'if it pleases God to bestow my Liberty upon me once more'. He imagined reunion with his parents ten years later, once his sentence had been served: 'it will be like a foretaste of Heaven itself'.[83]

Other convicts showed concern for the inner life of loved ones. In 1831 Richard Dillingham wrote to his sweetheart back home expressing the wish 'that God will be your leading star'.[84] Another, in a letter to his wife in 1835, noted solemnly that 'you and I have lived for a long time without God in our hearts'. He urged her to read to their children from the Scriptures, and selected certain passages for the purpose.[85]

Two final examples must suffice – but to my mind they are impressive ones.

In July 1834 a Supreme Court judge, William Westbroke Burton, went to Norfolk Island to preside at the trial for mutiny of some fifty-five convicts. According to the prosecutor they included 'characters of the foulest description', and in the event, fourteen of those convicted were sentenced to hang. Few feared death as such, but a number did fear dying before speaking to a prelate – whether Catholic priest or Protestant minister. To his credit, Justice Burton took steps to facilitate this. The Catholic priest, Father Ullathorne, reported later that those whose confessions he had heard 'manifested extraordinary fervour of repentance'.[86]

My last example of religious belief – and common decency – among the broad mass of convicts comes from 1862, near the end of the transportation era. The master of the *Norwood*, Captain Alfred Tetens, had treated all on his ship with unusual kindness and generosity. When the ship reached Western Australia he was presented with a letter signed by 270 convicts.

Addressing Captain Tetens as 'HONOURED SIR!', the convicts extended their thanks in effusive terms before concluding:

> We add the sincere wish that Heaven may grant you every earthly joy, that you may succeed in all your future enterprises, and while we must follow our unknown fate in an inhospitable land far from home and family, may the hand of the Almighty protect you and bring you back to a happy home.[87]

## Why religion mattered

Thus far I have tried to demonstrate that religious belief ran deep throughout all sections of colonial society – even among the convicts. Of course, some people were much more serious than others about the practice of their faith. But faith – even of a rudimentary sort – was the reflexive norm. The next question is whether religion actually mattered in the survival of colonial Australia, and, if so, how. I proffer nine ways in which religion did indeed matter – a great deal.

### The choice of New South Wales as the site of the colony

It not surprising that the English establishment of the 1770s and 1780s put Christian proposals for prison reform in the too-hard basket. When it comes to costly and unpopular social change, that, sadly, tends to be the way of the world. But if the penal colony option was always the more likely in the circumstances, the choice of New South Wales as the site most definitely was not. Numerous places were considered, including Canada, Nova Scotia, Florida, Greenland, the Falkland Islands, Madagascar and the Bay of Das Voltas (in modern-day Namibia).[88]

At one stage early in 1785 the British Government's preferred choice was Gambia, a slave-trade hellhole on the west coast of Africa. It is a little-appreciated fact that orders were actually signed to send British convicts there.

The West Africa scheme was defeated largely by one man, the great (small-c) conservative Edmund Burke (1729–97).[89] Much better known for his anti-Jacobite pamphlet *Reflections on the Revolution in France* (1790), the Irish-born Burke was a respected Whig politician (the member for Bristol in the House of Commons) and a voice of compassionate Christian conservatism on the notionally 'Left' side of British politics. 'There is but one law for all,' he once declared, 'namely that law which governs all law, the law of our Creator, the law of humanity, justice, equity – the law of Nature and of Nations.'[90] Burke objected to the West Africa proposal on the same grounds as he objected to black slavery: simple Christian charity. The convicts possessed human souls and should not lightly be sent to near-certain death in a place notorious for high mortality rates. It would be the ultimate hypocrisy to impose capital punishment 'after a mock display of mercy'.[91]

The fact that Botany Bay came to be considered a viable alternative site was largely attributable to the influence of another prophetic Christian voice – that of Sir Joseph Banks (1743–1820). He is recalled as the gentleman-naturalist who accompanied Cook on the *Endeavour*. Yet according to one of his biographers, Harold B. Carter, 'no man did more to ensure that the world map should include Terra Australis as a British settled region'.[92] Another biographer, J.H. Maiden, called him 'the father of Australia'.

By the 1780s Banks was an extremely eminent and well-connected man. He had risen to be President of the Royal Society, the highest honour open to a scientist. (Isaac Newton had also held the post.) When consulted by the government, Banks suggested New South Wales as a suitable site for a British colony. Many historians have pointed out that some of his claims for Botany Bay (as to the arability of the soil and so on) proved erroneous. Robert Hughes chastised him in *The Fatal Shore* for a 'farrago of optimistic distortions'[93] and David Hill has alleged that Banks was not a disinterested observer: he stood to gain from any settlement in New South Wales because he could expect to receive many more specimens of local flora and fauna, which would further elevate his prestige as a naturalist.[94] But these charges are petty. Banks was a visionary. If he made mistakes, he erred on the side of hope – and in the end he was proved right. He later corresponded regularly with all the New South Wales governors from Phillip to Macquarie, and was a source of immense wisdom and encouragement.

Did Banks' religious beliefs play any part in events?

Manning Clark thought so. In his assessment, Banks was a man who 'believed that every consideration that a man made of the works of the Almighty increased a man's admiration of his Creator'.[95] In other words, if Banks was motivated by scientific curiosity rather than the nuts and bolts of running a penal colony, this was so much to the good. Certainly, others who have written about Banks have noted his strong religious views. One of the world's leading Church historians, Diarmaid MacCulloch, has described him as a figure of the 'Anglican Enlightenment',[96] and this accords with the known facts. Banks privately expressed toleration in religious matters – his close friend and fellow naturalist on the *Endeavour*, the Swede Daniel Solander, was a practising Lutheran – and he appears to have held liberal views on some questions of doctrine and morality.[97] But he was a proud and loyal member of the Church of England and defended its established status. He believed, like many educated eighteenth-century Anglicans, that there was an 'Order of Nature' – a 'Chain of Creation' or 'Chain of Being' – that led inexorably back to God. His ancestral family home was Revesby Abbey in Lincolnshire. He was tutored as a boy by the Reverend Henry

Shepherd, Rector of Moorby, and attended Christ College at Oxford University.[98]

In short, the Church was in his blood. That was one of the main reasons his opinion carried so much weight.

### The voyage of the First Fleet

The vast majority of the 1500 or so people on the First Fleet made it to New South Wales alive and in decent health. Of the few dozen who died at sea, most were convicts who had boarded the ships in dire health to begin with.[99] Twenty-one babies were safely born on the voyage.[100] This was a remarkable achievement for the times. In itself, the physical survival of the First Fleeters remains one of the key facts in the whole history of Australia.

Consider, by contrast, the fates of the Second and Third Fleets. Some 273 people perished on the Second Fleet and 199 on the Third.[101] Many of those who arrived alive died soon afterwards or remained permanently incapacitated.[102] If the First Fleet had suffered a similar fate, it seems probable the whole venture would have foundered at the outset.

By such fine threads do the fates of nations hang.

Who deserves credit for the safe passage of the First Fleet? Principally, I maintain, just four people. Two were devout Christians. The other two were diligent and conscientious public servants, practising High Anglicans in the understated English way.

Arthur Phillip (1738–1814), the Fleet's commander, was in the second category. So was Evan Nepean (1752–1822), Sydney's youthful deputy at the Colonial Office, who had been given the job of getting the First Fleet safely to New South Wales and maximising its chances of survival once there. Phillip and Nepean had once been shipmates and it is probable that Phillip owed his appointment to Nepean's recommendation.[103] At all events, the two worked closely together in the vital stages of preparation for the long and arduous voyage – selecting and fitting the ships, commissioning the officers and crew, and laying in provisions. Almost all historians agree that both of them served New South Wales ably and honourably. Andrew Tink, a recent biographer of Phillip, judged him 'the key to the fate of [the] unprecedented operation'.[104] By contrast, in his book *1788* David Hill plumped for Nepean.[105]

The other two men who ensured the survival of the First Fleet were both staunch Evangelical Protestant Christians. One acted in the provisioning stage; the other at sea.

The name of William Richards Jr is all but forgotten today. He was a ship-broker based in South London when he tendered successfully for the overall contract to supply the First Fleet. This was an instance of blind luck, or Providence at work, for Richards was 'devoutly Christian'[106] and really cared about the success of the venture. In author Thomas Keneally's words, he was 'conscientious to the point of crankiness'.[107] All historians agree that the provisions he supplied for the First Fleet were 'of much superior quality to those usually supplied by a contract'.[108] In particular, there were decent quantities of fresh fruit and vegetables, which eliminated the risk of scurvy. No doubt Phillip and Nepean had a large role in this, but Richards' role should not be underrated. When he lost the contract to supply the Second and Third Fleets – a new Colonial Secretary, William Grenville, had ordered cost-cutting measures – what followed was 'one of the worst chapters in seafaring history'.[109] Amoral shysters supplied inferior ships, poorly fitted and provisioned. Worse, the shipowners were paid according to the number of convicts loaded onto the ships in Britain, not the number who landed alive in Sydney.[110] Conditions on board were appalling, with the fatal results I have mentioned.

The fourth hero of the First Fleet was John Hunter (1737–1821). In effect Phillip's deputy, he played a crucial role at sea. More than half the fleet would literally have been lost without him.

In early December 1787, shortly after leaving Cape Town for the easterly run across the Indian and Southern Oceans, Phillip decided to split the eleven ships into two convoys. The fastest four would go ahead under his command and establish a base at Botany Bay, several weeks ahead of the rest of the party. For this purpose Phillip transferred from the flagship *Sirius* to the smaller, faster *Supply* and took with him the three fastest convict transports.[111] He also took the Fleet's only chronometer (a timekeeper used for marine navigation). Hunter was given command of the *Sirius* and responsibility for the other six vessels.[112] In the event, and despite mountainous seas, both convoys arrived within two days of each other. Watkin Tench praised Hunter at the time for 'his accuracy as an astronomer and conduct as an officer'.[113] There is no doubt in my mind that Hunter's remarkable courage and grace under pressure were products of his deep faith.

This faith would be harnessed again at Port Jackson, to even greater effect. In the new colony's first year, Phillip sent him on an extraordinary voyage to Cape Town and back to obtain desperately needed food supplies. In the process, as historian Geoffrey Blainey has noted, Hunter 'effectively opened a sea route which was vital for Australian commerce in the next 100 or more years'.[114]

But it was a miracle he and his crew made it there and back at all.[115] Hunter wrote in his journal of one especially hazardous phase of the voyage:

> Every thing which depended upon us, I believe, was done; but it would
> be the highest presumption and ingratitude to Divine Providence,
> were we to attribute our preservation wholly to our best endeavours:
> His interference in our favour was so very conspicuously manifested in
> various instances, in the course of that night, as I believe not to leave a
> shadow of doubt, even in the minds of the most profligate on board, of
> His immediate assistance![116]

## The physical survival of the early colony in New South Wales

In retrospect, it is remarkable that the penal colony at Port Jackson (Sydney) survived. The conditions were harsh and terrifyingly unfamiliar. Food was scarce. The stores brought from England on the First Fleet quickly ran low, and, in the words of Robert Hughes, 'they all lived for five years on the bleak edge of starvation'.[117]

Yet the colony did not descend into nihilistic chaos. Instead, slowly, it took shape. As Watkin Tench remarked at the time, 'the behaviour of all classes of ... people since our arrival in the settlement has been better than could, I think, have been expected'.[118]

What kept things together? It would be silly to argue that religious faith was central to *everybody* in the way it was to, say, the North American Pilgrims. But committed individual Christians performed vital and heroic feats, quite disproportionately to their numbers. Further, despite claims to the contrary, institutional religion was far from unimportant.

For a start, there was the rule of law. All efforts to maintain good order in New South Wales were substantially based on it. As we shall see in Chapter 3, the rule of law is quintessentially a product of Judaeo-Christianity.

The sanctity of the Biblical oath was central to the function of the courts, and the formalities of baptism, marriage and burial were strictly observed. In the first four years these duties fell almost exclusively to the colony's chaplain, the Reverend Richard Johnson – a busy and compassionate man, though he always thought himself a failure. Within a fortnight of the First Fleet's arrival, fourteen marriages had been celebrated.[119] By October 1788 there had been more than fifty.[120] As for baptisms, Johnson himself once expressed pleasant surprise that even 'bastards' were brought to him for the purpose.[121] It was also his grim duty to say prayers before executions.[122]

The rule of law was harsh by today's standards, but even most of the convicts respected it. Indeed, if they could, they utilised it. The first civil case decided in New South Wales was brought by two convicts, Henry and Susannah Kable. They sued the captain of their ship, the *Alexander*, for the sum of £15: a parcel of clothes and other articles to that value had been deposited with him for safekeeping before the First Fleet's departure from England, but had vanished by the time the ship reached Sydney. The court found in the Kables' favour, despite the fact that they were convicted felons. Strictly, under a principle of English law called the doctrine of attaint, they should have been disqualified from bringing the case. But in its Christian wisdom, the court – Judge-Advocate David Collins (an extremely devout man), the Reverend Johnson and the colony's surgeon-general, John White – overlooked this.

Why? Their reasons were not explicitly stated, but it has been suggested that 'to deny convicts any form of civil rights would have made the development of the colony impossible'. It seems probable that after consultation with Governor Phillip, they were 'willing to adapt the law to give the colony its best chance of survival'.[123]

But beyond the rule of law, what of religion as such?

In terms of the survival of all Australia's penal colonies, I would point to one stark fact in particular: there was a general aversion to suicide. A few did resort to it; after drawing lots with others of like mind, the 'winner' got to be killed swiftly and efficiently. But most did not go to such lengths. Why? Robert Hughes suggested that, for many, 'suicide was unthinkable' on religious grounds. 'By killing themselves, they believed they would exchange the pains of [captivity] for a real and eternal Hell, from which there would be no release.' Hughes cited the testimony of the Norfolk Island felon Laurence Frayne: 'If ever once it had entered my mind that a Self-Murderer could obtain salvation, I would not have seen a 10th part of the misery I underwent.'[124]

What else? As far as feeding the colony went, *all* the key figures were serious Christians.

The best and most productive farmers – by far – were the two Anglican chaplains. Both Richard Johnson and Samuel Marsden had been raised on the land in Yorkshire, and believed it their duty to harness their God-given agricultural know-how. Johnson fed many from his personal stores ('few of the sick would recover if it were not for the kindness of the Reverend Mr Johnson,' wrote one convict[125]) but he returned to England in 1800. Marsden, who arrived in 1794, stayed in New South Wales for the rest of his life and founded a family dynasty.

Even the legendary James Ruse – the emancipated convict who grew a small crop of wheat and barley in 1790 and became 'the first authentic settler and farmer in Australia' – had a remarkable religious life. Ruse provides a beautiful early example of one of the themes I will explore in Chapter 4: the robust religious pluralism of early New South Wales. As an infant in Cornwall, he had been baptised an Anglican. When he married Elizabeth Perry in September 1790, it was an Anglican ceremony. Yet late in his life, in 1836, he was received into the Roman Catholic Church. Details are scarce, but it appears that as Ruse matured he became increasingly religious. He was buried at the Church of St John the Evangelist in Campbelltown, which had been established in 1822. His gravestone, parts of which he carved himself, revealed 'an understandably biblical pride'.[126] The inscription concluded: 'and now/ With my Hevenly Father I hope/For Ever to remain'.

This list goes on. It was a Scottish Presbyterian merchant, Robert Campbell, who 'virtually called into being the trade of Australia'. He also built the first shipyards.[127] But the most conspicuous models from this period of muscular but compassionate Christianity were the doctors. Each of the convict transports carried a 'surgeon', and many of these men became vital figures in the young colony. Surgeon-General John White kept a meticulous journal. It shows – among other things – that the medical challenges he and his colleagues faced were enormous. Soldiers, settlers and convicts all arrived in Sydney weak from the long sea voyage, and were unaccustomed to the Australian climate. Daily life was gruelling, the food basic at best, and standards of hygiene poor. Many people fell ill, scurvy and dysentery being two of the most common afflictions.[128] Others suffered sunstroke, snakebite and a variety of injuries from misadventure. Childbirth was an unavoidably hazardous procedure that some – mother or baby, or both – did not survive. Yet somehow the doctors coped.

These men were not well paid. Nor were there enough of them. Some of the most skilled arrived as convicts – usually for having committed some 'youthful, impetuous … action'[129] – and were soon emancipated. All were sustained by a sense of professional duty, and, in many cases, a strong Christian faith. Apart from White, notably religious figures included John Harris; Thomas Arndell, a Presbyterian at whose home the first regular church services in the Portland area were held;

and William Bland, for forty years the honorary surgeon at Sydney's Benevolent Asylum, the first free hospital for the poor.[130]

But perhaps the most outstanding figure was the emancipist William Redfern (1778–1833). A staunch Christian, motivated by a sense of charity and calling, he has been called, with justice, 'the father of Australian medicine'.[131]

From his arrival in Sydney in late 1801 (as a convict) to his retirement as a physician in 1826, Redfern performed service of incalculable worth, often for no pay. Undoubtedly his most crucial contribution to Australia's development came in 1814, when he attended to outbreaks of disease on three convict ships that arrived from Britain: the *General Hewitt* (in February), the *Three Bees* (May), and the *Surry* (July). One of the diseases was typhus.

If it had spread the colony might have been decimated. But Redfern put in place effective quarantine measures and later made an official report (commissioned by Governor Lachlan Macquarie) concerning conditions on convict ships. Its recommendations were taken up by the relevant British authorities, with the result that countless lives were saved on future voyages – and not only to Australia.[132] The medical historian Edward Ford has described Redfern's report as 'one of the major Australian contributions to public health'.[133]

### The first generation of native-born Australians

Bare physical survival was one thing. But what of the moral character of the first generation of native-born Australians – the so-called currency lads and lasses? Everyone agreed they grew up remarkably fine specimens, not merely physically but in terms of strength of personality. They were honest and decent and industrious.

This was another near-miracle. As Robert Hughes asked rhetorically in *The Fatal Shore*: 'How did the cankered stock of English criminality produce such fresh, green shoots?'[134]

Various theories have been proposed, some based on economic forces.[135] But in my view there were two main factors at play. First and foremost, huge credit must be given to their parents – especially their mothers.

Who *were* Australia's founding mothers? Most of them were young adults from the slums of London or other English cities. That made them underprivileged, but not necessarily stupid and certainly not the 'damned whores' of yore.[136] Though guilty of the crimes for which they were transported,[137] almost none of them were dangerous criminals.[138]

Most had been convicted for stealing food, clothes or other goods of low value.[139] John Nicol, a steward on the *Lady Juliana* (the first ship to reach Sydney after the First Fleet), commented favourably in his journal on the behaviour of the female convicts during the outward journey. There were 'not a great many very bad characters', he thought. Most of them had been convicted for being no more than disorderly.[140]

Nicol turned out to be right. In the different circumstances of the Australian colonies these women proved their worth. Some became school teachers; more became nurses and midwives. But it was as mothers that they performed their most vital and enduring role. Indeed, according to John Moore, 'in the colony's early days few things were more impressive than the courage and unfailing service of mothers'.[141] As Governor John Hunter rightly remarked at the time, 'if we estimate their merits by the charming children with which they have filled the colony they will deserve our care'.[142] In the latter connection, it is noteworthy that female convicts were assigned much less taxing physical work than the men and were exempted from work entirely while nursing babies. They also had the chance of escaping their station by marriage, as many did.[143]

It is true that a good number of the convicts (male and female) had been estranged from their own parents. At the least, in the words of L.L. Robson, many had paid the price for 'indifferent or non-existent parental control'.[144] That was why they had fallen into crime back in Britain. The women, in particular, were clearly aware of this, and were not going to repeat the same mistakes. Moreover – and this is the most important point of all – they were not innately wicked people. They were fallen people, in the Christian sense that we are *all* fallen people, but few if any were irredeemable monsters. As Russel Ward put it, 'most emancipist parents, though they commonly cohabited without clerical licence or divine blessing, were in other ways reformed and normally decent people'.[145]

I would add a further wrinkle. Though most female convicts were not observant Christians, still their bedrock thinking was Biblical. They feared divine judgment. I agree with John Moore: 'The church's education system [in Britain] was more effective than is often acknowledged. These women who were at the bottom of the social scale had at least a passing familiarity with its practices and teachings.'[146] They knew enough to understand where they themselves had gone wrong, and they passed on their hard-won wisdom to their children.

The second key factor in the success of the first Australian-born generation was education. William Wilberforce was one who saw its importance early on. Writing in November 1805 to the Secretary for War and the Colonies, Lord Castlereagh, he urged 'taking in hand the education of the colony's children [as] the way to improve things quickly and surely'.[147] Castlereagh agreed, instructing the incoming governor, William Bligh, that 'the Government should interfere in behalf of the rising generation and, by the exertion of authority as well as of encouragement, endeavour to educate them in religious as well as industrious habits'.[148] Yet even before Castlereagh's edict, steps had been taken to educate the children of New South Wales. Phillip established the first school in 1789.

It is notable that the early governors and the powers that be in England regarded the first generation of children in New South Wales as in more urgent need of education than the (lower class) children of England itself. The reasons were the 'convict stain' that so many of the former carried,[149] and their sheer numerical importance to the future of the colony. By the time of Macquarie, 'colonial children [got] a better schooling than their English cousins'[150] because both Church and State took steps in New South Wales that would not be taken in England for another forty years. On the part of the State, these steps included the construction of school buildings and the remuneration of teachers, both paid for by a combination of land grants, provisions from government stores and the payment of salaries.[151] It is true that in the colony's early decades only a minority of children received a formal education (that is, attended school during the week).[152] But that minority would prove, in the end, highly influential. (I have in mind later leaders such as John Batman, the co-founder of Melbourne; John Robertson, a five-time premier of New South Wales; and John Tebbut, a world-famous astronomer.) Moreover, the notion of education extended beyond attendance at a day school; it encompassed home instruction, trade apprenticeships, church attendance and Sunday school.

Now, this is the vital point. *Until the 1830s, the principal burden of providing education within the colony fell on the Church of England.* Effectively it acted as the agent of the State, or in partnership with it.[153] This was an era when 'religion and education were regarded as inseparable'.[154] The overriding aim of the governing classes was to produce a citizenry that was God-fearing, law-abiding and functionally literate. 'The ability to read the Bible was the principal goal.'[155] Today that may seem astounding, but it is a fact. Bible-reading was both a means to an end (the acquisition of basic reading skills) and an end in itself (the inculcation of Christian values).[156]

In any fair-minded view, the system worked. The colony simply would not have survived – let alone prospered – if the first native-born generation had all been amoral dolts.

## The era of Macquarie

Lachlan Macquarie (1762–1824) served as Governor of New South Wales from 1810 to 1821. I do not have space to list all his achievements, which are amply documented elsewhere.[157] Suffice to say, it was under his leadership that New South Wales went from being a penal colony, pure and simple, to a nascent free society. In short, he ensured Australia's long-term survival.

His best-known policy was to extend kindness and generosity to emancipated convicts. 'Once a convict has become a free man,' Macquarie believed, 'he should in all respects be considered on a footing with every other man in the colony, according to his rank in life and character.'[158] One of Macquarie's countless applications of this principle was his appointment of Dr William Redfern as a magistrate.

Like many great leaders – especially reformist leaders – Macquarie was a divisive, controversial figure during his lifetime. Despite his moral conservatism (he actively encouraged marriage, for example), snobs and money-grubbers resented him bitterly. Commissioner J.T. Bigge, dispatched by a reactionary Tory administration in Britain to report on the state of the colony, lambasted Macquarie's merciful attitude to convicts and emancipists (including Redfern's appointment) and his liberal expenditure on public works. This harmed Macquarie's reputation at the time, but today there is remarkable unanimity: his greatness is very rarely disputed. A feminist writer of the 1970s, Helen Heney, described him as 'the catalyst in [the] creation and growth of the Australian consciousness'.[159] Another hard taskmaster, Guy Rundle, an astringent voice of today's secular Left, has rated him 'unquestionably the country's second founder'.[160]

In a very recent book devoted to Macquarie, Luke Slattery wrote: 'Was he, then, a radical or a conservative? A nostalgist or a progressive? Macquarie challenges us to dispense with political nomenclature.'[161]

Precisely! But Slattery's puzzlement is a reflection of our secular age. The key point about Macquarie is simple – and far, far too often overlooked. He and his second wife Elizabeth (nee Campbell) were Evangelical Christians; she had been one since childhood, he was a late convert. And, indubitably, their religion mattered. In the words of biographer John Ritchie, by the time they reached New South Wales,

Macquarie harboured 'deep within him … a cardinal faith, augmented by Elizabeth, in a Christianity imbued with the eternal themes of atonement, absolution and redemption, as well as with the belief that all human creatures were equal in the sight of God'.[162] Moreover, as this faith grew, the governorship increasingly afforded him 'the means of translating his private values into a public sphere'.[163] In England he had the support of the pious Hunter (now returned from the colony) – who, it may be noted, 'set in motion the forces' that enabled the policies of Macquarie to be implemented.[164] Macquarie also had the support of the Clapham Sect (including William Wilberforce, with whom he corresponded regularly), and, in Sydney, that of the Reverends William Cowper and Robert Cartwright, and other Protestant clergymen.[165]

In defending himself against Bigge's charges, Macquarie did not dispute the central facts. He *had* been merciful to convicts and emancipists and had spent a lot of money on public works. But he was proud of his record. He stated expressly in a letter to the Colonial Secretary, Earl Bathurst, that his motives were in part religious.

## Exploration

Even today, the feats of our maritime and inland explorers are taught in schools and generally well known. So they should be: their achievements were essential to the survival, and eventual expansion, of the colonies. It is much less well known that almost all these men were practising Christians – some were truly fervent.

Charles Sturt (1795–1869), for example, the man principally responsible for the discovery of the Murray–Darling river system, was by every account an admirable gentleman and an utterly sincere Protestant believer.[166] The same was true of John Oxley and Edward John Eyre;[167] Eyre, indeed, was the son of an English clergyman. Several other notable Australian explorers were the sons of clergymen, including Charles Bonney, Peter Egerton Warburton, William Landsborough and John Septimus Roe. Thomas Mitchell, Ernest Giles and George Grey were Evangelicals and Ludwig Leichhardt a committed Lutheran. Matthew Flinders, the first circumnavigator of the continent – he stands with Abel Tasman and James Cook as one of the three most important cartographers in Australian history – was married to a parson's daughter.[168]

The religious faith of these men was not coincidental. In many cases their journals and autobiographies demonstrate that it was their faith that *sustained* them in the midst of quite extraordinary dangers and privations. They observed the Sabbath out in the desert and the scrub. They were also inspired by a sense of Providence or mission. For instance, when Mitchell discovered the fertile grasslands of Victoria (Australia Felix) he wrote that he believed they had been 'specially prepared by the Creator for the industrious hands of Englishmen'.[169]

Sturt – the greatest of all the colonial explorers – concluded the official narrative of his expedition to Central Australia as follows:

> I have recorded instances enough of the watchful superintendence of that Providence over me and my party, without whose guidance we should have perished, nor can I more appropriately close these humble sheets, than by such an acknowledgment, and expressing my fervent thanks to Almighty God for the mercies vouchsafed to me during the trying and doubtful service on which I was employed.[170]

### The wool industry

In order to become more than a struggling penal settlement, New South Wales had to develop a self-sufficient economy. It was the same in Van Diemen's Land, and, in due course, the other colonies. Until the 1850s, agricultural production – principally of wool and wheat – was the key. We needed exportable commodities. Wool came first, and its importance is hard to overstate. In the words of Keith Hancock, perhaps our finest economic historian, 'wool made Australia a solvent nation, and, in the end, a free one'.[171]

The point for present purposes is this. Most of the pioneers of the wool industry were serious practising Christians. In ascending order of importance they were the Reverend Samuel Marsden and John and Elizabeth Macarthur. To be clear: I rate Elizabeth's contribution above that of her more famous husband. The Australian wool industry would not have got off the ground without her.

All the evidence shows that Elizabeth Macarthur (1766–1850) was a thoroughly admirable human being and the backbone of the Macarthur family. She was in the mould of Jane Austen's best heroines. 'The first woman of education and sensitivity to reach the colony'[172] and beautiful in appearance, she raised five sons and three daughters while charming all who knew her. 'Impossible though it may seem,' wrote one biographer, 'she does not appear to have been mentioned by contemporaries except in praise.'[173]

But Elizabeth was not just delightful company. During her husband's two long absences overseas she was forced to take responsibility for management of their sheep operations at Camden Park. Biographer Jill Conway has argued that it was positively fortuitous for New South Wales that the couple were split between England and Sydney, especially in the years from 1809 to 1817: John was able to imagine the big picture and lobby the powers that be in the Mother Country while his wife – often but not always following his written instructions – did the hard yakka back in the colony. Most of the practical problems were at home, and in this formative period she (not he) had the tact, poise and patience to deal with them.[174] She also dealt with his increasing eccentricity throughout the 1820s, his baseless charges of unfaithfulness, and the melancholia that blighted his last few years. She had grace. It should have been her face, not John's, that adorned the old Australian two-dollar note. In any event it is hard to disagree with the assessment of Helen Heney: she was 'the greatest woman pioneer of all'.[175]

How did she do it? Having read her journals and letters – which are exquisite – and studied the details of her life, I am convinced she drew enormous strength from her Anglican faith. It was not a boisterous Evangelical form of faith, but it was constant and real, and seems to have been ingrained in her as a girl. She grew up in a small village called Bridegrule in southwest England, close to the border between Devon and Cornwall. But her father, a farmer, died when she was six, and her mother remarried. Elizabeth spent a lot of her childhood living with the family of the local vicar, the Reverend John Kingdon, who was an Oxford graduate and respected Biblical scholar.[176] It was almost certainly through the Kingdons that she acquired her religious education and – I would guess – her bright, good-humoured virtue.

Her letters are revelatory. Some were written to her friend Eliza Kingdon back in Bridgerule. Even during her early years in Sydney, which were frequently arduous and occasionally frightening, Elizabeth often expressed gratitude to God ('you see how bountifully Providence has dealt with us'[177] and 'I thank God we enjoy all the comfort we could desire'[178]). Her thanks sometimes extended to the Lord's bounty towards strangers. In 1790 she wrote of the fact that the colonists on Norfolk Island had found, in mutton birds, a much-needed source of food: 'so firm a reliance on the merciful dispensations of an Almighty, whose hand I think we may here trace without presumption'.[179] Four decades later, when her beloved husband had been confined to an asylum, she still expressed thanks. She confided to her son Edward: 'Let us be thankful to the Almighty, that a wholesome restraint was placed upon your beloved father before his malady had induced him to acts of greater violence.'[180] She was revered by her children, all of whom 'received careful and painstaking education, both secular and religious'.[181] From this the colony benefited in the long run.

It is hard to imagine that her husband could ever have coped without her. Even he – proud and haughty – seems to have understood this. In one tender letter (which incidentally suggests underlying deistic beliefs of his own), he wrote this: 'May God almighty reward you, both in this world and the next, and may the remainder of your life be free from those cruel cares and sorrows that have checkquered so many of the last ten years.'[182]

The twilight of her life was, in fact, quite happy. She survived John by sixteen years. On her death in 1850, her granddaughter wrote of her: 'Through all the difficulties and trials that beset her path, her Christian spirit shines forth, and in all her letters to her children, with whom she corresponded regularly until her death, there is found no complaining or ill-natured word.'[183]

### Charity and philanthropy

Apart from the release of food from government stores in the early decades, there was no State-funded social welfare in the Australian colonies for most of the nineteenth century. Nor was there any State-funded assistance to small business. It was not until the 1880s that any colonial government imposed a direct tax on land, income or wealth.[184] The relief of poverty and other social distress was left almost exclusively to the Churches, and to private benefactors and volunteers. They rose to the challenge, and kept countless destitute people alive.

The Bank of South Wales (now Westpac) and the Benevolent Society of New South Wales are two of the oldest still-extant bodies in Australia. They were founded in 1817 and 1818 respectively by Evangelical Protestants. (Many of the same people set up the Bible Society of New South Wales.) After 1820, numerous charities and other civic and community institutions were founded by the Catholic Church and the various Protestant denominations. Non-conformists were especially active: their lay members made huge contributions in all the colonies in terms of libraries, savings banks, schools, mechanics institutes (educational institutions, primarily for working men) and so forth. As the religious historian Ian Breward has pointed out, this is 'one of the most important ways of tracing the influence of the churches in Australia'.[185]

The dominant model of health insurance was that of the English friendly and mutual provident societies, invented by the Quakers of

Yorkshire in 1832. All such societies here, including the biggest, AMP, were established by small groups of devout Christians. Many private hospitals were (and still are) run by the Churches, sometimes as charities. The renowned St Vincent's Hospital in Sydney, for instance, was established in 1857 by the Irish Sisters of Charity as a place of free treatment for all comers, but especially the poor.[186] Three other hospitals followed shortly afterwards in Victoria, Queensland and Tasmania respectively.

Likewise, virtually without exception, the most generous individual philanthropists were motivated by Christian charity. The greatest of them all in this formative period was a woman, Caroline Chisholm (1808–77).

Chisholm's face appeared on Australia's first five-dollar note – and appropriately so. Her life has been scrutinised by biographers for over a century, in both Britain and Australia,[187] and her reputation remains very high. Put simply, she was a great woman – in Henry Kendall's phrase, 'a second Moses in bonnet and shawl'.[188] Unlike Elizabeth Macarthur, she did not leave behind a large estate or even a family dynasty. She and her husband died almost penniless. But the memory of her charitable work lived on in the minds of those she helped. She was also a shining example of the best sort of religious pluralism: in everything she did, her conscious motive was to 'serve all creeds'.[189]

Not even the anti-religious Russel Ward quibbled about Caroline Chisholm's achievements. On the contrary, Ward lauded her: 'By precept and example she did more than any other single human being to ameliorate ... the status of Australian women.'[190] That was a big call in 1982, and even now it is hard to disagree.

Chisholm was born Caroline Jones in 1808, to lower-middle class parents in rural Northamptonshire. Religion was central to her upbringing. Her mother Sarah was an Evangelical Anglican who stressed not only the duty the rich owe to the poor, but the duty the poor owe to the even poorer. Jesus' story of the widow's mite (Mark 12:41–44) was among Sarah's favourites.[191] Clearly the message resonated with her daughter, who took up philanthropic causes as a teenager; equally clearly, Sarah's brand of Anglicanism encompassed tolerance of other Christian denominations. When, in December 1830, Caroline married Archibald Chisholm – a British Army captain in India – she crossed over into his Church. Captain Chisholm was an unusual religious animal – a Scottish Roman Catholic. One of his brothers and several of his cousins were priests.[192] Becoming a Catholic was a significant decision for Caroline – feminists of today might argue that she ought to have been true to herself – but she seems never to have regretted it. Her faith was ecumenical in flavour. The one demand she made of her new husband was that she be permitted to continue with philanthropic work.[193] He agreed, and ever after supported her in her labours.

After a lengthy stint in India the Chisholms arrived in Sydney in April 1838, settling soon afterwards in Windsor. Caroline, then aged 30, was pregnant with their third son. Despite Windsor's distance from Sydney, and all the responsibilities of marriage and parenthood, Caroline travelled widely (mostly on horseback) and kept her eyes and ears open. She learned several disturbing things about the nascent society in which she had come to live – for one, that too many newly arrived female immigrants in Sydney were workless, homeless and friendless. Some were forced into prostitution. Caroline did not condemn them but resolved to help them, and – critically for present purposes – her motives were *religious*.

On Easter Sunday 1841, at St Mary's Cathedral in Sydney, she dedicated herself to a life of service: 'I was enabled at the altar of our Lord, to make an offering of my talents to the God who gave them ... I felt my offering was accepted.'[194]

In fact, Chisholm had already embarked on a life of service. This was but a *re*-dedication of her talents. In Sydney she had begun the practice of meeting incoming ships at Circular Quay wharf and greeting the female immigrants. Earlier in 1841 she had established the Sydney Female Immigrants Home, a combined hostel and employment registry. Over the next five years, until her (temporary) return to England in 1846, she found accommodation and jobs for thousands of new arrivals in the colony. Many of the jobs were outside Sydney, and frequently Chisholm herself accompanied the women to their new places of work. Within a couple of years she had established a dozen rural employment agencies, and her network had become so successful that she was able to close the home. She then devoted much of her time to travelling, collecting information from immigrants throughout the colony. The idea was to help prospective immigrants in Britain better understand what was in store for them and to formulate appropriate public policies to assist them.[195] Chisholm had morphed from charity-worker to social reformer.

Once back in England, she lobbied government figures fearlessly and founded, in 1849, her own Family Loan Colonisation Society. The squattocracy in Australia was suspicious of her egalitarian sympathies and blocked some of her proposals, but she won some eminent supporters in England, including Charles Dickens. Eventually, among other achievements, she was instrumental in improving the colonial postal service and shipboard conditions for immigrants. By the time she returned to Australia in 1854, this time to Port Phillip (Melbourne), she was 'one of the most famous women in England'.[196]

In Port Phillip she soon earned an even finer public reputation than she had in New South Wales. She was an early advocate of land reform – 'free selection before survey' – a measure implemented later in the nineteenth century. The idea was to unlock the land – to disperse struggling families from the cities to the country and enable them to 'start afresh with homes of their own'.[197] Populist political giants, such as John Robertson and Henry Parkes in New South Wales, and William Nicholson in Victoria, based their careers upon it.

Chisholm, then, was a selfless and courageous woman, ultimately quite radical in her political beliefs. She met opposition from numerous powerful men, both secular and religious. In many ways she should be a model for Australian feminists today. To some extent she is. Yet it is important to note that, consistent with her Christian faith, she always remained a staunch social conservative. She operated on the assumption that women needed husbands and homes. Further, she extolled marriage – and, better still, family life with children – as the best way to promote morality in Australian *men*. 'She believed that women – good women – had the power to civilise men through love.'[198] If they tried, and especially if their love was reciprocated, wives and mothers could assume their ideal role in colonial society – as 'God's police'.

Today, for some, this notion may seem patronising, even absurd. Yet Caroline Chisholm's vision substantially became reality. Australia changed, and for the better. Who would now wish it had happened differently? And who, knowing something of Chisholm's story, would dismiss her beliefs and principles out of hand?

### The survival of the Indigenous population

Saving the Indigenous population of Australia from total extinction may be the Christian Churches' most important collective achievement. Yet they get little credit for it. In fact, it seems a common misconception nowadays that the Churches have somehow been largely to blame for the plight of the Indigenous since 1788. According to Phillip Adams, 'mailed-fist missionary zeal created the tragedy of this country'.[199] But the facts, demonstrably, are otherwise.

My purpose in this section is not to strike another blow in the 'History Wars'. The denialist case does not hold water, but personally I cannot fully subscribe to a 'hard realist' or 'liberal fantasy' view either. (The terms are those of historian John Hirst.) Severe disruption to Indigenous society was inevitable once the British decided on colonisation. Even with the best will in the world – which is to say, even if the *terra nullius* principle had never been applied and fair compensation had been made for all traditional lands – dislocation and disruption were bound to happen. Western diseases wrought havoc and Indigenous warriors committed murders too (admittedly, or so their defenders would say, in pre-emptive self-defence). Nonetheless, the likes of Hirst set up a false choice. There is nothing hypocritical about the way the current generation of Australians feels shame and sorrow for the crimes and other misdeeds of the past – and seeks to atone for them now.[200]

Granted, non-Indigenous Australians would not be here today if British colonisation had not occurred. I am even prepared to concede that, once here, the British had a kind of duty to develop the continent. (J.D. Lang was one who held to this view.) In 1838 the *Sydney Morning Herald* opined:

> Where, we ask, is the man endowed with even a modicum of
> reasoning powers, who will assert that this great continent was ever
> intended by the Creator to remain an unproductive wilderness? …
> The British people found a portion of the globe in a state of waste –
> they took possession of it. And they had a perfect right to do so, under
> the Divine authority, by which man was commanded to go forth and
> people, and till the land.[201]

What – precisely – was wrong in this paragraph? Two things, I would say. First, Terra Australis before 1788 was neither unproductive nor in a state of waste; it had sustained millions of inhabitants for at least 50,000 years. Second, the British people did not have an unfettered right to 'take possession' of the land. They had a legal obligation to give fair compensation for any land they took – that, in essence, is what the High Court of Australia decided in the *Mabo* decision in 1992. More generally, they were obliged both legally and morally to effect colonisation in a far more humane way than actually occurred. Things could and should have been done more peaceably, more fairly, more lovingly – in short, in a much more Christian way. At the least, the attempt should have been made. As is always the case in Christianity, the key to any moral judgment is less the outcome than the motive.

Far too many white men on the frontiers had thoroughly evil motives. The crimes were worst in Van Diemen's Land, during the horror years from 1825 to 1831, but no colony was exempt. It was a view commonly held that the killing of Aboriginal people ought not to be regarded as a crime, let alone a capital crime.[202] In the Port Phillip district in the period from 1835 to 1850 only one European was convicted of shooting an Aboriginal, and he served only two months in gaol.[203] Yet we know that hundreds if not thousands of Aboriginals were shot. 'Every station,' recalled one settler, 'has some tragic tale connected with [it].'[204]

What were they thinking? At a public meeting in Mudgee, New South Wales, in the 1830s, a wealthy squatter named George Cox declared that the best measure towards 'the Blacks' would be to 'Shoot them all and manure the ground with them!'[205] A Victorian pastoralist explained himself to a missionary in early 1840:

> Mr Hutton avowed his [policy] to be terror; to keep the natives
> in subjection by fear; and to punish them wholesale, by tribes and
> communities. If a member of a tribe offended, destroy the whole. He
> believed they must be exterminated.[206]

The tragedy of this country was not created by well-meaning Christian missionaries, however obtuse and naïve some of them were. The suggestion is ludicrous. The tragedy of this country was created – principally, at any rate – by the perpetrators of deep-seated secular evil. Initially, lust for land, money and power was at the heart of things; later in the nineteenth century, convenient social Darwinism ('they are a doomed and inferior race anyway') also played a part.[207]

What it all boiled down to was widespread failure to observe the Golden Rule. That was the thrust of then Prime Minister Paul Keating's justly celebrated Redfern Speech of December 1992.

Unquestionably, the Churches and individual clerics must bear some of the blame. Too many 'respectable' Christians were dismissive of Indigenous people and complicit in atrocities. They were not, by and large, the instigators. But by their silence, their inaction, their turning of a blind eye, they let evil men get away with theft and rape and murder. Worse still, some co-opted Christianity to defend the indefensible. The Book of Genesis was invoked: Indigenous peoples were compared with the cursed descendants of Ham.[208] In Van Diemen's Land, the worst of the atrocities occurred on the watch of an Evangelical lieutenant-governor, George Arthur. Despite various arguments in mitigation, which I have detailed in an endnote,[209] Arthur and a number of other leading religious figures in the colony cannot be exonerated.

But the other side of the story must not be forgotten. Among the ranks of the small white minority who did speak out bravely on behalf of Indigenous peoples, it was Christians who dominated. They took to heart, in particular, a verse from Acts 17:26: 'God hath made of one blood all nations of men for to dwell on all the face of the earth' (KJV).

For a start, they were the only people who took a serious interest in Indigenous language and culture. I have mentioned the investigations of Tench and Dawes in Sydney in the first few years of colonisation. The next major discoveries were made by an earnest Congregationalist pastor, Lancelot Edward Threlkeld (1788–1859). Dispatched to the South Seas by the London Missionary Society in 1817, he arrived in New South Wales in 1824 and began living with the Awabakal people of the Lake Macquarie district. It may seem an obvious insight now, but Threlkeld believed it was crucial to learn a native language in order to maximise his prospects of evangelistic success. He translated Luke's Gospel into Awabakal, though, tragically, his translation was not published until 1892.[210] In the event, he made few converts and fell out with his superiors at the Mission Society (including its local agent, Samuel Marsden). But he made an invaluable contribution to understanding Indigenous language and culture[211] and was a brave spokesman for the general welfare of Aboriginals. So too were a pair of Lutheran missionaries at Encounter Bay in South Australia in the 1840s, H.A.E. Meyer and George Taplin, and the Presbyterian William Ridley, who ministered in both New South Wales and Queensland in the 1850s, and translated parts of the New Testament into the Kamilaroi language.[212]

Most of the missionaries who followed Threlkeld in the nineteenth century had similarly poor success with evangelism. But unlike most white settlers on the frontiers, who were ruthless, and most white residents in the cities, who were indifferent, the missionaries cared deeply about the fate of Indigenous peoples. Regrettably, few immersed themselves in Indigenous language and culture – sufficiently or at all – and this limited their effectiveness. Nevertheless, there were honourable exceptions. Three of the standouts were Karl Schmidt (d. 1864), a Polish missionary who led the Presbyterians' early efforts in Moreton Bay; Dom Rosendo Salvado (1814–1900), an extraordinary Spanish Benedictine monk who founded the New Norcia mission in Western Australia; and Carl Strehlow (1871–1922), a German-Lutheran pastor who served for almost 30 years as head of the Central Australian mission at Hermannsburg (later Ntaria). Strehlow assisted another Lutheran missionary, J.G. Reuther, in completing the first full translation of the New Testament into an Indigenous language.

Because the missionaries had taken an interest in Indigenous peoples as human beings, they were at the forefront of attempts to save them from extermination. So much is conceded by almost all serious historians, including some of the most eminent on the secular Left. These men and women have taken the trouble to study the facts. In some cases, I suspect, they have been surprised by what they found. Professor Henry Reynolds, one of the doyens of Indigenous history, has openly acknowledged what once seemed to him an 'intriguing point': the strongest advocates of Aboriginal rights were those most influenced by Christianity.[213]

Robert Kenny has been quite explicit:

> In the mid-nineteenth century a *secular* belief in a future for Aboriginal Australians, or a right to that future, was difficult to find. Those who believed in such a future were driven not by visions of 'democratic equality', still less by 'Enlightenment' philosophy, but overwhelmingly by dogged Christian faith [original emphasis].[214]

Consider, for example, these mournful words of John Bede Polding, Catholic Archbishop of Sydney, in 1845:

> I have heard it maintained … that it is the course of Providence, that blacks should disappear before the white, and the sooner the process was carried out the better, for all parties. I fear such opinions prevail to a great extent. Very recently in the presence of two clergymen, a man of education narrated, as a good thing, that he had been one of a party who had pursued the blacks, in consequence of cattle being rushed by them, and that he was sure that they shot upwards of a hundred. When expostulated with, he maintained that there was nothing wrong in it, that it was preposterous to suppose they had souls. In this opinion he was joined by another educated person present.[215]

Edward Stone Parker, a Methodist preacher, said this at a public lecture in Melbourne in 1854:

> Let the men of the world say, if they will … 'Let them die, as die they must,' and, as has actually been said to me, – 'The sooner they perish the better.' But let every Christian man … say with one voice, to the

government, the legislature, and the nation; – occupy the land, – till its broad wastes, – extract its riches, – develop its resources, – if you will; but, in the name of God and humanity, SAVE THE PEOPLE.[216]

To a large extent, people such as Polding and Parker failed. But it is strongly arguable that they and their kind spared Indigenous peoples an even worse fate than the one they suffered. As a surviving Aboriginal man from Gippsland said in 1858: 'Only for the missionaries there wouldn't be so many Aborigines walking around today. They're the ones that saved the day for us.'[217]

It was the same throughout the rest of mainland Australia: a terrible story overall, redeemed to a degree by the efforts of missionaries. Noel Pearson, one of today's most eloquent and respected voices for Indigenous Australia, is a self-described 'third-generation legatee of mission protection'.[218] Raised on a Lutheran mission at Cape York in Queensland, he is on record as saying that missions 'provided a haven from the hell of life on the Australian frontier while at the same time facilitating colonisation'.[219] More recently he has written bluntly: 'without the Lutherans my people would have perished on the Cooktown frontier'.[220] One cannot but admire Pearson's nuanced candour:

> As inheritors of the mission's religion and traditions, people like
> me necessarily hold complex perspectives on this history. The
> missionaries' kindnesses and humanity were mixed with the racialism
> of the time, and their objection to and support for various aspects of
> the colonial enterprise does not tell a simple story.[221]

There was an especially bad period of frontier terror in New South Wales in the years between 1837 and 1845, including the infamous Myall Creek massacre of 10 June 1838.[222] Twenty-eight unarmed men, women and children of the local Wirrayaraay clan were killed – trussed, shot, beheaded and then incinerated – by a posse of eleven assigned convicts and ticket-of-leavers. The ringleader was a free settler named John Fleming.

There was nothing especially unusual about this gruesome event, other than the aftermath. It was a very rare occasion when a measure of justice was done. Seven of the murderers (though not Fleming, who escaped from custody) were tried and – at their second trial – convicted. Subsequently they were hanged. This happened even though majority popular opinion was on the side of the accused and large amounts of money were contributed to their defence – including a contribution by the wealthy owner of Myall Creek Station, Henry Dangar.

The culprits were punished in this case because of a near-unique combination of circumstances and individuals. Several principled men took a stand in the face of private intimidation and public opprobrium, including a white witness, hut-keeper George Anderson, and two local stockmen, William Hobbs (the overseer at Myall Creek Station) and Frederick Foote, who reported what they had learned to the authorities. Equally crucial was the fact that four key public officials were serious Christians: the police magistrate at Muswellbrook, Edward ('Denny') Day; the attorney-general and prosecuting counsel, J.H. Plunkett; the presiding judge at the second trial, William Westbroke Burton; and the Governor of New South Wales, Sir George Gipps. When he sentenced the seven murderers to death, Justice Burton said: 'The law [against murder] is no conventional law, no common rule of life formed for human purposes; it is founded on the law of God.'

In 1999, the then deputy prime minister, John Anderson, made a gracious and penetrating speech in Federal Parliament in relation to the Myall Creek episode. Anderson was (and is) a practising Anglican, and his former electorate of Gwydir took in Myall Creek. 'In that incident,' he said, 'you see the very worst behaviour, but you also see the very best behaviour. I deeply and sincerely regret the worst, but I celebrate the hope that the best gives us.'[223]

Colonial Australia was not godless – far from it. It was rough and often irreverent, and much evil was perpetrated on its frontiers. But without religion, and committed individuals motivated by religion, it would not have existed – or not for long. The convicts would have been sent to their doom in West Africa, or the First Fleet would have foundered. The colonists, or those of them who arrived alive, would soon have starved, or fallen fatally ill, or committed suicide, or descended to impoverished barbarism. The first generation of native-born, those of them who survived childhood, would have grown up as lazy, unprincipled brutes. Sydney might have remained no more than a penal colony and most of the rest of the continent might have been left unexplored. And if, without religion, all of these hurdles had somehow been overcome, the Indigenous population would have been wiped out. The whole venture, in any of these ways, could have been a disaster.

# CHAPTER 2

# An enduring legacy to the West

The past which a historian studies is not a dead past, but a past which in some sense is still living in the present.

R.G. Collingwood, nineteenth-century English historian

The white mist dances in our eyes
But still, in every age and land,
His heart beats like a little child,
He writes of mercy on the sand.

John Shaw Neilson, Australian poet, 'He Was the Christ'

Non-Indigenous Australian society did not appear out of nowhere in 1788. Our British forebears were themselves the products of history. To understand why they were as they were – and why we are as we are – it is necessary to go back more than 2,000 years, to the time of Jesus. In the wonderful words of Ralph Waldo Emerson, 'the name of Jesus is not so much written as ploughed into the history of the world'.

You think that an exaggeration? It is not – and in the next two chapters I will explain why. This chapter will focus on the West in general. How was it that European countries such as Britain had the scientific know-how to colonise Terra Australis? And the necessary wealth? Why did all its citizens have such a strong sense of history and destiny? Why, in the minds of heroes like Lachlan Macquarie and William Redfern and Caroline Chisholm, was it imperative to extend charity to the lowly? Why did the Christian missionaries care about the Indigenous peoples?

These are questions that need answering. In doing so I will rebut a frequently repeated canard: that the West inherited its best ideas from the ancient Greeks and Romans. Consider this especially egregious example from a prominent Australian atheist, Tamas Pataki, in 2011:

> The fundamentals of our legal, political, civic and economic structures, as well as nearly every fruitful form of investigation, including moral exploration, we owe to Graeco-Roman civilization.[1]

That is wrong on every count. Australians should know why.

Let us start with some relatively uncontroversial facts.[2] Put to one side the reality or otherwise of Jesus' miracles, or of the Resurrection. It is generally accepted that Jesus was born in or about 5 BC, shortly before the death (in 4 BC) of King Herod the Great, the Rome-sanctioned ruler of Palestine. Between the age of about thirty and his death a few years later, Jesus established a following as an itinerant religious teacher. His supporters were small in number, but his activities generated much controversy. He came to the unfavourable notice of both the local Jewish authorities and the occupying Roman powers. He was put to death by crucifixion in or about AD 30, in Jerusalem, by order of the prefect of Judaea, Pontius Pilate, during the rule of Tiberius Caesar.

It is also generally accepted that Jesus was a man who kept unusually high moral standards and left behind a small band of people who had come, correctly or otherwise, to believe in his divinity. This group, the so-called Apostles, was led by Jews. It was they who 'invented' what came to be called Christianity, by attempting to reconcile Jesus with their existing faith, Judaism. They started preaching in Jerusalem, six weeks after the Crucifixion, and within 300 years their new hybrid faith was being practised by hundreds of thousands of people of many races throughout the mighty Roman Empire and beyond. In or about AD 312 it was adopted by the emperor himself, Constantine the Great, and in AD 380 it became the empire's official religion. These two decisions were as much strategic as spiritual ones: 'the vigour of Christianity' threatened the unity of the empire, so the powers that be went with the strength.[3]

Today, Christianity is practised by some 2.2 billion people worldwide. But while it is flourishing in Asia, Africa and South America, it is declining across the West. It seems probable that, within twenty years, the percentage of Australians identifying in the census as Christian will fall below 50 per cent.

Will that be the point at which all fair observers should be forced to admit that Australia has become a post-Christian nation? It depends on the criteria to be applied.

One noteworthy Australian who firmly rejects the post-Christian label is Edwin Judge, Emeritus Professor of History at Macquarie University in Sydney, and one of the world's more remarkable authorities on the first-century Church. Edwin Judge is a man to be reckoned with. In 1960 he advanced what was then a novel thesis. The prevailing view among historians, developed by the great Arnold J. Toynbee, was that the early Christian communities were primarily made up of, and directed by, the lower classes. In other words, Christianity in the first century spread from the bottom up. Judge questioned this view, pointing out that most early Christian writings in the Graeco-Roman world were directed at wealthy, literate and educated individuals. This suggested to him that the early Church spread from the top down. His theory attracted a good deal of academic comment, and in 1980 he put it forward again, in a modified and more sophisticated form. Subsequent research across the world has since refined his thesis. It has been called the 'new consensus'.[4]

Judge, then, speaks with authority. And he insists that it would be quite inaccurate to label Australia a post-Christian society – now or at any time in the foreseeable future. While not denying the waning influence of the institutional Churches, Judge points to Judaeo-Christianity's enduring *secular* legacies. In his words, 'contemporary ways of thinking and patterns of behaviour are in vital respects anchored in the Biblical understanding of the world'.[5] He is dismayed that these ways of thinking and patterns of behaviour are so blithely taken for granted in Australia, especially by agnostics and atheists.

I agree with him. While it is a commonplace that 'many social innovations, once established, become free of their origins',[6] it is important not to lose sight of those origins. We are all living off Judaeo-Christian capital. That capital includes the scientific method; the teleological view of history; parliamentary democracy; universities and mass literacy; the moral duties to be committed and charitable; and the primacy of individual conscience. Throw in music, the novel and naturalistic painting, and it is quite a package.[7]

## Judaism

Before Christianity there was Judaism. It was the faith Jesus was raised in. Its tenets were (and still are) laid down in a collection of writings sometimes referred to as the 'ancient Hebrew Scriptures'. Christians know them as the Old Testament. These extraordinary documents are, if nothing else, a history of the Jewish people. They cover the years from, roughly, 2000 to 400 BC. Admittedly, the Biblical account has been supplemented in large measure by centuries of careful scholarship and cannot at all points be read literally. But I cannot stress enough that even if one remains sceptical of its theological and supernatural content, the Old Testament is at core a record of real events, real places, real people.

The late American scholar John Bright cautioned that 'in attempting to describe how the people [of] Israel came into being we must at all costs avoid oversimplification'.[8] Despite that danger, I feel I must try. What follows is a bare-bones summary, drawn from Raymond Apple's book *The Jewish Way: Jews and Judaism in Australia*.[9] Apple, the Senior Rabbi of the Great Synagogue of Sydney between 1972 and 2005, was for more than three decades one of Australia's most eminent Jewish citizens. I have also relied on Bright's magnum opus, *A History of Israel*.

Human civilisation as we know it emerged about 10,000 years ago, in Mesopotamia. The area corresponds today with Iraq, Kuwait and northeastern Syria; it is centred upon the Tigris–Euphrates river system. Around 4,000 years ago, various tribal groups began to leave Mesopotamia. Let us call one of them the Hebrews, though that was not, then, what they called themselves. They were semi-nomadic peoples who made their living as breeders of sheep and cattle. In periodic waves they travelled westwards, in search of more land, to the region that ultimately became known as Canaan (modern-day Palestine). According to the Biblical account, which seems, at the least, 'demonstrably to embody a tenacious historical memory',[10] their first leader was a man named Abram (later called Abraham). When Abraham died he was succeeded by his son Isaac.[11]

During periods of drought and famine in Canaan, some of the Hebrews travelled further west, to Egypt. Isaac's son Jacob was one such early settler, along with his twelve sons and their families. (This is the origin of the 'twelve tribes of Israel'.) At first the new settlers co-existed with the Egyptians, but in time relations worsened and the Hebrews became enslaved. Others were brought to Egypt later as prisoners of war. After some hundreds of years in captivity a new leader, Moses, emerged among them. This probably occurred during the reign of the powerful Egyptian pharaoh Ramses II (c. 1290–24 BC). Moses led his people out of Egypt to Sinai and, eventually, after a circuitous 40-year journey eastwards, back to Canaan. This was the so-called Exodus – a seminal event in history regarded as marking the beginning of the 'nation of Israel'.[12] Moses himself did not quite reach the Promised Land. He farewelled his people within sight of it, at Mount Nebo in Moab.

According to Biblical tradition, it was Moses who wrote the first five books of the ancient Hebrew Scriptures, collectively known as the Torah – Genesis, Exodus, Leviticus, Numbers and Deuteronomy. Moses' authorship is now questioned by many scholars, and the date/s of the Torah's composition is also hotly debated. But it is probable that the *precepts* laid down in the Torah underpinned Hebrew society from the time of the Exodus until the time of Jesus.[13] The core precept was monotheism – the notion, embodied in the First Commandment, that there was only one God worthy of worship (Yahweh). That was not, I should emphasise, quite the same thing as believing that there was, in fact, only one God. That came later. As Bright points out, there are passages in the Old Testament in which the ancient Hebrews seemed to assume the existence of other gods. But from the beginning Israel believed in one god in a functional sense.[14]

The Torah contained the Ten Commandments and the far more detailed Mosaic Code, an intricate set of laws governing all aspects of life. Jesus summed them up thus: 'Love the Lord your God with all your heart and with all your soul and with all your strength and with all your mind; and, Love your neighbour as yourself' (Luke 10:27). It is uncanny to think that, over 3,000 years after they were first laid down, the Ten Commandments and some aspects of the Mosaic Code still underpin basic morality in the West.

After the Exodus, the Hebrews (by now the Israelites) reoccupied Canaan. It probably happened through a combination of brutal conquest (under a new leader, Joshua) and slow reintegration with the pre-existing Canaanite population (some of which was Hebrew in origin and culture).[15] At all events, soon after the conquest phase was completed, 'representatives of all components of Israel – both those who had worshipped Yahweh in the desert and Hebrews of Palestine who had newly joined with them – met at Shechem and there in solemn covenant engaged to be the people of Yahweh and to worship him alone'. They organised themselves into a loose confederation of tribes.[16]

The Israelites survived precariously for another 200 years or so (the period of the Judges). Then, around 1000 BC, came another key event in their history: the invasion of the Philistines. After decades of struggle a charismatic warrior named David led the Israelites to military victory, and, in the process, re-united the twelve tribes; he was proclaimed King of the United Kingdom of Israel. It was David who established Jerusalem as the nation's capital, and it was his son Solomon who, upon succeeding him as king, constructed the Great Temple there, on Mount Zion. This was a huge edifice and the spiritual centre of Judaism for centuries thereafter.

The destruction of Jerusalem in 586 BC by Babylonian invaders led by King Nebuchadnezzar II was 'the great watershed of Israel's history'. In Bright's words, 'at a stroke her national existence was ended and, with it, all the institutions in which her corporate life had expressed itself'.[17] The surviving Israelites, or all but a tiny remnant of them, endured another period of extended exile, in Babylon. It was not until 538–432 BC that they returned to their shattered homeland, in three stages. Gradually Israel was resettled and restored, and the temple at Jerusalem rebuilt – though on a scale considerably less grand than before.

By 165 BC or thereabouts, all of the Hebrew Scriptures had been written.[18] In addition to the Torah, there were the twelve so-called historical books (Joshua to Esther in the modern-day Protestant Bible); the five wisdom books (Job, Psalms, Proverbs, Ecclesiastes and the Song of Songs); and the works of the five major prophets (Isaiah, Jeremiah, Lamentations, Ezekiel, Daniel) and the twelve minor prophets (Hosea to Malachi).

As I have said, the notion that there is only one God can be traced back to the time of Abraham. But the first element of my definition of an essentially Christian view of the world (as outlined in the Introduction) is wider than that, and deliberately so. The Jewish God (Yahweh) is not a mere architect or watchmaker who set the Universe in motion and then stood aside. He is an all-knowing God who created and sustains the Universe, and who is vitally interested in the thoughts and conduct of each individual human being. He is a *personal* God. As Jewish scientist and author Robert Winston has explained, it took the Jewish people centuries to arrive at that conception: 'The ruination of their homeland and the repeated exiles they experienc[ed] eventually result[ed] in the Israelites arriving at a fresh understanding of God ... Their tortuous journey ... taught them the truth of monotheism.'[19]

## The Graeco-Roman world

It is critical to remember that in the ancient world the Jews were a small and relatively inconsequential group. In geopolitical terms, they were dwarfed by the Egyptians, the Babylonians, the Persians, the Greeks and the Romans (among others). Perhaps that is why they suffered so much.

When Jesus was born, around 5 BC, it was the Romans who ruled the roost. They had gained control of the Mediterranean basin in the war of 192–188 BC against the Seleucid king Antiochus III.[20] Roman rule over the Jews began in 63 BC. Troops commanded by Proconsul Pompeius Magnus (Pompey the Great) sacked Jerusalem and entered the Temple. Subsequently, Jerusalem and the areas surrounding it became a Roman 'client kingdom', and in AD 6 – when Jesus was a boy of eleven – parts of it became a province of the empire.[21] That was still the position when Jesus died, in or around AD 30, and it remained the position until AD 70. In that year the Romans laid siege to Jerusalem to crush a Jewish revolt. They destroyed the Temple and a Roman legion was garrisoned in the city.

The major challenges that faced Jesus' followers can now be enumerated. First, the dominant culture of the age was Graeco-Roman. I stress the 'Graeco' part of that formulation: despite the Romans' military might, Greek language and culture, and especially Greek philosophy, remained highly influential throughout the Mediterranean basin and beyond. Both the Greeks and the Romans worshipped a pantheon of gods of their own.[22] Second, the earliest of Jesus' disciples were Jews. They were members of a tiny, distrusted minority within the Roman Empire and their traditional religion, Judaism, was largely unknown to anyone but themselves. Third, even when they had made converts among Gentiles (non-Jews) in other parts of the Mediterranean basin, they were, from time to time, harshly penalised by the Romans. They were also actively disliked by the establishment Jews who had rebuffed Jesus during his lifetime and had engineered his execution.

An abiding complication was that it took the early Christians a long time fully to work out their own theological beliefs. Very few questioned Jesus' divinity[23] – a remarkable fact in itself – and by the end of the first century there was a general consensus among Christians that their God would judge every human soul in the afterlife. (Interestingly, the afterlife had not been a firm feature of Judaism and still is not;[24] the reality of divine judgment was a point hammered home by Jesus and his followers.) But there remained many secondary issues to be thrashed out. Paul of Tarsus, the author of most of the letters of the New Testament, made a vital contribution to this developing theology, but did not resolve all the issues. Far from it.

Even as Christianity spread, a vital and continuing challenge was reconciling Jesus' teachings and the circumstances of his life, death and resurrection with prevailing tenets of both Judaism and Greek philosophy. There was tension between the two great centres of intellectual power, Alexandria (in Egypt) and Antioch (in modern-day Turkey). Many early Christian thinkers proposed ideas that, while ultimately rejected, had to be grappled with. This process took centuries, though it was hurried along once Christianity had been sanctioned by the Roman Empire. The four key councils that debated and ruled upon these ideas were at Nicaea (AD 325), Constantinople (381), Ephesus (431) and Chalcedon (451).

For those interested in further details there are many good books on the subject.[25] Suffice to say, by the middle of the fifth century, an essentially Christian view of the world encompassed (at the very least) all three aspects of my definition: belief in an all-knowing God who created and sustains the Universe, and who is vitally interested in the thoughts and conduct of each individual human being; belief in an afterlife, in which each of us will be judged by God; and belief in the divinity of Jesus of Nazareth.

It is against this background that I can now examine Christianity's radical long-term impact on the West – Australia included. Adopting Edwin Judge's terminology, it is an exercise in comparison between (on the one hand) the main 'ways of thinking' and 'patterns of behaviour' of the Graeco-Roman or 'classical' world, and (on the other hand) those of the Christianised Western world.

The comparisons are stark. Indeed, the far-reaching implications of Christianity were not lost on classical thinkers of the first and second centuries. They were disgusted and disconcerted by this new faith. The very word 'Christian' was coined by them as a term of abuse. Christianity undermined or contradicted three basic features of the classical worldview; I will call them, with a nod to Edwin Judge, the 'closed Universe', the 'closed society' and the 'closed heart'. I should say that this exercise has been carried out at much greater length – and in quite breathtaking style – by the American Eastern Orthodox scholar David Bentley Hart. His 2009 book, *Atheist Delusions: The Christian revolution and its fashionable enemies*, is a tour de force. I will try to be more restrained in my rhetoric, though it is hard to disagree with Hart that 'it borders upon willful imbecility to lament the rise of Christendom'.[26]

## The closed Universe

Greek thinking was based on a fundamental axiom originally formulated by Parmenides of Elea in the early sixth century BC: change is impossible. Accordingly, to the Greek mind, the Universe itself was both eternal and perfect. Everything in it moved in pre-determined cycles, in infinite rotation. So said Empedocles, another pre-Socratic Greek philosopher, in the sixth century BC. It followed logically that nothing could be improved. A prime example was music. As Pythagoras of Samos first demonstrated, it is wired into the cosmos mathematically.

For the Greeks, science was not the rigorous discipline that we know today. It was a branch of philosophy, conducted not in a field or laboratory but in an armchair. One noticed a given phenomenon and sought to explain it by logic or analogy. The best and most elegantly argued explanation became accepted fact – when, and if, it was assented to by members of a tiny male elite. The key deficiency in this approach was that there was no such thing as experimental testing to confirm or disprove a given theory.[27] For example, Greek physicians never bothered to dissect a human body.

We now take for granted the so-called scientific method. The idea seems obvious: someone forms a hypothesis about the way an aspect of the physical world works, and decides how he (or she) will seek to prove it. This is done not by recourse to logic or analogy, or appeal to authority, but by demonstration. An experiment is devised and conducted, and the results are observed, recorded and published. One does not need to be a member of an elite to have one's theory accepted. The pre-existing consensus of received human wisdom should count for little, or nothing, if the experiment is sound.

Nicolaus Copernicus (1473–1543) is well known in the history of science. Famously, near the end of his life, he proposed that the Earth was not motionless but revolved around the Sun (and the Moon around the Earth). This heliocentric model of the solar system was not entirely novel – a Greek philosopher, Aristarchus of Samos, had made the suggestion in the third century BC – but Copernicus was the first person who seriously attempted to prove it. He spent years making astronomical observations and published a book, *On the Revolution of the Celestial Spheres* (1543), setting out his calculations. His theory was not accepted, principally because he lacked the necessary experimental tools. He worked with the naked eye and appealed principally to mathematical proofs rather than empirical data.[28] Copernicus was an instinctive genius, but failed to persuade most of his contemporaries of the falsity of the then-current geocentric model of the solar system, which had been laid down in the second century AD by a Greek philosopher named Ptolemy.[29]

The heliocentric model was proved definitively by Galileo Galilei (1564–1642), probably one of the two most important figures in the history of science. Only Isaac Newton is ranked higher on most experts' lists. Galileo's importance extended well beyond confirming Copernicus' theory. It was his method of doing so that mattered most. Galileo invented a new type of telescope, far in advance of the rudimentary Dutch prototypes, and backed up his arguments with observations that were more detailed and accurate than those of Copernicus. Galileo's subsequent book, *Dialogue Concerning the Two Chief World Systems* (1632), was a watershed. In the words of historian Michael Hart: 'Most previous natural philosophers, taking their cues from [the Greeks], had made qualitative observations and categorised phenomena; but Galileo measured phenomena and made quantitative observations.'[30]

It is for this reason that Galileo is sometimes described as the inventor of the scientific method. Others give that mantle to the English polymath Francis Bacon (1561–1626), and it is true that Bacon's key books extolling inductive reasoning – *The Advancement of Learning* (1605) and the *Novum Organum* (1620) – came first chronologically.[31] But Bacon was not a scientist. Apart from Galileo, two English scientists were among the first to employ the empirical method successfully: William Gilbert (1544–1603), the founder of the science of magnetism, and William Harvey (1578–1657), the first person to describe the circulation of blood systematically and in detail.[32]

It does not matter to which individual primary credit is given. The key point for present purposes is that the scientific method had its roots in Judaeo-Christianity. As Steve Bruce (an unbeliever) has put it, 'first Judaism and then Christianity were rationalizing forces'.[33]

Contemporary secularists might scoff at the notion that Judaeo-Christianity could be a rationalising force. But in the field of science, it was. It cut across several key aspects of the Graeco-Roman worldview that I have described. There is now a sizable body of literature dealing with Christianity's contribution to science,[34] but one of the more prominent and accessible authors is the American sociologist Rodney Stark, who in 2004 drew up a 'Roster of Scientific Stars'. Now well known (at least outside Australia), it is a list of the fifty-two most important scientists of the sixteenth to eighteenth centuries, the men who created science as we know it. Stark demonstrated that only two of them were religious sceptics. A clear majority were devout Christians and the rest (including Copernicus, Galileo, Gilbert and Harvey) were conventional Christians (neither nominal nor deeply devout).[35] It is an extraordinary list – well worth pondering – but of itself demonstrates the 'who' of modern science rather than the 'why'. To understand the causal link between modern science and Judaeo-Christianity it is necessary to delve a little more deeply.

The scientific method is a prime example of the pursuit of knowledge by inductive (or empirical) reasoning. This, unquestionably, was a by-product of Christianity. The main reason for its development was theological. For Christians, man lives in a fallen world. Man's powers of reasoning, while wonderful (and setting us apart from all other animals), are fallible. To know the truth of God's Creation, it is not enough to use human logic alone; it is also necessary to observe closely what God has created. God is not bound by human logic.[36]

Admittedly this insight was slow in coming. Medieval Christians developed many forms of clever technology without developing the scientific method as such.[37] It was not until the thirteenth and early fourteenth centuries that a quartet of Christian thinkers – Bishop Robert Grosseteste (c. 1168–1253), Roger Bacon (1214–94), William of Ockham (1285–1347) and Thomas Bradwardine (1295–1349) – began to articulate the key tenets of empirical thinking, and then only in a preliminary way.[38] A key step was taken in 1277, when a specially convened Church council formally rejected the Graeco-Islamic idea that (human) logic dictated what God could or could not do.[39]

Ironically, perhaps, it was a distinguished Greek authority on medicine way back in the second century, Claudius Galenus, who had first recognised this clash of worldviews. He is better known as Galen of Pergamon (AD 129 – c. 216). A record has survived of his observations about a new theory concerning the pulses in the human body, which had been proposed by a man named Archigenes from Apamea (in Syria). Archigenes taught in Rome early in the second century and had taken the trouble to devise a water clock to measure the pulse's rhythms. In short, he conducted experiments. His theory departed from received (Greek) wisdom, yet he still had the audacity to propose it. Galen complained: '[It is] as if one had come into the school of Moses or Christ!'[40]

There was another, related way in which Judaeo-Christianity acted as a rationalising force. Simply, it assumed an underlying rationality in the Universe. One all-knowing God – acting *outside* the Universe – was the author of everything. There existed within Creation fixed laws of nature, laid down by this God, which were there to be discovered. In the words of St Augustine of Hippo, writing in the fifth century, 'the ordinary course of nature in the whole of creation has certain natural laws'.[41] It was up to man to make the effort to find them. The Graeco-Roman gods, by contrast, were a flighty, capricious, all-too-human gaggle. They acted from *within* the Universe, often at cross-purposes, and had to be constantly appeased. They could not be relied upon for anything.[42]

The Judaeo-Christian concept of the rationality of God was given renewed emphasis by the so-called scholastic thinkers of the Middle Ages. (It was in this period that the Christian Church invented universities.[43]) But the clearest evidence of the potency of this idea came later – in the seventeenth century – from three giants in the history of science. All were devout Christians (and are so categorised in Rodney Stark's list). They all believed, like Galileo, that 'the laws of nature are written by the hand of God'.[44]

**First**, Johannes Kepler (1571–1630), the German astronomer who discovered the laws of planetary motion. Essentially he proved that planets move in elliptical rather than circular orbits. Kepler famously said: 'The chief aim of all investigations of the external world should be to discover the rational order which has been imposed on it by God.'[45]

**Second**, René Descartes (1596–1650), the French philosopher perhaps best remembered for a single aphorism: 'I think, therefore I am.' His greatest achievement was his treatise *Discourse on Method* (1637). In it, he popularised the notion of mechanical natural laws that govern everything except God and the human soul. He argued that such laws are ultimately grounded in mathematics, and must exist because God 'acts in a manner as constant and immutable as possible'.[46]

**Third**, Isaac Newton (1642–1727), perhaps the greatest scientist who ever lived. He was buried in Westminster Abbey, the first scientist accorded that honour. His achievements spanned optics, mathematics and (most importantly) physical mechanics. His magnum opus, the *Mathematical Principles of Natural Philosophy* (the *Principia*), was once described as 'preeminent above any other production of human genius'. In one of his many books of theology, *Observations on Daniel and the Revelation of St John*, Newton wrote thus of the Universe he did so much to explain: 'This most beautiful system of the Sun, planets and comets, could only proceed from the counsel and dominion of an intelligent and powerful Being.'[47]

Another way of testing the proposition that Christianity led to modern science is to pose a hypothetical question. Would modern science have developed, eventually, without Christianity? The general consensus is 'No'.[48] That is certainly the view of Edwin Judge. He points out that the Islamic world inherited the great corpus of Graeco-Roman wisdom in the early sixth century: after the Roman Emperor Justinian banned non-Christian teaching in AD 529, its leading exponents went to Baghdad, and took their libraries with them. This body of knowledge was preserved for centuries, and much of it was not rediscovered by the West until the 1300s. (Some classical learning, however, was preserved in Christendom during the so-called Dark Ages. The most important clerics in this regard were St Augustine of Hippo (AD 354–430), Boethius (AD 480–524) and John of Damascus (AD 676–749).)

Despite having this base of classical knowledge to build upon, and some very bright thinkers, the Islamic world never experienced a scientific revolution like that which occurred in the West. Nor did India or the Chinese Empire. In the eighteenth century, when Jesuit missionaries informed the Chinese about the state of scientific knowledge in Europe, the Chinese were astounded. 'For them the idea that the universe could be governed by simple laws that human beings could and had discovered was foolish in the extreme'.[49] What set the Judaeo-Christian West apart from the rest of the world – especially after the fifteenth century – was the scientific method.

Judaeo-Christianity not only transformed the ancient world's faulty approach to scientific investigation. Using the modern scientific method, man has been able to confirm empirically the truth of certain key Judaeo-Christian tenets and the falsity of some of those of the Greeks. One of the most striking examples is in the field of cosmology, where the Greeks believed that the physical Universe was eternal and unchanging. We now know that the opposite is the truth, on both counts.

The Universe had a beginning. Christian philosophers stuck to this view through thick and thin – John Philoponus, in the sixth century, was one such brave soul[50] – long before they were able to prove it scientifically. What eventually became known as the Big Bang theory was first proposed in the 1920s by a Belgian priest, Georges-Henri Lemaître (1894–1966). But Lemaître was ridiculed by disbelieving secularists in the scientific community who were repelled by the theory's obvious theological implications. 'Big Bang' was coined as a term of derision.[51] Until the 1960s most cosmologists stuck to the Graeco-Roman view of the Universe: what they called the Steady State theory. But by then the evidence against them had piled up. The decisive step was the discovery of cosmic background microwave radiation left over from the initial explosion of energy (singularity) some 13.7 billion years ago.

Modern science has also established that the Universe is not, as the Greeks thought, unchanging. Events are not pre-determined; change is possible.[52] In the nineteenth century, at the level of biology, Charles Darwin proved that change (evolution) is a fundamental feature of the living world. Darwin's successors proved that evolutionary change is brought about, at least in part, through indeterminate mechanisms (random genetic mutation). In the twentieth century, at the level of quantum physics, Werner Heisenberg showed that there is an element of randomness even in the sub-atomic world. He called this the Uncertainty Principle.[53]

I have barely scratched the surface here. For those wanting to explore the link between Judaeo-Christianity and the scientific method, one of the best books is *The Bible, Protestantism and the Rise of Natural Science* by Peter Harrison. It was published in 1998 by Cambridge University Press, and, notably, the author is an Australian. The impact of the book in relevant academic circles was considerable. It took Harrison from Brisbane to a chair in religion and science at Oxford, though he has since returned to the University of Queensland. He still contributes from time to time to this ongoing debate.[54]

### The closed society

The classical conception of a cyclical Universe extended to human society. The Graeco-Roman world was 'basically unhistorical'.[55] It was assumed that history infinitely repeated itself. Accordingly, the study of past events was more like psychology or social commentary: it amounted to meditation upon human behaviour. Curious writers would select notable people and events and pontificate about them in a rhetorical style. In this manner, Herodotus (c. 484–25 BC) wrote extensively about the Persian Wars and Thucydides (460 – c. 395 BC) about the Peloponnesian War between Sparta and Athens. But while their work was unusually thorough, it was still not history as we know it. As Edwin Judge has explained, 'although [ancient] historians were concerned with the truth of what had happened ... it was not part of their practice to lay out detailed evidence. They did not have to prove anything.'[56]

What was missing? A twentieth-century English historian, E.H. Carr, hit the nail on the head. Carr, it should be stressed, was a stern critic of organised religion. But he insisted that it was Judaeo-Christianity that brought into being the teleological view of history – the notion that events are moving towards a goal, that progress is not a mirage. For Carr, this was 'an entirely new element'; 'history thus acquired a meaning and purpose'.[57]

Of course, the idea of progress is malleable. It depends on the goal that one has in mind. For medieval historians, the goal was a religious one: the End of Days – the Second Coming of Christ. For post-Enlightenment historians, the goal was a secular one: the gradual improvement of man's state on Earth.[58] The majority of contemporary historians in the West (including those in Australia) fall into the second category. But there are still some who would argue that the notion of progress can, and should, encompass both goals simultaneously.

Either way, historians following the Judaeo-Christian model are obliged to prove their points. They must produce written work in a form that can readily be scrutinised. It was the early Christians who developed the codex, roughly the type of book we still use today. They converted it to the notebook form, an advance on the roll.[59]

Historians must also show how one thing led to another in the past, and, because history is not necessarily cyclical, might do so again in the future. This requires, at least, the specification of one's secondary sources. Ideally it also involves the use of *primary* sources – direct quotations from eyewitnesses (a technique employed in the Gospels) or the reproduction of relevant documents.

History books as we know them were anticipated by Titus Flavius Josephus (AD 37 – c. 100), a first-century Romano-Jewish scholar who was anxious to document the experience of the Jewish people under Roman law. Another key figure was Eusebius of Caesarea (AD 260–339), author of the first comprehensive history of the Christian Church.[60] However, according to Edwin Judge, it was not until the sixteenth century that 'the principle of proof from documentary evidence was established as the foundation for the scholarly study of history'. The main factor that led to this was the dispute between Catholics and Protestants as to who was the true heir to the practices of the early churches.[61]

The classical conception of the closed society was also transformed by Judaeo-Christianity in terms of sociopolitical norms. Greek city-state democracy was limited: only some men had the right to vote, and the system always degenerated within decades to mob rule. It was, in fact, rejected by Plato (c. 427–347 BC) and Aristotle (384–22 BC), two of the most influential Greek philosophers.[62] More fundamental still, throughout the classical world, people were not at liberty to attempt to better themselves. From leaders to slaves, one's destiny was to perform a given role, dutifully and honourably. According to Cicero (106–43 BC), a Roman philosopher–statesman of high rank, the basis of all good was honour – to seek it and to obtain it. Honour brought immortality. Only the honoured person would be commemorated. But there was no honour to be had in challenging the status quo. A person's station in life was pre-determined, fixed at birth.

Justice, accordingly, *was* the status quo. In the words of Aristotle, 'some men are by nature free, and others slaves, and for these slavery is both expedient and right'.[63] Seneca, a first-century Roman Stoic philosopher, went further: 'all slaves [are] our enemies'.[64]

The West today operates on quite different assumptions. In Australia we treasure the idea that we are an egalitarian society. We all have equal rights. Nobody is intrinsically 'better' than anyone else. If a person is prepared to work, and has some luck, he or she can rise above the circumstances of their birth. Everyone is unique, with their own special gifts and their own calling. Everyone is entitled to pursue their own search for personal identity.

These notions – now so utterly familiar – did not begin with universal suffrage in the twentieth century, or with the Enlightenment in the eighteenth, or even with the Magna Carta in the thirteenth. Historically, they are founded on the Judaic principle that each and every human being is made 'in the image of God' (see Genesis 1:26–27). This principle has nothing to do with physical anatomy.[65] Rather, in the words of Martin Luther King, 'the image of God ... is the idea that all men have something within them that God injected. Not that they have substantial unity with God, but that every man has a capacity to have fellowship with God. And this gives him a uniqueness, it gives him worth, it gives him dignity.'[66] We are not slaves of fate but independent free agents (see Genesis 4:7).[67] We are all severally (rather than jointly) equal in the sight of God, and each of us will be judged by God as individuals.[68]

The Christians of the first century, particularly Paul of Tarsus, built upon these ideas, in the light of their understanding of Jesus as the Saviour of mankind.[69] First and foremost, Paul insisted, Jesus had actually been God in human form. This was proof positive of man's special worth. Yet man was a fallen (innately sinful) creature.[70] Nobody, Paul taught, could hope for favourable judgment from God on their own merits: 'for all have sinned and fallen short of the glory of God' (Romans 3:23). But *anybody* could be saved if they placed their faith in Jesus: 'There is neither Jew nor Gentile, neither slave nor free, nor is there male and female, for you are all one in Christ Jesus' (Galatians 3:28).

I am not asking the reader to accept the theological truth of Paul's teachings. My point is that these teachings (expanding on principles in the Old Testament) were the beginning of egalitarianism as we know it.

The earliest Christians did not actively seek to challenge the hierarchical structures of Graeco-Roman society.[71] They were not in a position to do so. But among Christian converts, people from all sectors of society mixed together. This frequently happened within the households of prosperous Mediterranean landowners. In addition to the landowner's family, such households usually contained people of both sexes, several nationalities and all stations, including labourers and slaves. If the landowner himself became a Christian, so, often, did many of the people who lived with him.[72] Thus social barriers were broken down and people at every level of community life were brought together to a degree unprecedented in human experience.[73]

The early Christians were also remarkably generous to and respectful of each other. It was not just a matter of mixing freely on occasion, like CEOs and staff in a modern-day office. Within first-century Christian communities, high standards of moral conduct were expected. The sick were cared for, possessions were shared and sexual promiscuity was discouraged. Marriage was honoured in a way quite different from the Graeco-Roman norm. While the roles of husband and wife were different, marriage was seen as an *equal* partnership involving reciprocal rights and duties. Adultery by a husband was as bad as that by a wife.[74]

As Diarmaid MacCulloch has observed, it seems probable that many people in the earliest Christian communities were expecting the Second Coming of Jesus within their own lifetimes. But fairly quickly their horizons broadened. In the later documents of the New Testament there is a focus on how Christians could establish a form of society that might last for many generations and attract non-Christians.[75] It is an historical fact that, like Jesus Himself, the early Christians extended kindness to the lowest members of society, even those outside their immediate circle. Widows, prostitutes, tax collectors, slaves, beggars, orphans, cripples – all were welcome. So were unwanted babies. The early Christians spoke up strongly against the widespread Graeco-Roman practice of infanticide.[76]

The Graeco-Roman establishment was not attracted but repulsed. Celsus, a third-century Greek philosopher, described the typical early Christian community as being like a 'council of frogs in a marsh or a synod of worms on a dunghill, croaking and squeaking'. But this was the voice of fear and envy. The most renowned historian of the Roman Empire, Edward Gibbon (1737–94), ascribed the rapid spread of Christianity to a variety of causes, among them what he termed the 'pure and austere morals' of the early Christians. Rome could not compete.[77]

An even more novel aspect of the early Christian communities was the character of their leaders. True, they were patriarchal. But it was the 'patriarchialism of love'.[78] Great leadership, for the first Christians, was not about being masterful – conquering, showing strength, and thereby gaining honour. It was about being a servant, not only of one's immediate followers but of the common people. Humility was a virtue rather than a weakness, and the ultimate test of leadership was a preparedness to sacrifice oneself.[79] Jesus' openness and collegiality, and his suffering during the Passion Week, were their inspiration. By contrast, for classicists such as Celsus it was ludicrous that a lowly Jewish artisan – crucified and humiliated – could be an object of admiration, let alone of worship.

It took centuries for all the implications of Christian egalitarianism to be realised at the level of social structures, and there were many missteps along the way. The principal problem from the fourth century onwards was that the Church of Rome itself became increasingly hierarchical. But the process of democratisation was inevitable while Christianity flourished. 'Equality in the eyes of God laid the foundation for equality in the eyes of man and equality before the law.'[80]

Perhaps *the* vital catalyst for egalitarianism was the Reformation of the sixteenth century. The new Protestant theology inspired by men such as Martin Luther (1483–1546) in Germany and John Calvin (1509–64) in Switzerland led inexorably to the rise of the common man. There were two main factors involved. First, both Luther and Calvin preached a version of a doctrine that would become known, centuries later, as the 'Protestant work ethic'. Its central idea was (and is) that the humblest forms of work can be valuable in the sight of God, especially if they are performed in a devout spirit, 'as if you were serving the Lord' (Ephesians 6:5). In Luther's words, we can all of us be 'the fingers of God'; it is not necessary to be a priest or a monk in order to serve Him.[81] The task of each person is to find their calling or vocation, and to pursue it wholeheartedly, thereby contributing to the common good.[82]

In coming centuries, the British middle classes would live out this ethic as diligently as any other group of people in the world. And they would bring it with them to the Australian colonies.

Another crucial aspect of the Reformation, perhaps even more important in terms of promoting egalitarianism, was the reformers' insistence that the text of the Bible was the ultimate source of authority for the Church, and should be accessible to every believer. This caused the Bible to be translated from the fourth-century Latin of the Vulgate into contemporary European languages (German, English, Dutch, French and so on). This is in turn was a spur to wider literacy, because overwhelmingly the Bible was the book that ordinary people wanted to read.[83]

At the core of the Judaeo-Christian worldview, Protestant and Catholic, was an optimistic hope in a better future – not only in the afterlife, but in this life. The history of the West (including Australia) shows that, down the ages, exceptional Christians have displayed a singular determination to effect benevolent societal change.

The Huguenots of sixteenth-century France are a prime example. Brave Protestants in an overwhelmingly Catholic nation, it was they – *not* the secularist French philosophers of the eighteenth century – who first fanned the flames of rebellion against the despotic *ancien régime*. A modern-day Indian intellectual, Vishal Mangalwadi, has recently laid stress on the Huguenots' oft-forgotten role in the events leading up to the French Revolution. In three books known as the Trilogy of Freedom – Francois Hotman's *Francogallia*, Theodore Beza's *The Right of Magistrates* and the pseudonymously published *Vindiciae Contra Tyrannos* – Huguenot thinkers laid out many of the main features of liberal democracy and the rule of law. Collectively, these works were greatly influential in the creation of independent nation-states in Scotland and the Netherlands. According to Mangalwadi, 'after the Bible, *Vindiciae Contra Tyrannos* had the greatest impact in fuelling the American Revolution. It moved the pulpits that moved the pews to resist tyranny.'[84]

The abolition of slavery is another prime example of exceptional Christians effecting far-reaching societal change. Most of the key secular figures of the eighteenth-century Enlightenment *endorsed* slavery.[85] It was Christians who led the movement to abolish it. One of the first to articulate the abolitionist case, in 1700, was a Puritan judge in Massachusetts, Samuel Sewall; the first religious group to do so was the Dutch Quaker Church of Pennsylvania in 1758. The movement to end slavery in Britain and its colonies, in the late eighteenth and early nineteenth centuries, was led by Evangelical Christians – the so-called Clapham Sect. For leaders such as William Wilberforce – one of Lachlan Macquarie's mentors, remember – 'abolition was an act of moral revulsion which defied the strict commercial interests of European and Anglophone nations'.[86]

As we shall see, this mindset would have far-reaching implications for the Australian colonies. The slavery issue was highly topical in 1788, the year of New South Wales' founding. Governor Arthur Phillip famously referred to it in his journal[87] – 'there is one [English law] that I would wish to take place from the moment His Majesty's forces take possession of the country: That there can be no slavery in a free land, and consequently no slaves.' (In fact, in his admirable zeal, Phillip had got ahead of himself: the slave trade was not abolished in Britain until 1807.) It was also in 1788 that a former English slave trader named John Newton made this public statement: 'I am bound in conscience to take shame to myself by a public confession.'[88] Newton later became a parson. He wrote the hymn 'Amazing Grace'.

## The closed heart

The Graeco-Roman worldview was undermined by Christianity in a third way, perhaps the most fundamental of all. I have already touched upon it. Societal change would not have eventuated without the passion and compassion of individual men and women.

The concept of morality is notoriously controversial. Unbelievers dislike being lectured about it by Christians; they dislike, especially, the proposition that religion is necessary for morality. I would put the proposition another way: it is the existence of the supernatural (God), not the practice of religion, that is necessary for morality. There are two reasons for this.

The first is that human beings have free will. We are not automata forced to act in the way we do by the laws of physics, chemistry and biology. We can choose what we do or do not do. In the words of one of the world's most outspoken atheists, Michel Onfray, 'the very foundations of judicial logic proceed from Chapter 3 of Genesis' (the account of Adam and Eve's disobedience):

The premise that human beings have free will is the key to the cause-and-effect relationship between crime and punishment. For eating the forbidden fruit [and] disobedience ... flow from an act of will, and therefore from an act that can be reproved and punished. Adam and

Eve could have refrained from sinning, for they had been created free, but they chose vice over virtue.[89]

To put the point more bluntly still: 'if we cannot help being what we are then no one can blame us'.[90] The complete answer to any charge of immorality or wrongdoing – under any legal system in human history – would be: 'I couldn't help it'. That is one reason why atheists are forced to concede that, even if free will is an illusion, man must live on the basis that it is not. One of the key figures of the Scottish Enlightenment, David Hume (1711–76), was a sceptic in many things. But even he strove mightily to show that free will was not an illusion. Hume was a so-called compatibilist: he argued that free will could be reconciled with the findings of modern science and the impossibility of miracles. Few modern-day Australian unbelievers appear to have wrestled with this critical issue.

The second core assumption underlying Western morality – at least until recently – was that the *essential* rules of morality are fixed. They cannot be changed at the whim of man. The ancient Hebrews conceived of morality as a set of rules imposed by God, and thus to be treated with the gravest respect. They codified their laws and punished infractions dutifully. But the authors of the New Testament, echoing Jesus, emphasised the impossibility of total compliance with Jewish law, let alone with God's wishes. They also insisted that *every* human being is a sinner, regardless of formal compliance with man-made rules – and regardless of race, sex, wealth or social rank. In St Paul's famous words, 'God does not play favourites' (Romans 2:11). Luther and Calvin developed these notions further during the Reformation. They gave impetus to the attacks then being mounted against the medieval doctrine of the Divine Right of Kings. No one is above the law.

Some of this may seem obvious. But the Graeco-Roman position was quite different. For them, morals were man-made. The precepts determining correct and incorrect conduct were founded on law or contract and enforced by human authorities. Morality was fixed, but not by an all-knowing God. It was fixed because it was as it was. Unlike modern-day atheists of the Left, who would agree that morality is man-made but insist that perceived injustice be corrected, the educated Greek or Roman accepted the status quo. In the words of Epictetus, a first-century Greek philosopher: 'the good life is … a life reconciled to what is the case, a life which accepts the world as it is.'[91]

A related notion espoused by many philosophers in the Graeco-Roman world was that there was no such thing as evil, only error or extravagance stemming from an excess of passion. The key to leading a good life was moderation. That included limiting, as much as possible, the extent of one's contact with other human beings.

As I have said, the West has operated on quite different assumptions. Until very recently, it was taken as a given that morality emanated from God. The moral law was something to be obeyed, on pain of the wrath of God, whether or not it was immediately advantageous to do so in this world.[92] Most Westerners today no longer believe in God or the afterlife. But whether they realise it or not, their conception of morality remains much more Judaeo-Christian than Graeco-Roman.

'Everyone in the community,' insists Edwin Judge, 'has a powerful moral sense shaped by the Biblical tradition.'[93] A given action or thought is either right or wrong, according to the voice of individual conscience: 'in the last resort each person must take responsibility for deciding where truth [lies]'.[94] Thus, ultimately, no government or other human authority can dictate the substance of personal morality. Might is not right. There is such a thing as an unjust law. A person can do great evil even while acting lawfully; likewise, a person can do great good even while acting unlawfully. That is why Nazis who 'just followed orders' could be convicted at the Nuremberg trials, and why opponents of Nazism such as Dietrich Bonhoeffer are now regarded as heroes. It is why Poles such as Pope John Paul II (Karol Wojtyla) and Lech Walesa are revered for their indispensable roles in bringing about the collapse of the Iron Curtain in 1989.[95] In the words of Origen of Alexandria, a second-century defender of Christianity: 'It is not wrong to form associations against the laws [of the State] for the sake of truth.'[96]

So, the assumed basis of morality was for almost two millennia different in the West from that in the classical world. But that is not all. In several key respects, the substance of morality was different. I have already mentioned humility; I now offer four more examples.

**First**, in Judaeo-Christian thought, hypocrisy is a vice, not a virtue. And guilt, provided it is sincerely felt, is better than shame imposed by the sanctions of society. A thief should be remorseful whether or not he is caught. These notions are based on the New Testament idea that true goodness stems, not from compliance with the formal laws of the community, still less from outward appearances, but from inner motives: obedience to God, or the pull of conscience. That is what the word 'orthodoxy' means.[97]

**Second**, passion – or commitment – is a virtue, not a weakness. The English word 'passion' corresponds to the Greek *pathe*, meaning emotions or sufferings. For the Greeks, 'the good life [was] a life stripped of both hopes and fears'.[98] For the Christian, conversely, the good life is *based* on hopes and fears. Suffering for a good cause is a badge of honour. Paul boasted of his travails as demonstrating his commitment, and he urged his followers to do likewise: to 'offer your body as a living sacrifice' (Romans 12:1). That is the ideal today, among believers and unbelievers alike: to give something worthwhile your best shot.

**Third**, an idea related to the second: a life of work – with periods of rest – is better than a life of leisure. Each of us has a calling. This was originally a Jewish precept, but, as discussed earlier, it was taken up with renewed vigour during the Protestant Reformation. The central notion was that many forms of work can have dignity if, and because, they are done in obedience to God, for the satisfaction of genuine human needs. Jesus himself worked as carpenter and Paul as a tent-maker.[99] It was the opposite for the Greeks. Manual work was seen as a curse, a necessary evil to be carried out by the labouring and slave classes. In the words of Aristotle: 'the first principle of all action is leisure. Both are required, but leisure is better than occupation, and is its end.'[100]

**Fourth**, the most radical idea of all: compassion – a selfless concern for others – is a virtue, not a weakness. For the Greeks and the Romans, as we have seen, the status quo was just and right. Acts of beneficence usually took the form of grandiose civic philanthropy on behalf of the community at large.[101] The Judaeo-Christian position is that change for the better is possible at both community and private levels; in any event, mercy is better than strict justice. Old Testament Judaism laid emphasis on charity, but Jesus insisted that the duty to be charitable applied not merely to people of one's own kind. It extended to strangers, to foreigners, even to enemies. Paul ordered masters to treat their slaves well, a 'shocking exhortation' in the Graeco-Roman world.[102] During the smallpox epidemics of AD 165–180, Christians were widely noticed because they cared for the sick and dying – and often ended up dying themselves.[103] By the fourth century, charity was an essential element of the Christian life. The Clementine Homilies, an influential collection of early Christian writings, stated bluntly: 'He who wishes to be pious towards God does good to man, because the body of man bears the image of God.'[104]

In the long run, the Judaeo-Christian emphasis on charity would have far-reaching consequences in the West. It was in the monasteries of the early Middle Ages that a culture of care was first fostered as a practical ideal.[105] The development of modern medicine after the Renaissance was not solely or even mainly due to advances in scientific knowledge; it was also due to the Christian emphasis on using knowledge for compassionate purposes.[106] In due course this attitude led, on a massive scale, to hospitals, schools, poor relief, orphanages and the humane treatment of animals. The issue today is the extent to which charity should be provided by the State or privately, not whether charity itself is a desirable thing. It was the same in 1788.

## Two necessary qualifications

In concluding this chapter it is important that I make two qualifying points.

First, in 21st-century Australia, conventional wisdom is a *combination* of Biblical and classical norms. Aspects of the Graeco-Roman worldview are still with us; indeed, in recent decades, some have been making a comeback. One is the idea that work – especially menial work – is but a necessary evil, a way to make money. The ultimate dream of many Australians today is to become rich, as quickly and as easily as possible, in order to enjoy the rest of life in comparative leisure.[107] Such an ambition is very Aristotelian in flavour. Another classical tendency, more prevalent on the Right than the Left, is disdain for the less fortunate and for the (allegedly misplaced) compassion shown towards them. We see it in Australia today in the casually cruel distinction between 'lifters' and 'leaners' – or, more bluntly, 'wealth-producers' and 'bludgers'. Here there are strong echoes of Friedrich Nietzsche, the nineteenth-century German atheist philosopher who lambasted Christianity as a 'cult of resentment' and sneered at 'its active pity for all the failures and all the weak'. He rejected traditional morality as 'a biblical imposition on our culture'.[108]

My second qualification is this: laid over both Biblical and classical norms are the norms of the Enlightenment. The four main features or objectives of the Enlightenment have been usefully defined by the American historian Carlton Hayes.[109] All four have currency in Australia today:

- naturalism (the idea that natural explanations are to be preferred to supernatural ones)
- rationalism (belief in the power of human reason to discover the laws of nature)

- optimistic progress (belief in bettering or even perfecting humankind with the use of reason)
- humanitarianism (regard for each individual's natural rights).

I will nail my colours to the mast as regards each of these four sacred cows. Naturalism is a useful rule of thumb, provided the possibility of supernatural explanations is not excluded. Rationalism, like naturalism, too often morphs into scientism (uncritical application of the scientific method in inappropriate contexts). However, of itself, rationalism is not inconsistent with the existence of God or a religious view of the world. Indeed, as I have argued, rationalism assumes the existence of objective laws of nature which are there to be discovered, and highlights Man's unique capacity to discover them. Optimistic progress and humanitarianism are both products of Judaeo-Christianity, though the faith placed in progress during and immediately after the Enlightenment was excessive. If the tragedies of the twentieth century have proved anything, it is that human beings have an abiding propensity for evil.

Even so, I believe that progress is possible and that we should never cease to strive for it. The histories of Britain and Australia are proof of the idea's potency.

# CHAPTER 3

# Britain's debt to Judaeo-Christianity

The Christian religion – which, of course, embodies many of the great spiritual and moral truths of Judaism – is a fundamental part of our national heritage. For centuries it has been our very life blood.

Margaret Thatcher, Prime Minister of Britain 1979–90

I trust in the continuation of divine protection.

James Cook, discoverer in 1770 of the east coast of mainland Australia

Having surveyed Judaeo-Christianity's broad impact on the West in general, I will now offer a potted summary of the debt owed to it by Britain in particular – before, and as at, 1788. Only then can we fully appreciate the preciousness of our own inheritance. Admittedly, gratitude for the past is an insufficient basis for religious belief. But for many spiritually inquisitive Australians today, it might be a useful starting-point.

At any rate, what follows is history that all Australians need to know: most of the nineteenth-century British colonists were steeped in it, and, accordingly, our own story is unintelligible without it. It explains, for example, why there was such a thing as the rule of law and the Church of England; why, even more basically, Britain comprised four countries, not one; and how the land mass Terra Australis was discovered by the West. I believe I can guarantee a surprise or two.

## The creation of England

There was no such nation as England in AD 43, when the ancient Romans launched their invasion of Britannia – an area roughly corresponding to modern-day England and Wales, and the far southern areas of Scotland. These lands were home to at least fifteen Celtic tribal kingdoms, pagan agricultural societies of varying degrees of sophistication, with a total population of about 2 million inhabitants. The Romans came to refer to them collectively as Britons.

According to Diarmaid MacCulloch, 'we have no definite witness to Christianity in Britain before the early fourth century'.[1] Despite some intriguing evidence to the contrary,[2] the proposition makes sense. As we saw in the last chapter, Roman Emperor Constantine's conversion took place in AD 312, or perhaps a year or two earlier;[3] it was only then that the Romans began to take their new religion to all posts of the empire.

Nevertheless, there is an uncanny feature of first-century English history that bears mention. The Roman occupation of Celtic Britain in the first century coincided with the beginning of Christianity. Indeed, the two were interlinked. The Romans conquerors arrived in Britannia (at the extreme western end of their empire) only a dozen or so years after the crucifixion of Jesus in Jerusalem (at the extreme eastern end of the empire). While Christianity was getting started in that eastern region – a process facilitated by the stability of Roman rule – Britannia played a key role in sustaining the whole Roman Empire. Most crucial were the taxes exacted from its inhabitants and the exports dispatched from its southern ports – principally corn, metals and bricks.[4]

The Romans left Britain abruptly in the early fifth century, as their own mighty empire began crumbling on the Continent. By then Christianity had a toehold among the inhabitants of Britannia, though it barely survived the invasions of the fifth and sixth centuries by various Teutonic tribes from northern Europe. The Angles, Jutes and Saxons were all pagans. They did not try to convert the local inhabitants to their own religions, but within a short time their language (the base of modern-day English) had largely replaced both the Celtic and Latin dialects.[5]

Perhaps the key event in the creation of England was the conversion of the Anglo-Saxons to Christianity. Credit is traditionally given to Pope Gregory I, who dispatched a team of missionaries there in AD 596–97 headed by a monk named Augustine (later known as Augustine of Canterbury; not to be confused with St Augustine of Hippo). It is a complicated story, but by the end of the seventh century Roman Christianity had become the dominant religion throughout southeast

Britain.[6] Northumbria went over to Rome in 663, but, according to MacCulloch, the crucial decade was the 670s, when all the Anglo-Saxon kingdoms first voted as one at various ecclesiastical councils.[7]

Two generations later, in 731, a monk now known as the Venerable Bede completed his colossal book *The Ecclesiastical History of the English People*. It was Bede who initiated the practice (later adopted throughout the Western world) of reckoning years from the birth of Christ. Bede's *History* was the finest work of its kind written by anyone to that date, a prime example of the teleological style of history discussed in Chapter 2. Even more significantly, its very title demonstrated that, by 731, the notion of 'the English people' had well and truly come into being.[8]

And this is my overarching point. Increasing *religious* unity among the English people in the eighth century was the forerunner to *political* unity. In the words of one of its finest contemporary writers, Peter Ackroyd, 'England, as we understand it today, was created by the Christian Church.'[9] Except for this common factor, the seven kingdoms of Anglo-Saxon Britain (the Heptarchy) might have fought themselves back to barbarism. Instead, one wise king, Offa of Mercia (c. 730–96), strengthened ties with the Church in Rome.

Gradually, argues MacCulloch, there emerged a 'precocious belief among the English people in their special destiny'.[10] Not only did everyone (or almost everyone) now worship the same god. By the early ninth century the Roman Church was also their chief link to Europe, and literate churchmen had become the 'indispensable administrators of the state'. The cloister schools of the monasteries were the principal means of educating children.

In 829, the seven kingdoms were briefly united under a single 'wide ruler', Egbert of Wessex. There were sound administrative and military reasons for doing so. But the overriding cause was a religious one.[11]

It was also at this time – the ninth century – that the word 'Christendom' was coined. The Anglo-Saxons used it to express their part in the universality of a continent-wide (that is, European) culture focused on Jesus Christ. In time Christendom would extend beyond Europe to all parts of the globe, including Australia.

The story does not end there. It was because of Christianity that England survived – and was ultimately strengthened – by two potentially lethal foreign invasions.

The first was by the Vikings, the seafaring warrior peoples of modern-day Norway and Denmark. From the early ninth to the early eleventh centuries they launched a series of brutal attacks on the British islands and came to occupy much of northeastern England, an area that became known as the Danelaw. But the result was not genocide, for one main reason. After the Battle of Edington in May 878, at which the people of Wessex (in the south) won a rare victory, the Viking leader, Guthrum, agreed to be baptised as a Christian.[12] The leader of the Wessex forces, a man named Alfred, offered himself as Guthrum's godfather and called him his son. It was a symbolic act only but Guthrum was greatly moved by Alfred's magnanimity in victory.

Alfred knew that the Scandinavians were in England to stay and that the only long-term hope for his people was co-existence and, eventually, integration. Within two or three generations – admittedly, after some further bloodshed – the people of the Danelaw were converted to Christianity.[13] The process was facilitated by developments back in Scandinavia, including the conversion in 965 of the Danish king Harald Bluetooth, but, even so, Alfred deserves much of the credit for ensuring that Christianity survived and prospered in England. That is the principal reason why he is now remembered as Alfred the Great. In 927 his grandson, Athelstan, became the first Anglo-Saxon king of the whole of England.[14] The first Danish king of England, after the Anglo-Saxons were overthrown, was Canute, in 1016. He was not a believer himself but publicly converted to the local faith out of necessity. In the words of Peter Ackroyd, 'he needed the English Church as a way of maintaining his spiritual authority as a legitimate king'.[15]

The last successful invasion of England was by the Normans (of northern France) in 1066, under William the Conqueror. This was another watershed. It led directly to the introduction in England of the feudal system of land use. English language, law and culture became an amalgam of Teutonic (Germanic) and French influences.[*]

Again, Christianity was crucial to the process. The Normans were already Christians when they arrived in Britain. William was crowned King of England in Westminster Abbey on Christmas Day 1066,[16] but his absolute legitimacy was not confirmed until more than three years later. Three papal legates who had been sent to England by Pope Alexander met with William at Winchester, and agreed to crown him at

---

[*] Another, less welcome consequence was ongoing geopolitical rivalry with France. It became a fact of English life. The English Crown did not renounce its claim to the French Crown until the nineteenth century and suspicion of French territorial ambitions was rife at the time of the founding of New South Wales. This was a key factor in the creation of British outposts in Van Diemen's Land (Tasmania) and at King George Sound (Western Australia).

the cathedral there. The ceremony took place on Easter Sunday 1070. It has been powerfully argued that this act set the papal 'seal of approval' on William's kingship.[17]

After the Norman Conquest, the Christian Church in England did not merely survive. It prospered. Throughout the Middle Ages it was an indispensable source of comfort and continuity in a land racked by civil war (the period from 1135 to 1153, known as the Anarchy), famine (the worst periods were 1257–58 and 1314–16), and innumerable foreign military adventures of mixed success.

The ultimate test of Christianity's resilience in England came in the mid-fourteenth century. The Black Death (bubonic plague) killed almost half the population in 1348–49 and one-fifth of the remainder in 1361–62. The victims, disproportionately, were men between the ages of twenty-five and forty-five. Many were clergymen. Rather than interpreting this calamity as proof of God's non-existence and reverting to nihilistic barbarism, most people were *strengthened* in their faith. The plague was seen as an act of an angry God. The survivors felt enormous gratitude at being spared and intensified their efforts to display piety.[18]

If a similar calamity befell England today, would it survive in civilised form? Would Australia? I doubt it.

## The English legal system

The English legal system has been described as 'the greatest benefit that the English conferred on the world',[19] and it is hard to disagree. Many former English colonies have enjoyed the benefits that flow from having a settled and yet subtly flexible set of laws, impartially administered by trained judges, legal practitioners and police. The standout examples are the United States, Canada, Hong Kong, New Zealand – and Australia. India is on the road to catching up.

As we saw in Chapter 2, all Western legal systems were grounded on two core assumptions, both of them Biblically based: Man has free will, and morality is God-given. But the English went further. For centuries Christianity was recognised as an integral part of the law of the land. Chief Justice Sir Matthew Hale's statement to that effect in 1676 – 'The Christian religion is a part of the law itself'[20] – was still received wisdom when the First Fleet arrived at Port Jackson.

It is true that Hale's statement was made in the context of the law of blasphemy (the offending words were: 'Christ is a whoremaster and religion is a cheat … Christ is a bastard, and damn all Gods of the Quakers, etc.'). Even so, it had wider application. Hale's reasoning, repeatedly upheld until 1883 (as we shall see), was that 'such kind of wicked blasphemous words were not only an offence to God and religion, but a crime against the laws, State and Government'. To attack religion was 'to dissolve all those obligations whereby the civil societies are preserved'.[21]

Views changed in the nineteenth century about the desirability of punishing blasphemy – and rightly so. But the notion persisted that Christianity remained central to English society and English law, and the same was true of English colonies. In one of the first criminal trials conducted at Port Jackson, for the rape of an eight-year-old girl, the official indictment was framed in explicitly religious terms. One Henry Wright, a soldier, was alleged to have committed the crime while 'not having the Fear of God before his Eyes, but being moved and seduced by the Devil'. Moreover, when the victim was called to give sworn evidence, the following exchange ensued:

Q: Do you know it is wrong to speak an untruth?
A: Yes.
Q: What will happen if you do?
A: Go to the Devil.
Q: Where do you expect to go if you speak the truth?
A: To heaven.
Q: Can you say your Catechism?
A: Yes.
Q: The Lord's Prayer?
A: Yes.

The girl recited the Lord's Prayer and was duly sworn in. Wright was convicted.[22]

Such procedures continued to be followed long into the nineteenth century. It is therefore unsurprising that the notion that Christianity was central to English society and English law was widely held in the Australian colonies. In March 1898, during a debate at the Constitutional Convention in Melbourne, Sir John Downer of South Australia made this suggestion: 'The Christian religion is a portion of the English Constitution without any decision on the subject at all. It is part of the law of England which I should think we undoubtedly brought with us when we settled in these colonies.'[23]

These sentiments were repeated in 1901 by two eminent lawyers, John Quick and Robert Garran, in their *Annotated Constitution of the*

*Australian Commonwealth*: 'The Christian religion,' they wrote, 'is, in most English-speaking countries, recognised as a part of the common law.'[24]

In fact, Quick and Garran were in error, as Sir John Downer had been in 1898, regarding the then-current legal position in England. In a case decided in 1883, the future Lord Chief Justice of England had declared: 'It is no longer true, in the sense in which it was true [in the past], that Christianity is part of the law of the land.'[25] But Sir John Downer was right about the position in New South Wales in 1788, and in all the other colonies on the respective dates of their establishment.

Is this just quaint legal history, of no relevance today? Absolutely not. In numerous respects, the Australian legal system of 2015 is as it is because of the influence, in centuries past, of Judaeo-Christianity on the English legal system. In no particular order, I offer nine examples.

**First**, the notion that, to the extent practicable, the law should be administered at a local level rather than from on high. This idea began under the Anglo-Saxons, who developed an efficient system of local courts to administer their customary and written laws. The system might have been scrapped by the Normans after the 1066 invasion, but it was not. William the Conqueror retained it out of respect for the English Church's power and influence.[26] He needed to appease the local population, the ordinary men and women of England who associated their legal system with such venerated Christian kings as Alfred the Great and Edward the Confessor. Many of the written laws of England had been drafted by clerics.[27]

**Second**, the principle of the separation of Church and State. It was William the Conqueror who divided the courts spiritual from the courts temporal – again, out of deference to the English Church. This measure entrenched the king's autonomy over strictly secular affairs, such as taxation. But it also *increased* the Church's power over its own clergy and many aspects of everyday English life. From the eleventh century, England had a separate system of so-called canon law based on the Bible and the statutes of the Church. For centuries, canon law covered a wide range of matters including marriage, divorce, the legitimacy of children, wills and estates, and the punishment of mortal sins. All disputes were decided in the Church courts. To that extent, England was a theocracy! It may surprise some modern readers that, as far as matrimonial matters were concerned, this remained the position until 1857. In other words, it was still the position when the Australian colonies were founded. (Today, canon law is strictly confined to Church matters.)

**Third**, courts as we know them. As the legal historian S.F.C. Milsom has explained, 'the courts Christian … were the earliest in England which would have looked to us like courts of law'. Milsom points out that documents survive from actual litigation very nearly as old as the earliest rolls of the temporal courts. What we find is a single judge trying to ascertain the facts by considering and comparing the evidence of witnesses, and then applying to those facts rules of law that could be looked up in a book. That is what judges do today. For a long time the courts temporal were rustic by comparison. In Milsom's words, 'although [courts temporal] early lost the appearance of public meetings … centuries were to pass before they could be seen as ascertaining facts and applying known rules, before there were indeed systematic rules of substantive law that could be written down in books'.[28]

**Fourth**, the common law – perhaps *the* distinguishing feature of the English system of justice, and a basal part of Australia's justice system today. The key notion is that not all substantive law is decreed holus-bolus by a central authority; much of it is 'discovered' by individual judges on a case-by-case basis. The common law system became established in England under Henry II, grandson of William the Conqueror. As well as being a deeply religious man – 'the fear of eternal damnation, the hope of even greater realms beyond the grave, accompanied him from hour to hour'[29] – Henry II was, arguably, the most important monarch in the history of England. In order to promote reasonable consistency of legal principles and procedures across his realm, he ensured that all judges were drawn from a common pool. Crucially, almost all of them were clerics. The clerics' knowledge and experience of canon law made them well suited to the task. The system flourished and by the seventeenth century, though no longer administered by clerics, it was utterly entrenched.

At the time of the English Civil War (1641–53) eminent lawyers such as Sir Edward Coke felt emboldened enough to argue that the powers of both king and parliament were ultimately grounded in the common law. One form of this argument was that the common law, representing the customary wisdom of centuries, 'correspond[ed] most closely to the supremely rational laws of God'. In Coke's expression, it was 'tried reason'.[30]

**Fifth**, the notion of crime as being punishable by the State. Nothing could be more relevant to Australia: as we have seen, New South Wales was founded in 1788 as a dumping ground for convicts, as were all the other colonies except South Australia and Western Australia. Yet until the twelfth century the punishment of crime in England was a haphazard affair; much was left to acts of private vengeance. Again, it was Henry II who changed things. Wrongs could be committed, he maintained, against society at large – by violation of the 'king's peace'.[31] It is vital to understand that the system that thus evolved was not purely, or even mainly, utilitarian. The king's peace was not to be maintained at any price: no one could be convicted of a crime unless they were found to have had a guilty mind (*mens rea*). This was a religious idea. As criminologist C.R. Jeffery explained, 'the concept of *mens rea* was derived from the Christian view of sins of the mind. Sin can be punished individually not collectively, so that the individual and not the clan or family is responsible.'[32] So here we have another legacy of English Christianity. In Jeffery's succinct words: 'The concept of crime thus developed as it did as a result of [the] interaction of the Church and State. However, it was the State, not the Church, that became the agent for punishing sin.'[33]

**Sixth**, the jury system. Henry II also instigated the use of juries – a Norman custom – in conjunction with his royal judges. The system took time to develop into its current form, but was popular immediately with the broader citizenry and made the king's courts still more attractive.[34] Juries were an alternative to 'the barbarous and unchristian custom of duelling'.[35]

**Seventh**, the Magna Carta. The agreement reached in 1215 between King John and the rebellious English barons remains part of the law throughout England and Australia, and was the forerunner of many future statements of essential civil liberties.[36] The barons' claims would not have been acceded to but for the support of the English Church. The Archbishop of Canterbury, Stephen Langton, played a central role in negotiating the terms of the Magna Carta. He acted as a mediator between the barons and the King. Winston Churchill once lauded Langton as 'the indomitable, unwearying builder of the rights of Englishmen against royal, baronial and even ecclesiastical pretensions'.[37]

**Eighth**, the Bill of Rights. This seminal enactment of 1689 established once and for all that parliament – not the king – was England's supreme lawmaking power. The Civil War of the 1640s and 1650s had been fought, essentially, over this issue. There were many twists and turns in the period following the Civil War, leading up to the so-called Glorious Revolution of 1688 in which Catholic King James II was overthrown, but the clinching argument for the supremacy of parliament was essentially theological. It revolved not around the common law – as some argued – but around God's law. A consensus developed that kings and parliaments and judges were alike 'bound by the laws of God and nature'.[38] It was that implicit recognition that enabled all three to co-exist in some sort of workable harmony. The 1689 Bill of Rights remains in effect in all Commonwealth realms, including Australia (which has no bill of rights of its own).[39]

**Ninth**, Equity. As well as the common law, English law was and is distinguished by another body of substantive law – that known as Equity. The notion of the trust – pursuant to which one person holds property for the benefit of another – is part of it. A distinguished twentieth-century legal historian, F.W. Maitland, praised the trust idea as 'the greatest and most distinctive achievement performed by Englishmen in the field of jurisprudence'.[40] I agree, yet trusts were but one creation of Equity, albeit the most versatile and ubiquitous. The key point for present purposes is that Equity was quintessentially a product of Christianity. For centuries it was administered by the king's lord chancellor, and until 1625 the lord chancellor was nearly always a churchman of high stature.[41] This meant that he was trained not only in theology but also in canon law, and, as we have seen, canon law was for centuries the most carefully administered body of law in England. Equity benefited as a result. It also benefited from the fact that the lord chancellor's expected role, especially in the early phases, was to 'soften the edges' of the common law. He was 'the repository of a monarchical prerogative of justice and clemency [and] thus acted explicitly in the name of morality and justice'.[42] In practice, he exercised reasoned compassion according to his Christian conscience.

This survey makes sense, I think, of some wise words uttered in 2008 by a former chief justice of the High Court of Australia, Murray Gleeson (a lifelong Catholic):

> On a couple of occasions over the last 20 years or so, some journalists have asked me whether my application of legal principles was affected by religion and I usually answered no but added something that seems to have been overlooked: that religion itself has had an extensive influence on the law. Anybody who applies established legal principle is, in that respect, responding to influences that as a matter of history have included religious influences.[43]

## The Church of England

The institution created by Henry VIII in 1534 was, of itself, a benefactor to the English people. Since before the Norman Conquest the Church *in* England had had its own character, distinct from Rome; but after 1534 the Church *of* England was formally independent and played an integral part in creating the English national character. In Robert Bolt's 1960 play *A Man for All Seasons*, the Common Man famously describes the Church of England as 'that finest flower of our Island genius for compromise; that system, peculiar to these shores, the despair of foreign observers, which deflects the torrents of religious passion down the canals of moderation'.[44]

The Church of England was, of course, a product of the Reformation. The theology of Luther and Calvin was important, and Henry VIII's wish to obtain a divorce from Catherine of Aragon played a part, but the pivotal catalyst was the mass production of an English translation of the Bible by an Oxford scholar named William Tyndale (c. 1494–1536). The first copies were smuggled into England from Geneva in 1526–27 and a decade later there were some 16,000 in circulation – about one for every 150 people. According to Diarmaid MacCulloch, 'nothing else was so important in creating a popular English Reformation which was independent of Henry's whims'.[45] Indeed, few things were as important as Tyndale's Bible in the whole history of Christianity. All subsequent English translations – including the peerless King James Version of 1611 – were based on it.

A document only slightly less seminal was the Book of Common Prayer. Adopted in 1549, it was a form of vernacular liturgy for use in churches throughout England.[46] Revised several times, it remains in use today, most often for traditional weddings and the beautiful Anglican ritual known as Evensong. The 1662 version was current when New South Wales was founded in 1788 – there were more than one hundred copies on the First Fleet – and most educated Australians were familiar with it until well into the twentieth century.

All English literature from the mid-sixteenth century onwards was inspired, shaped or influenced by these two books – Tyndale's Bible (as incorporated into the King James Version) and the Book of Common Prayer. So much is usually conceded, even by atheists as radical as Richard Dawkins.[47] But what of my broader claim, that the Church of England was principally responsible for shaping the English national character?

It is a huge subject, but, again, many roads lead back to the Reformation. The Church of England, in the form in which it evolved, was a *compromise* between the claims of still-loyal Roman Catholics on the one hand and radical Puritan reformers on the other. In 1559, by the Acts of Supremacy and Uniformity, the Church of England was established.[48] But Queen Elizabeth I and her wiser counsellors were cautious in the pace of further Protestant reform. The Thirty-Nine Articles of 1563, which still define the official doctrine of the Anglican Church, were a middle way in terms of both theology and clerical practices. In the opinion of a contemporary Australian writer, Muriel Porter, this choice represented the 'genius of Anglicanism'.[49] Australia's greatest founding father and second prime minister, Alfred Deakin, often made the same point.[50]

Roger Scruton has argued that it was not merely sagacious politics on Elizabeth's behalf. She had, in fact, correctly read the temperament of most of the English people. 'What mattered to them,' Scruton has written, 'was less the clarity and certainty of a religious faith, than the shared experience of sanctity, which blessed in familiar but elevated tones the country and society that was theirs.'[51] He has a point, but only half of one. There were many Protestants in England who *did* yearn for the 'clarity and certainty of a religious faith'. Some stayed within the Church of England, but in the seventeenth century others – in search of religious freedom – went to North America. These people, the Pilgrims, founded the colonies that became, in 1776, the United States.

By 1788 the Church of England was roughly split into two factions. The fact that both could co-exist in the same institution was, of itself, remarkable.

The so-called 'High' Anglicans were dominant among the senior ranks of clergy. They followed the middle way between Calvinism and Catholicism, and were backed by most members of the upper echelons of English society. They inclined to liberalism or tactful imprecision in theological matters, and, in Diarmaid MacCulloch's words, 'emphasised the solemn performance of public liturgy and the offering of beautiful music in settings of restrained beauty as the most fitting approaches to God in worship'.[52] They also emphasised the importance of episcopal authority in the giving of the sacraments and in the guidance of the common people on matters of public and private morality. In short, they were 'the establishment'.

The 'Low' Anglicans – also referred to as Evangelicals – were of a rather different mindset. Today, in Australia, they are epitomised by the Sydney Diocese of the Anglican Church, whose spiritual ancestors they are. The Evangelical movement emerged as a significant force in England in the late seventeenth century, in reaction against the perceived failings of the High Anglicans and the Tory Party.[53] They were principally concerned about the secularisation of English society and the breakdown of private morality. Like the High Anglicans, they were predominantly of the ruling classes and motivated by 'moral and national duty'.[54] However, they tended to place much more emphasis on impassioned voluntary activity in the cause of the gospel. Theirs, in the words of MacCulloch, was 'a religion of the heart and of direct personal relationship with Jesus Christ, in consciousness of his suffering on the Cross'.[55] Missionary work was particularly important to them, both within and outside Britain.

In the mid-eighteenth century, and in the years leading up to Australia's colonisation, two of the leading figures in the Low Church wing were John and Charles Wesley. Their influence on Britain and Australia was so important – remember the great prison reformer John Howard, whom we met in the Introduction – that it merits special mention here.

As well as being brothers, the Wesleys were both Anglican clergymen; so too was another leading Evangelical figure with whom they collaborated, George Whitefield. John Wesley and Whitefield possessed sharp theological minds and the gift of oratory. Charles Wesley would become immortal as a prolific composer of hymns, many of which are still sung in Protestant churches across the West. Their movement, dubbed 'Methodism' by its early detractors, would eventually result in the creation of a separate Church. However, it is important to remember that Methodism began *within* the Church of England. Indeed, the Wesleys, who had had been raised in the High Anglican tradition, never left the Church of their birth. But in May 1738 each of them underwent a further conversion experience and emerged with renewed passion for evangelism.

Methodism involved, on an increasingly large scale, the teaching of the Gospel to the middle and lower classes of Britain by a combination of local and itinerant preachers. Their hallmark was enthusiasm – but directed, applied enthusiasm. They were labelled 'Methodist' because of the extra-zealous way they used rule and method to go about their religious affairs. They preached in basic chapels or outdoors, as the situation demanded, and encouraged the boisterous singing of communal hymns. Morally they were conservative and theologically they were orthodox. Most insisted that salvation was available to everybody. But they tended to emphasise the roles played by God and the individual believer in effecting conversion, and to downplay the role of any institutional Church.[56]

Another point of departure from the High Anglicans – and of commonality with the Low Anglicans – was a willingness to support broad-based popular causes, such as the abolition of slavery. John Wesley was a prominent spokesman for the abolitionist cause. His *Thoughts on Slavery* (1774) went into four editions in two years and in August 1787 he wrote to the Abolition Committee of the House of Commons to express support. In 1788, when the abolition campaign in England was in full swing, he preached a famous sermon in Bristol, one of the main slave-trading ports.[57]

As I have said, Methodism began as a form of Anglicanism. But as the movement grew it caused serious ructions within the Church of England. These were coming to a head at the very time – the late 1780s – that New South Wales was founded. When John Wesley died, in 1791, there were some 70,000 Methodist members in Britain. They were mainly from the middle and lower middle classes, but there were also significant numbers from the working class.[58] Wesley's successors had to decide what to do. Some chose to stay in the Church of England as part of its Evangelical or Low Church wing.[59] Others left to found a new entity, the Wesleyan Methodist Church. It was, in some respects, a radical body – but nowhere near as radical as its secular equivalent in France. Indeed, it has been argued powerfully that by offering working-class people an outlet for their idealism, Methodism saved England from revolution in the 1790s. If so, it certainly also saved Australia.

As we shall see, both of these groupings – the Low Church Anglicans and the Methodists – were highly influential in the early Australian colonies. So, to a lesser extent, were other Protestant Non-conformist sects that had grown in strength during the eighteenth century, such as the Congregationalists, the Baptists and the Quakers. There was also a small but influential Jewish community in England: after being expelled from the country by King Edward I in 1290, Jews had been readmitted by Oliver Cromwell in the 1650s. They, too, were represented in New South Wales from 1788.

## Wales, Scotland and Ireland

Britain in 1788 was comprised of four great peoples, not one. And each of those peoples was a racial polyglot. The English, as we have seen, were a mixture of Celtic, Roman, Anglo-Saxon, Scandinavian, Norman and Jewish blood. The differences between the four nations of

Britain were partly racial, partly political, but as much as anything else they were a result of different takes on the Christian religion.

## Wales

The home of many of my own British forebears, Wales can be dealt with fairly briefly. Of all the members of the United Kingdom, its history has generally borne the closest resemblance to England's. It, too, was occupied by the Romans. The seeds of Christianity were first planted in that period, but the Welsh Church, entrenched by the work of St David (c. 500–89), soon developed its own distinctive identity and a spirit of independence. At the height of the invasions of England by the Anglo-Saxons and the Vikings, British Christianity had a stronghold among the Celts of Wales. England conquered Wales in 1282, and three centuries later, against all the initial odds, Protestantism came to Wales fairly seamlessly. In 1536 Wales was legally united with England, but the main reason for Protestantism's swift integration was the publication in 1588 of William Morgan's excellent Welsh translation of the Bible.[60]

## Scotland

Scotland was never effectively Romanised. Indeed, over the period AD 122–28, the Romans of Britannica built Hadrian's Wall, a massive structure some 73 miles long, in order to protect themselves from the marauding tribe to their immediate north – the Picts. Christianity was brought to the Picts, not by Roman occupiers, but by missionaries. According to tradition, the first conversions were made by an ascetic named Ninian, a Briton who had been educated in Rome. In around AD 400 he established a mission at Whithorn, in what is now southwest Scotland.[61] But the main work in Scotland was done in the sixth century, by the Gaels of Ireland. The central figure was St Columba (521–97).

Scotland, like England, survived invasion and occupation by the Vikings. The process was more complicated and protracted there than it was in England, and is less clearly understood by historians.[62] What can be said with some certainty is that the Norse pagan religions were never widely practised in Scotland, even in the far north where the Viking presence was strongest. By the mid-eleventh century[63] the Vikings themselves had converted to Christianity back in Scandinavia, and throughout Scotland the Christian Church had been firmly re-established.

The Church in Scotland always had its own identity, tied in part to the character of Scotland's clan system and, from time to time, the proclivities of its monarchs. In the early stages of the Reformation the Scottish Crown stayed loyal to Rome, but eventually the people prevailed and Scotland made a decisive switch to Protestantism.

The key figure from the mid-1540s was John Knox, a renegade priest who spent long periods in exile in England, Switzerland and Germany. He returned to Scotland in 1559 to lead a coalition of interests (religious and secular) dedicated to eradicating papal jurisdiction over the Scottish Church. In August 1560 the Scottish Parliament established the Reformed Church of Scotland (known informally as 'the Kirk'). It was a Church conceived along Calvinist lines, much more so than the Church of England. Not only was its theology thoroughly Protestant, its system of strict but democratic Church government ('Presbyterianism') was modelled on the one implemented in Geneva by John Calvin himself.[64]

Mary Queen of Scots (1542–87), a devout Catholic, tried but failed to resist the Kirk's establishment. Famously, she abdicated, went into exile, and ultimately was martyred. Scottish Protestantism was entrenched during the reign of her son and successor, James VI (James I of England and Ireland).

It is crucial to understand that the Act of Union of 1707 – under which England and Scotland joined together to form one sovereign State, 'Great Britain' – was possible *only* because Scotland was Protestant. The argument for union was in any event a close-run thing, just as it was at Scotland's independence referendum of 18 September 2014. But the consequences in 1707 were enormous. If not for the Act of Union, England would not have benefited so directly from Scotland's extraordinary achievements in the eighteenth and nineteenth centuries. These were quite disproportionate to its small population. One thinks of titanic figures such as Adam Smith (economics), James Watt (the steam engine), James Clerk Maxwell (physics), Alexander Graham Bell (the telephone) and Alexander Fleming (the co-discoverer of penicillin). One also thinks of the large Scottish presence in the upper ranks of the British Navy and Army. If England alone had settled the Australian colonies, figures such as John Hunter, Lachlan Macquarie and Thomas Brisbane – to say nothing of the Reverend J.D. Lang – would not have played a part.

## Ireland

The fourth constituent part of Britain, Ireland, was different again. Here, religious differences were central. What follows should help to shed further light on the harsh treatment of the Catholic convicts discussed in Chapter 1. Again it must be stressed: this religious backstory was front of mind for the British colonists of the eighteenth and nineteenth centuries.

Christianity had reached Ireland by the fifth century. Certainly, the Christian faith was being practised among the Gaels of the western and northern regions not long after the Romans left Britannia, in the early fourth century. Dual credit is traditionally given to two missionaries: Palladius of Gaul, who worked in Ireland in the first half of the fifth century, and the venerated St Patrick, who came after him. The details of Patrick's early life are uncertain, but it is likely he was born in Britannia, the son of a Romano-Celtic deacon.[65]

As we have seen, it was the Irish who brought Christianity to Scotland, in the sixth century. They also introduced it to parts of northern England, and even to Europe. They exported their own rigorous monastic system, and placed upon it their own special stamp. As Diarmaid MacCulloch has explained, some of the most iconic Irish-Catholic rituals – including the system of penance – began in this era.[66]

As in England and Scotland, the Irish Church survived Viking raids between the early ninth and early eleventh centuries. Dublin was founded as a Viking settlement. The Viking era effectively ended in Ireland on Good Friday 1014, when local forces prevailed at the Battle of Clontarf.

As almost everyone knows – or should know – most of the people of Ireland remained loyal to Rome during the Reformation. A (Protestant) Church of Ireland was established in 1536, but it never had anything approaching majority support. There are few more important facts in Australian history. By 1788, England, Scotland and Wales were mostly Protestant, at all levels of society. Ireland, on the other hand, was mostly Roman Catholic – and, *at the lower levels of society*, overwhelmingly so.

The causes of hostility between England and Ireland were not wholly religious. But religion was key. During the English Civil War, English armies invaded Scotland and Ireland to suppress royalist sentiment.[67] The methods used in Ireland were singularly ruthless, and there was a harsh sectarian aspect to the conflict. The ravages of Oliver Cromwell – and of William III in the period 1689–92 – were deeply resented for generations thereafter.[68] Huge tracts of Irish land were confiscated by the Crown and sold to English Protestant loyalists. English soldiers and traders became the new ruling class, and in due course its richer members came to control the Irish Parliament. Religious freedoms were severely curtailed.

By the 1790s it was no longer illegal to say or attend Mass, and persecution was rarely violent. A few wealthier Catholics in England were held in high esteem. Even so, there was still a huge amount of anti-Papist feeling. As Robert Hughes lamented in *The Fatal Shore*, for most of the eighteenth century 'no Catholic could sit in Parliament, on the bench or on a jury; none could vote, teach or hold an army commission. They were disabled in property law.'[69] Some of this legal discrimination was ameliorated late in the eighteenth century, at the very time of New South Wales's founding, by the Roman Catholic Relief Act of 1791. But prejudice and sectarianism remained strong. In Ireland, the Catholic peasantry had been 'beaten into the clay'. Although Protestants were a small minority in Ireland, they came almost exclusively from the ruling classes. Ireland was divided, wrote Edmund Burke, 'into two distinct bodies, without common interest, sympathy or connection'.[70] Ireland's admission into the United Kingdom in 1800 did not change this.

I have said that this chapter is about Britain's debt to Judaeo-Christianity, and so it is. But in the interests of balance I cannot omit the dark side. Sectarianism within Britain from the Reformation onwards did much harm. Even so, I shall also argue that Australia's experience in dealing with inherited sectarianism was, on balance, a cause of national strength.

## The Age of Exploration
Until the Reformation, England was, in world terms, a middle-ranking power only. It was the combined Protestant strength of England, Scotland and Wales that made Britain so formidable, especially after the 1707 Act of Union. But the Reformation did not merely empower Britain; it also led to greatly intensified competition between all the Protestant and Catholic powers of Europe. Each strove to extend its territorial reach – to create a colonial empire.

To be sure, much of this competition was commercially motivated.[71] But there were also evangelistic factors at play. The desire to convert the native peoples of other continents to the 'correct' form of the Christian faith was another common objective, particularly, though not exclusively, on the Catholic side. (Abel Tasman's official instructions from his Dutch Protestant masters in 1642 alluded to an ongoing effect of Spanish and Portugese colonisation in the South Seas: 'numberless multitudes of blind heathen have been introduced to the blessed light of the Christian religion'.) It is also beyond dispute that many of the individual seafarers who performed mighty feats were sustained by their personal faith. One outcome of these competing forces was the discovery of the Australian continent. And while Britain would eventually be the main beneficiary of that discovery, a number of other Christian countries were involved.

I have space here for only the barest summary of events – enough to make the point that (non-Indigenous) Australia owes its existence to the Christian religion in general, and British Christianity in particular. But the full story bears closer study. It is far more interesting than primary-school history lessons might have made it seem. It so fascinated Manning Clark, when he began research in the 1950s on the European Age of Exploration, that he was inspired to base his six-volume *History of Australia* around metaphysical themes.[72]

In very brief terms, the sequence of events was this. In 1492 Spain's Christopher Columbus – acting, so he later swore, under 'inspiration … from the Holy Spirit'[73] – discovered the Americas. He thereby opened up a New World for exploration via a westwards route from Europe. The two great Catholic powers – Spain and Portugal – were now in direct competition. Pope Alexander VI brokered a peace in 1493 by fixing a line of demarcation through the centre of the Atlantic Ocean – roughly halfway between Europe and the Americas. In the following year, this 'Papal Line' was adjusted slightly in Portugal's favour by the Treaty of Tordesillas, later sanctioned by Pope Julius I. Any territory to the west was Spain's – which included most of the Americas – and any to the east was Portugal's. But until 1529 the Papal Line did not extend to the other side of the globe (the side containing Australia). Instead, Spain and Portugal were entitled to claim any new territory they might first discover on that other side, Spain by sailing westwards or Portugal eastwards, even if they passed each other on the way.[74]

For the next thirty-five years, competition was unchecked, and there were major long-term consequences for Australia. A key event occurred in 1498, when Portugal's Vasco de Gama found an eastwards route to India via the Atlantic and Indian Oceans, around the Cape of Good Hope. In ensuing decades other Christian explorers took this route and proceeded beyond India, to the East Indies (modern-day Indonesia). Among them were the Dutch. By the late sixteenth century the Netherlands had broken away from rule by Spain and become a major Protestant power, with a trading base at Batavia (Jakarta). It is well known that it was Dutch sailors – Willem Jansz in February 1606 and Dirk Hartog in October 1616 – who first made landings on, respectively, the northern and western coasts of the continent of Australia. Both landings were unplanned – in Jansz's case, he thought he was in New

Guinea – but over the next twenty years several other Dutch ships stopped at various points on the western coast between Cape Leeuwin in the south and Willem's River in the north.[75]

The land mass was named New Holland. For centuries Europeans had suspected the existence of a Great South Land, but it was not clear until the late eighteenth century that this and New Holland were, in fact, one and the same. In 1626 a party led by Peter Nuyts mapped a long stretch of the previously unsighted southern coast, between the modern-day towns of Albany in Western Australia and Ceduna in South Australia. Then, in 1642, came a resourceful seafarer–merchant named Abel Tasman. A fleet under his command was dispatched from Batavia by the Dutch East India Company for 'the often attempted discovery of the unknown South-land'. Sailing eastwards, well beyond the point reached by Nuyts, Tasman's crew sighted the island that is now named after him – Tasmania – but which Tasman dutifully named Van Diemen's Land, after the then Governor-General of Batavia. That was on 24 November 1642. A fortnight later the fleet was the first to reach New Zealand. On a second voyage in 1644, Tasman mapped the northern coast of New Holland.[76]

The Dutch, of course, never settled in New Holland. Simply put, they did not much like what they saw. The new territory was deemed uninhabitable and otherwise unpromising. Manning Clark once remarked that there was a certain 'stern justice' in this grave miscalculation. The Dutch were motivated too much by greed ('insatiable covetousness'), and not enough by God.[77] Thus they missed their chance to claim a region whose mineral riches were not at first apparent, and would remain largely undeveloped for three centuries or more.

Yet the British themselves formed a similar low opinion of New Holland in the light of William Dampier's explorations of the northwest coast in 1688 and 1699. It was not until 1770, when the more temperate east coast of the mainland was discovered and claimed for Britain by James Cook, that Europeans began seriously to consider that the land might be worth occupying.

So, it was the discovery of the *east* coast that was the watershed. And here plain geography looms large. It was always much more likely that the east coast would be sighted by sailors coming *west* across the southern Pacific Ocean. And so it eventually proved. But first a sea route had to be found from Europe into the Pacific, either through or around the Americas. Columbus had never found one. It was here that the Roman Catholic Church was critical in the discovery of Australia. After de Gama's discovery in 1498 of an eastwards route to Asia, Portugal's Catholic rival Spain was desperate to discover a westwards route. Remember, it had to be a westwards route in order that Spain might comply with the Pope's edicts and the Treaty of Tordesillas.

Ferdinand Magellan found such a route for Spain in 1519. A fleet under his command negotiated the treacherous 600-kilometre-long strait that passes through the South American continent at latitude 52 degrees south. Magellan named it All Saints' Channel, because his fleet traversed it on All Saints' Day (1 November). Today it is called the Strait of Magellan.

Now, consider the role played in these events by Christianity and the Church. Apart from the background of Spanish–Portuguese rivalry, it was twofold. First, in 1518, when Charles I of Spain was hesitating over the cost and viability of Magellan's expedition, he was persuaded to give his consent by the advice of his royal chaplain, Cardinal Juan Rodriguez de Fonseca (1451–1524). The Cardinal (later an archbishop) was the acknowledged expert in Spain on matters pertaining to exploration of the New World. He had organised Columbus' voyages, among others. On this occasion he procured the backing of a wealthy merchant, Christopher de Haro, who provided a portion of the necessary funds.[78]

Equally important was the religious fervour of Magellan himself. He took an oath of allegiance to Spain in the Church of Santa María de la Victoria de Triana in Seville, and gave a large sum of money to the monks of the monastery there in order that they might pray for the success of the expedition. His personal motivation was 'to contribute to the glory of Almighty God and His church by converting barbarous nations to the Christian faith'.[79] When his depleted fleet eventually reached the Philippines, in 1521, Magellan lost his life in that cause, killed by natives. Indeed, for various reasons, only eighteen of the original 237 men under his command made it back safely to Spain. They, however, were the first people to have circumnavigated the Earth.

All Australians, Catholic or not, owe a debt to Magellan. True, in 1612, the Dutch found a better, safer route into the southern Pacific Ocean, around Cape Horn (Drake's Passage). (This was the route taken by Cook on the *Endeavour*.) But Magellan's was the vital breakthrough. In the admiring words of Manning Clark, the discovery of the east coast of Australia was 'a long-term by-product of Magellan's voyage'.[80] Other devout Catholics, all 'seeking the glory of God',[81] followed him into the Pacific and nearly made it to Australia – de Mendana in 1568, de Quiros in 1606, Torres in 1607. Later came the Dutch, the French and the British. It is entirely appropriate that the Catholic church in the town of Lismore, New South Wales, is in Magellan Street.

## James Cook and the voyage of the *Endeavour*

England had its own Magellan in James Cook (1728–79). He is a uniquely important figure in both British and Australian history, and merits careful attention. My blood boils when secularists claim him as one of theirs. Cook was the very embodiment of a certain kind of virile, intelligent yet understated Protestant Christianity.

Almost all historians regard Cook as one of the finest navigator–explorers of all time. His achievements may not have been as significant globally as those of Columbus or de Gama or Magellan, but no one was more important in the discovery of Australia. His is also a household name in Canada and New Zealand, and in the US States of Hawaii, Oregon and Alaska. On the first of his three voyages of exploration, in 1768–71, he claimed the east coast of New Holland for Britain, having crossed 'a sea so vast that the human mind can scarcely grasp it'.[82] His ship, the *Endeavour*, was just 32 metres long – one and a half cricket pitches. The Americans named a space command module and a space shuttle after it.

The context of Cook's first expedition befitted the Age of Enlightenment. Its aims and setting were metaphysical in scope. There had been two expeditions to the South Seas dispatched by Britain earlier in the eighteenth century: George Anson's in 1740–44 and John Byron's in 1764–66. A third, led by Samuel Wallis and Philip Carteret, was still in progress when Cook set out.[83] Wallis and Carteret had been charged with the task of finding new territory, but for Cook exploration was only a secondary purpose. His primary purpose was a scientific one: to observe the transit of the planet Venus on 3 June 1769 from an ideal vantage point in the southern Pacific Ocean, Tahiti. This remote but beautiful island had been discovered by Wallis just two years earlier.

The Royal Society (as the Royal Society of London for Improving Natural Knowledge, founded in 1660, has almost always been known) had several representatives on board. One was the esteemed astronomer Charles Green. Observations of the 1761 transit had whetted scientific appetites, and it was known that there would not be another transit for more than one hundred years. The information to be gleaned would help resolve some momentous geographical and cosmological issues, including the so-called problem of longitude (then very difficult to determine at sea) and the measurement of the distance from the Earth to the Sun. The French were equally interested and had sent out their own expedition to the South Seas, commanded by Louis-Antoine de Bougainville. As well as observing the transit, both expeditions were equipped to gather other sorts of scientific data. Cook was accompanied by two famed naturalists – an Englishman, Joseph Banks, and a Swede, Daniel Solander – and Bougainville by the no less distinguished Philibert Commerçon.[84]

The British observation of the transit went according to plan. Cook then opened sealed orders that required him to conduct further exploration of the South Seas. 'There is reason to imagine,' his orders read, 'that a Continent, or Land of great extent, may be found to the Southward of the Tract lately made by Captn Wallis … or of the Tract of any former Navigators.'[85] This was a reference not to New Holland but the eponymous Great South Land, the possible existence of which many geographers still insisted upon. Cook himself was sceptical, but dutifully followed orders and sailed south until he reached latitude 40 degrees. Then he sailed west. The Great South Land was, of course, nowhere to be seen, but the route eventually brought the *Endeavour* to New Zealand. Cook and his men were the first Europeans to set foot there since Tasman's party in 1642. They spent six months exploring and mapping both islands, and by March 1770 were free to sail home whichever way Cook saw fit. He chose to continue sailing west, with the aim of reaching the east coast of Van Diemen's Land and then making his way north to the East Indies.

Then came another act of fate – or Providence. The currents of the Pacific Ocean pushed the *Endeavour* slightly north of Cook's intended route and on 19 April 1770, a crew member named Hicks sighted land at a point corresponding today to Cape Everard in Victoria.[86] Cook had discovered the east coast of New Holland. He continued sailing north, looking for somewhere to land, and finally weighed anchor on 28 April at the place he would name Botany Bay. His men stayed there for a week, alternately exploring and resting. Cook then sailed all the way up the east coast, reaching Cape York on 22 August. He had proved, among many other things, that New Guinea and New Holland were separate islands.[87] He claimed the entire coastline he had traversed for the English Crown.

The *Endeavour* eventually got back home on 12 July 1771. During the entire voyage not a single man was lost to scurvy – 'a feat without precedent in the history of seafaring'.[88] Cook had taken precautions that too many ships' captains before him had neglected, even though the benefits of citrus fruits in warding off scurvy had been known since the 1590s.

## Was Cook a Christian?

Cook's religious views are disputed to this day. Personally I think they can confidently be inferred, but it is arguable territory because the man himself mostly stayed silent: 'he held his tongue and pen on most questions affecting the inner man'.[89] His most eminent biographer, J.C. Beaglehole, concluded over-cautiously that he 'had, so far as one can see, no religion'.[90] Others have confidently asserted that he was an active unbeliever, perhaps an atheist. According to Russel Ward 'there is no evidence that he had any belief in, or even respect for, divine revelation and its earthly components'; Ward considered Cook 'the noblest-natured son of the Enlightenment in the European Age of Reason'.[91] Manning Clark took a similar view.[92]

There are, however, some quite different schools of thought. One Christian commentator, Matthew Verschuur, has held up Cook as 'a godly man' for whom 'the secret of … success was the Word of God'.[93] One of his recent biographers, Frank McLynn, thought him 'probably' a deist,[94] while Guy Rundle has described him as 'a man of enlightenment *and* faith', postulating that 'in encountering his crew as human beings' Cook was 'a product of the rise of Protestantism'.[95] Still others have felt able to claim him as a kind of saint or martyr. He was killed on St Valentine's Day 1779 by native Hawaiians who had initially believed him to be a fertility god.

A rare theological statement by Cook, written in his journal in 1769 while the *Endeavour* was at anchor in Tahiti, is intriguing rather than decisive: 'the Histories of most Religions are very dark and not easily understood even by those who profess them'.[96] Some have put this forward as proof of Cook's unbelief, but I beg to differ. It is little more than a sage statement of fact, the qualifying word 'most' leaving room for Christianity to be considered an exception to the rule. It would be unsafe to read too much into the sentence either way, especially when there are other fascinating religious aspects to Cook's life story. He was influenced not only by the Church of England but by various strands of Protestant Non-conformism, and he owed much to the graces bestowed on him by some thoughtful Christian men.

Like many English naval officers of his era, he was a man of humble origins. Born on 27 October 1728, in the Yorkshire village of Marton-in-Cleveland, he was the second of eight children to a farm labourer and his wife. Little is known of his parents' religious views, but young James was dutifully exposed to Protestant rites and beliefs. He was baptised in the village church of St Cuthbert (Anglican), and as a boy received a basic secular and religious education at the Postgate School in Great Ayton. This schooling was paid for by the principal landowner in Ayton, one Thomas Skottowe, who employed Cook's father. Skottowe must have been a man of some religious sensibility: he took the trouble to build an Independent chapel at the back of his residence, Ayton Hall.[97]

Cook worked for some years with his father, as a farmhand. Then, in 1745, when he was sixteen, he moved 20 miles to the fishing village of Staithes, where he was apprenticed as a shop boy to a grocer and haberdasher named William Sanderson. But Cook was not suited to indoor work. The following year he began a three-year apprenticeship to Sanderson's friend John Walker, a ship-master in the nearby port of Whitby. Walker was a committed Quaker and a 'sober and benevolent soul'.[98] He placed supreme value on morals and integrity. Cook lived with the Walker family for six years after his apprenticeship had ended, and, according to another biographer, John Gascoigne, it was under Walker's tutelage that he 'acquired his grounding as a seaman and much of the personal discipline that made him an effective leader of men'.[99] Walker remained a lifelong friend and mentor. It was due mainly to Walker's example that Cook acquired the traits of benevolence, thrift, temperance and resourcefulness.[100]

So much is usually conceded, even by secularists anxious to claim Cook as one of their own. But what of the adult Cook? It can be said with certainty that he was not an Evangelical Christian. If he was a believing Anglican – as I think he was – then he was firmly of the High Church wing. He displayed no enthusiasm for missionary activity in the South Seas. Certainly – and this is to his credit – he was remorseful about the spreading of disease by his sailors among New Zealand natives. 'What is still more to *our* Shame as civilised Christians,' he wrote in his journal, '*we* debauch their Morals already too prone to vice' (emphasis mine).[101] This comment is revealing on several levels, not least because Cook counted himself a 'civilised Christian'.

There is no doubt he was familiar with Biblical terms. Several of the place names that he bestowed in New Holland were derived from the days of the Church year on which the *Endeavour* reached them – the Whitsunday Passage, Trinity Bay, the Pentecost Islands.[102] He observed the religious formalities of his era. In 1762 he married Elizabeth Batts, an innkeeper's daughter from Wapping in east London. The wedding ceremony was conducted at the parish church of St Margaret's, in nearby Barking, and when the Cooks settled down to live in east London they worshipped at St Paul's Church in Shadwell, traditionally known as the Church of Sea Captains. Their eldest son James was baptised there in 1763.[103] The marriage seems to have been a happy one. Although husband and wife were separated for long periods while Cook was at sea, they had six children, and in her widowed old age, Mrs Cook cherished her husband's memory. She is reputed never to have spoken ill of him.[104] One of her treasured possessions was the Bible he had taken with him on his voyages, which she had given him.[105]

Historians have long argued about Cook's Bible-reading habits. W.H. Fitchett wrote in 1917 that he 'was accustomed to read [from it] every Sunday to his crew'.[106] But an earlier biographer, Heinrich Zimmerman, who travelled with Cook on his third voyage in 1777–79, claimed that he seldom celebrated the Sabbath.[107] It is true that there are few references in Cook's journals to his having taken Sunday service, but that does not mean he did not do it more often than it is mentioned. We know from Joseph Banks' journal that Cook initiated divine service on 14 May 1769, when the *Endeavour* was in Tahiti.[108] Another of Zimmerman's claims – that Cook would not 'permit' any chaplain on his ships – was simply wrong. The Navy did not provide chaplains for modest-sized ships like the *Endeavour*. Religious duties were performed by the ship's commander.

I believe that Cook often read aloud from his Bible, if only because he was accustomed to following orders. Before departing on the 1768–71 voyage in *Endeavour* he had received written advice from Lord Morton, the President of the Royal Society:

> Ships of so small a rate, not being furnished with Chaplains, it were
> to be wished that the Captain himself would sometimes perform that
> office, and read prayers, especially on Sundays, to the Crew; that
> they may be suitably impressed and with a sense of their continuing
> dependence upon their <u>Maker</u>, and all who are on board, passengers
> and others should be obliged to attend upon those occasions.[109]

It is to be noted that the President of the Royal Society was a man of faith. James Douglas, Lord Morton, was an astronomer and long-time President of the Philosophical Society of Edinburgh, and Cook named Moreton Bay in Queensland after him. (The 'e' is a carry-over from Cook's original spelling error.)

What, though, of Cook's personal beliefs? The hard evidence is sparse, admittedly, but what evidence there is strongly suggests belief in an Almighty God. In his journals Cook made occasional reference to the divine – 'It pleased GOD at this very juncture to send us a light air of wind', 'Providence had conducted us through these rocks'[110] – and in an obituary he wrote for a young sailor he used the expression 'had it pleased God to have spared his life'.[111] Five letters survive from Cook to his Quaker mentor John Walker, in which the existence of God is assumed. In one of these Cook wrote: 'I trust in the continuation of the divine protection.'[112]

Of particular interest – and poignancy – is a letter that Cook wrote in July 1776 to the Reverend Dr Richard Kaye, chaplain to King George III. It was shortly before Cook's departure on what would turn out to be his last voyage. He thanked Reverend Kaye for his 'kind tender of ... service to Mrs Cook in my absence', and promised to name a landmark after him [Kaye] 'if it please God to spare me till I reach the place for Discoveries'.[113]

Dan O'Sullivan's recent biography contains an interesting section on 'Cook and Divine Providence'. In the eighteenth century there was an ongoing debate in British Christian circles regarding the nature and extent of God's 'supervision' of Creation. All participants took God's existence for granted but there was disagreement about God's methods. The minimalist view was that He never intervened directly in human affairs: He was indirectly responsible for everything that happened, because He had set in place the immutable laws of nature, but that was all. The more expansive view (sometimes called 'particular Providence') was that God might, and sometimes did, directly intervene in human affairs – whether in answer to prayer or of His own volition. O'Sullivan leaned towards the view that Cook believed in the minimalist notion of Providence only.[114] But the statements I have quoted above are open to a broader interpretation.

I regard it as a near certainty that Cook believed in God. Did he believe in Jesus Christ as the Son of God? Here there is a gap in the record – but for two indisputable facts. First, Cook was evidently a man of unimpeachable integrity. Second, as a precondition to his retaining a commission in the Royal Navy, he must have taken Holy Communion at least annually.[115] Here it is worth taking note of the sheer rigour of the Church of England's Communion service. Cook would have stood in church and prayed, in the words of the Nicene Creed from the 1662 Book of Common Prayer, that he believed 'in one Lord Jesus Christ, the only-begotten Son of God'. The prayer continues:

Begotten of his Father before all worlds, God of God, Light of Light, Very God of very God, Begotten, not made, Being of one substance with the Father, By whom all things were made: Who for us men, and for our salvation came down from heaven, And was incarnate by the Holy Ghost of the Virgin Mary, And was made man, And was crucified also for us under Pontius Pilate. He suffered and was buried, And the third day he rose again according to the Scriptures, And ascended into heaven, And sitteth on the right hand of the Father. And he shall come again with glory to judge both the quick and the dead: Whose kingdom shall have no end.

Along with the rest of the congregation, Cook would also have been warned by the presiding cleric that it would be better not to take Communion at all than to take it insincerely:

Dearly beloved in the Lord, ye that mind to come to the holy Communion of the Body and Blood of our Saviour Christ, must consider how Saint Paul exhorteth all persons diligently to try and examine themselves, before they presume to eat of that Bread, and drink of that Cup. For as the benefit is great, if with a true penitent heart and lively faith we receive that holy Sacrament; (for then we spiritually eat the flesh of Christ, and drink his blood; then we dwell in Christ, and Christ in us; we are one with Christ, and Christ with us;) so is the danger great, if we receive the same unworthily.

I simply cannot believe that the upright Cook would have gone through this solemn ritual in bad faith, even if others did.

Cook did not live to hear of the British Government's decision to establish a penal colony in New South Wales – the name he had bestowed upon the east coast of New Holland. As we have seen, he died in Hawaii in 1779. The decision to colonise was not made until 1786. But Cook, and the various Christian men who had guided his career, had paved the way.

CHAPTER 4

# Passage to Federation

I do not believe in any people becoming a great people without a profound faith.

Henry Parkes, the 'Father of Federation'

Righteousness exalteth a nation.

Proverbs 13:14 – lifelong motto of Vida Goldstein, Australian suffragette and feminist

We saw in Chapter 1 that religion was crucial to the survival of the Australian colonies. But once that initial hurdle had been overcome, what then? I will argue in this chapter that religion's role became, if anything, still more important. The achievement of Federation in 1901 was due, in large measure, to Christianity. It played a central part in the shaping of our national character – a character that has endured in the essentials and evolved in the details.

Let us count the ways. Without the abolition of the convict system, without cultural and religious pluralism, without strong marriages and the civilising influence of women, without parliamentary democracy, without a self-supporting yet civic-minded middle class, without an empowered and decently treated working class – without any of these things, there would have been no serious possibility of establishing a functional nation in 1901. At least, not a *civilised* nation to which most people were proud to belong. In that sense, these were all preconditions to Federation.

## The abolition of the convict system

Ending the convict system was perhaps the first key step in the Australian colonies' path to nationhood. It is true that the assignment of free convict labour to settlers was an integral aspect of colonial society during the formative period from 1800 to 1840. The system had a certain fiendish energy. In Van Diemen's Land, in particular, it was popular with ambitious emigrants from Britain – and continued to be until its abolition there in 1853.[1] In Western Australia, the system was actually introduced in 1850 in an attempt to revive the settlement's moribund economy. It stayed in place there until 1868.[2]

But as Robert Hughes and others have incontrovertibly shown, it was a system rotten at its core. It worked up to a point, but was plainly immoral. Assignment was akin to slavery. A different though related issue was the 'convict stain'. As the years went on, the criminals transported to Australia tended to be more serious offenders. And their often brutal and degrading treatment, especially at netherworlds such as Norfolk Island, Port Arthur and Moreton Bay, became an embarrassing disgrace.

The abolition of transportation was quintessentially a *moral* issue. Certainly – and this is my central point – it was religious, not secular, voices who spoke up most loudly for the cause. Evangelical Protestants and Catholics were united around it, in both England and Australia.

In 1837–38 a select committee of the House of Commons, chaired by Sir William Molesworth, deliberated on the matter. Ultimately it recommended the cessation of the assignment system and of transportation to the eastern mainland, though the system continued in Van Diemen's Land – in fact, after 1840, it was expanded there. Persuasive evidence had been given to the committee in person by two prominent colonial clerics. One was John Dunmore Lang, the 'father' of Presbyterianism in Australia; the other was W.B. Ullathorne (1806–89), a Benedictine priest who served as Vicar-General in New South Wales from 1831 to 1840. Perhaps the most vital work of all was done by two Quaker missionaries, James Backhouse and George Walker. They had compiled copious documentary evidence about the cruelties of the convict system, including a damning report by the great Christian penal reformer Alexander Maconochie, who, for a time, had implemented remarkably benevolent measures as commandant on Norfolk Island. All this material was supplied to the committee.[3]

Consider Ullathorne's plea, based on concern for the souls of both the convicts and their enslavers:

We have been doing an ungracious and ungodly thing. We have taken a vast portion of God's earth, and made it a cesspool; we have taken the oceans, which, with their wonders, gird the globe, and made them a sink ... The eye of God looks down upon such a people, such, since the deluge, has not been.[4]

Despite such pleas, and the Molesworth committee's ruling, attempts were made to revive transportation to the eastern mainland in the ensuing decade. Opposition in Sydney and Port Phillip respectively was led by an up-and-coming Henry Parkes and the Superintendent of Port Phillip, Charles La Trobe (1801–75). La Trobe was a devout man from a family of Moravian missionaries, descended from Huguenots in France. In Van Diemen's Land, the leaders of the abolitionist cause were a Congregationalist minister, John West,[5] and the first Catholic bishop of Hobart, Robert Willson. Willson travelled to London in 1846–47 to give evidence before a House of Lords committee.[6] La Trobe also lent his support to the cause in Van Diemen's Land: during a brief stint there in 1846–47 as Acting Lieutenant-Governor, he formed the view that he owed a 'sacred and imperious duty' to check the vices to which the penal system gave rise.[7]

Transportation to Van Diemen's Land finally ended in 1853.[8] As historian A.G.L. Shaw once pointed out, it would have been better for the local economy if transportation had continued. But 'moral considerations triumphed over material'.[9] Three years later the colony changed its name to Tasmania, in an effort to rid itself of the convict stain. Thus, 'the mid-nineteenth century evangelical view of Christianity became inextricably associated with Van Diemen's Land'.[10]

Thereafter, Tasmania became an especially pious – even puritanical – place. Many leading politicians and judges were staunch Anglicans. One, Thomas Reibey (1821–1912), bears special mention: he held high office in both the Church of England (as Archdeacon of Launceston) and in politics (as premier and colonial secretary). Somehow this seems appropriate: Tasmanians had a lot to atone for.

## Religious and cultural pluralism

Another precondition to Federation was establishing a society in which free people of diverse backgrounds could contentedly co-exist. In short: a culture of tolerance. Some readers may be surprised to see this subject mentioned in the context of nineteenth-century Christianity. Nowadays, indeed, many of the strongest supporters of multiculturalism are the strongest detractors of Christianity. Sometimes, sadly, Christians blame non-British immigration since World War Two for Australia's secularisation. Both mindsets spring from the grave misconception that Australia was once a monocultural place – boring or idyllic, depending on your point of view.

Donald Horne – author of the seminal 1964 critique of modern Australia, *The Lucky Country* – scotched this heresy. He observed near the end of his life that 'the "settlement" of Australia was a multicultural experience long before the word was invented'.[11] He was right. Ethnically and culturally, few of the colonists from 1788 onwards thought of themselves as British – that came much later. In the early decades they were English or Scottish, Welsh or Irish.[12] And before too long there were other identifiable sub-groups, such as the German-Lutherans in South Australia. From the start, all of the Australian colonies were melting pots or patchwork quilts – or, to use Noel Pearson's preferred metaphor, places of 'layered identities'.

It is perhaps as well that I define what I mean by multiculturalism. I am happy to adopt the definition of one of its former opponents, Tony Abbott. By his own admission, the Prime Minister came to see that 'multiculturalism was just a new term to describe what had always been Australia's social reality: that significant numbers of people from quite different backgrounds were assimilating into Australian society in their own way and at their own pace'.[13] In colonial New South Wales, virtually from the beginning, there were five distinctive religious groupings: Anglicans, Catholics, Presbyterians, Methodists (and other Protestant Non-conformists) and Jews. Within each of those groupings there was a high degree of factionalism and dissent. Thus, there were the High and Low Church Anglicans; the English- and Irish-Catholics; the traditionalist and progressive Presbyterians; the many strains of Protestant Non-conformism (Methodists, Congregationalists, Quakers, Baptists, Lutherans and so on); and orthodox and cultural Jews. The clearest religious divide was that between Protestants and Catholics (see Appendix B). But apart from doctrinal differences there were also sharp cultural factors at play.[14] Most Catholics in Australia were Irish and working class. Most Presbyterians were Scottish and middle class. The English spanned all denominations and classes, though English-Catholics were a small minority. The Welsh, meanwhile, had their own brand of Protestantism.

The Protestant–Catholic divide played a huge part in our history from 1788 until as late as the 1970s – as, to a lesser extent, did other religious and cultural differences. Sometimes these differences flared up in ugly ways. But for the most part – putting Indigenous relations to one side – they were managed peaceably. And in the end, through fractious diversity came strength. Australia's robust multiculturalism is a key feature of our Judaeo-Christian heritage.

In religious terms, Australia was never likely to become a pale imitation of England. It is doubtful as a matter of law whether the Church of England was *ever* the established Church of New South Wales – but the matter was put beyond any doubt in 1836. In that year Governor Richard Bourke passed the Church Act, 'the most significant ecclesiastical legislation in Australia's history'.[15] Described at the time as 'the Magna Carta of Australia's religious liberty',[16] it entrenched the principle that the State should not favour any one Christian denomination over any other. Henceforth, in New South Wales, all of the main denominations received government support on roughly equitable terms. Van Diemen's Land followed suit soon afterwards, as, in due course, did the other colonies.

Bourke's legacy to Australia is underrated. In a profound sense, he was the author of multiculturalism. Secular historians are happy to praise his liberality – and rightly so. What many overlook is that his motive in passing the Church Act was to advance the cause of the Christian religion. In the words of David Stoneman, a recent biographer, he 'believed in the divine purpose of Britain and his responsibility in that mission'.[17]

What made Bourke unusual in the 1830s was not his fervent Christianity but his ecumenism. He regarded Catholics not as enemies but as fellow Christians; he feared that denigration of Catholic beliefs would prejudice not only the overall cause of religion, but the maintenance of good moral standards in the colony. Born into the Irish aristocracy in 1777, Bourke himself was an enlightened Anglican, but by 'enlightened' I mean generous and humanitarian, not wishy-washy in his core faith. Bourke stopped well short of an open-slather approach to religious truth, once warning against 'an overly tolerant spirit' that 'endures all manner of eccentric wanderings from the Christian orbit'. He believed that God was his 'dear great friend'; that His mercy and providence guided each individual's life. He believed in the Holy Trinity (Father, Son and Holy Spirit) and in life after death.

Bourke's wife Elizabeth was a fellow Evangelical. When she died, in May 1832, Bourke wrote to a friend: 'I closed her eyes and kissed her forehead and left her with her God. Those eyes I trust will open upon me at the Resurrection and that we shall both be finally accepted thro' God's mercy in Christ our Saviour.'[18]

The full flavour of Bourke's Christianity – and its importance to Australia – is evident in this passage:

> We should remember that Christ is the way; and that the Roman Catholic is a Christian: and while our views have led us to a different road from his, we ought not to think and speak irreverently of that, which our fellow Christian may as piously have preferred it. It, on the contrary, becomes us to rejoice humbly and sincerely, that both roads may lead the faithful to salvation.[19]

It should also be noted that Bourke's attorney-general, John Hubert Plunkett (1802–69) – the man who actually drafted the Church Act – was himself a Catholic. Indeed, until the mid-1850s, he was the leading Catholic layman in Sydney. Religion was central to his view of the law – 'to him the law in its essence came from God as the only source of authority'.[20] And, despite his proud Catholicism, Plunkett's presence in the colony helped to reduce religious tensions. One reason was his own open-mindedness ('intolerance in religious matters was always anathema to him'[21]), but, more generally, he impressed all who knew him with his competence, diligence and decency. In the words of historian Bede Nairn, 'his very career … provided clear evidence of the open nature of the colonial society'.[22]

The Church Act continued the process of 'reorientating New South Wales from a penal colony to a settler society'.[23] But, of course, it was not a cure-all. As I have said, the Protestant–Catholic divide would remain an important feature of Australian life for more than a century.

Observers of Australian history, both religious and secular, have tended to denounce sectarianism as an unmitigated evil. It is true that some manifestations of religious bigotry were appalling; the worst, perhaps, occurred during the conscription campaigns of World War One (see Chapter 7). It is also true, as Steve Bruce and other secularisation theorists have noted, that the post-Reformation trend towards 'fragmentation' – 'competing [religious] perspectives and institutions' – coincided with the decline of religious belief across the West overall.[24] Yet there are other ways of looking at this issue.

From a religious perspective, unity for its own sake should not be the lodestar. It may be that the best way to increase raw religious numbers in a given society is by imposing some sort of authoritarian theocracy.

But such arrangements are inimical to religious freedom and true religious enlightenment.

The ideal – as Richard Bourke clearly saw – is informed ecumenicism. If that has never quite been the position in Australia, a strong case can still be made that destructive sectarianism has always been most harmful at the top – among over-zealous Church leaders[25] and opportunistic politicians. The default position has been ecumenicism/multiculturalism. I agree with John Hirst that, from the earliest days of British settlement in Australia, the mass of the common people sought reasonable harmony in their daily lives. This included sincere religious believers of all kinds. For most of them, conditions here were tough enough already and memories of religious schisms in Europe ran deep.[26] There were so many significant religious groups that no one of them could reasonably hope to overwhelm all the others. Thus it was in most people's interests to get along, especially as mixed marriages were frequent. Ian Breward has called it 'the ecumenicism of need'.[27]

Modern-day atheists, and others hostile to the Churches, might wish that sectarianism had been *more* virulent and destructive than it was. Judaeo-Christianity might not have survived at all. But that is not what happened. A hardy, healthy religious pluralism eventually developed.

This feature of Australian life was perhaps most pronounced in Queensland. 'Probably in no other colony,' reflected Michael Hogan, 'was Catholic integration in the general society so well developed.'[28] Once it had cast off its penal origins and become a separate colony in 1859, Queensland soon developed a robust, pluralistic society. The first premier, Englishman Robert Herbert (1831–1905), observed in a letter to his aunt in the late 1850s that 'the people here seem to be more religious than in many places'.[29] Herbert himself, only twenty-eight when he assumed office, was a staunch High Anglican with the finest of religious and political pedigrees. Importantly, he was a cultivated ecumenicist like Bourke in New South Wales: all denominations in Queensland received aid on fair terms. As well as Catholics, Presbyterians and Methodists made their presence felt in that colony. In addition, significant numbers of Lutheran immigrants arrived from Prussia and Scandinavia in the 1860s and 1870s.[30] Similar trends are evident in the early history of Western Australia.[31]

This attitude of grudging tolerance spilled over into other aspects of civil society. An eminent historian of the mid-twentieth century, A.G.L. Shaw, argued that religious pluralism fostered egalitarianism and democracy in Australia:

The relative weakness of the 'official' Church of England [...] shattered any idea of creating in the antipodes a replica of English society. Wealthy landowners and government officials were too few, and the Anglican Church too much opposed by Roman Catholics, Presbyterians and Dissenters alike, for these groups to reproduce a ruling class like that of England; the strength of the combined 'opposition', Irish, Catholic, non-conformist, Chartist, emancipist and radical, was such as to encourage the building up of a democratic ... ideology.[32]

In short, the Church Act proved to be not only a charter of religious liberty; it was also 'a charter of social equality'.[33]

## The founding of Victoria and South Australia

An excellent contemporary historian, James Boyce, has shown that 'Melbourne's birth, not Sydney's settlement, signalled the emergence of European control over Australia'.[34] He has also established that the process by which that happened cannot be understood properly, or at all, outside the context of Evangelical Christianity. The story is not, I am the first to admit, a wholly edifying one. Indeed, in several respects, it is tragic. But it demonstrates how much Christianity mattered in early Australian history as a motivating force for powerful individuals. It also reveals how, 'on the ground', beyond the civilising influence of missionaries and the Churches, secular evil held sway.

The original land grab in 1835 by John Batman's Van Diemen's Land syndicate was a thoroughly opportunistic exercise; the crucial question was whether it would be ratified by those in authority. There were three sets of officials to be mollified: those in Hobart (Lieutenant-Governor George Arthur) and Sydney (Governor Richard Bourke), and the ultimate decision-makers back in London. The key issue was the position of the Kulin people, the Indigenous inhabitants of Port Phillip.

We have already seen that both Bourke and Arthur were Evangelical Christians; Arthur, moreover, nursed a guilty conscience over the fate of the Indigenous population in Van Diemen's Land (by now approaching extinction). The situation in the Mother Country was pivotal. Not since the Civil War had Evangelical Christianity played such a dominant role in English politics as it did in the 1830s. In 1833 slavery – the archetypal Evangelical cause of the pre-Victorian era – had finally been abolished throughout the British Empire. When Lord Melbourne's Whig government came to power in Britain in 1835, it was dominated at the highest levels by liberal Evangelical reformers – men such as George Grey; Thomas Spring Rice (a very close friend of Bourke); James Stephen; Charles Grant, Lord Glenelg; and Thomas Fowell Buxton.[35] With slavery dealt with, they turned their minds to new causes.

Chief among them were the future of penal transportation (already discussed) and the welfare of 'native peoples'. Buxton, an Anglican–Quaker, chaired a House of Commons committee on the latter subject in the period 1835 to 1837.[36] Its members were motivated by the belief that the British Empire existed 'for some higher purpose than commercial prosperity and military renown'. The empire, to their minds, was called 'to carry civilisation and humanity, peace and good government, and, above all, the knowledge of our true God, to the uttermost ends of the earth'.[37]

These men genuinely cared about Indigenous peoples. But they believed the key to their welfare was the settlement of the Australian colonies by men in their own image – middle-class, law-abiding, enlightened, devout. Settlers of that ilk would treat the natives properly and might even convert them to Christianity – 'a blessing exceeding all which mere philanthropy has ever accomplished'.[38] In that way, a repeat of the Tasmanian experience could be avoided.

The reality proved horribly different. A treaty of sorts was negotiated with the Kulin people by Batman in June 1835.[39] But it was swiftly repudiated,[40] and from 1836 Port Phillip 'effectively became the new frontier in the Tasmanian war' against Aboriginal people.[41] By 1842 a local cleric was lamenting: 'judging from present appearances, by the time the missionary shall have acquired the language, so as to be able to preach the Gospel, he will have no one to preach to.'[42] Before white settlement there had been some 11,000 to 15,000 Indigenous people living in the area south of the Murray River (modern-day Victoria).[43] By 1845 virtually all the grazing land had been occupied by white settlers and the native population had been decimated.[44] In 1851 Victoria would become a separate, thriving colony, but the price paid was high indeed.

What went wrong? It was not an excess of Evangelical zeal but the tragic lack of it in practice.

One stark fact stands out. In the first few years after 1835, the white settlers of Port Phillip were *not* upright middle-class people of the sort the English Evangelicals had been led to believe they would be. On the contrary, most of them were rough, bush-hardened ex-convicts from Van Diemen's Land.[45] In this respect, Governor Bourke in Sydney and the colonial authorities in London were operating under a misapprehension.

Moreover, because of the slowness of communications in that era, they were frequently called upon to make decisions after the event.

Bourke soon formed the view that colonisation was inevitable and that (pending a final decision from London) he should try to make the best of things. In May 1836 he announced government protection of Port Phillip's Aboriginal population.[46] But the system was never adequately resourced or policed. This must stand as a major stain on the otherwise honourable record of Charles La Trobe, the first superintendent of the Port Phillip District (and, after 1851, Victoria's first lieutenant-governor). I agree with Boyce: 'The lack of a local commitment to the Protectorate or even to traditional missionary work after 1839 is a deeply troubling dimension of the early history of Port Phillip.'[47]

It is true that more enlightened white settlers came to the area after the first few years, but, even then, many of them clustered in Melbourne or regional centres such as Geelong, Bendigo and Ballarat. The churches there quickly gathered strength. But in more distant rural areas it was too often a different tale. In the critical formative period there were nowhere near enough civilising influences: men of faith and education, churches, or women. Missionaries did follow later, and some did fine work. But by then huge and irreparable damage had been done.

To – for my purposes – a happier story.[48] South Australia was the only Australian colony to which convicts were never sent. On the contrary, in December 1836, it was founded as a province for free settlers of a certain mindset. The intention was to make it a 'Paradise of Dissent'.

The expression comes from Douglas Pike's seminal book of that title, published in 1967.[49] The dissent in question was *religious* dissent. South Australia was the first colony in the British Empire not to be aligned officially to the Church of England.[50] Its founders were dominated by non-Anglican Protestants, principally Methodists, Congregationalists and Baptists. In the words of George Fife Angas (1789–1879), the most important founder of all:

> My great object was, in the first instance, to provide a place of refuge
> for pious dissenters of Great Britain, who could in their new home
> discharge their consciences before God in civil and religious duties
> without any disabilities.[51]

And so it proved. There would be plenty of Anglican settlers and some Catholics. But Non-conformists were over-represented at all levels of society, including at the top (premiers, judges etc.). The whole place retained a notably 'religious' character until well into the twentieth century. Adelaide has often been referred to proudly as 'the City of Churches'.[52]

Several other points about South Australia are worth noting.

While most of the early colonists were British, there was from the beginning a strong German Lutheran presence. The full story is told in Everard Leske's fascinating book, *For Faith and Freedom*.[53] Many of these godly men and women settled in the Barossa Valley, and were pivotal in the creation of the now-enormous Australian wine industry. More generally, in the latter half of the nineteenth century, South Australia became the powerhouse of Australian agriculture. The most famous agriculturalist, John Ridley (1806–87), was an English-born lay preacher. In 1843 he invented the Stripper, a labour-saving machine that efficiently removed the heads of grain from wheat stalks. It proved 'of inestimable benefit to Australia'.[54] Crucially, the generous and upright Ridley refused to profit by his idea: he did not seek an exclusive patent, thereby allowing anyone to copy his invention.[55] Yet Ridley was just one of many among the colony's productive and pious farmers. Between 1860 and 1880 the South Australian wheat crop equalled that of all the other colonies combined.[56]

In the 1870s another devout and civic-minded South Australian, Charles Todd (1826–1910),[57] was responsible for another achievement of huge consequence to the whole continent. He supervised the construction from Darwin to Port Augusta of Australia's first overland telegraph, a massive feat of technology and engineering. It enabled all the colonies to communicate with each other – and the world – in a matter of minutes. Until then it had taken weeks or even months.[58]

## The rise of the middle class

George Fife Angus, John Ridley and Charles Todd are good examples of a key religious and social type: the hard-working, successful yet civic-minded man of the middle class. Such men were utterly crucial in the history of nineteenth-century Australia. They were prominent not only in South Australia, but in all six colonies. They were benevolent doers. They built not merely personal wealth, but also institutions and societies. The common thread? They were devout. They looked well beyond their own material comfort and that of their immediate families; they looked to their employees, their fellow citizens, their churches, their souls, their God.

The emergence of a flourishing moral middle class was another precondition to nationhood. The process began in the 1830s with the mass immigration of free settlers, and intermarriage between them or their descendants (on the one hand) and emancipists or the native-born (on the other). In 1828 the ratio of convicts and ex-convicts to free settlers was an untenable five to one. By 1851 it was two to five, and the process of urbanisation was well under way.[59] So was the movement towards self-government and the extension of the franchise beyond the squattocracy to 'respectable' men of modest wealth and income.

In New South Wales, these causes were led not by the squattocracy – indeed, most of them resisted change – but by the leaders of the rising middle class. The upper-middle class coalesced around the leadership of Charles Cowper – son of the Reverend William Cowper – a man who would serve five terms as premier and earn the title 'patrician democrat'.[60] The more radical lower-middle class was fired up by figures such as Henry Parkes and the Reverend John Dunmore Lang.[61] In the words of Peter Cochrane, whose book *Colonial Ambition* is the definitive account of the period, 'the link between the Protestant faith and liberal politics was a powerful one'.[62]

The gold rushes of the 1850s sharply accelerated these trends. In that decade Victoria turned into an economic powerhouse, its population rising from 76,000 in 1850 to 540,000 in 1860.[63] Initially, some sections of colonial society had been concerned that gold would have a deleterious effect. There were fears – based on the experience in California – that a get-rich-quick mentality would take hold and that the vices of prostitution, drinking, gambling and fighting would proliferate on and around the fields. The Anglican Bishop of Melbourne, Charles Perry (1807–91), feared for 'the destruction of social order'.[64]

In the event, these fears proved exaggerated – and the Churches can take substantial credit. The Eureka Stockade of 1854 notwithstanding, behaviour on the goldfields was not nearly as rowdy or immoral as feared. The Sabbath was well observed – this, indeed, was a condition to the granting of mining licenses – and many religious speakers addressed large and attentive audiences. J.D. Lang himself spoke to some 3,000 miners at Sofala in October 1851 ('the most numerous I had ever addressed in the colony'[65]) and several Methodist preachers and Catholic priests took up postings on the fields.[66] One of the earliest discoverers of gold was the Reverend W.B. Clarke, the minister at St Thomas' Anglican Church in North Sydney, and one of the colony's few formally trained geologists. Ultimately, gold was a huge plus not only for the colonies but for the cause of Christianity: it 'gave a major fillip to religion in Australia'. The main reason was that the educational standard of the immigrants who arrived in the colonies after 1850 was, on the whole, 'far better than before; so was the degree of religious understanding'.[67]

Considered as a group, the emergent middle class was much more religiously observant than the convicts or the military had been in the early days of the various colonies.[68] The presence of women in large numbers was critical in this regard, a point to which I shall return shortly. Among men, the best of them in both the artisan/shopkeeper class (lower middle) and the farming/business/professional class (middle and upper middle) were steeped in a particular version of the Protestant work ethic. As we saw in Chapter 2, this ethic had its roots in the Reformation. In nineteenth-century Britain, the key text espousing and extolling this ethic was Adam Smith's *The Wealth of Nations*, first published in 1776. Especially among Scottish Presbyterians and other Non-conformists, the values of thrift, modesty and self-improvement were paramount.[69]

The squattocracy was supplanted in its own field, agriculture, by some hardy post-gold pioneers. In Victoria, for instance, there were three critical figures; all were stout Presbyterians, infused with the Protestant work ethic. George Hall Peppin (1800–72) bred the sturdy Wanganella strain of sheep in the 1860s;[70] Hugh McColl (1819–85) was a visionary pioneer of irrigation programmes in the 1870s and 1880s;[71] and in 1884 H.V. McKay (1865–1926) invented the Sunshine Harvester, an improvement on John Ridley's seminal design. The significance of McKay's invention is hard to overstate: it encouraged wheat farmers nationwide to sow more extensively and helped the Australian colonies survive the 1890s recession. For many years the Victorian factory in which McKay's workforce manufactured the machines was the largest in Australia, and McKay was Australia's leading industrialist.[72]

At the top of this tree there emerged a body of enterprising and wealthy men who were also well educated, ethical and public-spirited. There were dozens in every colony, but by way of example I would point, in New South Wales, to men of the calibre of David Jones (1793–1873) and John Fairfax (1804–77); in Victoria, to William Westgarth (1815–89), David Syme (1827–1908) and H.V. McKay; in Queensland, to Robert Christison (1837–1915) and William Knox D'Arcy (1849–1917); in South Australia, to Robert Barr Smith (1834–1915) and Thomas Elder (1818–97); in Western Australia, to Walter Padbury (1820–1907) and John Henry Monger (1831–92); and in Tasmania, to Henry Jones (1862–1926). Almost always they were ardent Christians. Not nominal or conventional – ardent. So were most of their wives and children. It is a combination not often seen today. Not only the economies, but also the religious, cultural and social institutions of each and every colony owed a great deal to men such as these. They were moral and financial giants.

Robert Barr Smith of Adelaide (1834–1915) is as good an example as any of the sort of benevolent, larger-than-life man I am talking about. A son of the Reverend Dr Robert Smith, of the Free Church of Scotland in Renfrewshire, he remained a staunch but ecumenically minded Christian all his life. His father had taken pains to see that 'the religious and secular training of his son was of the most thorough character',[73] and the Reverend's efforts paid off. According to one admirer, 'he had got by heart the apostolic injunction, "Whatsoever thy hand findeth to do, do it with all thy might" [Ecclesiastes 9:10 (KJV)]'. Soon after migrating to Melbourne in 1854, Barr Smith married Joanna Elder, a highly cultivated – and devout – woman in her own right. (She became a close friend and supporter of Mary MacKillop.) She and Barr Smith would have thirteen children together and start a family dynasty.

Joanna was the sister of Barr Smith's long-time business partner, Thomas Elder, with whom he built up from nothing the vast conglomerate known as Elder, Smith & Co. In the half-century before Federation the company was central to Australian banking, commerce, shipping, agriculture and mining. But Barr Smith was no mere thrusting tycoon. He refused a knighthood ('I have done nothing to earn it, and the acceptance of it would be inconsistent with the spirit of my whole life'[74]) and there is no reason to doubt the sincerity of his motives. His obituary in the Adelaide *Advertiser* speaks for itself:

> There is not an industry in the State that does not owe much to him,
> either directly or indirectly … He always had a high sense of his duty
> and his responsibilities, and he bore without abuse the grand old name
> of gentleman. No whisper of a dishonourable transaction was ever
> associated with his name.[75]

Barr Smith's charitable activity was legendary. Indeed, he was arguably the greatest philanthropist in Australian history. 'No one ever went to him with a genuine story of distress who came away empty-handed, and often his gifts were as spontaneous as they were unexpected.'[76] The more notable causes that he supported included the University of Adelaide, the Adelaide Botanical Gardens, the Overland Telegraph Line, the Queen Victoria Maternity Hospital, numerous exploratory expeditions (such as Douglas Mawson's to the Antarctic), the Adelaide Trades Hall ('he realised that labour as well as capital has rights'[77]) and – significantly – the Anglican Church. He gave £10,000 – an enormous sum in those days – towards the cost of completing St Peter's Cathedral.

Men such as these, together with their professional advisers (lawyers, accountants, doctors etc.) and their elected representatives in the colonial parliaments, became the ruling class. They thus supplanted forever the pretensions of the squattocracy. In Western Australia, for example, the strength of middle-class Protestantism may be gathered from the composition of the so-called six hungry families – the Leakes, the Stones, the Shentons, the Lefroys, the Burts and the Lee Steeres – who dominated the colony's legal and political affairs by the late nineteenth century. Most were pillars of their various churches. Although the moniker 'hungry' was first used as term of derision by populist critics (a reference to their alleged hunger for money and power), there can be no question but that these families made a massive contribution to Western Australia.

## The empowerment of the working class

The Australian trade union movement now has a tarnished reputation, but its contribution to the nation should never be forgotten. For over a century it played a vital role in improving working and living conditions for millions of vulnerable people. Modelled on the movement in Britain, it gathered strength in the 1870s and 1880s and quickly achieved success – indeed, more success than its British counterpart.[78] At the leadership level, the movement was dominated in the fledgling stages by devout Protestant Christians from the working classes. These men were the original 'Christian socialists' – the genuine article.

A key figure in Australia was the Scottish-born W.G. Spence (1846–1926).[79] He came to prominence in Victoria through the miners' and shearers' associations and later founded the Australian Workers' Union (AWU). Spence led the seminal Maritime Strike of 1890. Its failure was a turning point in Australian history, because it convinced the working classes that to achieve their goals they needed representation in parliament. Spence is remembered as 'perhaps the greatest union organiser in Australian history'.[80]

The key to his approach (like Bob Hawke's many decades later) was moderation. He eschewed the language of violent class struggle, preferring to emphasise Christian ideals of justice and charity. A lifelong Presbyterian, his great-grandfather and his uncle had both been noted preachers in Scotland and his parents were also devout. His mother taught him to read from the Bible. Spence himself became an elder, secretary and Sunday school superintendent at the Creswick Presbyterian Church, and in the 1880s often preached with the Primitive Methodists (a Methodist breakaway group).[81] He once said: 'New Unionism [is] simply the teachings of the greatest of all social reformers, Him of Nazareth, whom all must revere.'[82] He believed that 'he was doing what Jesus would have him do for the downtrodden of society'.[83]

Spence was not a lone wolf. Many of Australia's early union leaders were cut from the same Christian cloth. They went on to form the Australian Labour (later Labor) Party.

The ALP was founded in the late nineteenth century as the political arm of the trade union movement. It enjoyed amazingly rapid success in its first twenty years, and it is crucial to understand why. This was not solely, or even mainly, a matter of economic determinism in action, as Marxist theory would have it. The ALP's founders were little influenced by the radicalism of Continental Europe. There was a streak of racism in their thinking and some American populist elements as well. (The latter were mostly derived from Edward Bellamy's best-selling science fiction novel, *Looking Backward from 2000*, first published in 1888.[84]) But, in large part, their success was due to religious causes.

The party's founders embodied two potent streams of contemporary Christian thought. There was the Catholic social justice tradition – Pope Leo XIII's ground-breaking encyclical of 1891 about labour and capital, *Rerum Novarum*, was highly influential – and Protestant Christian socialism, of the sort espoused by men such as W.G. Spence. This dual appeal was broad – and it needed to be. In the words of John Hirst, 'the success of the Labor Party depended on its ability to keep Protestant and Catholic working men together'.[85] The party achieved this feat in the early decades because its leaders spanned both camps. Agnostics and secularists were there too, but in nothing like the numbers of today. As a foreign observer wrote in the year of Federation, 1901: 'Many of the supporters of the Labor Party say grace before every meal, go to church on Sundays and strictly observe the Sabbath as a day of rest. They would not tolerate the principles of Christianity to be questioned.'[86]

John Christian Watson (1867–1941), the party's first federal leader and (in 1904) the country's first Labor prime minister, embodied in his own person all three strands of thought: Protestant, Catholic, rationalist. But Watson – who emigrated to Sydney from New Zealand in 1888 – was an unusual hybrid. He had a German-Lutheran father, a Scots-Presbyterian stepfather and an Irish-Catholic New Zealand-born mother. He was twice married in a Unitarian church in Sydney and late in life made a formal conversion to Catholicism. Watson was well versed in theology but rarely went to church, and may have been a deist or an agnostic. I would class him as a fellow traveller with Christianity.

Three of Labor's most vital early figures were, in contrast, solid, conventional Protestants. Each rose steadily through the union movement, and, after Federation, each became prime minister: Andrew Fisher (Presbyterian), Joseph Cook (Methodist), and W.M. (Billy) Hughes (Anglican). The greatest of these was Fisher. In his native Scotland he had been a child coalminer. In the early 1880s, as a young union leader, he worked closely with Keir Hardie, one of the founders of the British Labour Party and (from 1892) its first member of the House of Commons. Hardie was one of the original Christian socialists – a member of the Evangelical Union Church, a lay preacher, and a prominent figure in the temperance movement. Famously, he claimed during World War One that 'I now understand what Christ suffered in Gethsemane as well as any man living'.[87]

Another early giant in Australia was J.T. (Jim) McGowen (1855–1922), the first Labor premier of New South Wales and the leader of the party there for almost twenty years from 1894. Billy Hughes once said that 'there was not a great reform on the statute books of this country – no great achievement made by industrial labour – that had not its foundation in some act or support of Mr McGowen ... When he took the Labor Party in hand it was nothing: when he left it it was everything.'[88] McGowen was a boilermaker by trade and an Evangelical Protestant by religion. He was a prominent member of the congregation at St Paul's Anglican Church in Redfern, serving as its Sunday-school superintendent for thirty-two years, and a close friend of the long-time minister there, the Reverend Francis Bertie Boyce.[89] According to one biographer, McGowen 'never allowed his public duties to interfere with his Church attendance or his work in the Sunday school'.[90] Once, at a public lecture in London, McGowen commented on the link between the ALP and Christianity:

A representative body of a civilised Christian community should so legislate and work that each succeeding generation will be better,

happier and more comfortable. We ask you to believe that this
Religion of Humanity is practical in ways such as the Nazarene
Carpenter demanded … We raise our hats and bow our heads with
reverence to the Commandments as they came down from Mount
Sinai. But we believe that the Eleventh Commandment is the
Commandment that we want above all others to practise, and that
is, to love our neighbour as ourselves and to do to others as we would
they should do unto us.[91]

There were equivalent Labor figures in the other colonies. In 1899,
Queensland elected the first Labor government anywhere in the
world. There were also some notable Protestant ministers of religion –
admittedly a small minority – who spoke up proudly for the ALP and
progressive causes generally.[92]

In one key respect Australia may owe its very existence to the ALP.
At the least, Federation could have been delayed for a long time but for
Labor's rise in the 1890s. I shall say more about Federation's debt to
religious sensibilities later in this chapter and confine myself here to two
main points.

First, the ALP's early successes in colonial elections, especially in
Queensland, helped to appease the more radical social reformers in the
Labor movement, many of whom were suspicious of Federation as a
bourgeois distraction. Second, in New South Wales, during the crucial
period 1894 to 1899, the ALP kept George Reid's relatively progressive
Free Trade government in office. (Labor MPs supported Reid on the
floor of the Legislative Assembly.) Public opinion on Federation was
evenly divided in New South Wales; it was the swing colony. Reid – yet
another Protestant clergyman's son, by the way – vacillated for years,
but eventually he supported Federation. If William Lyne's powerful
anti-Federation faction had gained power, the course of events might
well have been different.[93]

Thus, the early ALP of the idealistic Christian socialists was not
merely an agent of social reform for the working class; it was also a
unifying influence for the whole nation.

## The civilising influence of women

For decades after 1788 women were massively outnumbered by men.
In 1830 the ratio was still a staggering one to three. It was down to one
to two by 1840 but still skewed by as much as five to seven by 1860.
Despite the carnage of two world wars – which overwhelmingly took

male Australian lives – the Australian population did not reach perfect parity until 1980.[94] (There are now more women than men.)

The reason for this long-term imbalance towards men was our origin as a penal colony. Most of the convicts (about 80 per cent) were men, and although many of them were married, their wives were not allowed to accompany them. Permission was routinely denied. This may well have been the cruellest and most anti-social aspect of the whole transportation system – the rule of law taken to a nasty, un-Christian extreme. Certainly it was a cause of immense human sorrow.[95] (It is worth noting that clergymen, not lawyers, made most of the formal pleas to the authorities on behalf of such couples.[96])

The gender imbalance was similarly pronounced throughout the convict and the non-convict populations. All of the naval personnel were men, and only some in the lower ranks of the Marines brought out their wives and families. A few more women came when the New South Wales Corps replaced the Marines, including well-educated women such as Elizabeth Macarthur, who was an officer's wife. But for a long time such women remained a small and conspicuous minority. Clearly, this was a completely unviable way to build a functional society.

The first to realise this were the Anglican chaplains, even if some of them looked down superciliously on the female convicts and emancipists. The Reverend Samuel Marsden, a father to five daughters, appreciated early on that there could be no long-term future for a colony populated largely by the offspring of low-born female convicts.

On an extended trip to Britain between 1807 and 1810, Marsden took pains to alert the Colonial Office to the gender imbalance in the New South Wales population. The lack of non-convict women, he insisted, posed a danger to public and private morals. Over time, the imbalance would be reduced by natural means. (Native-born children were, of course, evenly split between male and female.) But this would take too long. What the colony needed in the short term were many more non-convict women, especially well-born, middle-class women.

This was not mere puritanism but sound and prescient advice, and soon afterwards it bore modest fruit. When Governor Lachlan Macquarie arrived later in 1810 he brought 300 soldiers and most came with their wives.[97] In the longer term, Australia benefited after about 1830 from the influx of large numbers of emigrant women. They – along with the original core of officers' and other free-settler wives, and their daughters and granddaughters – came to constitute the most pious group of people in the community. They civilised the colonies and started a trend. Ever since, and until the present day, middle-class women have been our most faithful churchgoers and our most solid, law-abiding citizens.

Today, some 60 per cent of Australian churchgoers are female – and increasingly they are from the better-educated sections of society.[98] Historically, women in Australia have been much better churchgoers than men. The average churchgoer is a thoughtful woman. Studies have also shown that women tend to pray more often than men.[99] 'It has been said,' noted Hans Mol, 'that if not for women, Australia would be a much less "religious" nation.'[100] Certainly in rural areas – which until the late nineteenth century were the least religious parts of Australia – it was women who made the decisive difference. On isolated farms and stations it was usually wives who insisted on Sunday observance and family prayers.[101] And they passed on their piety to their daughters.

Why was it so? Why is it still so? One theory, popular in the nineteenth century, was that 'women's ability to bear children [keeps] them both less rational and more spiritual than men, closer to nature and to God'.[102] The Anglican Archbishop of Melbourne from 1877 to 1886, James Moorhouse, was one who held to this view. Moorhouse, it should be stressed, was very much a liberal in matters of theology and social progress[103] – a nineteenth-century version of, say, Tim Costello. But at least in one thing Moorhouse was a conservative, certainly by today's secular standards. The woman of a family, he thought, was 'the nurse, the comforter, the sanctifier'. A man might have headship of the family, and be worldly-wise, but his wife was his religious and social equal – and often his moral superior.[104]

Was that hopelessly patronising, or a great compliment? It depends on your point of view. The thing I would emphasise is that many Australian women of the nineteenth century – and beyond – proudly saw themselves in such terms. Their faith sustained them through many hardships, and the men in their lives (deservedly or not) benefited immensely as a result. So did Australia.

Consider one real-life example from the very apex of society. The most important statesmen of the late colonial era was Sir Henry Parkes (1815–96). Though a political titan, five times Premier of New South Wales and the individual most responsible for the achievement of Federation, it would be a stretch to call Parkes godly. In the political arena he was a street-fighter and opportunist; in his private life, a financial failure (thrice bankrupted) and womaniser. Yet his achievements were phenomenal, and he owed almost everything to the two staunch Christian women who dominated his life in Australia: his first wife Clarinda (nee Varney) and his oldest daughter, also named Clarinda but known as Menie. His older sister Sarah was also a rock, though her direct influence waned after their childhood years in England.

Now, this is the vital point. Any one of these women could easily have brought Parkes down; there was plenty of ammunition. But they did not abandon him or seek to sabotage his career. Instead, time and again, they propped him up. They drew strength from their faith and obeyed what they saw as their spiritual and familial duties. Parkes was grateful to them and – in his own way – to God.

Of the three, Clarinda, whom Parkes eventually outlived, was the most important figure in his life. A woman of 'deep and uncomplicated Christian convictions',[105] she had served for seven years as a Baptist Sunday school teacher in Birmingham before her marriage to Parkes in July 1836.[106] A year or two later she fell in with her young husband's proposal that they make their life together in the distant Australian colonies. It was Clarinda who procured (from the Reverend Cheadle, a Baptist minister in Birmingham) the necessary reference from a clergyman. They had little money, and this reference enabled them to immigrate to New South Wales on a free passage.[107]

Henry and Clarinda eventually had twelve children together, though five died in infancy. Their oldest child, Menie, was born aboard ship on 23 July 1839, just a few hours before her parents arrived in Sydney.[108] The lifelong favourite of her father, Menie was intensely religious from girlhood. In 1869 she married a Scottish Presbyterian clergyman, William Thom, to whom she was devoted.[109] Thom was killed only eight years later in a horse-and-buggy accident on 23 July 1877 – Menie's birthday.[110] But neither that tragedy nor anything else life threw at her ever shook her faith.

Menie's letters to Parkes are extraordinary. Her Evangelicalism shines through, as does her devotion to her father. Time and again, in a loving way, she praised his accomplishments while gently rebuking his failings – especially his spasmodic religious life. 'My own dearest father,' she wrote once, '[do] not be offended if I ask this question frankly, Is not my father's trust with his child's, in Christ the Saviour?'[111] At times she seemed to doubt it. On another occasion, when Parkes' spirits were low, she implored him:

If you once said 'I leave my future in the hands of Jesus Christ, and rest my every hope on him for salvation' then I say yours has been no wasted life, but the brave beginning of a holy eternity. Father, you *must* share eternity with me, and through the Saviour's blood is the only entrance to a happy Eternity.[112]

Parkes' most eminent biographer, A.W. Martin, doubted whether Parkes was able fully to meet Menie's expectations. The historical record is incomplete because most of his letters to her do not survive.[113] What can be said with certainty is that father and daughter were extremely close. Parkes drew great strength from Menie, just as he did from Clarinda.

Parkes' dearest female confidantes operated behind the scenes, as did countless other wives, mothers, sisters and daughters in colonial Australia. But what of the more public stars?

We have already looked at the foundational contributions of Elizabeth Macarthur and Caroline Chisholm, and I will come presently to the campaigners for temperance and female suffrage, crusaders such as Catherine Helen Spence. At this point it is convenient to pay tribute to Mary MacKillop (1842–1909), perhaps the brightest star of all. On 17 October 2010, she was canonised as Saint Mary of the Cross at a Mass celebrated in Rome by Pope Benedict XVI. She thus became Australia's first official saint, and remains its only one today, though moves are still afoot in relation to Caroline Chisholm.

Mary MacKillop is not only important in her own right; she is also representative of another cohort of women who made a massive and unpaid contribution to nineteenth- (and twentieth-) century Australian life. I refer to Catholic nuns and, within the Protestant tradition, deaconesses, Anglican Sisters, female missionaries and – ubiquitously – the wives of Protestant clergy.[114] The nuns (and equivalent Protestant figures) of Australia deserve special mention, I think. In their freely chosen roles as nurses and teachers and charity-workers, they sacrificed sexual fulfilment and personal comfort. They lived for others. Who does not, deep down, share the view of American agnostic Jo Piazza? 'I may not believe in God,' she has written, 'but I do believe in nuns.'[115] Germaine Greer has expressed similar views (see Appendix A). In a sense it is unfair to single out any one person or any one order.

Much has now been written about St Mary MacKillop. The details of her achievements have been amply recorded in many books and newspaper articles,[116] but I suspect that, even today, they are insufficiently appreciated. She was born in Melbourne to middle-class parents. In March 1866, as a 24-year-old school teacher, she founded the Sisters of St Joseph of the Sacred Heart, a Roman Catholic order dedicated to the education of poor children. Beginning in rural South Australia, the order rapidly established schools, convents and charitable institutions throughout the continent. Mary took classes herself while still attending to heavy administrative duties. But, much more than that, 'she trained the first generation, not only in the art of teaching but in the art of holiness'.[117] Mary was invalided by a stroke in May 1901 and died in 1909. However, the order she had founded, and for which (in 1873) she had personally obtained papal approval, continued on with its work.[118] It is still in operation today.

Hundreds of thousands of Australian children have been educated by the Josephites, including one grateful prime minister: Paul Keating. As a primary school student in the 1950s at St Jerome's, Punchbowl (in western Sydney), Keating experienced at first hand the nuns' love, devotion and commitment. In a public speech in 1997 he extolled their 'fidelity to the poor, and [their] belief in God's interest in them, Christ's interest in them, and their intrinsic importance as his children'.[119]

It is fair to ask: what about sexism? Did not Mary herself experience it in spades? I will deal with the subject of sexism and religion more fully in later chapters, but the key point as regards St Mary MacKillop is this. While she was the victim of terrible sexism, she did not allow it to defeat her. Famously, and very sadly, she fell out with the man who had encouraged her to establish the Sisterhood of St Joseph in the first place, Father Julian Tenison-Woods (1832–89). Woods was a visionary in his own right – a high-class scientist and historian as well as an educationalist – but he did not treat Mary fairly in their dispute concerning the Rule of Life within the order. Substantially more unfair and obtuse was Bishop Shiel of Adelaide, who excommunicated Mary in September 1871 for alleged insubordination. That order was rescinded in 1872, but she faced other rebuffs thereafter, mostly from diocesan bishops jealous to protect their patches.[120]

Mary could separate divine wheat from human chaff. She once said: 'Do all you can with the means at your disposal and calmly leave the rest to God.'[121]

*This is all very well*, I can hear sceptics muttering. But did any of it help women collectively? Or did the acceptance by many individual women of the 'meek' role assigned to them by Christian tradition operate against the real interests of their sex?

These are fair questions, and the answers are illuminating. Apart from the creation of the ALP, the other crucial development in Australian politics prior to Federation was the move towards the enfranchisement of women.

It is well known that Australian women were among the first in the world to be granted the right to vote – a right now regarded as one of the most fundamental of all. At a national level it was New Zealand that acted first, in 1893. But just a year later, in 1894, the province of South Australia followed suit, introducing full female suffrage for elections to its colonial parliament.[122] In 1902 the Commonwealth Parliament did likewise for federal elections and by 1908 all States were in line.[123] This was a truly seminal democratic achievement. By way of comparison, American women waited until 1920 to be conferred equivalent rights, and British women until 1928.[124]

Why did events move so quickly in Australia? Clearly there were worldwide factors at play, but here, at least, the role of Christianity was central. Two concurrent and related phenomena bear mention.

First, the institution of marriage had done its work. As a result of the influx of female immigrants from the 1830s onwards, and the speedy closing of the gender gap in all colonies, the social norm in Australia was, increasingly, marriage. Christian marriage. But in the special and challenging circumstances of a young settlement like Australia, it was Christian marriage with a twist. John Hirst has called it 'companionate marriage'. Especially but not exclusively in rural areas, husbands and wives worked together closely and formed very tight bonds. These were not patriarchal arrangements but true partnerships, based on mutual sympathy and understanding. Husbands earned the money, but wives ran the home, a task that in those days involved many hours a day of arduous labour. Some in the upper and middle classes had domestic servants, but even with their help, the regimen of shopping, cooking, washing, cleaning, mending and child-rearing was all-encompassing. (Remember, there were no cars or electrical appliances until the twentieth century; outside the major cities, most nineteenth-century homes lacked even running water.) Many mothers also acted as accountants, home-schoolers and nurses, especially in the bush.

In these circumstances, decisions about the family as a whole were made jointly by husbands and wives. In Hirst's opinion this was 'the key precursor' to the extension of the franchise.[125] The Marxist historian Russel Ward thought the main motive of those involved in the movement for female suffrage in Australia was 'the protection of the idea of the

Christian bourgeois family'.[126] Ward meant this as a criticism, but as an historical observation it was substantially correct.

The second factor was the role played in colonial society by activist Christian women. In the words of historian Hilary Carey, 'women religious were the most significant group of independent women in ... the late nineteenth century'.[127] Nuns such as Mary MacKillop were standouts, but there were also many Protestant women – single and married, and from both the middle and working classes – who entered the public arena. They did so, from the 1850s onwards, in support of law reform in areas such as divorce, gambling, sabbatarianism, the care of orphans and the raising of the age of consent. But the biggest issue of all was temperance – restrictions on the sale of alcoholic drinks.

The key bodies were the various colonial arms of the Women's Christian Temperance Union. In the 1880s they were the catalyst for the first large-scale involvement of Australian women in sociopolitical affairs. Women ran their own organisations and spoke out publicly – not only on the evils of alcohol, which disproportionately affected women, but many other issues besides, including those listed above. Thus 'the temperance movement became the forum for feminist ideas'.[128] When the amalgamated Women's Christian Temperance Union of Australia was founded in 1900, its constitution stated:

> We believe in total abstinence for the individual, prohibition for the
> state and nation, equal standards of purity for men and women, equal
> wages for equal work without regard to sex, the ballot in the hands of
> women, arbitration between nations ... [and the] Holy Bible as our
> standard faith.[129]

It is always instructive to personalise social trends. In Australia, as overseas, many of the leaders of the temperance and female suffrage causes were seriously religious women.

In South Australia, where the initial breakthrough was made on female suffrage, the leaders of the cause included Mary Lee (1821–1909), Mary Colton (1822–98), Catherine Helen Spence (1825–1910), Serena Lake (1842–1902) and Elizabeth Webb Nicholls (1850–1943). Admittedly they spanned a wide range of spiritual positions. Lee was a committed Irish Protestant, strongly influenced by Primitive Methodist preaching in Adelaide. Colton was a Wesleyan Methodist, and one of the first Sunday school teachers in South Australia. Spence, though born into the Church of Scotland, became a prominent Unitarian preacher. When she died on 13 April 1902 she was widely mourned as 'The Grand Old Woman of Australia'.[130] Lake was a so-called Bible Christian; she married a minister of that denomination and also preached herself. Nicholls was a conventional Methodist.

It was the same in all the other colonies. In New South Wales, Eliza Pottie (1837–1907) was a Quaker. Mary Windeyer (1837–1912), the daughter of a Church of England minister, was a devout Anglican. Louisa Lawson (1848–1920), Henry Lawson's mother, had a strict Methodist upbringing but in later life threw her energies into progressive spiritualism. In Victoria, Margaret McLean (1845–1923) was an active member of Collins Street Baptist Church in Melbourne. Annette Bear-Crawford (1853–99) was a conventional Anglican. Bessie Harrison Lee (1860–1950) was an Evangelical Anglican who had undergone a profound conversion experience as a teenager. Vida Goldstein (1869–1949) had a mixed Presbyterian–Unitarian upbringing before adopting Christian Science at the age of thirty; she helped to found its church in Melbourne.[131] In Queensland, Elizabeth Brentnall (1830–1909) was a devout Methodist, married to a clergyman. Margaret Ogg (1863–1953) was a passionate Presbyterian, the daughter of a minister. In Western Australia, Janetta Foulkes, Emily Hensman and Christina Clark were Anglicans. In Tasmania, Jessie Spinks Rooke (1845–1906) was a Presbyterian and President of the Women's Christian Temperance Union of Tasmania.

The common thread was religious sincerity – often real fervour – translated into practical action. Lake, for instance, believed sexual equality to be 'the original design of the Creator'.[132]

It is true that there were other important suffragettes not personally motivated by religion, at least not primarily. Henrietta Dugdale (1827–1918) in Victoria and Emma Miller (1839–1917) in Queensland were active secularists.[133] But they were exceptional. Most of the women involved were at least respectful of religion. Rose Scott (1847–1925), for instance, moved away from the intense Anglicanism of her upbringing in the Hunter Valley of New South Wales. But her character had been much influenced by Christianity and she maintained an interest in Spiritualism and Theosophy.[134]

If the movement for female suffrage had been dominated by women of radically irreligious bent, it undoubtedly would have failed. Neither men nor women would have supported it in anything like sufficient numbers. Change occurred because many Australian men in positions of power and influence – including conservatives – respected the core values of most of the female activists. So did their wives and sisters and daughters, the people in their family circles most able to influence them. Indeed, it is fair to say that practising Christian men from the middle class were *more* likely to support votes for women than working-class men. The former group had much more in common with the suffragettes than did the latter, at least as regards issues such as temperance, sabbatarianism and gambling. To grant women the vote would increase the likelihood of furthering those causes.[135]

Thus, at an inter-colonial temperance convention in Melbourne in 1888, the Reverend David O'Donnell moved a motion that the franchise be extended to women, 'to make the will of the people the law of the country'.[136]

## The vote for Federation

Federation was not inevitable. Henry Parkes had laid the groundwork, but he was a very old man by the 1890s and died in 1896. Younger leaders had to step in – Edmund Barton, Alfred Deakin and others – even as many mercantile 'hardheads' were arguing against the cause. They favoured a customs union as a way to deliver the benefits of free trade without the complications of nationhood.

Fortunately the founding fathers – and a majority of the populace – did not think in such narrow economic terms. Inspired by a form of civic patriotism – 'dignified, earnest, Protestant'[137] – they harboured nobler aspirations. The Federation cause inspired a great deal of poetry, and one is struck by the religious flavour of much of it. Two standout examples were John Farrell's 'Hymn of the Commonwealth' (sung by the choir massed in Sydney's Centennial Park for the celebrations on 1 January 1901) and William Gay's sonnet 'Australian Federation'.[138]

One thing can be stated with certainty. If any of the major Australian churches had opposed Federation, it would not have happened. Instead, many clerics participated in the process, and, in the end, all the Churches lent their institutional support. The price they exacted was the insertion into the preamble to the Constitution of the phrase 'humbly relying on the blessing of Almighty God'.

It is instructive to review the sequence of events leading up to 1901, which demonstrates beyond doubt that religion was a highly potent force in Australia at the time of Federation. What follows is a bare summary, but those wanting more detail can find it in Richard Ely's excellent book *Unto God and Caesar: Religious Issues in the emerging Commonwealth 1891–1906.*

At the People's Convention in Bathurst in late 1896 – a sort of preliminary Federation talkfest – the Anglican and Catholic archbishops of the town, C.E. Camidge and J. Byrne, were among the vice-presidents. A local Wesleyan minister, A.J. Webb, acted as the secretary and the special guest speaker was Cardinal Patrick Moran, the Catholic Archbishop of Sydney.[139] On the last day the following motion was passed:

> That this Convention, acknowledging the Government of the World
> by Divine Providence, commends the cause of Federation to all
> who desire, not only the material, but also the moral and social
> advancement of the people of Australia.[140]

The next step in the process, in March 1897, was the election by popular ballot of delegates to the Federation Convention, where the draft Constitution would be discussed. Most unwisely, if for admirable motives, Cardinal Moran stood for election. He hoped to be chosen as a representative Christian, not a Catholic. But there was considerable Protestant opposition and he failed to win a place.[141] This rebuff to the colonies' most senior Catholic prelate posed a potential threat to the Federation cause. I shall come to back to it.

The convention met in Adelaide in April 1897. Queen Victoria herself (through an intermediary) sent a message to the delegates. They learned that Her Majesty 'takes special interest in their proceedings and hopes that *under Divine Guidance* their labours will result in practical benefit to Australia' (italics mine).[142] Most of the delegates were lawyers and politicians, but in the lead-up to the convention the Protestant Churches had begun campaigning for recognition of God in the draft Constitution. Some wanted a provision specifying that God was 'the supreme Ruler of the world, and the ultimate source of all law and authority in nations'.[143] Petitions in support were signed by tens of thousands of citizens. The Reverend Professor Andrew Harper published a book on the subject, *Australia Without God: An Appeal to the Churches of Australia to Secure an Acknowledgment of God in the Australian Constitution*.

Yet, at the first meeting of the Constitution Committee in Adelaide, all reference to God was left out of the draft. Some days later a Catholic delegate from South Australia, Patrick Michael Glynn, was prevailed upon to move a proposal that God be recognised. It was rejected eleven to seventeen at a vote of the full convention. Most of those who opposed it were not unbelievers. They were sophisticated thinkers – perhaps overly sophisticated – and believed its inclusion unnecessary or problematic or even sacrilegious.[144]

The Churches were appalled. It was one instance when most Catholic and Protestant clerics were united. The Churches' newspapers and journals became organs for the cause, and sympathisers in the mainstream press also weighed in, a *Sydney Morning Herald* editorialist declaring on 14 April 1897 that 'no Christian could in conscience vote for a Federation Bill that did not recognise God'.[145]

In due course the Churches developed a clever strategy. They knew that the draft Constitution would be submitted for approval to the parliaments of each of the colonies before finally being put to a popular vote. It was essential that a recognition provision be inserted in the draft Constitution before the colonial parliaments made their decisions. But as well as lobbying politicians, the Churches appealed to public opinion. Their hope was that pro-Federation activists would not wish to buck majority sentiment, whatever their personal views on recognition might be.

In the end, the strategy worked. By the time of the next convention, held in Melbourne in February to March 1898, a sufficient number of pro-Federation delegates had been persuaded that 'excluding God might dampen popular support'.[146] A majority approved the insertion of words of recognition in the preamble, and there is crystal-clear contemporary evidence of their motives. The delegate who moved the key motion, Patrick Michael Glynn, wrote in his diary that 'it was chiefly intended to secure greater support from a large number of voters who believe in the efficacy for good of this formal act of reverence and faith'.[147] Melbourne's *Argus* newspaper reported that delegates 'thought it safer to defer to the strong expression of public feeling in favour'.[148]

Other delegates then expressed concerns about a possible undermining of the principle of the separation of Church and State. After lengthy debate another change was made to the draft: the insertion of the provision that ultimately became section 116. It provides: 'The Commonwealth shall not make any law for establishing any religion, or for imposing any religious observance, or for prohibiting the free exercise of any religion, and no religious test shall be required as a qualification for any office or public trust under the Commonwealth.'

Looking back, I believe the delegates got it right. At any rate, if the preamble had not referred to God, we may be sure that a prediction made in the *Presbyterian Monthly* would have come to pass: 'The omission will in future be made the ground for asserting that our new Constitution was deliberately founded on the negation of God.'[149] Section 116 was an important precaution, though its limited scope is widely misunderstood. It is a guarantee of freedom *of* religion against Federal Government power, not freedom *from* religion in the public square.

There were still two hurdles to overcome. As mentioned, the draft Constitution, thus amended, needed to be approved by the various colonial parliaments. This was achieved. Finally, the proposal for Federation had to be put to a popular vote in each colony. 'Yes' majorities were considered certain in Victoria, South Australia and Tasmania; the likely outcome in Queensland and Western Australia was unpredictable. The pivotal colony was New South Wales. At the first vote, in June 1898, the 'Yes' vote was not sufficiently large to meet the required threshold. But at the second attempt, in June 1899, it was.

What made the difference? Various factors were at play, but perhaps the most vital was the attitude of Cardinal Patrick Moran. Remember, voters had snubbed him in May 1897. Yet for many Catholics, his opinion was still highly influential. In 1898 he stayed neutral. But a year later he was persuaded publicly to support a 'Yes' vote. Just three days before the June 1899 poll the *Catholic Press* reported: 'He is confident that only blessings can follow the acceptance of Federation on the present lines.'[150]

# CHAPTER 5

# The making of modern Australia

I would also crave to do something for my country and my kind, if ever so fractional, and pray to be shattered and crucified, rather than aid anything contrary to Thy will and their elevation.

Alfred Deakin, founding father of Australia, praying in 1890

'What does it profit you to give God one thing if he asks of you another? Consider what it is that God wants and then do it.' … These words are still as valid today as ever.

Paul Keating, commenting in 1997 on the words of St John of the Cross

On the eve of Federation, 31 December 1900, a Catholic man named George M'Clure wrote in his diary: 'A real wild night. How much we should pray for the guidance of the Holy Spirit in the affairs of Federated Australia that she may be an example to all sections of the British Empire.' The next day, M'Clure and his brother made their way to Sydney from Wallsend, near Newcastle, by steam train and ferry. They took Holy Communion at St Mary's Cathedral before finding a vantage point to watch the Federation Day festivities.[1]

Such tiny incidents, we may be sure, were not atypical. When the country of Australia was born, on 1 January 1901, some 96 per cent of citizens identified as Christian. We now know that this figure had already peaked. Rates of churchgoing, while still very high (about 50 per cent of the adult population), had begun declining in the mid-1890s, and that trend would continue throughout the century to come.[2]

Yet, until the 1970s, belief in the Christian God remained the default position for the vast majority of Australia's citizens.[3]

In this chapter I will make the case that Christianity played a vital role in the making of modern Australia – not just in the 'olden days', but right up to recent times. My focus will be on domestic affairs (other than education, which is the stand-alone subject of Chapter 6). I shall examine pivotal institutions and social movements, and outstanding individuals.

## The Australian legal system

I have argued in earlier chapters that the rule of law – a product of Christianity – was one of Britain's most precious gifts to the Australian colonies. I have also noted the amazing incidence in Australian history of influential high achievers who were the sons of Protestant clergymen. Two of the most critical figures in twentieth-century Australian history tick both boxes. Each was an extremely distinguished lawyer and (you guessed it) the son of a Protestant clergyman – a Welsh Congregationalist and an Irish Wesleyan Methodist respectively. I refer to Samuel Walker Griffith (1845–1920) and Henry Bournes Higgins (1851–1929).

Both Griffith and Higgins served on the High Court – Griffith, indeed, was its first chief justice – but that is not the principal reason for their importance to the Australian nation. Griffith's most enduring legacy is the Commonwealth Constitution: he was its principal draftsman. Higgins' legacy was the *Harvester* basic-wage decision of 1907, which he made in his capacity as a judge of the Commonwealth Court of Conciliation and Arbitration.[4]

It is impossible to overstate the significance of either the Constitution or the *Harvester* decision. Let us take the latter first. Although Higgins' judgment in that particular case was later overturned on appeal,[5] the basic principle he laid down held sway in Australian industrial relations for another eighty years. It underpinned what author Paul Kelly has called 'the Australian settlement' – the sociopolitical compromise struck at, and following, Federation, between the constituent classes of society. It is no wonder that, when Higgins died in January 1929, his demise was discussed throughout the country, 'in trains and trams and … workshops and offices'.[6]

At issue was how to calculate the minimum wage of a male worker. The relevant statute provided only that the amount be 'fair and reasonable'. Higgins held that account should be taken of 'the normal needs of the average employee, regarded as a human being living in a civilised community'. His wages should be sufficient to buy food, clothing and 'a condition of frugal comfort estimated by current human standards'.[7] Higgins added: 'A wage that does not allow for the matrimonial condition for an adult man is not fair and reasonable'.[8]

There were several basic Christian concepts wrapped up in this ruling. Higgins' personal religious beliefs have been the subject of debate (see Appendix A), but, for present purposes, the key point is this. Although a Protestant, Higgins had been deeply influenced by Pope Leo XIII's seminal encyclical on labour and capital, *Rerum Novarum* (1891). In 1896, Higgins had spoken about it approvingly and at some length in a public lecture, 'Another Isthmus in History'. In the *Harvester* judgment some eleven years later he adopted its sentiments and some of its language, including the expression 'frugal comfort'.[9] Thus, the moderate position of the Catholic Church became, in effect, the secular law of Australia. Economic hardheads on the Right – for whom the maximisation of employer profitability has always been paramount – have been complaining about Higgins' judgment ever since.[10] But the incontestable fact is that the *Harvester* principle was popular: parliaments did not dare to overturn it.

Higgins was a deeply religious man – if not in an orthodox sense. The source of his compassion and idealism was the Christian well. One of his closest friends once said that he had never met anyone 'so aloof from religion in any sense of creed, whose life lay so deep in the things of the spirit'.[11]

The same might be said of Samuel Griffith. A case can be made that he is *the* greatest Australian who ever lived.[12] Sir William Deane has so argued, and I would disagree only because of Griffith's patchy record on Indigenous issues. Even so, his overall contribution to Australia is imperishable. Apart from the Constitution, and his decades of legal service, Griffith was an effective premier of Queensland in the 1880s during the colony's formative years. He stood on a progressive platform: 'The great problem of this age,' he said at the time, 'is not how to accumulate wealth, but how to secure its more equitable distribution.'[13]

The key to understanding Griffith is, again, his religiosity. As in the case of Higgins, his deepest personal beliefs have been disputed. There seems no question he was not as fervently orthodox as his parents, but his basic Christian values mattered greatly to him. His platform as Premier of Queensland, quoted above, was based on principles of natural law.[14] More generally, according to biographer Roger Joyce, 'his Christian upbringing had introduced him to the concepts of sin and evil, and he … never eliminated the influence of such ideas. Law was needed to control society.'[15]

Near the end of his life Griffith wrote and published an essay entitled 'The Social Problem'. He sent copies to many friends and acquaintances, including the Anglican Archbishop of Brisbane, St Clair Donaldson.[16] In the essay Griffith restated some basic principles of natural law, and his belief in a society ruled by fraternity rather than power. His instinctive belief was that conscience points to God: 'every living sentient creature,' he wrote, 'is equally subject to an unformulated and unknown law which it is unconsciously bound to obey.' He added (quoting Isaiah 53:6): 'All we like sheep have gone astray.'[17]

Griffith's and Higgins' colleagues and successors on the bench of the High Court of Australia have included a disproportionate number of seriously religious men and women, both Protestant and Catholic. I have not (yet) conducted an exhaustive survey, but some of the most eminent legal minds in our history are among them. In the modern era I would nominate Ronald Wilson, Gerard Brennan, William Deane, Murray Gleeson, Michael Kirby and J.D. (Dyson) Heydon. Brennan and Gleeson were chief justices, and Deane also served as governor-general. At the State and Territory level there are far too many names to list, but one name requires special mention. Roma Mitchell (1913–2000) was the first woman in Australia to be appointed as a QC, to sit as a judge of a superior court (the Supreme Court of South Australia), and to serve as a State governor. She was also an extremely devout Catholic, having been educated as a girl by the Mercy Sisters in Adelaide. Her 'school days were saturated with religion'. She regarded 'the promulgation of Church doctrine [as] the most supreme social service', and said late in life: 'I'm sure religion has helped. It is always there, somewhere in the background.'[18]

I should note that the man some would nominate as Australia's finest-ever legal mind, Owen Dixon (1886–1972), was an agnostic. Yet his grandfather had been a lay preacher with his own chapel, the Zion Independent Church of Lower Hawthorn, and his father-in-law was an Anglican minister. In the words of Dixon's biographer, Phillip Ayres: 'Dixon … was not one of those who wished not to believe in God. He was perfectly happy for his wife to maintain her religious views, and it is interesting that *Agamemnon*, a work steeped in religious feeling, was his favourite. He found aggressive atheists distasteful. It was simply a matter of his being unable to satisfy himself of the validity of religious propositions.'[19]

This congruity between religious belief and the practice of law at the highest level ought not, perhaps, to be surprising: the more eminent the lawyer, the deeper their understanding of morality is likely to be. As Gerard Brennan said at an ecumenical church service in Canberra in 1992: 'the nobility of our profession depends, in the ultimate analysis, upon our fidelity to God'.[20]

## The moral middle class

The contribution to Australia of the educated Christian middle class was just as critical in the twentieth century as it was in the nineteenth. During the passage to Federation it supplied the great political leaders, men like Edmund Barton, George Reid and William Lyne in New South Wales; Alfred Deakin in Victoria; James Dickson in Queensland; Charles Kingston in South Australia; and John Forrest in Western Australia. The greatest of these was Deakin (1856–1919), thrice prime minister before World War One (1903–04, 1905–08, 1909–10) and the single most important figure in the bedding down of the Australian settlement.

Deakin was also the most religiously minded prime minister in Australian history. An unorthodox Protestant with an encyclopaedic knowledge of all faiths, he wrote hundreds of private prayers in which, collectively, one can see his soul laid bare. The closest Deakin ever came to distilling his core religious beliefs was in the following passage:

Three things are certain –
1. God is love – Infinite, all-embracing, eternal.
2. God is a Spirit, though manifest in all nature and humanity, and specially in all life and mind.
3. God is our Father and our Mother, including all that in us is various or contradictory, or imperfect, complete and perfect to his perfection.

It cannot be stressed enough that Deakin's religiosity was no mere distraction or affectation: it went to the core of his being and profoundly influenced the course of Australian history. I have written about Deakin in detail in my book *In God They Trust?*. Here it must suffice to say that what he believed *became* Australia: a lively patriotism, the rule of law, a strong defence, assistance for Australian industry, and a reasonable safety net for the working classes and the elderly. And – the big blot on his record, though even this must be understood in its historical context[21] – the White Australia Policy. Deakin regarded these achievements as the fulfilment of his, and Australia's, divine destiny – the practical implementation of the Lord's Prayer, the coming of God's Kingdom on earth. That is what he wrote in his journal in January 1908.[22]

The high-minded ethos that Deakin embodied has sometimes been termed 'small-l' liberalism. In my view – given Deakin's staunch belief in the protective role of the State, and the support that his first two governments received from the ALP – that characterisation is inaccurate. Deakin was a believer in what used to be called the 'mixed economy': a judicious balancing act between free-market capitalism and government regulation. But even that term does not give the full flavour; it is too secular. The kind of men and women whom Deakin most admired and who built on his legacy over ensuing decades – in politics and the wider community – were not mere technocrats obsessed with the bottom line. They believed in philanthropy, traditional morality and a fastidious code of personal honour. They were adherents of a creed that I would describe as benevolent Christian conservatism.

To put a face on it, think of giants in federal politics such as S.M. Bruce, Joseph Lyons, Enid Lyons, Robert Menzies, Richard Casey, Paul Hasluck, John McEwen and Malcolm Fraser.[23] There were many equivalents in business and the professions: G.J. Coles, Norman Cowper, Warwick O. Fairfax, Fletcher Jones, Dame Elisabeth Murdoch and Sidney Myer, to name a few.

For over a century, until the 1980s, this 'moral middle class'[24] was mostly Protestant – proudly so. It formed the rock-solid electoral base of the non-Labor side of Australian politics and was supported strongly by the Protestant Churches, especially the Church of England. For fifty years its political groupings went under many names – Protectionist, Free Trade, Anti-Socialist, Fusion, Nationalist, United Australia – until Menzies created the Liberal Party of Australia in 1944. In doing so he pronounced that 'there is no room in Australia for a party of reaction'.[25]

A few words about Menzies, who is not normally remembered for religion but who was a Bible-believing man raised by devout parents in the Presbyterian–Methodist tradition.[26] In mid-1942 he resuscitated his (then) flagging career with a celebrated series of radio talks. There were thirty-seven in all, and they often mentioned Christianity directly or in passing.

In 'The Forgotten People', his first and most famous talk, delivered on 22 May 1942, Menzies outlined a vision for post-war Australia. He argued powerfully that society had to be constructed around the middle class, which he called the 'the backbone of the nation', emphasising the old Scots Protestant virtues of thrift, independence and free enterprise. But also central to Menzies' analysis was a Biblical proposition: 'we are all, as human souls, of like value'. This required a temperate, *moral* liberalism – not dog-eat-dog. Menzies spoke movingly of the less fortunate in society and of the critical importance of education. He laid heavy emphasis on family and the arts. He lauded 'homes material, homes human and homes spiritual'. As to the last, he declared that 'human nature is at its greatest when it combines dependence upon God with independence of man'.

In another address, 'Freedom of Worship', he expressed himself in even more explicitly Christian terms (remember the second limb of my definition of minimum belief): 'There is a consciousness in most of us that someday all will come to light and he shall be judged.' But Menzies' was an ecumenical form of faith. In the same 'Freedom of Worship' address he quoted Christ's words in John 14: 'In my father's house there are many mansions.'

In broad terms, as John Howard is fond of saying, the Liberal Party has been ever since the 'custodian' of the two main strands of non-Labor ideology in Australia: liberalism and conservatism. But, to put it mildly, conservatism (or, more accurately, neo-liberalism) is now in the ascendency – at least at the all-important federal level. The Liberal Party has moved from being the dutiful party of the moral middle class to the populist party of the super-rich and of go-getting 'aspirationals' and 'tradies'. Xenophobia is one of its main weapons. The reasons for that state of affairs are beyond the scope of this book, but I would note one intriguing fact. While the Liberal Party since about 1985 has become increasingly neo-liberal, it has also become rather less benevolent and much less Protestant. Its senior federal parliamentary ranks are now dominated by a curious mix of shallow, market-driven secularists and nominal or selectively doctrinaire Catholics (selective in the sense of endorsing the Vatican's teachings on some things – divorce, homosexuality and abortion – while ignoring or flouting others – war, climate change, social justice, refugees). The National Party, while still well-meaning, is impotent and shrinking. The vote of the moral middle class has long since splintered.

All this is unprecedented in Australian history, and I believe it has been a significant factor in secularisation. Mainstream Protestant Christianity has been marginalised on the Right of Australian politics almost as much as it has been on the Left. (The Evangelical Liberal Premier of New South Wales, Mike Baird, is a welcome throwback, an oddity who proves my point, and his high personal popularity should tell us something.) I shall address this issue further in Chapter 10.

Yet however grim things currently look, let it not be forgotten what the Liberal Party once was – nor the importance of its Christian roots.

## Egalitarianism and the relief of poverty

In the twentieth century, as in the nineteenth, Christianity continued to be a vital force in alleviating inequality in Australia. This happened in two ways: in the political arena, and through charitable and advocacy work by the Churches.

In Chapter 4 I outlined the two strands of religious thought that dominated policy-making at the highest levels of the ALP at the time of its formation. Right through to the present day, a high percentage of Labor prime ministers, federal Labor treasurers (whose names I have indicated with a 'T'), and federal Labor opposition leaders ('OL', those who never made it to the top job), have come from one of two great left-wing religious traditions:

- Protestant Christian socialists or those in that mould – Andrew Fisher, William Higgs (T), Billy Hughes, Frank Tudor (OL), Frank Crean (T), Kim Beazley (OL), Kevin Rudd[27]
- Practising Catholics who imbibed the Vatican's social justice teachings as part of their faith – James Scullin, E.G. (Ted) Theodore (T), Joseph Lyons (T), Ben Chifley, Arthur Calwell (OL), Paul Keating. (It is too early to judge Bill Shorten (OL).)[28]

In a third category are those who might best be described as fellow travellers with Christianity: they were either raised in the faith as children or maintained or developed an interest in religion as adults. In this group I would place Chris Watson, Matthew Charlton (OL), John Curtin, H.V. Evatt (OL), Gough Whitlam, Bill Hayden (OL), Bob Hawke, Simon Crean (OL), Wayne Swan (T) and (despite her professed unbelief) Julia Gillard.[29] Of course, some of them travelled much more closely with Christianity than others. Perhaps the three standouts in that regard were John Curtin (a lapsed Catholic who made a late conversion to Protestantism under the pressures of World War Two), Gough Whitlam and Bob Hawke. Both Whitlam and Hawke became agnostics, but each was utterly steeped in religion, having been raised by a beloved and devout Protestant father. (The Reverend Clem Hawke was a Congregationalist minister.)

It is not, I think, much of a stretch to say that we owe to Christianity such basic aspects of the Australian social safety net as old-age pensions (Fisher), unemployment benefits (Chifley), Medicare (Whitlam, Hawke, Keating) and employer-funded superannuation (Keating). Scullin and Lyons led the nation through the Great Depression and Rudd through the Global Financial Crisis. For all the opprobrium Rudd has since received, he erred during the GFC, if at all, on the side of compassion. Add the National Disability Insurance Scheme, admittedly still in the formative stages, and it is an impressive package.

Below the leadership level, it must be said that Labor's religious electoral base has long been the Catholic Church. As Michael Hogan once observed, until the creation of the Democratic Labor Party in 1955, 'Australian Catholics did not adopt a European model of separatist Catholic politics'.[30] Overwhelmingly – except during the prime ministerial era of Joe Lyons – they supported the ALP. And ALP leaders regularly consulted senior Catholic figures, giants such as Archbishop Daniel Mannix (1864–1963) in Melbourne. That is why the DLP breakaway was so disastrous. DLP preferences (to the Coalition) cost Labor the 1961 and 1969 federal elections. Many of these voters were still, at heart, of the Left; they were certainly not free marketeers. But, understandably, they felt extremely strongly about State aid to Catholic schools and – above all – the Cold War, and did not like the ALP's stance on either issue. As Mannix wrote in 1950: 'With me the Communist menace is no mere political matter: it threatens the Christian way of life.'

What of the earnest Catholics – men such as Scullin, Theodore, Chifley, Calwell and Keating – who stuck with Labor despite everything? What did *they* stand for? In very rough terms, they were conservative on most social and moral issues but leaned to the Left on questions of economic justice. Most, too, were highly suspicious of anyone who beat the drums of war – but especially if they were English or American. Their achievements, and their failures, are best understood in terms of an overriding Irish-Catholic motivation – as Ronald Conway put it, 'their urgent desire to cast off the stigma of communal inequality'. Sometimes this made them appear defensive and tribal, but, as Conway rightly thought, 'Australia would be far poorer politically and socially were it not for their frustrations'.[31]

\*

So much for politics. What of the Churches themselves as agents of economic justice?

Secular progressives argue that the relief of poverty and disadvantage should primarily be the duty of the State. To leave the care of the underprivileged to the Churches or private philanthropy is, they say, a right-wing cop-out, a ruse to keep taxes low. It is certainly arguable that the State should do more in this regard, but there is no good reason why the Churches and the State cannot work together.

That, indeed, has been the reality throughout Australian history. To be sure, some clerics and congregations have, over the years, been more generous than others. But those who have shone in this area have made a real difference, and have been revered by those they have helped. There are few more cherished institutions than the Salvation Army. Even today, when some loud voices in the media allege that the State already does far too much, the Churches fill many voids. There are some 12,000 religious charities currently active in Australia.[32]

At an individual level, three of the greatest-ever Australian charity-workers were Protestant ministers: the Reverend R.B.S. Hammond (1870–1946), an Evangelical Anglican based in inner-city Sydney after whom HammondCare, a Christian charity specialising in aged care, is named; the Reverend Dr John Flynn (1880–1951), Presbyterian missionary and founder of the Royal Flying Doctor Service of Australia; and the Reverend Alan Walker (1911–2003), a Methodist/ Uniting Church leader of genuine world renown. All 'firmly believed that there was no dichotomy in the ministry of Jesus between faith and works'.[33] Hammond and his legions of followers became famous during the Great Depression of the 1930s; they helped countless thousands of destitute people by providing food, clothing and shelter and assisting with job-seeking.[34] Walker's myriad achievements included the founding of Lifeline, the suicide-prevention charity, in 1963.[35] Flynn – whose face appears on the twenty-dollar note – is probably the most famous Presbyterian in our history. A former governor-general of Australia, Sir William Slim, once said that Flynn's hands were 'stretched out like a benediction over the Inland'.[36]

What, though, of social reform more broadly? It has been argued with some force that until recent decades the Australian Churches – especially the Protestant Churches – tended to focus too much on alleviating the symptoms of disadvantage and not enough on tackling its underlying structural causes. During the Depression of the 1890s and the General Strike of 1917 most Protestant Churches were, as institutions, hostile towards the aims and methods of the trade union movement.[37] It was little different during the Great Depression of the 1930s. In the Menzies era from 1949 to 1966, Churches both Protestant and Catholic did little to aid the Labor cause.

But it would be a gross exaggeration to say that the Churches – or Coalition governments, for that matter – were uniformly and implacably hostile to *any* social reform. The arguments were usually about the pace of change and the methods to be used to achieve it, not the desirability of change itself. Even among Protestants there were some important trailblazers: J.D. Bollen's study, *Protestantism and Social Reform in New South Wales 1890–1910*, traverses some of the early ground. The Australian Student Christian Movement, established in 1896, has been a consistent voice of progressive, ecumenical opinion for over a century.[38]

Among Protestant clerics one thinks of mighty figures such as the Reverend Charles Strong (1844–1942), a liberal Presbyterian from Melbourne who later founded the Australian Church and was a religious mentor to (among others) Alfred Deakin. Strong gave priority to the relief of poverty and deprivation, through bodies such as the Social Improvement Friendly Help and Children's Aid Society, the Working Men's College, and the National Anti-Sweating League; he was also an outspoken opponent of the Boer War and World War One. C.R. Badger's biography of Strong, published in 1971, is a must-read for any Australian Christian of liberal Protestant bent.[39] A man of even higher stature was the Reverend Ernest Burgmann (1885–1967), for many years the Anglican Bishop of Canberra and Goulburn. (A college at the Australian National University in Canberra is named after him.) Peter Hempenstall's biography of Burgmann, *The Meddlesome Priest* (1993), paints an inspiring portrait of a man both utterly secure in his faith and completely committed to progressive social reform. During the Great Depression of the 1930s, Burgmann championed the unemployed and the evicted, and wrote for newspapers and magazines on the Church's responsibility for the welfare of the nation. One of Burgmann's Scriptural heroes was the Old Testament prophet Amos, who railed loudly and often against the smug, rich establishment figures of his day.[40]

Strong and Burgmann were unusual, to be sure. But they did not stand completely alone. In their day each of them had numerous followers and admirers (as well as many detractors), and in all eras there have been others sympathetic to progressive causes – even, in a few cases, at very senior levels of clergy. Most of them were Catholics.

I have mentioned Daniel Mannix; Cardinal Patrick Moran also gave vital early support to the ALP. So, early in his term, did James Duhig (1873–1965), the long-time Catholic Archbishop of Brisbane; he was a close friend of Queensland's powerful Labor premier, T.J. Ryan.[41] Norman Gilroy (1896–1977), another Catholic archbishop of Sydney, worked hard behind the scenes to maintain Labor unity in the 1950s. Bishop James Patrick Carroll (in the 1960s and 1970s) and Father Frank Brennan (from the 1990s to the present day) have been other influential voices of Catholic progressivism.

On the Protestant side, as I have said, strongly progressive voices were relatively unusual until the last generation. The creation of the Uniting Church in 1977 was a turning point in this regard: it has provided a natural home for people of liberal theology and left-leaning political sympathies. Before 1977 such people were always a minority within the mainline Protestant Churches. The exceptions, especially at a clerical level, stood out. I have mentioned Strong and Burgmann, but there were others cut from similar cloth.[42] Today, one thinks of the likes of Tim Costello – Chief Executive of World Vision Australia since 2004, and, for twenty years before that, a prominent Baptist minister in Victoria at churches in St Kilda and Collins Street, Melbourne. My favourite Costello quote is this one: 'How did the message of Jesus ever become aligned with big business, military spending, gun ownership, tax cuts and disdain for the environment?'

## Twentieth-century Christian women

The first half of the twentieth century was terribly cruel to Australian men. Two hideous world wars sandwiched the Great Depression of the 1930s, when one-quarter of male breadwinners lost their jobs.

Of course, such suffering afflicted men throughout the Western world. The difference in continental Europe was that women shared a great deal of their men's pain. By contrast, most Australian women were insulated from the worst. A small minority volunteered for overseas service, principally as nurses, but most stayed at home, where they were safe. Thankfully, our continent was neither occupied nor concertedly invaded. (The attacks on Darwin on 19 February 1942 and on naval vessels in Sydney Harbour on the night of 31 May to 1 June 1942 were one-offs.) Women in Australia endured grief and austerity, but not genocide, carpet-bombing, torture, starvation, maiming and mutilation, disease, mass rape or the pillage of their homes.

In Chapter 7 I shall explore the insidious effects of war on the religious faith of Australian men, and Christendom in general. Here I merely note an interesting flipside. From the early twentieth century onwards, Australian women became even more active – at least by comparison with men – in their religious devotions. They maintained their enthusiasm. True, they were still shut out from the highest clerical positions. But they made up for this in other ways. Indeed, as Hilary Carey has demonstrated, the gradual result by 1945 was 'the feminisation of religious culture'.[43] Carey has documented this phenomenon in detail. Yet as she herself has conceded, 'it is difficult to do justice to the complexity and depth of women's church-based organisations'.[44] I will not try, other than to list some of the most significant. The names themselves are resonant.

Apart from the all-powerful temperance unions, there were the various State branches of the National Council of Women in Australia (federalised in 1925). Their guiding philosophy was the Golden Rule: 'Do unto others as you would that they should do unto you.'[45] The first branch of the Mothers' Union in Australia was formed in 1892 by a Mrs L'Oste, the wife of the Rector of Christ Church, Cullenswood, in Tasmania. The original Mothers' Union was founded in England in 1876 by Mary Sumner, the wife of the Anglican Vicar of Old Alresford in Hampshire. Mrs Sumner's (then novel) idea was that groups of young mothers should meet together regularly to discuss their challenges, in order to help and encourage one another and to realise more fully their responsibilities as wives and mothers. In its original conception, the women were also helped to understand the significance of the sacrament of baptism and the teaching of the Christian faith to their children. Other key bodies were the Girls' Friendly Society (established in Australia in 1879), the Young Women's Christian Association (1880), the Presbyterian Women's Missionary Association (1891), the Methodist Women's Auxiliary for Foreign (later Overseas) Missions (c. 1891), the Catholic Women's Association (1913), the Red Cross (1914), the Country Women's Association (1922), the Federated Association of Australian Housewives (1923), the Girls' Brigade (c. 1925), and the Presbyterian Women's Association (1954).

It is important to note that the leadership and membership of most of these bodies spanned both the moral middle class and the more progressive feminist elements of Australian womanhood. Many of these organisations still exist today, though some are shadows of their former selves. In not a few cases their original Christian aims have become secularised or forgotten.

Bodies of this kind, while publicly visible and hugely influential, were in a sense the tip of the iceberg. At the level of local congregations, countless women took the lead in activities such as fund-raising (the ubiquitous church fetes) and pastoral care (the visiting of the sick, the feeding of the hungry and so on). As Carey has emphasised, these activities were not trivial. Taken collectively, they constituted 'one of the most important and long-lived products of Australian religious culture'.[46] And – a point I cannot stress enough – such activities are still carried out today, across the country, in all healthy church congregations. It is a beautiful thing to behold.

## Protective social policy

Writing in 1988, Edmund Campion suggested that 'the longest-lasting impact religion has made on our public life came in the social legislation of the early twentieth century'.[47] I disagree: there were longer lasting and more important effects. But, certainly, that legislation can be added to the list of ways in which religion has shaped Australia.

Until recently the majority of political activists from the Protestant Churches – and a significant minority within the Catholic Church – threw their energies into causes that, to many people, must now seem quaint. Even at the time they were far from universally popular, particularly among working-class men. The emphasis was on discouraging and restricting – even banning entirely – certain conduct deemed to be immoral. In the nineteenth and early twentieth centuries the focus was on gambling, prostitution, the consumption of alcohol, and *any* work or leisure activities carried out on Sundays (Sabbatarianism). Itinerant evangelists such as the Englishman Henry Varley (1835–1912) and Victoria's own William Henry Judkins (1869–1912) were household names. Judkins was perhaps 'the most effective wowser Australia has known'.[48]

The political influence of such campaigners, especially before the 1970s, was considerable.[49] Take temperance, for example. In the century or so after 1850, many colonial and State elections were fought on issues such as 'local option' (giving local communities the power to make their own special laws regarding alcoholic drinks), and more general restrictions on the opening hours of public houses and bottle shops. There were also a good many referendums on such issues. In 1915 a majority of South Australians voted in favour of six o'clock closing; New South Wales, Victoria and Tasmania followed suit a year later. These and similar laws remained in place for decades.[50] No Australian

State ever enacted total prohibition (which was the legal position in the United States between 1920 and 1932), but it was a relatively close-run thing. At a referendum in Queensland in October 1923, 37 per cent voted 'Yes' to prohibition.[51] The closest result came in the Victorian poll of March 1930, when the vote for 'Yes' was 42 per cent.[52]

Although these more extreme measures failed to carry majority support in the community, other temperance laws did. Likewise proscriptive laws concerning gambling, prostitution and censorship. Until the 1960s, or even later in some States, restrictions remained in place on commercial trading and the holding of sporting events on Sundays. These laws had broad-based support.

Was all this for the better or the worse? On the one hand, there is a case for saying that some wowsers went too far and used unfortunate rhetoric. By prioritising issues such as temperance and gambling, and neglecting or even opposing more broad-based social reform, they alienated working-class people. Hilary Carey has written of an overall Christian tendency to explain poverty 'in terms of the vices of the poor'.[53] In *The Great Australian Stupor*, Ronald Conway was more scathing: 'The churches quickly assumed the character of social ghettos or lobbies in which fringe obsessions such as temperance, gambling … and sexual conduct were pushed, to the embarrassment of governments and the jeers of secularists and ordinary blokes.'[54] In Conway's view, 'these largely unconnected strains of inhibition had little to do with a genuine spiritual awareness or a sense of God'.[55]

This was interesting commentary, but I do not think the issues were ever so clear-cut. Put to one side issues of sexual morality; I will come to those in Chapter 8. It is important to remember (as mentioned earlier) that causes such as temperance were supported overwhelmingly by vulnerable women. As wives and mothers, they were often the innocent victims of drunkenness, gambling and other hedonistic excesses. Likewise teenage girls and young women forced into prostitution. Looking after their welfare was *not* a fringe obsession, and the motives of many religious people were as much altruistic as vengeful or disapproving. Some established vitally needed rehabilitation programmes.

Again, let us focus on temperance. Drunkenness was, and still is, a genuine scourge in Australian life. The first Premier of Queensland, Robert Herbert, described it in 1860 as 'an endless evil which is always at the bottom of all Australian mishaps'.[56] He was exaggerating, of course, but his central point was sound. Among male supporters of temperance there were some unimpeachably progressive figures, such as Henry Parkes in New South Wales and George Higinbotham in Victoria. As we shall see in the next chapter, Higinbotham was an especially thoughtful, well-educated and idealistic man. He and many temperance advocates like him were well aware that some people are able to drink in moderation, without ill effects. But there will always be many people who cannot. Thus, their argument went, restrictive laws are necessary for their sake and the common good.

Taking this reasoning to its ultimate conclusion, a conscientious Christian may insist that all Christians should abstain from alcohol, so as to set an example. Total legal prohibition may even be called for.[57] Personally I do not share this view. What I am suggesting is that many who held it in times past were not mean-spirited but well-intentioned – and at least half-right.

A more common view – the one that ultimately prevailed – was that substantial restrictions on personal liberty were warranted. This case is made persuasively in Ross Fitzgerald and Trevor Jordan's study *Under the Influence: A History of Alcohol in Australia* (2009). There is persuasive evidence that, from the 1880s, thanks in part to the temperance movement, the Australian population as a whole began to consume less alcohol per head – and certainly much less spirituous liquor.[58] In any fair-minded view, this was no bad thing. Yet alcoholism remains prevalent, as does public drunkenness. The latter problem seems to be getting worse, especially among the young – both men and women.

In recent generations there has been a fascinating development in community attitudes to many of these lifestyle issues. Religious 'wowsers' are no longer on their own. The trend of progressive opinion – especially progressive feminist opinion – is increasingly against an open-slather approach to alcohol, pornography and gambling. Thus, within the last decade, there have been well-publicised campaigns in relation to 'alcopops', the opening hours of clubs and hotels on Friday and Saturday nights, access to pornography on the Internet, poker machine limits, and television advertisements by betting agencies during sporting matches.

Objections to law-making in these areas come mostly from right-wing *secular* voices. Their chief concerns are the making of money (*Who cares if drunken teenagers hurt each other, so long as I can sell them grog at 4 a.m.?*) and unlimited personal freedom (*If I want to blow a thousand bucks at a casino, who gives a s—t?*) For such people an unregulated 24/7 economy is ideal. Many progressives in 2015 have much more in common with the likes of William Henry Judkins than they might realise.

In 1988, when Edmund Campion commented on the importance of the social legislation of the early twentieth century, he added: 'The dismantling of these laws in recent years points to a rejection of the religious impulses which produced them.'[59] In retrospect, it may not have been a conscious rejection so much as a rejection by default. The underlying impulses are still there – and are once again being articulated. But they are less likely to be articulated in religious terms.

## Racial tolerance

During the course of the twentieth century, Australia went from strict enforcement of the White Australia Policy to a racially-blind immigration programme and general acceptance of multiculturalism. We also, if belatedly, made substantial progress in reconciliation with Indigenous peoples. It is not sufficiently appreciated that the Christian Churches – and individual Christians – deserve much of the credit for making these things happen.

Among left-wing secularists in Australia who give free rein to their views, few opinions are expressed more often than the one that 'Christians are racists'.[60] A somewhat more charitable view is that, while most Christians are not racists, most racists are Christians. In fact, the truth is otherwise. I would go this far: if you are a racist in the twenty-first century, you cannot be a true Christian. You may be a nominal Christian, but you have not yet been born again. Many of the most passionately anti-racist figures in Australian history have been devout. By contrast, the Australians most likely to exhibit racist attitudes are *irreligious* – a sociological fact proved empirically by Hans Mol's research of the 1960s and 1980s.[61]

As Marion Maddox has observed, churchgoing Christians are more conservative than other Australians on various moral issues – abortion, for instance, or euthanasia, or sex outside marriage – but they are more liberal on issues of race.[62] All Christian Churches here sponsor missions and charities overseas, and congregations are updated regularly about their activities. This builds knowledge and fosters empathy. An unusual consensus has developed in recent decades between regular churchgoing Christians (mainline Protestant and Catholic) and far-Left secularists of activist bent. Each group is highly suspicious of the other, but often they find themselves arguing for the same things on matters affecting refugees, say, or foreign aid.

In Australia today, the people most likely to hold racist or xenophobic views belong to the large group in between – purely nominal Christians and the religiously (and socially) apathetic. In Mol's words: 'the non-churchgoing, modal Australians tend to look less beyond their shores and more to what is of immediate advantage to them personally'.[63]

Why, then, is religion associated with racism, and racism with religion? How could a writer as distinguished as Christopher Hitchens hope to get away with the line that *all* religion is 'intolerant, allied to racism and tribalism and bigotry'?[64] Since 9/11 the issues have been complicated by Islamic terrorism, but I still think this is a distraction from the main game – at least in Australia. Let me explain why.

### Indigenous relations

We saw in Chapter 1 that during the nineteenth century, a sorry pattern developed in Indigenous relations. Official good intentions towards the 'natives' and nominal legal protection coincided with a ghastly reality on the frontiers, followed, somewhat later, by Christian atonement of a limited kind. It was more or less the same in every colony, with local variations on the theme. Queensland's was an especially awful story. The original Indigenous population of around 100,000 had been reduced, by the 1890s, to only 15,000.[65]

Frontier killings in Western Australia continued well into the twentieth century;[66] likewise in the Northern Territory, which was only separated from South Australia in 1911.[67] It did not help that, following Federation, and until 1967, the Constitution (section 127) explicitly provided that Aborigines were not to be counted in population censuses. Unmistakably, this 'bore the implication that [they] were less than human beings'.[68] One of the very few white Australian organisations to complain about section 127 *at the time* was the New South Wales Aborigines Mission, an Evangelical Protestant group.[69]

No segment of Australian society comes out of this history especially well. But I venture to suggest that serious Christians emerge rather better than most – in the twentieth century even more so than in the nineteenth. Three main points are worth making.

First, as to frontier killings and other physical mistreatment of Indigenous peoples, often it was brave missionaries – and *only* them – who spoke up. A notable example was the redoubtable Anglican Ernest Gribble (1868–1957),[70] who raised hell after the Forrest River massacre of June 1926, in outback Western Australia. But, to put it mildly, majority white opinion was not on Gribble's side. Indeed, when it came to exposing such atrocities, the majority was rarely on any missionary's side. For too many people in the coastal cities it was a case of out of sight, out of mind. In rural areas, Aboriginals – and their over-passionate defenders – tended to be disdained. One contemporary wrote of Gribble: 'He treats them as the equal of whites. He continually puffs up blacks and has been a source of great mischief in the Wyndham district. That is why he is so cordially hated by those amongst whom he has lived for thirteen years.'[71]

During the twentieth century the nature of the Aboriginals' plight gradually changed. Under various federal and State systems of official protection, their lives became much less at risk from outright murder. Piecemeal efforts were made to improve their living standards and – after World War Two – to assimilate them into Australian society. But other kinds of wrongs were done to them in the process. Infamously, between about 1909 and 1969, these wrongs included the separation of thousands of Aboriginal children from their families. These were the so-called Stolen Generations, the subject of the Human Rights Commission's seminal report of 1997, *Bringing Them Home*, and of Prime Minister Kevin Rudd's national apology of 2008. Revisionist historians have attempted to explain away the treatment of the Stolen Generations,[72] and it is questionable whether the term 'genocide' was appropriate to describe what happened. But there can be no doubt whatever that this was another dreadfully sad chapter in Australian history.

It is also undeniable that the Churches played a central role in the process. The motives of those involved were, on the whole, altruistic. But that did not lessen the intense pain and suffering of the victims. Sir Ronald Wilson, president of the Human Rights Commission from 1990 to 1997 and the principal author of the *Bringing Them Home* report, realised this fully. He had no axe to grind with the Churches; on the contrary, he was a deeply religious man. To their credit, the institutional Churches were among the first to apologise once the full facts came to light.[73] It was *secular* institutions – in particular, the Australian Government – that dragged the chain.

Christians' second great contribution to Indigenous relations came in enlarging our knowledge and understanding of pre-contact Indigenous societies. Few things were more important in scotching the canard that Indigenous people were 'savages'.

The initial breakthroughs were made by a mere quartet of men. In time, they came to be described as 'the band of brothers ... who laid the foundations of Australian anthropology'.[74] In ascending order of importance they were A.W. Howitt (1830–1908), Lorimer Fison (1832–1907), Francis Gillen (1855–1912) and W. Baldwin Spencer

(1860–1929). Indigenous religion was one of their main sub-specialties, and, in the long term, their findings pricked and shaped the Australian conscience. In the words of one modern-day admirer:

> Their anthropology allowed them to detect a spiritual world of
> unsuspected extent, complexity and feeling, a revelation that made
> possible the eventual transformation of racism into pluralism. Their
> anthropology's empiricism was, in its way, a search for truth, the
> beginnings of an effort at comprehension that has continued ever since.[75]

The point I would stress is that all four members of this band of brothers were well equipped theologically to tackle their subject. Each was a practising Christian or had been raised in that tradition.[76]

Later in the twentieth century, other anthropologists built on their legacy. Three of the most distinguished were men of the Church, Anglican, Catholic and Lutheran respectively. Adolphus Peter Elkin (1891–1979) was an Anglican clergyman and Professor of Anthropology at the University of Sydney. Though an assimilationist, his writings[77] were of enormous value in shaping white attitudes for the better. Father Ernest Worms (1891–1963), a Catholic missionary for many years in the Broome region of Western Australia, was another titanic figure. Justly described as 'the anthropological jewel in the tiara of the Pallottine missions',[78] he and numerous colleagues contributed a great deal to our understanding of Indigenous society. T.G.H. (Ted) Strehlow (1908–78) was the son of a renowned German-Lutheran missionary in the Northern Territory. His masterpiece, *Songs of Central Australia* (1971), was an attempt to 'sing and elucidate the soul of the first inhabitants'.[79]

But the most consequential of all Australian anthropologists was W.E.H. (Bill) Stanner (1905–81). It was Stanner who coined that superbly resonant term 'The Dreaming' to encapsulate the essence of Indigenous religion. It was a variation on Spencer and Gillen's term 'The Dreamtime'. Stanner took out the word 'time' because the concept was (and is) timeless. 'One cannot fix The Dreaming *in* time,' he later insisted, 'because it was and is everywhen.' It is an eternal and continuing process:

> The Dreaming is many things in one. Among them, a kind of
> narrative of things that once happened; a kind of charter of things
> that still happen; and a kind of *logos* or principle of order transcending
> everything significant for Aboriginal man.[80]

On another occasion he described the Indigenous worldview thus:

> The celebration of a *dependent* life which is conceived as having taken a wrongful turn at the beginning, a turn such that the good life is now inescapably connected with suffering ... the Aborigines ... [give] the impression of having stopped short of, or gone beyond, a quarrel with the terms of life [emphasis mine].[81]

There are clear similarities here with the opening chapters of Genesis (the accounts of Creation and the Fall) and the Gospel of John (the Divine Logos). Stanner's original fifteen-page essay on The Dreaming (first published in 1956) has been described by John Hirst as 'the finest achievement of European civilisation in Australia'.[82]

Stanner embodied an ideal mixture of Christian and Enlightenment values. He was a conservative, but not a reactionary: he 'drew on the West's foundational traditions rather than its relatively recent political derivatives'.[83] As a man he exhibited rock-solid integrity: when it came to Indigenous questions, there was not a racist bone in his body. He deplored the 'Great Australian Silence' about post-1788 relations with Indigenous peoples. As author Dean Ashenden has observed, 'There was something of the Old Testament prophet about [Stanner], calling down a plague on all our houses, an element of what right-wing critics have called (but failed to see in themselves) "moral vanity".'[84] Stanner's deepest personal beliefs are a matter of conjecture, but his knowledge of religion was profound and some of his closest colleagues were devout.[85] Certainly, an atheist or an uninformed agnostic could not have achieved what he did.

Australian Christians' third and most important contribution to Indigenous relations has been in the field of evangelism. This has been the key to such limited reconciliation as has been achieved.

I expect that some secular readers may be scoffing. But the facts are incontrovertible: over the last two generations, Indigenous people themselves have voted with their feet, hearts and minds. They are now *more* Christian than any other segment of Australian society. As commentators such as Noel Loos have demonstrated, a vibrant 'Black Church' has emerged.[86] In the 2011 census, 62.3 per cent of Indigenous respondents classified themselves as Christian; only 1.3 per cent identified with 'Aboriginal spirituality'. In truth, many Indigenous Australians have combined aspects of both traditions – they have brought 'Christ into The Dreaming' or 'The Dreaming into Christ'.

This is the crux of so-called Rainbow Spirit theology, the roots of which can be traced as far back as the 1840s. It is an incarnational, Creation-centred theology – in short, it focuses on the wonders of Nature and the example of Christ.[87]

One of the keys to this phenomenon has been the translation of the Bible – or at least important New Testament sections of it – into Indigenous languages. The process began in earnest in 1961 with the establishment, by Wycliffe Bible Translators, of the Australian Society for Indigenous Languages. The Bible Society of Australia and the Uniting Church have also played important roles.[88]

There is a fascinating discussion of these issues in Gideon Goosen's book *Australian Theologies*.[89] It highlights some key questions with which all thinking believers must grapple: how to reconcile Christianity with other faiths, and how to determine the likely 'test' of salvation, especially for people who lived before the coming of Christ or who were never made aware of Him. These questions are quintessentially relevant to Australia. One Indigenous suggestion is that 'the Holy Spirit is present in all cultures' – and always has been.[90] Another is that Jesus may be understood as 'a Dreamtime hero': He is 'present not only in ceremonies which explicitly celebrate him, but also in those which express human yearning for the sources of life and goodness'.[91]

The essence of Rainbow Spirit theology was described by Goosen as follows:

[It] assumes that the Creator Spirit has been speaking through Aboriginal culture from the beginning. It sees Christ as the life-giving power of the Creator God made present in the Incarnation. And this Aboriginal Christ, because he brings life, leads them back on the journey of rediscovering the good in their culture and of discerning the presence of the Creator Spirit in their ancestral stories.[92]

Among trendy white defenders of Indigenous spirituality, I suspect there are very few who have considered such questions. Most are atheists, or lazy agnostics, prone to casual ridicule of the Christian Churches. Contrast their shallowness with the practical wisdom of a revered Indigenous woman such as 'Mum Shirl' Smith (1924–98). Born at Erambie Mission, near Cowra, she founded in New South Wales both the Aboriginal Legal Service and the Aboriginal Medical Service, and was known in later life as the Black Saint of Redfern. She was not blind to the faults of the Churches, but remained a believing Catholic all her life. 'There's nothing out of plumb with the Catholic religion,' she once said. 'It's the way Catholics practise it.'[93]

How, in the end, did the Christian Churches reach people like Mum Shirl Smith? How did we get to the position recorded in the 2011 census – 62 per cent Indigenous affiliation with Christianity, admittedly down from 73 per cent in 2006 – and a vibrant Black Church? It seems a near-miracle, given the injustices suffered by Indigenous peoples since 1788.

In 1845, Sydney's Catholic archbishop John Bede Polding tried to explain to a parliamentary committee the lack of early success by Christian missionaries. He blamed 'the bad feeling and want of confidence, naturally caused by the mode in which possession has been taken of their country – occupation by force, accompanied by murders, ill-treatment, ravishment of their women'. In short, claimed Polding, the major obstacle was 'the conviction in their minds that the white man has come to his own advantage, without any regard to their rights'.[94] This was a remarkably modern insight. And the overall treatment of Indigenous peoples did not markedly improve until more than a century later. The still-existing material plight of many Indigenous communities, in both rural and urban areas, is notorious.

Even so, Indigenous attitudes to Christianity have now been transformed. Credit belongs chiefly to the Indigenous peoples themselves, who have demonstrated a remarkable capacity to keep sight of the big (spiritual) picture. In the end they separated the wonderful message from the deeply flawed messenger. But the efforts of the Churches were crucial too. The vital point is that the Churches' more passionate members took their faith seriously. The best of them were the opposite of racist. They never saw Indigenous peoples as sub-human creatures, to be ignored or exploited or exterminated, but as human beings made in the image of God. As Messrs Tyerman and Bennett of the London Missionary Society asked rhetorically in the 1830s: 'Doth no men care for their souls? "Have they souls?" it may be superciliously asked. We answer … "The Lord knows that they have!"'[95]

A must-read book for anyone interested in this subject is John W. Harris' monumental work *One Blood: 200 years of Aboriginal encounter with Christianity – A story of hope*. It is a detailed history not merely of missionary efforts from 1788 but of the impact of white settlement on all aspects of Indigenous life. Harris does not spare the Churches from criticism – far from it – but gives praise where it is due. Importantly, he starts from the premise that 'it was the duty of the Christian Church to bring the gospel of Jesus Christ to the Aboriginal people'.[96]

In very broad terms, the Christianisation of Indigenous peoples was a two-stage process. The first phase spanned the period from 1788 to roughly 1965. Missionaries led the way, using a wide range of methods, from haughty paternalism to enlightened co-existence. They endured countless setbacks: throughout the nineteenth century, and a good deal of the twentieth, most of their efforts failed. Apart from the attitudes identified by Archbishop Polding, the next biggest problem was the language barrier. There was no full translation of the New Testament into any Aboriginal tongue until 1899,[97] and, understandably, many individuals became discouraged. (The Reverend Samuel Marsden was one.) But some intrepid souls persisted for decades.

Most importantly, the Churches *as institutions* kept trying.[98] One of their earliest and most celebrated success stories was the conversion, in 1860, of a young man belonging to the Wotjoballuk clan of the Wergaia people, in the Wimmera district of Victoria. Two Moravian Methodists, Friedrich Hagneuer and Friedrich Spieseke, had established a mission in the region in 1858. The young man, who took the name Nathaniel Pepper, had witnessed as a child the murder of his mother by a white settler. Later he became a lay preacher to his people. The full story is rousingly told in Robert Kenny's *The Lamb Enters the Dreaming.*

As the decades wore on, various landmarks were reached. In 1925, at St George's Cathedral in Perth, James Noble (1876–1941) became the first Aboriginal to be ordained as an Anglican minister.[99] In 1929, David Unaipon (1872–1967), a Ngarrindjeri man who had been raised at the Point McLeay mission in South Australia, became the first Aboriginal to publish a book in the English language. For many years an Anglican lay preacher, Unaipon's face appears on the fifty-dollar note.[100] In the 1930s a man of the Yorta Yorta people, Doug Nicholls (1906–88), came to public prominence playing Australian Rules football for Fitzroy in the Victorian Football League. Later he became a Church of Christ pastor and, in 1972, the first Aboriginal to be knighted.[101] In 1975 a young Yawuru man from Broome, Patrick Dodson (b. 1948), became the first Indigenous priest of the Roman Catholic Church. He is now widely regarded as the 'father of Australian reconciliation'.

The achievements of Nicholls and Dodson – and several others like them – take us into the second phase of the process of Indigenous Christianisation. I date its beginning at, roughly, 1965. But there had been an important transition period in the years following World War Two.

During the war many more Aboriginals had come into contact with white Australians, in the armed services or as employed labourers. A view developed that Aboriginal people should no longer be kept isolated on missions but should gradually be assimilated into Australian society. The notion of assimilation is frowned upon now, but it was regarded at the time, correctly, as an enlightened advance on past practices. Paul Hasluck (1905–93) – a truly eminent Australian, later Governor-General – adopted it as official government policy after he became Minister for Territories in the Menzies Government in 1951. He held this position for twelve years, and was extremely influential in an area of public policy that had never before been taken so seriously.

It is important to understand that Hasluck's parents had been officers of the Salvation Army, dedicated to social justice causes. They ran a boys' home at Collie, in the rural southwest of Western Australia, and among its workforce was a Nyoongar man known affectionately as 'Black Paddy'. He converted to Christianity. One of Hasluck's biographers, Geoffrey Bolton, has suggested that it was 'in these years the young Hasluck may have first formed the idea, not then widely shared, that Aborigines could be as good as white people'.[102] At any rate, as a young man, Hasluck became an active member of the Western Australian Aboriginal Amelioration Association. His assimilation policies were an important precursor to more progressive reform, including the gradual conferral of full rights of citizenship. The right to vote was granted in 1962, and, on 27 May 1967, more than 90 per cent of Australians voted 'Yes' at a landmark referendum to amend the Constitution. The overriding purpose, according to the official 'Yes' case, was to remove 'any ground for the belief that … the Constitution discriminates in some ways against people of the Aboriginal race'.[103] More specifically, Aboriginals would be counted in the census and the Federal Parliament would be empowered to legislate for the benefit of Aboriginal people. Until then it had lacked that power.

The Churches strongly supported the 'Yes' case. Admittedly, in the end, so did all the major political parties, but Church spokespersons were especially eloquent – and influential. Some had been in the vanguard for many years. Among them was Pastor Doug Nicholls, who, almost a decade earlier, on 29 April 1958, had chaired the first public meeting of the Aboriginal-Australian Fellowship at Sydney Town Hall. That occasion saw the launch of one of the original petitions calling for Constitutional reform.[104]

An associated post-war development was the movement towards Aboriginal land rights. This cause, too, was adopted early on by some prominent and enlightened Christians, including a Methodist missionary in Arnhem Land, Edgar Wells,[105] and Kim Beazley Senior, the Labor MHR for Fremantle and a staunch lay Anglican. Famously, in 1963, Beazley suggested that the Yirrkala people send a bark petition to Federal Parliament in support of their cause. They did. The petition failed in the short term but fostered a great deal of publicity and debate.

The key point is this. During the 1960s, there was a transformation in white Christian attitudes to Indigenous people. Always well-meaning, Christians became less paternalistic and more empathetic. A National Missionary Council pamphlet published in 1963 stated without equivocation: 'It must never be forgotten that, for the most part, Australia was taken from the Aborigines by force without payment or compensation or recognition of their inherent title to the land.'[106] In 1965, the Australian Council of Churches published a seminal booklet written by the Reverend Dr Frank Engel called *The Land Rights of Australian Aborigines*,[107] and within a few years almost all the mainline Churches had declared their broad support for the cause.

Federal Government action followed in the 1970s under the Whitlam and Fraser Governments, in regard not merely to land rights but also to anti-discrimination generally. In the 1980s and 1990s, the Hawke and Keating Governments built on this legacy. The High Court delivered the *Mabo* judgment on 3 June 1992, overruling the *terra nullius* principle and establishing a common law basis for native title claims. On 10 December that year, Prime Minister Paul Keating gave his Redfern Speech. It was laced with Christian themes: there were strong parallels with Pope John Paul II's address at Alice Springs in 1986.[108] In 1993 the re-elected Keating Government passed the Native Title Act, codifying and clarifying the principles laid down in *Mabo*. It has been powerfully argued that the reasoning of three of the majority justices in *Mabo* – Brennan, Deane and Gaudron – was influenced by Catholic natural law teachings.[109] James Franklin has contended that *Mabo* represented 'the most dramatic outcome of Catholic philosophy in recent times'.[110]

We now come to another point insufficiently appreciated by left-leaning secular critics of the Australian Churches. As institutions, they have firmly and consistently supported reconciliation with Indigenous peoples – the language of Prime Minister Bob Hawke's motion of reconciliation in 1988 was taken from a text proposed by fourteen Church leaders.[111] They have just as firmly and consistently opposed the greedy, xenophobic backlash. This backlash began in the early 1980s as a campaign led by big mining companies, but it was not successfully popularised until the mid-1990s. Unscrupulous politicians were to blame. The twin nadirs were the Hindmarsh Island Bridge affair of 1995–97 (the infamous clash between developers and Indigenous residents over 'secret women's business', and a truly disgusting episode in our national life)[112] and the Howard Government's legislative response, in 1997–98, to the High Court's decision in the *Wik* case.[113]

*Wik* had decided that native title could in certain circumstances co-exist with pastoral leases, but that, in the event of inconsistency, the pastoral lease prevailed. The Howard Government's Ten Point Plan to overturn *Wik* was condemned by Australian church leaders across the denominational spectrum, including the Sydney Diocese of the Anglican Church to which Howard belonged.[114] In the event, an imperfect parliamentary compromise was negotiated. An independent senator from Tasmania, Brian Harradine, cast the deciding vote. Harradine was a staunch Catholic who consulted during the process with a Catholic priest, Father Frank Brennan. Although he and Brennan were heavily criticised (famously by Keating himself), Harradine insisted that he voted as he did to avoid the possibility in 1998 of an ugly race-based federal election.[115] The legislation survived a High Court challenge, though the government stooped to arguing that section 51(26) of the Constitution could be utilised to make special laws *to the detriment* of Indigenous peoples. It was a ghastly flouting of the spirit of the 1967 referendum, to say nothing of plain Christian charity.

Politics aside, the moral of the story is this. Once the Australian Churches became loyal champions of Indigenous rights, they had far greater success with evangelism. The surge in Indigenous identification with Christianity coincided with the legal and sociological developments I have outlined. Historian Roger C. Thompson has argued that it was the establishment of the Aboriginal Christian Fellowship, in 1971, that 'signified the emergence of Aboriginal Christianity'.[116] I would go back a little further – to 1965, when the Australian Council of Churches took its stance on land rights.

## Multiculturalism

Unlike the history of Indigenous relations, the history of Australian multiculturalism – at least since World War Two – is an almost unqualified triumph. It is true that a strain of anti-immigration sentiment has always existed in Australia, invariably directed at the most recent cohort of arrivals. Yet, today, a vast majority of citizens (according to one recent survey around 85 per cent) agree with the proposition that 'multiculturalism has been good for Australia'.[117] Many rate it our finest national achievement. The percentage of the Australian population born overseas is approaching 30 per cent – up from about 10 per cent in 1950 – and almost all countries of the world are represented. The top fifteen are the United Kingdom, New Zealand, China, India, Vietnam, Italy, the Philippines, South Africa, Malaysia, Germany, Greece, Sri Lanka, the United States, Lebanon and Holland.[118] (Many of those countries – notably the UK and the US – are now racially diverse themselves.)

The resulting enrichment of Australian life, across all aspects of society, has been utterly profound. Yet the belief persists that multiculturalism has come at the expense of Christianity. Or that Christians and the Christian Churches have, on the whole, been opponents of multiculturalism. In fact, on both counts, the opposite is true.

Prior to 1945 there was some non-British immigration (Germans to South Australia, for instance, and Chinese to New South Wales and Victoria during the gold rushes), but this was always on a small scale. After 1945, immigrants came in waves – initially from southern and eastern Europe, later from southeast Asia, Africa and the Middle East. Australia was well placed to handle the consequent societal change because, in managing the Protestant–Catholic divide, we had a textbook model to follow. (See the section in Chapter 4 on the roots of multiculturalism.) Indeed, post-war immigration coincided with the gradual improvement of sectarian tensions.

The story of Australia's post-war immigration programme has been told many times. But I would lay stress on the religious aspect of it. It is not emphasised enough that the Australian Churches – the Catholic Church in particular – were pivotal in the whole process. Australia's post-1945 experience is an excellent example of one of the most important *secular* functions of religion: for immigrants it can serve as a comforting link between the old country and the new.[119] At their best, the great religions are colour-blind. Belief in the same God transcends all other differences.

The first wave of post-war immigration – that from southern and eastern Europe – was actively facilitated by the Catholic Church. Over a million practising Catholics came to Australia, many with the assistance of the International Catholic Migration Commission.[120] As many Irish-Catholics in earlier generations had relied on the Church as a point of continuity in their new country, so it was in the 1950s and 1960s for the Greeks, the Italians, the Yugoslavs and others. 'The church actively helped them settle in their new land and promoted welcoming policies.'[121]

Another little-known fact of Australian history: it was the Democratic Labor Party – the party of B.A. Santamaria and his fellow right-wing Catholics – that first advocated the abolition of the White Australia Policy. Author and political commentator Gerard Henderson has contended that this was a natural response to the culture of the Church. For decades, through regular contact with the Vatican in Rome – and Europe and the world more broadly – Australian Catholics had become comfortable with non-British culture.[122] This trait manifested itself again in the late 1970s and early 1980s. More than half of the Vietnamese and other Indo-Chinese refugees who arrived in Australia in that period were Catholics – some 85,000 in all. The St Vincent de Paul Society played a major role in their resettlement.[123] In the words of Edmund Campion: 'Thus the Catholic community became a potent factor in achieving a multicultural society in Australia.'[124]

Protestant churchgoers were, on the whole, slower to embrace multiculturalism. Sad to say, among some older and more nominal adherents, Britain's Anglo-Celtic culture was (is) more deeply cherished than the Gospel. But, for the most part, it has been a different story at the level of the clergy and among Evangelical believers. True, such people may be suspicious of people of other religions. But race *per se* is not a factor in this. My own Presbyterian Church has become – since the split of 1977 – a deeply conservative institution. But as far as issues of race are concerned, its thinking is impeccably progressive. First- and second-generation Asian immigrants are completely welcome within its walls and have a large presence. It is the same in the Uniting Church and in most Anglican and Pentecostal churches also.

## National character

Few people in any era – even devout Christians – have associated Australia's unique national character with religion. Our most popular myths are secular ones. Nevertheless, religious laymen and laywomen have always been prominent in fields like history and the creative arts.

For example, in the field of Australian history, it is true that the average member of a university faculty today is far more likely to be an atheist or an agnostic than is a random member of the community.[125] Yet many of the truly outstanding and influential Australian historians of the twentieth century – giants such as W.K. (Keith) Hancock (1898–1988), C.M.H. (Manning) Clark (1915–91) and Geoffrey Blainey (b. 1930) – were (or are) steeped in Christianity. As I noted in the Introduction, perhaps the greatest of them all – Clark – was the son of an Anglican minister. Ultimately his work was a search for meaning and his 'guiding conception was taken from Dostoyevsky'.[126] Despite his lionisation by the secular Left, he in fact disdained much of its shallow vitriol – 'men without reverence were not likely to improve the world'[127] – and recognised the crucial place of religion in Australian history. In the words of biographer Stephen Holt, he 'remained an incurably Protestant idealist'.[128] Blainey, one of Clark's most eminent former students, has summed him up best: 'He was devoted to and hostile to Christianity. He belonged to both the left and the right.'[129]

I would make the same general observation about Australia's greatest creative writers – not the fashionable fly-by-nighters, but the enduring greats. The depth of their work transcends easy political labels. And, without exception, they were (or are) steeped in Christianity – even if not all of them practised it faithfully.

Think of poets such as Banjo Paterson (1864–1941), Henry Lawson (1867–1922), Christopher Brennan (1870–1932), John Shaw Neilson (1872–1942), Dorothea Mackellar (1885–1968), A.D. Hope (1907–2000), Gwen Harwood (1920–95), Bruce Dawe (b. 1930) and Les Murray (b. 1938). Hope is an excellent example. When he died on the eve of the third millennium, 'Australia lost its greatest living poet' – or so suggested a fellow poet and close friend, Kevin Hart, in 2008. Hope's exact rank in the pantheon is a matter of opinion, but few dispute his greatness. In one of his finest poems, 'Exercise on a Sphere', he touched upon the very theme that I am attempting to address in this book: the West's slow loss of faith in a materialistic age. The poem concludes:

Man's need for certainty is a disease past cure.
Where are those fixed world-pictures of the past
Which, as they changed, gave place to others as sure?
Christmas is over, Christmas is over at last!

The sentiments expressed in the first and last lines of that stanza were too pessimistic. But the question Hope posed in the middle was – and is – spot-on.

Think also of Australian novelists and short-story writers – the likes of Henry Handel Richardson (1870–1946), (Stella) Miles Franklin

(1879–1954), Martin Boyd (1893–1972), Patrick White (1912–90), Ruth Park (1917–2010), Christopher Koch (1932–2013), Thomas Keneally (b. 1935), Helen Garner (b. 1942) and Tim Winton (b. 1960). Miles Franklin, for example, was a lifelong quester for spiritual truth. Her enigmatic motto became: 'It takes a greater mind to find God than to lose Him.' Patrick White, Australia's only Nobel Prize winner for literature, underwent a profound mid-life conversion experience. Though never quite an orthodox Christian, he became a deeply spiritual man and his novels reflected the fact. In 1970 he wrote to a friend: 'I suppose what I am increasingly intent on trying to do in my books is to give professed unbelievers glimpses of their own unprofessed faith.'[130]

I would also point to publishers such as George Robertson (1860–1933), the co-founder of Angus & Robertson in the mid-1880s and its driving force until the 1930s. The iconic publishing and bookselling firm that Robertson created proved of incalculable worth to Australian cultural and intellectual life: until Angus & Robertson, almost all books were imported. Even book*sellers* were comparatively rare in the colonies until Robertson came along. But he principally earned his place in history as a visionary publisher of aspiring Australian authors. Before the 1880s their main option was to seek a publisher in Britain – never a straightforward exercise.

All of these icons, I repeat, were thoroughly versed in religion. Many were passionate believers and some made metaphysical themes central in their work. If you doubt me, the details are in Appendix A. But, to further give the flavour, consider these words of Christopher Koch, another candidate for Australia's greatest-ever novelist:

> I suppose I'd admit to one preoccupation that's been constant: an interest in the invisible world that in my view lies all around us – a dimension often sensed or glimpsed by those who are attuned to it. In *The Boys in the Island* I called it the Otherland. In Christian terms – and I remain a kind of unsatisfactory, non-Churchgoing Christian – it's the search for Paradise. James McAuley called it 'the Edenic urge'. Critics tell me I'm preoccupied with duality – and I'd plead guilty to that. In one novel, *The Doubleman*, I made it my main theme. I believe that we live in a Universe of dualities, and may be torn between two inner natures. Possibly my focus on this was made inevitable because of my own background: half German, half Anglo-Irish; half Protestant, half Catholic. I gave this conflict most notably to Billy Kwan, in *The Year of Living Dangerously*.[131]

I shall not repeat the exercise by making reference to Australian painters, musicians or film-makers – though I will point out that one of Australia's greatest composers of instrumental music, Peter Sculthorpe (1992–2014), once wrote: 'To me ... it has always seemed clear that the highest forms of music on this planet stem from religious belief.' (Sculthorpe was raised an Anglican; later in life he explored Zen Buddhism and Shintoism.)[132]

Hopefully the point is made. In the fields of history and the creative arts – as in every other field of significance – Christians and Christianity shaped modern Australia.

PART TWO

# THE SECULAR JUGGERNAUT

# CHAPTER 6

# Ignorance

How can they believe in the one of whom they have not heard? And how can they hear without someone preaching to them?

Romans 10:14

My long-standing interest in religion was never anything other than prudential, moral, or simply curious. I say prudential since, if there is a God or gods who involve themselves in human affairs, it would be madly imprudent not to try as far as possible to keep on the right side of them.

Antony Flew, *There is a God: How the World's Most Notorious Atheist Changed His Mind* (2007)

It is time to look at the first of the major causes of secularisation in Australia. Rocket science this is not: as St Paul asked rhetorically of his followers in Rome, way back in AD 57, 'How can they believe in the one of whom they have not heard?' The 'they' to whom Paul was referring were citizens of the empire who had not yet been told about Jesus of Nazareth.

The situation in Australia in 2015, it may be argued, is not quite as cut-and-dried as that. Almost everybody has *heard* of Jesus – and, for that matter, of Mohammad and the Buddha. Paul himself insisted that there was no excuse for total ignorance of God: contemplation of the natural world, and the inner voice of conscience, ought to be enough to get anyone thinking (Romans 1:20, 2:14–15). But a vague feeling that there must or may be something more is a far cry from mature knowledge of religious teachings. I emphasise the word 'knowledge'. It is often alleged that religious faith is blind, but the opposite is true. The strongest faith is necessarily built on solid, detailed knowledge.

Sir John Forrest (1847–1918) was one of Australia's key founding fathers. The Premier of Western Australia throughout the 1890s, he had been a notable inland explorer as a young man and was blessed with robust common sense. By the time of his premiership all the colonies except Western Australia had withdrawn financial aid to religious schools and (to varying degrees) had secularised their State schools.

Forrest was an Anglican, though not an especially pious or intellectual one. Yet he resisted strenuously, for as long as he could, the pressure placed on him to go the way of the other colonies. Not only did he advocate the continuation of State aid to Church schools, Protestant and Catholic; in 1893, he also proposed that clergyman of all denominations be permitted to go into State schools and teach during school hours. The howls of complaint from Protestants astonished Forrest, but he came to realise he was outnumbered. He withdrew his proposal about clergyman getting access to State schools, and, in 1895, agreed reluctantly to legislate for the abolition of State aid in Western Australia.[1]

I believe that Forrest foresaw the big picture much more clearly than most. He had witnessed the practical effects of education reform in the other colonies. His basic point was simple: 'if youngsters were not taught some religion at school, they probably would not get it afterwards'. In one parliamentary debate he asked a rhetorical question of his opponents: 'Did they wish to see the rising generation brought up without any religious teaching at all?'[2] That was the crux of the matter then, and, in my opinion, it remains so today.

## Is religion worth knowing about?

As basic as it might seem, this is a crucial preliminary question. I stress again that what we are here considering is not religious faith but religious knowledge – the huge corpus of human learning and discourse that has accumulated over three millennia or more. This includes the arguments against the existence of God as well the arguments in favour, and the teachings of all the major religions, not just Christianity. It is a body of knowledge spanning theology, philosophy, sociology, science and history (both ancient and modern). Without at least a basic grasp of this body of knowledge, it is hard to see how anyone can arrive at an informed answer to the most important questions of life.

At the end of my book *God, Actually* I proffered a list of such questions. It did not purport to be an exclusive list; apart from anything else, it was skewed towards a consideration of Christianity. But, with a few modifications, both believers and atheists have since endorsed it as a useful starting point. Those questions include:

- Why is there something rather than nothing?
- How did that something come into being?
- Why are the fundamental physical laws that govern the Universe just right for life?
- How and why did life on Earth begin?
- Does Darwinian evolutionary theory fully explain the organised complexity of life on Earth?
- Why do human beings have a conscience?
- Is free will an illusion?
- Is faith a mere incidental by-product of Nature?
- Is love a mere incidental by-product of Nature?
- Will science ever be able to explain everything?
- Granted that Jesus of Nazareth lived, who or what was he, if he was not divine?
- How otherwise do you explain the reports of the Resurrection?
- If the Resurrection did not happen, how do you explain the Apostles' conduct, St Paul's conversion, and the establishment of the Christian Church in the face of overwhelming odds?
- How do you explain the correlations, which are sometimes striking, between many of the prophecies of the Old Testament and certain key events described in the New Testament?
- How do you explain the reports of personal religious experiences by many millions of people down the ages?
- If there is no God, why do people pray when their lives are in imminent danger, including many unbelievers?
- Why has man not yet been destroyed by nuclear holocaust?
- How do you account for the fact that atheism is, and always has been, an unpopular minority creed?
- How do you account for the many commonalities between different religions, and in particular the commonalities between Judaism, Islam and Christianity?
- Is there an afterlife, or is the rough 'justice' meted out by nature and by man all that we can ever hope for?
- If there is no afterlife, why is man capable of imagining it?
- If there is an afterlife, will all persons be subjected in it to some form of divine judgment?
- If there is divine judgment, what will be the likely 'test' of salvation?

Are they not questions worth considering? If you think that they are, the next question is whether anyone is equipped to answer them unaided. For that is what most Australians today attempt to do – if they make an attempt at all.

## Should we be satisfied with current levels of religious knowledge?

Among both the general population and public figures who should know better, current levels of religious knowledge in Australia are extremely low. They are lower, indeed, than levels of religious faith.

I make that statement with absolute confidence despite the fact that, in Australia, we have no equivalent of the Pew Forum's comprehensive Religious Knowledge Survey, last carried out in the United States in 2010. It revealed surprising levels of ignorance: for instance, only 45 per cent of adult Americans could name all four Gospels; only 16 per cent knew that Protestants believe in salvation by faith alone.[3] There are no grounds for believing that knowledge in Australia is better. Almost certainly it is worse. On this point I am inclined to take Phillip Adams at his word. In *Adams vs. God* he had this to say about the letters he receives regularly from irate Christians: 'It matters little if they're aggressive or patronising … These correspondents have one thing in common. They know far less about Christianity than the atheist they're writing to. Theirs is a comfortable, cosy Sunday school Christianity.'[4]

Consider Hans Mol's seminal research into Australians' religious knowledge, carried out in the mid-1960s. It can safely be assumed that the low levels of knowledge Mol then uncovered have not improved since – in fact, the overwhelming likelihood is that they are now lower still.

Mol put a series of propositions to his test subjects and asked them to respond to each in one of three ways: 'Agree', 'Disagree' or 'Don't know'. One proposition was as follows: 'The Book of the Acts of the Apostles gives an account of Jesus's life on earth.' Only 15 per cent of Australians surveyed gave the correct answer. Indeed, only 25 per cent of regular churchgoers gave the correct answer.[5] Yet for anyone with a basic knowledge of the New Testament, it was a simple question. A rough equivalent about, say, politics would be: 'Hansard is a record of proceedings in the Legislative Assembly and the Legislative Council.' A rough equivalent about lexicology would be: 'A thesaurus is a useful tool for looking up the source and meaning of words.'

(The correct response to each proposition is 'Disagree'. In the case of Mol's proposition, the reason is this: it is the four Gospels, not Acts, that give an account of Jesus' life on Earth. Acts is an account of events immediately following Jesus' death and resurrection – it describes, in substance, how the Christian Church got started.)

Consider some more recent Australian data. In April 2010, the Christian Research Association produced a report entitled 'Bible Engagement Among Australian Young People'. The report, which had been commissioned by the Bible Society of South Australia, defined a young person as someone between thirteen and twenty-four years of age. The principal finding was that 'around 4 per cent of young people read the Bible daily, another 6 per cent read it weekly, and 15 to 20 per cent read it very occasionally'.[6] In other words, 70 to 75 per cent read it not at all. It is hard to know much about Christianity if you do not read the Bible.

Let us not pick on the young. What of the well-educated, well-informed baby boomers? A usually erudite Australian writer and broadcaster, Michael Cathcart, gave us a telling glimpse into their mindset in 2012. During an ABC Radio interview with Salman Rushdie, Cathcart ventured this aside: 'There's no doubt that Mohammad was a real person, whereas Jesus is a person who is *at least* ambiguous in the question of whether he existed or not' (emphasis mine). As John Dickson subsequently pointed out in an article for the ABC's Religion and Ethics website, this was 'amateur hour'.[7] There is not a qualified historian in the world who doubts Jesus' existence as a man who lived in first-century Palestine. One may as well doubt the existence of Alexander the Great or Julius Caesar (or Mohammad). Cathcart, to his credit, later recanted. But it is amazing how often this suggestion is made. In *The God Delusion*, even Richard Dawkins allowed that 'Jesus probably existed'.[8] The argument will continue because of the (undeserved) prominence now being given by atheists to American Richard Carrier's 2014 tome *On the Historicity of Jesus*. Dickson has demolished it too.[9] (As a minister of the Anglican Church, an Honorary Fellow of the Department of Ancient History at Macquarie University in Sydney, lecturer on the Historical Jesus in the University of Sydney's Department of Jewish Studies, and perhaps Australia's best-known Christian author, Dickson is well placed to set such specious arguments to rights.)

Such gaffes are not confined to commentators of the Left. In the same year, 2012, Dickson pounced on similarly naïve comments by an icon of the Right, Andrew Bolt. Bolt had rehashed another tired canard: that the two accounts of Creation in the opening chapters of Genesis are 'contradictory'. Evidently he was unaware that theologians for 2,000 years have argued against a literalistic interpretation of those passages. Each addresses a different issue: the origin and nature of the Universe on the one hand, man's place in the Universe on the other.[10]

It is unnecessary to multiply examples. Let us take it as a given that levels of religious knowledge are low. What follows from that? In her book *Taking God to School* (2014), Marion Maddox posed this question: 'If today's young Christians slowly drift from their faith, is it the state's business?'[11] The thrust of her answer was 'No' – a debatable position in itself – but I am not sure she asked the right question. A better question is this: 'If today's generation of school students is not taught adequately or at all about religion, is it the State's business?'

My answer to that question is 'Yes – it *is* the State's business.' And the reason is not that low levels of religious knowledge are a cause of low levels of religious faith (though that is true).

I proffer two main reasons. The first is that a decent knowledge of religion is a necessary ingredient of a decent knowledge of literature, science and history, including Australian history. The second reason, and even more important, is that every Australian child deserves the chance to make a considered and informed decision about matters of religious faith. Admittedly these are value judgments of sorts. They involve rejecting the view of some on the secular Right that the role of education is purely vocational – that the State's duty is confined to ensuring that employers get 'suitably shaped human fodder to feed the national work force'.[12] It also involves rejecting the view of many on the secular Left that religion is not a serious subject for study – that it is all so patently nonsensical, if not downright dangerous, as to be beneath contempt. (Marion Maddox, I hasten to say, does *not* hold that view. She is of the Christian Left, though I find some of her thinking on the education question to be puzzling.)

At its core, the provision of universal education is about maximising equality of opportunity. The principle should apply to religion as much as any other aspect of life. As things stand, religious ignorance among the young leaves them exposed to indoctrination – both religious and secular. They do not, as adults, get to exercise a genuine choice. Usually, by the time they are adults, the die is cast. If they have been raised in a Sunday school version of faith, they may never adequately question it or be able properly to defend it. A much-underrated Anglican bishop of Sydney, Alfred Barry, saw this danger way back in the 1880s. 'He welcomed … questioning and doubts because they forced Christians to re-examine their faith and to distinguish between what was central and what was merely traditional.'[13] He formed an interdenominational Christian Evidence Society. Regrettably, this spirit of enquiry caused him to be distrusted by many of his colleagues.

I agree to this extent with the likes of Phillip Adams: religious indoctrination is a bad thing. But the thorough imparting of knowledge – the exposure of young minds to all the main facts, arguments and counter-arguments about a given subject – is not indoctrination. It can only ever be a good thing. Certainly – and this applies to minds young and not so young – people who have never been sensibly taught about religion are much more likely to fall victim to charlatans and extremists. They will not be equipped to sniff danger, if and when they are exposed to one-way urgings by exploitative Christian cults, say, or about Islamic jihad. But likewise, they are also much more likely to be taken in by false *secular* assertions – that Jesus never lived, say, or that most wars are fought over religion, or that scientists can fully explain the origin of the Universe and the origin of life.

A particular danger in modern Australia is that bright and idealistic students entering university (especially in the humanities faculties) are sitting ducks for proactive atheists, those who know little about religion but 'assume as a matter of course that their horizons are the widest'.[14] Another danger for people who are unschooled in religion is their underrating of human evil, especially at the highest levels of commerce, the trade unions and government. A commentator of the secular Left, Mark Davis, has identified the problem without realising its ultimate source: Australians today have 'a childish tendency to turn away and to doubt the facts when confronted with the more malevolent aspects of politics'.[15] Either that, or they go to the other extreme – cynicism and disengagement.

## How is religious knowledge imparted to children?

A small minority of children in Australia today grow up in homes where religion is taken seriously. They learn about it from their parents and, in most cases, at the churches to which they go with their parents. The findings of secularisation theorists are clear-cut and unsurprising: there is a strong correlation between churchgoing as a child and religious belief as an adult.[16] In the words of Steve Bruce: 'the socialisation of children is vital, for it accounts for most of the variation in the fates of different religions'.[17]

The State, quite properly, does not have the right to dictate to Australian parents what they should teach their children inside the family home (religion or no religion), or whether they should send them to church. But the State does have the right to require that parents send their children to school. For most children in Australia today, school is therefore the only place where they *might* receive a religious education. But as things stand, this depends on the choice of school – and that choice is made by parents.

As at March 2013 there were approximately 3.5 million school students in Australia. Of these, about 700,000 attended schools operated by the Catholic Church. Another 500,000 attended so-called independent schools, most of which are aligned with a Protestant denomination. (But not all of them: there are also independent schools run by non-Christian organisations, including some that are religiously neutral.) The remaining 2.3 million Australian school students – about 65 per cent of the total – attended schools run by the various State and Territory governments.[18]

We now come to the crux of my argument in this chapter: that religious ignorance is a major factor in secularisation. Children who are taught about religion at home or sent to church on Sundays are, by and large, the *same* children who attend Church schools (especially at the secondary level). They learn something about religion both at home and at school. On the other hand, children who are not taught about religion at home and who do not go to church – that is, most Australian children – are probably attending a government school. The plain truth is that they are most unlikely to have the gaps in their religious knowledge filled at such a school.

These blunt words of Patrick O'Farrell are as applicable today as they were in 1988: 'The secular school system is to blame for the non-philosophical tenor of Australian society. It is also responsible for the remarkable ignorance of religion.'[19] Government schools are now largely religion-free at both the primary and secondary levels. This has been the case for decades. Religion is not taught as part of the compulsory curriculum, though at the time of writing, moves were afoot on the part of the Federal Government to address this situation. Its expert panel has recommended that there be, in the history curriculum, 'greater focus on the impact and significance of Western civilisation and Australia's Judeo-Christian heritage, values and beliefs'.[20] (For reasons I will develop in Chapter 10, this proposal seems to me welcome but inadequate.) At present, students at government schools are offered one period a week of instruction about religion (what, in the 1970s, my generation used to call Scripture). These classes are optional – parents can and frequently do withhold their consent – and are mostly taught by well-meaning volunteers; at least in some States there are also genuine grounds for concern about the theological quality of the materials, especially at the primary-school level.[21] Most students do not take the classes seriously because the subject is not examined. Back at school in the 1970s, my mates and I used to regard Scripture as a free period – a joke.

At government high schools in some States there is a more substantial subject offered to students in Years 11 and 12 as an option for the Higher School Certificate or its equivalent: General Religious Education. GRE involves a comparative, non-confessional study of at least two of the world's major religions. It is, as Marion Maddox has written, 'a start'. But very few government school students take the subject, or are even aware of it. By the time they get to Year 11, religion is not on their radar.[22]

Going to a private school is no guarantee of a decent religious education either. Certainly, most students who go to these schools do not leave them with any sort of living faith. About a third of all Australian children go to private (mostly 'Church') schools; yet, as we have seen, only a small fraction of graduates emerges from them as regular churchgoers. Indeed, according to one study, 'there is little evidence … that attendance at a religious school has an effect over and above the influence of the religious beliefs and activities of parents'.[23]

Why? There are several reasons.

The wealthiest independent schools do little more than pay lip service to religion. True, most employ full-time chaplains, who are qualified people. But they hover in the background, their talents under-utilised. For the rest, religion is barely mentioned except on specified occasions. In the words of Ronald Conway: 'The habit of teaching religion in a separate compartment from secular knowledge fail[s] to create a natural relationship between Christian belief and the routine of daily life.'[24] At most independent schools, primary and secondary students are expected to attend only one period a week of religious instruction (Christian Studies or some such) and one chapel service. Some schools offer GRE to students in Years 11 and 12, but, again, this is only an option – and it is one that comparatively few students at elite Protestant schools take up. Moreover, most of the students who do take it up are those who need to the least. (They come from religious homes.) Incredibly, some elite Protestant schools do not even offer

GRE. They seem to cop little criticism for this, no doubt because many of the parents who can afford to send their children to such schools are uninterested in religion. Notionally Protestant schools have become, at the elite level, vocational factories for the upper-middle class – a ticket to wealth and prestige.

The low-fee Protestant schools, and their counterparts in the Islamic and Jewish communities, take religion rather more seriously. They began opening in the late 1970s but have exploded in popularity since the mid-1990s, chiefly as a result of the Howard Government's policies in relation to the opening and funding of new independent schools, policies which were continued by subsequent federal governments. It is true that most of the parents who send their children to these schools are more interested in discipline and 'traditional values' than they are in theology as such.[25] Be that as it may, a lot of the low-fee Protestant schools make no secret of their Christian emphasis. I am convinced that their existence is the main reason why levels of religious belief in Australia have not fallen even further than they already have. Yet in *Taking God to School*, Marion Maddox takes aim at them for representing 'a quite different strand of Christianity from the one in which I was raised'.[26] (She is the daughter of a Methodist clergyman.) To some extent I share her concerns – especially as regards the teaching at certain schools of six-day, young-Earth Creationism.[27] It is a great pity that there are not many more low-fee independent schools operated by the mainline Protestant Churches (Anglican, Presbyterian, Uniting), which would be more likely to avoid such teaching. Even so, Maddox exaggerates the 'fanaticism' of the low-fee independent schools – especially the Pentecostal ones.[28] And in questioning whether they should be funded by the State, she fails, in my opinion, to see the bigger picture.

Some form of positive religious education, even if it is not to one's own personal taste, is better than none at all. Why? Because it means students may be nudged away from a position of near-total ignorance, and begin to think along non-materialist lines. A few, if their interest is sparked, will pursue further investigation for themselves. Yes, there is a risk of indoctrination – but it is a risk that can, with goodwill, be minimised. In any event, it is a risk that *all* Australian school students currently run.

Let us be honest on that score. Everyone has a religious worldview, even if it is one of contempt or apathy. All schools impart a religious worldview. What most students get today – by default – is a form of soft *secular* indoctrination. Sometimes it is overt. The parents who reject this option for their children deserve, I think, rather more credit than Maddox is prepared to give them. I agree with teacher and commentator David Hastie that she 'asks us to regard a large and diverse demographic of Australians as sub-intelligent, based on loose guilt-by-association with small fringe groups'.[29]

Generally speaking, the schools that take religion the most seriously are those in the Catholic system. The subject is taught from Kindergarten to Year 12 and there is far less of a tendency to compartmentalise it. Further, no pretence is maintained that a magic line can be drawn between, in Hastie's phrase, 'students being informed *about* something and them actually starting to believe it'.[30] At many Catholic schools, Year 11 and 12 students are required to study GRE. All this is consistent with *Gravissimum Educationis* (1965), the Second Vatican Council's Declaration on Christian Education, and subsequent pronouncements. One declared that 'what makes the Catholic school distinctive is its religious dimension, and that this is to be found in *a*) the educational climate, *b*) the personal development of each student, *c*) the relationship established between culture and the Gospel, *d*) the illumination of all knowledge with the light of faith'.[31] These principles have been reaffirmed in Australia by the National Catholic Education Commission. One of its foundational understandings is that Religious Education is 'an area of learning on a par with ... other defined areas of learning'. In many dioceses it is specified as being 'the first ... in priority'.[32]

It is no accident, we can be sure, that rates of church attendance among Australian Catholics remain higher than those who belong to the mainline Protestant Churches. That said, those rates are declining and Catholic schools are not what they used to be. The ongoing revelations about child sexual abuse (about which more will be said in Chapter 8) must have damaged their reputation, along, perhaps, with the self-confidence of some of the people who run them. For better or worse, Catholic schools are no longer staffed by brothers, priests and nuns, at least not primarily.

## How did we get to where we are?

The history of the education system in Australia is not of mere academic interest. Our current system is not set in stone: things have been done differently in the past and might be done differently in the future. The issues we face today are not entirely new, though what emerges from an historical survey is this: religion has never been taken less seriously in schools than it is today.

But a second fact also emerges clearly: the Churches, for the most part, have only themselves to blame. They all botched the great education debates of the 1860s and 1870s. In the words of Russel Ward (writing in 1982), 'most schools might still be under religious control if it had not been for the seemingly irreconcilable differences between different bodies of Christians and even, at times, between those within the same churches'.[33] Once government education had been made 'free, compulsory and secular', the Protestant Churches then botched things further by running down their own school systems. By the 1970s they were mostly serving children of the conservatively minded middle class only – and a minority of them at that. The non-Catholic children of the progressive middle class and the entire working class were, in effect, abandoned.

### Building a school system from nothing

In Chapter 1 I mentioned the vital role played by the Churches in early New South Wales in educating the first generation of native-born Australians. Governor Phillip established the first school in 1789. A so-called Dame's School for very young children, it was run by a 35-year-old female convict named Isabella Rosson. Her only teaching aid on the first day was a single sheet of paper, on which was printed the alphabet, figures from one to nine in Roman and Arabic numerals, a few simple words, and the Lord's Prayer. A second Dame's School was opened at Parramatta in 1791 by another female convict, Mary Johnson.[34]

But, as we saw in Chapter 1, the principal burden of providing education fell on the Anglican Church; effectively it acted as the agent of the State, or in partnership with it.[35] As in the case of agriculture, the Reverends Richard Johnson and Samuel Marsden were vital early figures. Johnson taught some children himself and supervised Isabella Rosson and Mary Johnson (no relation) at the Dame's Schools. Together with Marsden, he also organised and staffed most of the first primary schools and procured precious financial grants from religious groups in England, such as the Society for the Propagation of the Gospel. Such grants supplemented the funds provided by the State.[36] By 1797, when there were almost a thousand children in the colony, six schools were being run by the Church. Parents were asked for a small amount of money to offset costs, but, crucially, these were egalitarian institutions. The school founded by Johnson in Sydney – a room attached to the church he had built in the town centre – was explicitly 'Open to Children of all Descriptions: of Soldiers, Settlers or Convicts'. Catechisms, hymns and prayers were a compulsory part of the curriculum.[37]

In 1800 a committee was formed to deal with the problem of orphans. By then there were several hundred in the colony.[38] The Governor's wife, Mrs King, chaired the committee, but again, the Church took the leading role. Samuel Marsden was the treasurer of the committee and gave generously of his time. In August 1801, when a female orphan house was opened at Parramatta, Marsden himself gave the religious instruction. He wrote after the first night: 'New South Wales while I was performing this duty appeared more like a Christian Country than it had ever done since I first entered it.'[39] By 1820 there were several orphan schools.

In these early years, one of the hardest problems was finding suitable teachers. Where possible, clergymen took on the role: in the early 1800s, the Reverends W.P. Crook (Congregationalist) and John Harris (Anglican) took up posts in Sydney and Green Hills (Windsor) respectively.[40] But sometimes (as in the Dame's Schools), educated convicts were employed for the purpose. More often than not they were women, because men were harder to spare from manual labour, but this was not always so.[41] In 1793, the first teacher at Richard Johnson's school was a male convict named William Richardson. (He was Isabella Rosson's husband; they had been married by Johnson on 5 September 1789.) But perhaps the most celebrated of the pioneer school teachers was Thomas Taber (1763–1842), a watch-finisher by trade who came to Sydney as a convict in June 1797. An Anglican, he was persuaded soon after his arrival by Richard Johnson to teach at Johnson's school in Sydney. Taber was an immediate success and taught at various institutions over the next twenty-seven years. On his retirement in 1824, Governor Thomas Brisbane awarded him a (then-rare) pension for 'unremitting attention to your duty as Schoolmaster in this colony'.[42]

Macquarie's governorship was vital for education, as for all else. He gave teachers full status as government employees[43] and exhorted parents of means to assume responsibility for erecting schools, promising matching government funding if they did. The result was the establishment of several day schools and boarding schools in Sydney and surrounding areas.[44] Marsden played a leading role in many of these ventures as organiser and subscriber.[45] He later wrote proudly: 'We have ... schools established in almost every district so that the rising generation will be brought up in the principles of the Protestant religion.'[46] Among them were five so-called charity schools for the poor, in Sydney, Richmond, Windsor, Liverpool and Wilberforce respectively,[47] and a school for Indigenous children, the Native Institution, opened at Parramatta in 1815 under the supervision of a Congregationalist missionary, William Shelley.[48] Its aims were shamelessly paternalistic, and it closed in 1826, but in the interim dozens of children were at least taught to read and write. In 1819, when all the colony's children were examined, an Indigenous girl received the top mark.[49]

Another Protestant clergyman, the Reverend Thomas Reddall, arrived in Sydney in September 1820. An Anglican, married with seven children, he had been despatched by the Colonial Office as both a chaplain and a school master. His task was to implement the so-called Madras or Bell system of instruction in New South Wales, favoured by the Church of England because it involved (among other things) compulsory use of the Anglican Catechism.[50] Reddall soon opened a fine private school in Liverpool that utilised the system – the Macquaries sent their son there[51] – and excelled as a minister at St Peter's Campbelltown. In August 1824 he was appointed by Governor Thomas Brisbane (himself a most godly man) to the imposing position of director-general of government schools. However, Reddall served for less than two years and never succeeded in implementing the Madras system beyond a handful of places.[52]

Nor did the Anglicans have it all their own way with Sunday schools. In fact, in the early years, these were dominated by Nonconformists. In May 1813, Thomas Hassall – son of Rowland Hassall, one of the original missionaries to come to Sydney from Tahiti – opened in his father's house at Parramatta the first Sunday school in the colony. The venture proved very popular, and in December 1815 a group of leading Dissenters and Methodists, including Hassall Senior, formed the New South Wales Sunday School Institution. Thomas Hassall acted as both secretary and superintendent.[53] Among the teachers under his charge were Samuel Marsden's spirited daughter Ann (Hassall's future wife) and a doctor's daughter named Lucy Mileham, who married his brother.[54] Despite his Methodist upbringing, Thomas Hassall was ultimately ordained as an Anglican minister – the first ever Australian-born candidate. He preached his first sermon in February 1822.

The Sunday school movement had wide significance. Not only did it reach many children, for some of whom Sunday school was the *only* formal education they received. It was also an important outlet for the talents and energies of the currency lasses. In the words of Helen Heney, 'To teach in Sunday school was an acceptable social activity for girls otherwise confined to home duties.'[55]

The Anglicans made their boldest attempt to assert religious hegemony in the colony a few years later. In May 1825 Thomas Hobbes Scott arrived in Sydney, not merely as the first archdeacon of New South Wales but as King's Visitor of Schools.[56] Soon afterwards, in accordance with a plan drawn up by him, the whole care and conduct of education in New South Wales was effectively assigned to the Church of England. A new regulatory body was set up, the Church and School Lands Corporation, which was endowed with one-seventh of all surveyed Crown land.[57] The idea was to develop a vast network of Anglican schools – a virtual monopoly – under the Archdeacon's direct supervision.

In the event, the scheme came to little. The operations of the corporation were suspended in 1829 and the corporation itself dissolved in 1833. Scott was industrious, and some new schools were built, but the corporation was hampered by lack of capital and delays in the surveying of land.

In any case, Scott's grand plan had always been doomed. The fundamental obstacle was the spirit of religious pluralism that already permeated the colony. New South Wales was not England. True, the other Christian denominations had, as yet, few schools of their own. But the Catholics had been working hard in that direction since the arrival of Father Therry in 1820. Therry's 'great nightmare was the Protestantizing of the whole colony', and he would have ten schools up and running within a decade.[58] The Presbyterians, under J.D. Lang, would open their first primary school in 1826 and their first secondary school, the Australian College, in 1831.[59] The Non-conformists had pioneered the Sunday school movement, and since the colony's earliest days had provided some of the most respected day-school teachers (John Hosking, W.P. Crook, Thomas Bowden). All three groups resented the privileged status accorded the Anglicans, and the haughty Scott was the worst possible salesman for such a set-up. He was persistently attacked in the liberal press (the *Australian* and the *Monitor*) and did not even get on with his own clergy.[60]

Yet there are several points to be made in defence of Scott and the Anglicans generally. Their vision was flawed, and rightly thwarted, but their intentions were honourable. At heart, they had the interests of children in mind.[61] They had done most of the vital work in the colony's first few decades and, even after 1829, maintained a dominant share of responsibility for educating the colony's children. The cause was close to the heart of William Grant Broughton, Scott's successor,[62] and to that of an exceptionally talented teacher and headmaster, William Timothy Cape (1806–63), whose stellar career in Sydney spanned the period 1823–56. He had been intended by his parents for the Anglican ministry, but found his true calling as an educationalist. At one stage in the late 1820s, when a number of public school teachers from rural areas were brought to Sydney for training, Cape was given charge of them, though barely over twenty himself. For more than thirty years he taught many of the boys who would grow up to shape Australia's future. Cape has been justly described as 'the best known and best beloved of Australia's early teachers'.[63]

So, the Anglican contribution to education continued. But increasingly it was a *shared* contribution alongside the other denominations. Governor Richard Bourke's seminal Church Act of 1836 did away forever with the possibility of institutionalised favouritism. In due course, all four main denominations (Anglican, Catholic, Presbyterian and Methodist) received government support – including funding for their schools – on roughly equitable terms. In effect it was a pound-for-pound subsidy for private sources of school income,[64] designed to 'subsidise genuine religious effort in the colony'.[65] The impact was profound, in both the short and longer terms. The numbers of schools and clergy increased rapidly; indeed, at first they increased faster than the population. This happened across all denominations, and not only in New South Wales but in the other colonies as well.[66]

As we shall see, there were ongoing sectarian rivalries. But all the Churches – before and after 1836 – deserve credit for the effort they made. Even their bickering, fierce and ugly at times, was proof of their passion and commitment. And although they differed stridently on some issues of theology, they had always agreed on the basic moral values to be taught in schools. In the words of Michael Hogan, these encompassed 'a respect for authority, a hierarchy of status, and a conformity to a code of conduct … [of] honesty, industry and chastity'.[67] I would add sobriety and frugality as well. It sounds old-fashioned, but would anyone seriously suggest it ought to have been different, given the social mores of the time?

### The evolution of the 'dual' system

After the passing of the New South Wales Church Act of 1836, and equivalent legislation in Van Diemen's Land and South Australia, denominational Church schools multiplied. This ensured that the children who went to them got a basic religious education. But there was a major practical problem: government funding did not keep pace with the growth in population. Increasingly, the Churches were forced to rely on financial support from their flocks. Some denominations fared better than others in that regard: supposedly tight-fisted Presbyterians proved much more generous than Anglicans, for instance.[68] But even with such support, the Churches still could not supply nearly enough schools to educate all children – especially in rural areas.

It soon became evident that the colonial governments would need to establish schools of their own, at which, ideally, children of all denominations would be taught together. But a key question then arose: what form of the Christian religion would they hear about? Successive governors of New South Wales reasonably advocated a 'non-denominational' system – Governor Richard Bourke's proposal was based on the Irish model, Governor George Gipps' on that of the British and Foreign School Society. In effect, each proposed 'combin[ing] secular and religious schooling'.[69] But Bourke faced trenchant opposition from the Anglican Church[70] and Gipps from both the Anglican *and* Catholic Churches.[71]

Eventually, in 1848, the colonial government of New South Wales compromised. It set up a so-called dual system. Denominational Church schools would continue to be supported financially. But the government would also fund its own national schools, at which the Christian religion would be taught on a non-denominational basis, along the lines of the Irish model. Separate boards would administer each system.[72]

When Victoria became a separate colony in 1851, and Queensland in 1859, each inherited the dual system. Tasmania also adopted it.[73] In this period, the only colony that did away with State aid was South Australia, in 1851. But South Australia – the Paradise of Dissent (see Chapter 4) – was a special case. The Protestant Non-conformists who dominated its affairs put their faith in the voluntary principle – naïvely, I would argue, but for honourable *religious* reasons. The system of national schools they set up was not religion-free; on the contrary, it was 'based on the Christian religion, apart from all theological and controversial differences on discipline and doctrine'. Teachers regularly read out passages from the Bible.[74]

### The education debates and their aftermath

We now come to a pivotal period in Australian history as regards religion: the 'education debates'. The Churches' collective failure to strike a reasonable compromise – with colonial governments and between themselves – has had lasting, unintended consequences.

It is vital to understand the main issues at stake and the context in which the debates took place. For a start, individual churchmen were not motivated by financial self-interest. There were two aspects to State aid. The first was payment of clergy's salaries by the colonial governments. Rightly, in my view, this was phased out. Indeed, the Churches did not put up much of a fight over that issue.[75] The intense arguments were about continued government funding and supervision of Church schools, and the religious curriculum at national schools.

Few maintained that the status quo was satisfactory. Under the dual system, there had been significant growth in the number of Catholic schools. In some urban areas, where the government, the Anglicans and the Non-conformists also ran schools, there was wasteful duplication. But, across the board, especially in rural and regional areas, the Anglican system had not kept pace with demand. Nor had the national system. Too many teachers were unqualified and too many colonial children were still not getting an education. To give the flavour: in Victoria, in the mid-1860s, less than 60 per cent of children between the ages of five and sixteen were attending school.[76] The situation was worst in New South Wales, and Henry Parkes' Public Schools Act of 1866 was directed at the problem. Laudably, it involved a substantial injection of funds – for the building of new national schools in areas not already serviced, and for the payment of qualified teachers to staff them. State aid to Church schools would continue.[77] So, also, would religious instruction in national schools.

Henry Parkes is too often held up as a champion of secular education. In fact, he never opposed religious instruction *per se*. As his principal biographer, A.W. Martin, was at pains to stress, 'Parkes genuinely believed in the moral and social efficacy of Christian training.'[78] The form of 'common Christianity' taught after 1866 in national schools in New South Wales was more comprehensive than it had been previously.[79]

It was at this point that the Churches began to make serious errors of judgment. The Catholic and Anglican Churches erred in their over-the-top opposition to Parkes' reforms in New South Wales. Both complained bitterly that the national and denominational systems were now to be supervised by one body, the Board of Education. The Catholics had an additional objection: that the brand of Christianity to be taught in national schools would be too Protestant in flavour. Some Anglicans thought it would be too wishy-washy. There was 'an ecclesiastical storm'[80] but the Act passed regardless. So it should have. In the ensuing decade, the number of national schools in New South Wales rose sharply, from 259 to 892.[81]

The Anglican Church made some even more serious mistakes. Instead of bolstering or at least preserving its own system of parish schools, it allowed that system to disintegrate. It declined to attempt the private fund-raising that would have been necessary to preserve the system, hoping complacently that the new national schools could be effectively Protestantised. In the decade after 1866 the number of Church schools in New South Wales fell from 310 to 181 – and most of those remaining were Catholic.[82] Across all the colonies, the relatively few good schools that the Anglicans kept up were for the sons and daughters of the wealthy. Most unforgivably of all, too many Anglican schools were neglecting *religious* education. This was glumly admitted by no less a figure than the Anglican Bishop of Melbourne, Charles Perry. In a letter to clergymen in 1865, Perry wrote: 'I have been painfully impressed with the conviction that the Church is guilty of a great neglect of duty in not providing as it ought, for the religious instruction and Christian training of the pupils in its Common Schools.'[83]

It was against this background that the education debates were conducted. The combatants lined up as follows.

The Catholic Church's position was straightforward and its spokesmen implacable. Catholic schools were deserving of financial support by the State, but the State should not interfere in the running of them. As for public schools, the Church wanted nothing to do with them, since in its mind the very notion of education was inseparable from doctrinal instruction. Catholicism was not open to inclusion in any common form of Christianity that might be taught in public schools.

Protestant leaders were divided. Generally speaking, the Presbyterians and Non-conformists supported, or did not oppose, the withdrawal of State aid from *all* Church schools. (As we saw in South Australia, a lot of them had long favoured the voluntary principle.) Many Anglicans, on the other hand, still expected to receive State aid. There were also differences of opinion on the teaching of common-form Christianity at public schools. Presbyterians and Non-conformists mostly fell in with the idea, as did some Anglicans, but other influential Anglicans opposed it with vehemence.

Protestants were united on only one thing: their distrust of the Roman Catholic Church. Some held out a vague hope that the abolition of State aid would cause the Catholic school system to collapse. It was in the 1860s, or thereabouts, that an iron law was laid down in this country. Geoffrey Blainey has called it the 'First Commandment of Australian Protestantism' and it was followed, more or less assiduously, for a century: 'Do not allow the public purse to subsidise private schools because such schools are mostly Catholic.'[84] It has even been suggested that 'the founding of state schools was specifically designed to justify the withdrawal of state aid to Catholic education'.[85]

I would not go that far. The principal reason for the founding of State schools was to ensure that all Australian children received an education. And, in the circumstances, since the population was growing rapidly and this was before the days of income tax, this probably necessitated the end of State aid to religious schools. The colonial governments would have been stretched to fund both systems adequately – though, for a long time, Henry Parkes in New South Wales was prepared to try. As for secondary motives, anti-Catholicism played a part on the Protestant side. But – and this is crucial – the purpose of the exercise was *not* to attack or undermine the overall cause of religion.[86] That is a 21st-century invention. At the time, 'few people maintained that religion was wrong or religious teaching undesirable'.[87] State schools were not made secular because most Australians felt hostility towards religion, or were indifferent about it, or did not want their children exposed to it. The difficulty was that, because so many people took religion seriously, it was hard to reach a consensus on important and delicate issues. In the end, secularism won by default.

This is such a crucial point that I will flesh it out a little through the personal experience of a remarkable man. In 1866, a youngish politician named George Higinbotham was appointed by the Victorian Government to try to solve the religious difficulty facing the colony's schools. He headed a Royal Commission that investigated all aspects of the matter and, in the following year, reported back to parliament.

Higinbotham (1826–92) would become one of the most distinguished statesmen of the latter nineteenth century. Of Irish heritage and a barrister by profession, he had immigrated to Melbourne in 1853 and worked for a time as both a lawyer and a journalist. At the age of thirty-five he was elected to the Victorian Parliament and, in a long career, served in various ministerial capacities, including as attorney-general. In later life he was appointed as a justice (ultimately chief justice) of the colony's Supreme Court.

Higinbotham was a cultivated yet forthright person whose views did not please everyone. A rough twentieth-century equivalent would be Gough Whitlam. Politically, he was a progressive free-trader: his sympathies lay with the merchant and working classes and disenfranchised women, rather than with the wealthy pastoralists or the city elites. Some dubbed him the 'red radical'. But everyone acknowledged his intellect, his integrity, his personal courtesy – and his superb oratory. When Higinbotham died, all realised that a unique individual had passed away. The Victorian Premier, William Shiels, assessed him Australia's 'noblest if not its greatest man'.[88]

The key to Higinbotham was his profound faith. Biographer Gwyneth Dow adjudged that 'the essence of the man [was] to be found in his religious nature'.[89] He belonged to the Church of England, and, although a liberal ecumenicist, was 'never tempted by the prevailing mood of agnosticism or scepticism'.[90] He once wrote of God as his 'secure and indestructible abode'. God, for him, was 'revealed to the intellect in every minute movement of matter, and in all the phenomena of this vast Universe'.[91]

But Higinbotham was no mere deist. He added in the same passage:

God [is] revealed anew to the intellect, and also to the responsive
human heart, as the Father, the Friend, the Guide, and the Support
of our race, and every member of it, in the simple but profound
philosophy, and also in the sublimest life, of Jesus of Nazareth, the
Light of the World.[92]

Now, was such a man likely to desire the total secularisation of Victorian schools? Of course not. Higinbotham wanted to find a compromise solution. He did not oppose the principle of State aid to religious schools. But he accepted that the government's resources were not unlimited and, almost certainly, would have to be reallocated. For the present they were most needed to fund national schools: it was plainly unacceptable that almost half of Victoria's children did not get any formal education.

But, equally, Higinbotham did not want to strip the State system of any and all religious content. To the contrary, that prospect horrified him:

Any attempt on the part of the Legislature to separate itself from
religion, to disown religion in its acts – to adopt … the principle that
the State has nothing to do with religion except not to notice it – will

be altogether a failure. When I speak of religion, in a country like this … I speak of it … to mean … the religion which recognises the religious sentiment of all without the fanaticism of the sects.[93]

Similar views were held by three of Higinbotham's Protestant colleagues on the Royal Commission. J.E. Bromby, Alexander Morrison and James Corrigan were the headmasters of Melbourne Grammar School (Anglican), Scotch College (Presbyterian) and Wesley College (Methodist) respectively.[94] All believed, like Higinbotham, that 'moral training and religious education were inseparably linked, that religion held a central place in the child's education, and therefore that the state could not interest itself in education without religion'.[95] Were parents screaming for godless schools? Again, the answer is 'No'. The tenor of the evidence given to the commission was that Victorian parents either actively desired some religious instruction in public schools, or at least were prepared to accept it.[96]

The stage seemed set, then, for a compromise solution. What went wrong? The basic problem was that the Churches – and to a lesser extent the Royal Commissioners – could not agree on key points. The Catholic Church was of no help: Catholics invited onto the Commission refused to serve, and Bishop J.A. Goold, the senior Catholic in Victoria, refused to give evidence before it.[97] The Anglican Church, in the person of its senior cleric in Victoria, Bishop Charles Perry, likewise spat the dummy. It would not countenance the proposed withdrawal of State aid, nor even the provision of aid with strings attached. It rejected any notion that common Christianity should or could be taught in national schools. In Perry's view, it was impossible 'that religious instruction … be separated from what is called a "Church"' – in other words, denominationalism.[98] Anything else led to the propagation merely of 'a sickly something',[99] 'the deism of educated infidels'.[100] (It is vital to note that, unlike Perry, both Higinbotham and Bromby were liberal Anglicans.) The Non-conformists agreed that State aid should go, but split on other issues. Who would provide religious instruction in public schools: teachers or visiting clerics? What would be the content of religious teaching? What use would be made of the Bible?

In its final report, delivered in 1867, the commission urged a compromise. It recommended that State aid to religious schools be withdrawn, but that public schools be permitted to provide 'religious education', along lines to be determined by elected local committees.

Religious education as defined in the report was, admittedly, a fairly amorphous concept:

> The drawing out, in the mind of the child, of the sense of its relation to God, and of the duties which flow from that relation – the inculcation, by words as well as the example of the teacher, of a reverent and truthful tone of thought, feeling and expression – and the enforcement, by gentle yet constant pressure, of cheerful obedience and habits of discipline.[101]

The commission contrasted such education with, on the one hand, 'the process of imparting mere intellectual knowledge' (which might include, legitimately, religious knowledge) and, on the other hand, 'instruction in dogmatic or sectarian theories'. The latter should not be attempted in State schools – even though, in the commission's view, it was an essential part of any child's education.

The proposal was no one's ideal, but, with goodwill on all sides, it could have been made to work. Most of the Protestant Churches were broadly in favour, and even secularists (still a small minority) were prepared to live with it.[102] But opposition from the Catholic and Anglican hierarchies was unflinching.

In the event, the Victorian Parliament never voted on the Bill submitted to it, which was based on the commission's report. Higinbotham withdrew the Bill from its consideration. In ensuing years, he became, with extreme reluctance, a supporter of secular public education as the lesser of two evils. As he saw things – perhaps too pessimistically – the alternative was that many Victorian children would continue to get no education at all. He was appalled by the self-interest of the Anglican and Catholic Churches; to his eyes they presented a 'melancholy spectacle'.[103]

Just five years later, in 1872, Victoria enacted legislation for the withdrawal of State aid from all religious schools, and the establishment of a completely secular system of compulsory public education. The Catholic Church was horrified by the withdrawal of State aid, but by then it was powerless: the education issue had brought down the government of Charles Gavan Duffy, a liberal Catholic, in 1871.[104] In 1875 similar legislation was enacted in South Australia and Queensland.[105]

The passing of the Public Instruction Act of 1880 in New South Wales was a watershed. Henry Parkes was responsible for it, but it is vital to remember that he introduced it after a change of heart: for many years he had favoured retention of his 1866 compromise, which maintained State aid for religious schools and a substantial amount of religious instruction in national schools.[106] Parkes' hand was forced, or so he asserted, by strength of Protestant public opinion.

Throughout the 1870s there had been virulent criticism of national schools by spokesmen for the Catholic Church. The Archbishop of Sydney, Roger Bede Vaughan, famously denounced them as being 'seed plots of future immorality, infidelity, and lawlessness'.[107] Understandably, this angered many people who had attended such schools and emerged from them as decent citizens. An equable young lawyer named Edmund Barton – who would become, a generation later, the first prime minister of Australia – was one who spoke out.[108] There was a Protestant backlash against State aid. By this time, at least in New South Wales, most Anglicans had formed the view that they could afford to do without it: it was more important to stop the Catholics from getting it. Even if the Anglican school system continued to fall away, they reasoned, Protestant religious instruction for the young could be provided adequately in the home, in Sunday schools, and, to an extent, in national schools. (In the event, Parkes did not go as far as the legislators in Victoria, South Australia and Queensland: he kept provision for a substantial amount of religious instruction in national schools.[109])

In retrospect, the Anglicans miscalculated. Their optimism may have been warranted in the short term – but not in the medium to long term. Here, I must confess to sympathy and admiration for an old-school Anglican, Bishop Frederic Barker (1808–82), the man after whom Sydney's Barker College is named. Barker was not a crude sectarian, but he believed in his Anglican parish schools and regretted the loss of State aid. Above all, 'he could not bring himself sufficiently to trust the ... State'.[110]

He was right. Even dogmatists such as Perry and Vaughan – who, by their intransigence and exaggerations, harmed the general cause of religion – were not entirely wrong. The twentieth century proved that trust in the State *was* misplaced. As Roger C. Thompson has put it, the schools legislation of the 1860s and 1870s 'sowed future seeds of secularist indifference to Christianity'.[111]

There were two short-term consequences of the schools legislation passed in the period 1870–80, both deleterious to the cause of religion. It was not immediately obvious that religion had been dealt a mighty blow, for reasons to which I will come. But the early warning signs were there. Ironically, in Victoria, both the Catholic and Anglican Churches were soon railing against the 'infamous tyranny'[112] resulting from the 1872 Act – a tyranny they had largely brought about by their own pigheadedness.

First, State schools became largely secular. It would not be right to say that, after 1880, Australian State schools became entirely religion-free. Nor that, across all the six colonies, 'school textbooks were stripped of their religious content'.[113] That did happen in Victoria – 'so comprehensive was the … cull that even literary works mentioning God or Jesus were purged'[114] – and in South Australia and Queensland religious instruction was severely curtailed.

But the measures were less drastic in other colonies. In New South Wales and Tasmania, religion remained on the agenda: class teachers were still permitted to give general, non-denominational instruction and clergy could visit once a week.[115] And, as we saw at the outset of this chapter, State aid was not abolished in Western Australia until the mid-1890s, when John Forrest's will to resist was finally overwhelmed.

A clear trend had set in, however. In New South Wales, Bishop Barry's dream of a 'Christianised state system'[116] came to nothing. In time, across the country – admittedly in fits and starts – the various education departments played things more and more safely. They came to teach 'a history, an ethics, and a religion that were so vague and pallid as not to encourage the interest of boys and girls in the great questions of life'.[117] And that was in States where such questions could be posed at all.

The second major consequence of the education debates was that the Protestant Churches closed most of their parish schools. I have mentioned the vision of Bishop Barker (Barry's predecessor in New South Wales) as regards the small Anglican parish schools. He loved them and wanted to retain them. But the withdrawal of State aid soon killed most of them off – the ones, that is, that had not been closed before 1880. It was the same for the Anglicans and the other Protestant denominations in the other colonies. Within a generation, the surviving Protestant schools catered mostly for parents of the middle class who could afford to pay for them. Many were wonderful schools, and some even took religion seriously, but relatively few Australian children went to them.

Australia's children did not become godless overnight. For many decades, the changes made to the school system were masked or offset by other factors. Most importantly, the community at large remained broadly committed to Christianity, so religious parents kept educating their children at home. And there were several other factors at play specifically related to education. I will deal with them in descending order of importance.

### The Catholic school system

After the withdrawal of State aid, the Catholic Church did not give in. Instead it staffed its schools with nuns, priests and brothers vowed to poverty, many of whom were immigrants from Ireland.[118] The system flourished, in spite of, or perhaps because of, 'a developing Protestant accord'.[119] I agree with Edmund Campion that, after about 1880, this system became 'the single most distinctive feature of Australian Catholicism'.[120] More than that, low-fee Catholic schools, staffed by priests and nuns, became an intrinsic and indispensable part of the Australian social contract. Literally millions of Australian citizens spent their formative years in these schools, from prime ministers down. Only in the 1970s did the Protestant Churches begin the task of creating a comparable system of low-fee religious schools.

In the decades after 1880, and well into the twentieth century, a strange trend developed. Protestant children, even those of highly religious parents, went to increasingly secular schools. Catholic children, even those of parents who were not particularly religious, 'found themselves drawn into the [Catholic] network'.[121] The Church convinced many parents that *not* to utilise the Church's schools was of itself a serious sin.[122] And within Catholic schools, even greater emphasis was placed on religion than had been the case under the old system.[123] In the words of the formidable long-time archbishop of Melbourne, Daniel Mannix, the Catholic school became the 'antechamber of the Church'.[124]

The vast network of Australian Catholic schools survives to this day, and has played a significant role in ameliorating the effects of secularisation. The Church never stopped fighting for the reinstatement of State aid – after 1955, it was one of the chief goals of the DLP – and it finally won the battle in the 1960s, almost a century after having first lost it. Ironically, in the political arena, the two men chiefly responsible for achieving the breakthrough were Protestants: on the Coalition side, Sir Robert Menzies (a Presbyterian) and, on the Labor side, Gough Whitlam (a lapsed Anglican).

## The Sunday school system

Among Protestant children, this was the most important factor operating against secularisation (aside from parenting). After the withdrawal of State aid in the 1870s and 1880s, all the Protestant Churches greatly expanded their Sunday school operations. Before then these schools had catered mainly for working-class children not otherwise reached by the Churches. Thereafter they catered for everybody and became, in time, 'venerable institutions'.[125] Rates of attendance were very high until the 1960s; even a great many non-religious Protestant parents sent their children to Sunday school, at least in their early primary school years. I was one such child myself.

## New Protestant schools

We have seen that, after the withdrawal of State aid, many Protestant schools were closed. The process was offset to a degree by the opening of new schools. This took time and money – apart from the cost of land and buildings, teachers at Protestant schools had to be paid – but gradually it happened. In Sydney, for instance, the Anglican Church established such notable boys' schools as Shore (1889), Barker (1890), Trinity (1913) and Cranbrook (1918); the Presbyterian Church opened The Scots College in 1893 and Knox Grammar in 1924. There were equivalents for girls, such as (in Sydney) the Wesleyan Ladies College at Burwood (1886), SCEGGS at Darlinghurst (1895), and the Presbyterian Ladies' Colleges at Croydon (1891) and Pymble (1916).

Some of these schools, as I have noted, came over time to cater for the wealthy. Certainly, most of the venerable old schools that *survived* the withdrawal of State aid were in that category. (Across the colonies, I have in mind the likes of King's and Newington in Sydney; Scotch College, Melbourne Grammar and Wesley College in Melbourne; Geelong Grammar; St Peter's College in Adelaide; and Bishop Hale's School in Perth.) But at least some of the newer Protestant schools – for both boys and girls – were accessible to parents of more modest means.

For much of the twentieth century, albeit with a few exceptions at the very apex of the system, Protestant school fees were not unreasonable. Very few children from the working class attended these schools, but many middle-class children did, especially at the secondary stage. Their parents were prepared and able to make the financial sacrifice. It may be true, as Russel Ward once sniped, that 'in practice boys and girls learnt to set more by "good form" and "right thinking" than by the example of the Judean carpenter'.[126] Nevertheless, Christianity was kept on their radar.

It is only in the last generation that some private school fees have become absurdly high (as much as $30,000 per annum per child). This has resulted in too many once-accessible Protestant schools being put out of the reach of middle-class parents. That is one reason why the low-fee independent schools have become increasingly popular – and why, since the 1970s, they have operated as another modest check on secularisation.

### Relaxation of secular restrictions in State schools

After Federation, as a result of lobbying by the Protestant Churches, the formal bans in some States on religious instruction were gradually lifted or eased. In Queensland, a referendum was held in conjunction with the 1910 federal election on the question of Bible-reading in State schools. 'Yes' won by 74,228 votes to 56,681, with the result that the word 'secular' was removed from the Queensland Education Act.[127] Victoria finally followed suit in 1950, allowing religious instruction in class time by visiting clergy or their delegates. Indeed, by 1960, all States allowed some right of entry to religious instructors.[128] By then, however, Scripture classes were largely token – or heading that way.

### University colleges

From the beginning, universities in the Australian colonies were secular institutions – run and funded by the State rather than the Churches. Sydney University was founded on that basis in 1850 and Melbourne University in 1853.[129] The Churches were not amused, and managed to win certain concessions – chief among them the right to establish, at their own expense, residential colleges on campuses at which religious instruction could be provided.

Most Australian universities followed this model, and, ever since, despite their elite status, these institutions have been moderately helpful for the cause of religion.[130] Not a few future Australian prime ministers had their views shaped there: Menzies, McMahon, Whitlam, Rudd, Abbott. The Australian Student Christian Movement, mentioned in Chapter 5, has been another influence at universities working against secularisation. So, too, the Australian Fellowship of Evangelical Students.

## The tipping points

None of these ameliorating factors has been sufficient, in the long term, to halt the Secular Juggernaut. Sometime in the 1960s things began to go awry; by 1990, or thereabouts, the process was complete. A perfect storm of factors combined to take us to where we are today. Again, I will address each factor in descending order of importance.

### The near-total secularisation of State schools

This, undoubtedly, has been the critical factor. Over the course of roughly a century, following the withdrawal of State aid, State schools became, on the whole, increasingly secular. But it has only been in the last two generations – Scripture classes notwithstanding – that they became almost totally secular. The change was as much cultural as formal. In the words of Christian author Hugh Jackson, 'through to the sixties, teachers in government primary schools were charged with the responsibility of inculcating in children moral principles drawn from the Christian religion'.[131] As religious teaching went, this may have been vague and pallid, but it was something. From the 1970s onwards, even this faded away.

I am not suggesting that State schools became ethical wastelands. My point is that the moral principles that (most) government school teachers continued to inculcate became divorced from their Judaeo-Christian roots. Why? Because, as time went on, fewer and fewer teachers had themselves been raised in that tradition. And a significant minority were (and are) actively hostile towards it. In 1971, my Third Class teacher at a State primary school had us recite the Lord's Prayer every morning. Today that would be inconceivable; perhaps illegal.

Religious knowledge is no longer conveyed to many students adequately or at all. This, it is crucial to stress, need not have happened. Indeed, as Marion Maddox has demonstrated, a series of expert reports in the 1970s recommended that it not be permitted to happen. The Overton Report (1971) in Tasmania, the Steinle Report (1973) in South Australia, the Russell Report (1974) in Victoria, the Nott Report (1977) in Western Australia, the Rawlinson Report (1980) in New South Wales – the thrust of them all was that the teaching of 'General Religious Education' should be beefed up in State schools. It should be taught as a fully fledged academic subject, by qualified teachers, as part of the general curriculum. *It should be tested.*[132]

Tragically, all these reports were ignored. Both militant Christians and militant secularists raised Hell; State governments put the matter into the 'too hard' basket. Ever since, for the last thirty or forty years, millions of Australian children have grown up not learning about religion.

## The collapse of the Sunday school system

At around the same time – the late 1960s and early 1970s – levels of attendance at Protestant Sunday schools and youth groups began to drop sharply across the country.[133] The reasons why this happened are unclear, but the long-term effects are not. Tom Frame rates the decline of the Sunday school system in Australia as one of the main reasons for secularisation – most children did not find any alternative source of religious enlightenment, and 'churchgoing became alien to them'.[134]

## Protestant tokenism

I have already remarked upon the tendency towards religious tokenism in Protestant schools – especially those catering for the upper-middle class. Of course, there have always been honourable exceptions. But, by the late 1960s, children at Protestant schools fared little or no better on tests of religious knowledge than children at State schools.[135] Nor were their levels of professed belief or churchgoing appreciably higher.[136] In 1971 Ronald Conway remarked that male adolescents exhibited 'profound indifference ... to religious, altruistic, or aesthetic questions'; this was so 'even among a great many students from private schools'.[137] I would argue that private school students today do, in the main, have a reasonable appreciation of altruistic and aesthetic questions. But their indifference to religion is as marked as ever.

The Protestant Churches have largely failed to capitalise – in an evangelistic sense – on the reintroduction of State aid. Their schools, especially at the upper end of the spectrum, have become businesses first, vocational factories second and social clubs third. Most provide a good secular education. But they are a very long way from being Church antechambers. And it must be conceded that, despite the sky-high fees, many parents want it that way. Market forces have triumphed.

## The changed character of Catholic schools

Even Australia's Catholic schools – while still the most conscientious about religion – are not as religious as they once were. Apart from the secularisation of society as a whole, which has affected Catholicism along with all other branches of Christianity, a crucial factor has been change in the composition of teaching staffs. In 1950, a staggering 95 per cent of the teachers at Catholic schools were nuns, brothers and priests. By 1984 the figure was down to 10 per cent,[138] and now it is lower still.

The vast majority of teachers today in Catholic schools were trained at secular universities and colleges. While, in a strictly technical sense, this has probably improved the overall standard of instruction (and, in the case of male teachers, reduced the risks of sexual abuse), the consequences for religion must have been negative.

Reforming Australia's education system should be part of any attempt to slow down the Secular Juggernaut. I will make some suggestions in Chapter 10. But schools are far from the only challenge. Up to a point, they are a symptom of secularisation – not a cause. Let us turn to other factors that have affected not only children, but Australian society as a whole.

# CHAPTER 7

# War and nationalism

The Christian church has been powerfully damaged by letting itself be confused with love of country and the making of great wars.

Peter Hitchens, *The Rage Against God*

As a Christian who is partly Jewish, and who ... spent five years behind the racists' barbed wire, I weep for the folly of Australia's leaders. They have learnt little from history: for them, it seems, the struggles of mankind begin and end with the framework of American-style diplomacy – beyond which nothing else matters.

Bernard Durrant, letter to *The Australian*, 4 May 1965, on the Vietnam War

In early 2003, as the US-led Coalition of the Willing prepared to launch its invasion of Iraq, Christian leaders around the world did their best to prevent a tragedy from unfolding.[1] Both Pope John Paul II[2] and the Archbishop of Canterbury voiced strong opposition. On 21 February 2003, the Executive Committee of the World Council of Churches declared that 'war against Iraq would be immoral, unwise, and in breach of the principles of the United Nations Charter'.[3]

In Australia, very few[4] mainline Church bodies were in favour. Yet the Howard Government pressed ahead regardless. It was unquestioning in its support of the Bush Administration, deterred not a whit by ecclesiastical (or secular) warnings. A disastrous[5] war duly ensued.

The whole episode was a perfect illustration of the waning power of the Churches. Once upon a time, it would have been highly problematic for a Coalition government in Australia to flout their near-unanimous admonitions – especially as regards so grave a matter as the waging of war.

Yet it must be said that this was another instance – like education – in which the Churches largely had themselves to blame. Over the previous century, in Australia and overseas, they had undermined their own collective credibility on the most important public policy issue of all.

In this chapter I shall argue that war and its poisonous corollary, nationalism, have been major causes of secularisation since 1914. Each of the two big drops in levels of religious belief in Australia was preceded by our involvement in an utterly horrendous war: respectively, World War One (1914–18) and Vietnam (1962–72). It was no coincidence that the Churches, for the most part, strongly supported our role in both.

Census statistics are a raw guide only: while the religion with which people identify is recorded, the census does not measure the extent of their involvement or commitment. Even so, the pattern is clear enough. In 1911, identification with Christianity was almost total. By 1933, 13 per cent of Australians declined to specify any religion.[6] Even more tellingly, in the years immediately after World War One, church attendance fell.[7] The 1920s have been described as a 'mean decade', an 'uncertain, cautious and shabby era',[8] and there is plenty of evidence that a good many people were disillusioned. At the 1922 federal election, only 58 per cent of eligible voters bothered to cast a ballot.[9] The nation, in Joan Beaumont's sad expression, was 'broken'.[10]

The second and much bigger big drop in religious belief in Australia began in the early 1970s. Between the censuses of 1971 and 1981 there was a large rise in the percentage of respondents who nominated 'No religion' or who declined to answer the question. That trend has continued, more or less inexorably, ever since. Was the initial cause related to Vietnam? No doubt there were several factors in the mix, but Vietnam was one of them. It was 'the great catalyst for change in Australia',[11] and arguably, hit institutional religion even harder than had World War One. It presaged another sharp decline in respect for authority, especially among the young.

I expect that some readers will need a lot of convincing on this point. One possible objection is that war has been a fact of human life for millennia, and religion still survived. That is true enough, though the Old Testament itself records periods in Jewish history when the ravages of war caused many people to question God. (See, for example, the Book of Lamentations, written in the aftermath of the Babylonians' destruction of Jerusalem in 586 BC.) In any event, what we are here considering is a particular period in human history (the twentieth and early twenty-first centuries) and the impact of war on a particular religious society (Christian Australia). One aspect of our situation is truly unprecedented: since 1945, all Australians, along with the rest of humanity, have had to live with the existential threat of nuclear annihilation. That threat has not gone away.

Before making my case in further detail, it is as well to scotch certain myths about war in general and the wars of the twentieth century in particular. These myths are too frequently propagated by people on both sides of the religion debate.

## A secular myth: religion causes most of the conflict in the world[12]

Among the so-called New Atheists, this is a common theme. The late Christopher Hitchens was a particularly strident advocate of it. Phillip Adams once wrote: 'More than 160 million people died during the twentieth century's wars and genocides and many, if not most of these conflicts were either triggered or intensified by religious intolerance.'[13]

Adams' adroit use of language left some wriggle-room. But basically this argument is bogus.[14] I have read no better refutation of it than that proffered by Karen Armstrong, a former Catholic nun, in her immensely wise book *Fields of Blood*.[15] In essence, she points out that although some wars are started by proponents of religion *for religious reasons*, most are not. The seminal wars of the twentieth century were certainly not wars of that sort.

The same point has been made by other writers, including Christopher Hitchens' brother, the anti-war Christian conservative Peter Hitchens. 'The only general lesson,' he concludes, 'is that man is inclined to make war on man when he thinks it will gain him power or wealth or land.'[16]

World War One was fought for all three of those reasons. As for World War Two, the Cold War, and the Korean and Vietnam Wars, the Nazis were essentially pagan and the Soviets, the North Koreans and the North Vietnamese were committed atheists. So were the Chinese Communists. There is a much better case that these wars were caused by *irreligion* than the other way around.

Rightly or wrongly, Australia fought in all the major wars of the twentieth century, and in Iraq.[17] In each case we did so for geopolitical reasons. Iraq aside, the Australian Government was not to blame for *starting* these wars – still less the Australian Churches. We participated because our major ally (Britain or the USA) wanted us to participate. A kind of self-interested loyalty, not religion, was the key motivating factor. (I hasten to add that the Pacific War of 1941–45 had another dimension: many Australians genuinely and reasonably feared invasion by the Japanese.)

## A religious myth: war can be a holy and even glorious thing

So, the wars of the twentieth century in which Australia participated were not caused by religion. But nor, I would argue, were they ennobled by religion. As we shall see, the Australian Churches, like many Australian politicians, repeatedly attempted to justify them on a Christian basis. But this proved a massive and tragic mistake. The sanctioning of large-scale destructive violence as a solution to conflict between sophisticated nation-states had become, by 1914, close to untenable on orthodox theological grounds.

In the Christian tradition there are only two valid approaches to war: pacifism and the 'just war' doctrine.[18] The latter was a thirteenth-century invention of St Thomas Aquinas, who built on certain ruminations of St Augustine 900 years earlier. The Catholic Church has since refined the doctrine substantially: various criteria have been laid down in respect of just entry into a war (*jus ad bellum*), just conduct by combatants once a war has begun (*jus in bello*) and just terms of peace after a war has ended (*jus post bellum*). Needless to say, these are always honoured in the breach. Once the dogs of war are unleashed, the vilest human sins are inevitable. Pacifism, for all its apparent impossibility, comes much closer to the examples of Jesus and the pre-Constantine Christian Church.[19] It cannot be emphasised enough that Jesus eschewed physical violence to the very end, and – an unambiguous historical fact – the early Christians did too, for the best part of 300 years. On one view, 'nonviolence is constitutive of what it means to be a disciple of Jesus' – but one must be prepared to suffer and die for it.[20]

For good reasons, neither World War One nor the Vietnam War has many wholehearted defenders nowadays – secular or religious. But there are still a few.[21] A small cohort of Australian Christians point with pride to the role played by the Australian Light Horsemen in fighting against Ottoman forces in the Holy Land from 1916 to 1918. The highlight was the recapture of Jerusalem by British Empire forces under General Edmund Allenby, in November–December 1917. (Around 200 fallen Australian servicemen were buried in the Holy City, near the Mount of Olives.[22]) One would not wish to deny the valour of these soldiers, but their feats, however symbolic, scarcely made up for the calamity of the Great War.

At least the story of the Light Horse is true. An amazingly common misconception is that World War Two was fought by the Allies to save the Jews from extermination by the Nazis. The truth is quite different. The Holocaust was a *consequence* of World War Two, of the fact that Germany was fighting on two fronts from early 1941 after the invasion of Russia, and, from late 1941, following the Americans' entry into the war in Europe, doomed to defeat. It was this confluence of circumstances that caused the Nazi high command to implement the Final Solution.[23] Less than a week after the bombing of Pearl Harbor, Joseph Goebbels wrote in his diary: 'With respect to the Jewish Question, the Führer has decided to make a clean sweep. The world war is here, and the annihilation of the Jews must be the necessary consequence.'[24]

Moreover, total war covers many sins.[25] The Nazis could not have perpetrated the Holocaust during peacetime. The situation was exacerbated after the Casablanca Conference of January 1943 by the Allies' insistence on unconditional surrender by the Axis powers. In the words of a leading American historian, James Carroll, this policy 'guaranteed that the war would last long enough for the genocide nearly to succeed'.[26]

At any rate, none of the Allied powers, at any stage, was motivated primarily or at all by concern for the Jews.[27] Most Western governments, including Australia's,[28] had been stingy in the 1930s in dealing with pleas by or on behalf of would-be Jewish refugees, desperate to escape Germany or Eastern Europe.[29] The Evian Conference of July 1938, convened to discuss the issue, was a dismal failure.[30] In the words, forty years later, of former US vice-president Walter Mondale: 'At stake at Evian were both human lives – and the decency and self-respect of the civilized world. If each nation at Evian had agreed on that day to take in 17,000 Jews at once, every Jew in the Reich could have been saved.'[31]

It is true that one effect of the Holocaust was the strengthening of the Zionist cause and the creation of the State of Israel in 1948 – a process in which Australia, through H.V. Evatt and others, played a noble part.[32] But it is vital to get the timeline straight. For religious defenders of World War Two, there is precious little comfort here. Mr Durrant, the Holocaust survivor and letter-writer to *The Australian* in 1965, whose words are quoted at the beginning of this chapter, seems to have understood these things much better than most people.

None of this means that the outcome of World Wars One and Two did not matter. Plainly, once the wars were being waged, it was essential that the Allies prevail or that peace be brokered on terms with which the

Allies could live. (The tragedy of the Allies' insistence on unconditional surrender during World War Two was that it effectively precluded the latter possibility.) And, as I have said, Australia's participation in the Pacific War was a different thing again: after the Japanese bombed Darwin on 19 February 1942, Australia was acting in self-defence.

It is also proper to acknowledge that war always gives rise to feats of individual courage and heroism. Naturally, and rightly, these are honoured. But it seems to me highly significant that Australia's most exalted war heroes have been non-combatants. Military aficionados apart, we do not dwell overmuch on the feats of those who killed efficiently. How many can you name? Instinctively, we look elsewhere. We hail, instead, the stretcher-bearers, the doctors, the nurses, the POWs, the repentant old Diggers,[33] the 'fuzzy-wuzzy angels' of New Guinea[34] – those who most conspicuously embodied the life-affirming virtues of love and compassion. John Simpson Kirkpatrick (1892–1915), for example, he who led that donkey at Gallipoli. Or Dr Edward 'Weary' Dunlop (1907–93), the saviour of so many sick and dying on the Burma–Thailand railway. Or Damien Parer (1912–44), the gallant cameraman of the Kokoda Track, who won a posthumous Academy Award for the footage he took.

General John Monash (1865–1931), the commander of the Australian Corps on the Western Front after May 1918, may be the exception who proves the rule. He *was* a soldier. Yet even Monash is best remembered for helping to *end* World War One, and for striving to protect the lives of his own troops. He is also vitally important in Australian history for a religious reason: in the words of Russel Ward, 'his life helps to explain why there is probably less anti-Semitism in Australia than in most other English-speaking countries'.[35] (Though, as Hans Mol observed, levels of anti-Semitism in Australia were still considerable until the 1960s.) Indeed, Monash's own life story is a fascinating religious case study. He was exposed at various stages of his life to both orthodox and cultural Judaism, and his personal beliefs oscillated. In old age, it appears that he settled on an amalgam of deism and traditional morality. (See Appendix A.)

The religious lives of both Weary Dunlop and Damien Parer are also of remarkable interest. In a nutshell, Dunlop was a fellow traveller with Christianity, a disciple of Christ rather than the Christian religion. (See Appendix A.) Parer was a devout Catholic – a daily communicant and a member of the Campion Society in Sydney. In camp he prayed on his knees every night. According to his friend Ron Maslyn Williams: 'When Damien did all that scrupulous work on his cameras, preparing them as a priest might the chalice, he wasn't doing it for himself, but for God. His faith was limitless.'[36]

Heroes and guiding lights aside, the central point remains. War as a whole is Hell, a shocking and degrading affront to the Christian vision. And patriotism is not the same thing as faith. At a bare minimum, on the Christian view of things, war should always be an absolute last resort, waged on rock-solid grounds. The lives of non-combatants should be respected. Any opportunity for peace should be explored; any peace struck should be fair and merciful. None of the major wars of the twentieth century, nor the Iraq War, came near to fulfilling these conditions. And among the many victims were the Christian Churches.

Of religion in England, Peter Hitchens has written:

> I think it safe to say that the two great victorious wars of the twentieth century did more damage to Christianity in my own country than any other single force. The churches were full before 1914, half-empty after 1919, and three-quarters empty after 1945.[37]

The story in Australia was not quite the same – but it was close enough. Let us look at what happened in its horrid, inexorable sequence.

## The 'martial spirit' in the colonies

The first thing to understand is that Australians were lambs for the slaughter when World War One broke out in August 1914. There was never any serious prospect that we would question the wisdom of the war, let alone break from Britain. Legally, it is doubtful whether Australia *could have* broken from Britain, at least not without undermining its status as a British dependency.[38] Labor prime minister Andrew Fisher had said as much in August 1911: 'If the Empire is at war the Commonwealth de facto is at war.'[39] True, on the same occasion, Fisher also insisted that it was 'for the Dominion parliaments to say how far they will actively participate in any war, and how they will dispose their forces'.[40] But he provoked a public outcry in saying even that.[41]

Even if the Christian Churches here had been minded to act as prophets of caution in 1914, they would have faced a huge challenge. As Alfred Deakin wrote approvingly on the eve of Federation, in his book *The Federal Story*: 'The martial spirit is strong in all the colonies.'[42] During the nineteenth century Australian troops had proudly fought for Britain in various foreign engagements: the Maori Wars in New Zealand in the 1840s; Crimea in 1853–56; the Sudan in 1885. The 'crimson thread of kinship' – Henry Parkes' phrase to connote local loyalty to the British Empire – almost always took precedence over faith or ethics. A common catchcry of the age was, in fact, shamelessly amoral: 'The Empire right or wrong.'[43]

The Boer War of 1899–1902, in which Australia also participated, *did* have a few local opponents. But voices from the institutional Churches were not notable among them, despite the dubious nature of Britain's cause.[44] (The Boer War, in essence, was about which foreign Protestant power – the British or the Dutch- and German-descended Boers – would control southern Africa.) Ironically, it was the anti-clerical *Bulletin* that hit the nail on the head: 'Truly it is time for England to burn the Bible publicly by the hands of the common hangman, and go back to the worship of THOR and ODIN, so that its faith may square with its foreign policy.'[45]

To put it mildly, this was not how most Australian Christians saw things. Loyalty to Britain was widely regarded as synonymous with loyalty to the Christian religion, especially the Church of England. In the years before and after Federation, the Reverend W.H. Fitchett of Melbourne became famous for his books lauding battle and derring-do. His most popular by far was a collection of essays entitled *The Deeds that Won the Empire*. First published in 1897, it ultimately ran to thirty-five editions and sold 250,000 copies.[46]

Things did not change after Federation. If anything, the imperial spirit intensified. The infant Australia had colonial ambitions of its own, and acquired British New Guinea (later renamed Papua) in 1902.[47] The British Empire League was instituted in 1905 – the founding president in Australia was a prominent Anglican minister in Sydney, Canon F.B. Boyce[48] – and, from that year forward, Empire Day was celebrated annually.[49] A conscious decision was made to inculcate schoolchildren with the spirit of empire, along the lines followed in, of all places, Japan.[50] Again, apart from *The Bulletin* (which dubbed Empire Day 'Vampire Day'), there were few voices of dissent. And such dissent as there was tended to be along secular, anti-imperialist lines.

The martial and imperial spirit was fostered in other ways. Two especially fateful developments were the push for compulsory military training – eventually introduced in 1910[51] – and the creation, in 1911, of the Royal Australian Navy. Interestingly, the latter step was opposed by Britain itself.[52] But Australia had caught the militarist bug. In August 1908, the arrival in Sydney Harbour of sixteen American warships – the 'Great White Fleet' – had been an occasion of pure celebration.[53] The Churches joined in with most everybody else: lavish banquets were held along denominational lines, one for Catholics and another for Protestants.[54] When Australia's very own navy first sailed into Sydney Harbour five years later, there was another ecstatic celebration.[55]

None of this, incidentally, had much if anything to do with the diplomatic situation in Europe. Even as late as June 1914, general war was not expected there. Australia's actions were motivated by suspicion of Japan – 'Beware of the East, O Christian, for the sake of your fairest and best,' wrote Henry Lawson in 1913[56] – and, above all, by misplaced patriotism. Lawson might have had a racist streak, but he also harboured a wise, melancholy foreboding of the self-inflicted horrors to come. In 'The Star of Australasia' (1895), he anticipated that Australians would not be satisfied until they had 'proved themselves' in war. Until then, our flag would remain 'bloodless': we would 'rot in a deadly peace', on which 'the scorn of Nature and curse of God are heavy'.

This, the second stanza, is representative; but the whole, quite incredible poem should be read in full:

> There are boys out there by the western creeks, who hurry away from school
> To climb the sides of the breezy peaks or dive in the shaded pool,
> Who'll stick to their guns when the mountains quake to the tread of a mighty war,
> And fight for Right or a Grand Mistake as men never fought before;
> When the peaks are scarred and the sea-walls crack till the furthest hills vibrate,
> And the world for a while goes rolling back in a storm of love and hate.

Lawson's nightmarish vision was realised by World War One, the seminal event of modern history. As the Cold War statesman George F. Kennan once remarked, all lines of enquiry lead back to it.

## World War One

The events preceding the outbreak of the war in Europe need not here concern us. Few Australians were much interested in the fine details anyway, at least in the early stages. War came, indeed, during a tight federal election campaign. The Prime Minister of the day, Joseph Cook, said on the hustings:

Whatever happens, Australia is part of the Empire right to the full.
Remember that when the Empire is at war, so is Australia at war ...
I want to make it quite clear that all our resources in Australia are in
the Empire and for the Empire and for the preservation and security
of the Empire.[57]

Andrew Fisher, by then the Labor Opposition Leader, responded in
kind. He did not attempt any nuance, as he had done to his cost in 1911.
Instead he said this: 'We shall pledge our last man and our last shilling
to see this war brought to a successful issue.'[58]

Both Cook and Fisher were decent men and earnest Christians.
Each had risen from working-class poverty in Britain, and it would be
quite unfair, with the benefit of hindsight, to judge either of them too
harshly. They were products of their time, and Fisher (who became
prime minister again a month later, when Labor won the election on
5 September) ended up quite shattered by the war. He resigned from
politics in late 1915 for reasons of ill health.[59] Nevertheless, his and Cook's
knee-jerk pronouncements in August 1914 now seem obscenely glib, for
the scars of World War One have never fully healed. The 15 million
dead, and 20 million other casualties, proved just the beginning. The
unjust and unwise Versailles Treaty of 1919 led directly to Nazism and
World War Two with all their attendant horrors – the targeted bombing
of civilians in large cities, the Holocaust, Hiroshima and Nagasaki, the
Cold War, Vietnam. Even the instability of today's Iraq can be traced
back directly to the carve-up of territory in the old Mesopotamia after
World War One.[60]

The only force that might have prevented World War One – from
starting in 1914, or at least from escalating so horribly in 1915 – was
Christianity.

The Vatican failed, but failed honourably.[61] The main Protestant
Churches across the West failed and failed pathetically. They asked
few questions; on the contrary, in each nation, pastors and priests led
prayers for the victory of their own side and the decimation of the other.
Australia, as we shall see, was no exception.

## Cause and effect

Why, exactly, did World War One contribute so much to secularisation
in Australia? In no particular order I proffer six inter-related reasons.

## The deaths of Christian men

Some 60,000 Australian combatants were killed during the war: about one in every twenty across the entire male population between the ages of eighteen and forty-four. It is to be stressed that these men were all volunteers, and they spanned all classes of society. It is impossible to know how many potential leaders were among them, but it seems a safe assumption there were some, in all fields of endeavour – including religion. Certainly, there were many documented cases of heroism among fervently religious men, a good proportion of whom did not survive.[62]

## The surviving soldiers

In addition to the 60,000 dead there were around 155,000 other casualties – the maimed and the shell-shocked. Even those who emerged uninjured (clinically speaking) had witnessed unspeakable horrors.

Ronald Conway mused that terrible suffering in combat must have sparked 'the nearest to spontaneous inner questioning ever experienced by Australian men … peering into the faces of the obscenely wounded, the grotesquely fallen, the common soldier was forced to ask for an answer to the meaning of life'.[63]

Some did react in this way – but the weight of evidence suggests they were in a small minority. In the main, the Australian soldiers exhibited little enthusiasm for religion in any conventional sense.[64] In the abominable circumstances in which they found themselves, most replaced the Christian code of ethics with their own: a combination of fatalism and mateship. The chaplains (padres) of all denominations were not actively disliked, but they tended to be judged as individuals, for their qualities as men. Bravery, and a preparedness to share privation uncomplainingly, were the qualities most admired.[65] Christianity as such was not a binding force.

How could it have been otherwise, when all involved (except the chaplains) had assumed a duty to kill? It was principally for this reason – not so much the attenuated deprivations – that the direct experience of war proved antithetical to faith in Jesus, the ever-loving Prince of Peace. That, and the inevitable 'questioning of conventional religious teaching about God and providence' that must work in a soldier's mind.[66] In the words of Kenneth Henderson, an Anglican chaplain, 'the battlefield does not give to ninety-nine men out of a hundred any immediate apprehension of the Divine. Very much the reverse is the truth.'[67] If a soldier wants to survive and help his mates, he must deaden his conscience.

I mean this as no sort of criticism of the Diggers. Their attitude was understandable, and certainly did not manifest itself in the glorification of war. They knew the awful reality much better than anyone. Those serving at the front voted *against* conscription by a margin of three to one. But the fact remains it was mostly men, not women, who drifted away from the Churches after World War One, and many were ex-servicemen.[68]

## The Churches' loss of status

A broader effect of the war was that all institutions lost credibility – but none more so than the Churches. They had acted not as courageous advisers to the State, but as cheerleaders and apologists. The Lord Bishop of London, A.F. Winnington-Ingram, had hailed the war as 'a great crusade – we cannot deny it – to kill Germans', and called upon the Church of England 'to MOBILIZE THE NATION FOR A HOLY WAR'.[69] For their part, the Australian Churches positively welcomed the outbreak of hostilities. Michael McKernan's indispensable study *The Australian Churches at War: Attitudes and activities of the major Churches 1914–1918* makes for disturbing reading.

With a tiny number of exceptions,[70] Protestant clergy of all stripes ostentatiously linked the war effort with the cause of the British Empire. Even the German Lutherans in Australia declared their loyalty – but they received no favours in return. Many were interned; their schools were closed and the speaking of the German language was banned in their churches.

There was much talk of 'national prestige',[71] but little serious analysis. In McKernan's tart assessment, 'a discussion of Australian theology or ethics in regard to the war would make a very slim volume indeed'.[72] To give the flavour: in August 1914 four Anglican bishops of the Victorian Province made this not unrepresentative pronouncement: 'Into the causes which have plunged our own Empire and the greater part of the civilised world into war, *we need not enquire*, but we feel the justice of our Empire's cause' (emphasis mine).[73] Catholic clergy, at least in the early stages of the fighting, were no less keen to show their loyalty. In fact, they may have been even keener, in order to dispel any suspicion of disloyalty. Another relevant factor for them – or so they rationalised things to themselves – was that Britain's allies Belgium and France were Catholic countries.[74]

In 1914 some of this insouciance and jingoism was excusable. Almost nobody expected the war to drag on for four horrific years. The more unpardonable cheerleading came later, when the realities of trench warfare were known to all. As we shall see, the Catholic Church's support began to fracture, here and in Europe; but very few leading Protestants ever changed their tune. They had locked themselves in to backing a side and had demonised dissenters.[75] To admit error was unthinkable. This happens time and again in wartime: 'to acknowledge [that] a policy or strategy was mistaken is thought to betray the sacrifices made by those who, as a result of the policy, died'.[76]

Perhaps the Australian Churches' biggest failure came in 1918 to 1919, with their near-complete indifference to worldwide discussion about the terms of the peace.[77] They also ignored the immoral means used by the Allies *after* the Armistice, to secure German agreement to the terms of the Versailles Treaty – an eight-month naval blockade, from November 1918 to June 1919, that caused the deaths by starvation and disease of tens of thousands of German civilians, and embittered a generation.[78] The First Lord of Admiralty, Winston Churchill, actually boasted of his aim: 'to starve the whole population – men, women and children, old and young, wounded and sound – into submission'.[79]

Of course, the Australian Churches were not alone: they were a small part of a worldwide failure. By 1918, in the words of Diarmaid MacCulloch, the war had 'damage[d] the concept of Christendom irreparably'. Why? Because 'four years of slaughter revealed where the power lay between nationalism and religion'.[80]

During the war, only a few Protestant clergymen in Australia – exceptionally wise and exceptionally brave – had foreseen this outcome and spoken up. Among them were the Reverend James Gibson, the editor of the *Messenger of the Presbyterian Church of Queensland*, and the Reverend S. Martin, a follower of Gibson. They argued that the Church was betraying Christ – and damaging itself – in blessing the war.[81] A handful of like-minded souls across Australia warned against a future in which 'patriotism is the virtue which takes the place of Christian Brotherhood; the State replaces God; and the National flag replaces the Cross. Its supreme law is not the law of God, but the military safety of the country'.[82]

## Wowserism and hypocrisy

The Australian Churches did not merely persist in defending an increasingly brutal war on the grounds of patriotism. Many Australians supported them in that. The Churches also persisted in thoroughly ill-conceived attempts to link the conduct of the war effort with domestic moral causes – temperance, sexual abstinence, anti-gambling and so forth. These causes were not unreasonable in themselves. But to pursue them so sanctimoniously in the context of the war was a turn-off for many people – the Diggers especially. When on leave, here or abroad, they sought solace when and how they could.[83]

From the beginning the Churches had portrayed the war as a consequence of sin and as an opportunity for all citizens to atone for that sin. Henry Howard, Adelaide's most prominent Methodist, welcomed 'any discipline, whether of war or pestilence, of famine or fire, of drought or flood, that breaks down our trust in the material and strengthens our faith in the spiritual'.[84] Fair enough. But people of this ilk had in mind churchgoing and clean living – and little more. In 1916 the Anglican Bishop of Bathurst, George Merrick Long, took this logic to an absurd extreme: 'I say we want to free our country from the German menace and I say that is going to be done far more quickly by closing the bars at six o'clock.'[85]

But even these sorts of appeals had their share of supporters. There were two aspects of the Australian Churches' war effort that won them very few friends. One was the widespread practice of co-opting clergymen to deliver news of the death or disappearance of servicemen to their next of kin. The very sight of a 'man of the cloth' approaching a dwelling place was apt to invoke terror, dread or rage in the minds of its occupants.[86]

Worst of all were the clergymen of fighting age who stayed at home but urged other men to enlist – often in bellicose or unctuous terms. These were the 'would-to-God-that-I-could-go' brigade.[87] As one bush worker recalled:

> I can remember one man, a young clergyman about 25, a splendidly made fellow over 6 feet high, and as sound as a bell. He went around advising every young fellow to go to the war yet he never volunteered himself, not even as a chaplain. Such hypocrisy one cannot forget.[88]

## The conscription debates

Another deleterious effect of World War One was heightened religious sectarianism, along Protestant–Catholic lines. There is evidence that a good many twentieth-century Australians were put off religion as a whole by wearisome bickering between the denominations;[89] to the extent that this is true, World War One was at the root of it.

As I have said, most Australian Catholics supported the war in 1914 – but by 1916 some were having second thoughts. A combination of factors was at play, including the Easter Rising in Dublin in 1916, which was harshly suppressed by English troops. This episode introduced another nationalist element into the mix: a re-igniting of Irish hostility towards England.[90] Later in the same year, Pope Benedict XV – who had regarded the war from its outset as 'the suicide of civilized Europe'[91] – tried to mediate a general peace. But the key issue in Australia was conscription for overseas service. Twice, in national plebiscites in October 1916 and December 1917, the Australian people narrowly rejected the proposal.

The campaigns were virulent. A leading figure for the 'No' case was Melbourne's coadjutor archbishop (later archbishop), Daniel Mannix. His opposition to conscription was on secular grounds, but he also mused publicly about the justice of the war on traditional Catholic principles. He made the important point that 'a war which was just at the beginning may become unjust before it is over'.[92] Mannix was vilified by many advocates of the 'Yes' case – as, increasingly, were 'Papists' generally. Protestant churchmen overwhelmingly favoured conscription,[93] and not a few invoked some dubious theology. An especially poor argument was that employed by the Reverend Andrew Law, an Anglican in Victoria: 'Christ, in his sufferings, was a conscript.'[94] Christ, of course, was the very opposite. He could have saved Himself, but *chose* to die. He was a volunteer.

Too many Protestant leaders used hateful words to describe men who declined to enlist: shirker, coward, slacker, traitor, parasite, and even murderer.[95] Too many resorted to wholesale condemnation of 'seditious' Catholics.[96] The Reverend James Carruthers, for example, a prominent Methodist preacher in New South Wales, declared in 1916 that the outcome of the vote would determine 'whether the lower, baser and disloyal elements in Australia are to prevail or be defeated'.[97]

In fact, some prominent Catholic churchmen supported conscription and others remained neutral.[98] Moreover, many – if not most – of the Catholic laypeople in Australia who opposed conscription did not do so on religious grounds. Working-class resentment of war-profiteering and unequal sacrifice was a far more common basis of objection.[99] In England, taxation had risen fourfold to finance the war effort; in Australia, it had risen barely at all.[100] Queensland's (Catholic) premier, T.J. Ryan, voiced the views of many: 'If you have conscription of the individual you must also have commandeering of wealth.'[101] There were also secular opponents of conscription who based their case on quasi-religious grounds. The editor of *The Worker*, Henry Boote, was among the foremost Australia-wide publicists for the 'No' case. He himself was a rationalist, yet he maintained that the best argument against conscription was that it was 'an outrage to the sanctity of the soul'.[102]

W.M. Hughes, prime minister after October 1915 and *the* leading proponent of conscription, exacerbated the situation by deliberately inflaming religious passions. He spoke in hateful terms, calculated to enrage Catholics and other opponents of conscription and stoke the basest of prejudices. The 'No' victories embittered him – and he never forgot or forgave. 'There are in this country,' he declared at war's end, 'sheep and goats, those who have earned salvation, and those who have done nothing.' He promised honour and financial rewards for those who had backed his war policies. Then, again blasphemously invoking one of Jesus' parables, he addressed 'those who passed by on the other side of the road'. His message was uncompromising: 'I say let them do what they will. But as far as I am concerned they need not look to me.'[103]

Hughes' conduct of the war effort had at least two notably bad consequences for religion in Australia. One was his personal role in the heightening of Protestant–Catholic sectarianism. Partly as a result of Hughes' rhetoric, and that of his many supporters, an insidious mindset gained currency. Edmund Campion has described it as 'the typecasting of any Catholic as potentially disloyal'.[104]

But Hughes' other legacy – less frequently commented upon – was arguably even worse. He precipitated the de-Protestantisation of the ALP, and the working class in general. We saw in Chapters 4 and 5 that the ALP began its life as a product of Protestant Christian socialism. When Hughes (an Anglican) led a mass walkout of the Federal Parliamentary Labor Party in October 1916 over the conscription issue, he took with him much of the party's Protestant base. Indeed, the war 'tore the evangelical Labor Party leaders apart'.[105] Thereafter, the ALP became closely associated with Irish Catholicism and the non-Labor parties attained a de facto hold on the Protestant vote. This not only harmed the ALP, but, in the long run, it also harmed Australian Protestantism. In the minds of several generations of progressive Australians, Protestantism – and especially Anglicanism – became associated with stuffy, reactionary right-wing politics.

One organisation must be exempted from any general charge of inciting sectarianism. The Returned and Services League of Australia (RSL), founded in 1916, has always welcomed members of all denominations. John Hirst has described the RSL as 'the other great Australian institution of the twentieth century'[106] – alongside the ALP. On balance I agree with him, the bombastic excesses of the Bruce Ruxton era notwithstanding.

## The cult of Anzac

Another product of World War One was Anzac Day, which has been held on 25 April every year since 1916. As this book goes to press, the centenary of the original landing at Gallipoli (on 25 April 1915) looms large.

To many Australians, Anzac Day has always meant a great deal. Evidently it still does. The occasion is sometimes denounced by commentators of the Left as a celebration or glorification of war but, at least until recent times, I never thought that criticism fair or accurate. Certainly, most of the veterans themselves – or those who had seen serious combat – did not see it that way. Other criticisms are that Australians have much better national achievements to celebrate than a failed, British-led military campaign in World War One,[107] and that the whole occasion is excessively male-centred.[108] I will not pass comment, other than to say that many Australians in 1915 genuinely believed that the Gallipoli campaign marked some kind of watershed (or 'baptism of fire'). The contemporaneous evidence is clear. To that extent, the Anzac legend is based on fact.

My own reservations about it are different. True, Anzac Day itself has Christian roots. Canon David Garland of Brisbane, an Anglo-Catholic, was one of the key people involved in its establishment,[109] and the 'honour boards' that can still be seen in churches throughout Australia testify to the Christian faith of many soldiers of earlier generations. But I believe that the Anzac legend is now manipulated for crass and venal reasons. Genuine memories of war have faded or disappeared; comparatively few Australians alive today can have any conception of what military combat is really like, or the extent of the sacrifices borne by the whole nation during both world wars. Today, families seem to attend Anzac Day marches for a fun day out. Sports stars invoke the Anzac legend for self-aggrandisement. Politicians do too, and call media conferences to commemorate the deaths of individual soldiers, when and however they happen.

All this encourages a new form of secular nationalism, 'unreflective, earnest, often sentimental'.[110] It may be truly felt, but it is shallow and ephemeral, and unlikely to prompt serious metaphysical thought. War memorials, as Ken Inglis has argued, have become, for many, more sacred than churches.[111] The idealised figure of the Anzac has become a sort of national pagan god and Anzac Day a quasi-religious festival. The spiritual inclinations that modern-day Australians still harbour are channelled into it, or into other inferior substitutes for the real thing (a theme I will explore in Chapter 10).

## Blows upon a bruise

The Churches – indeed, most Australians, and most normally decent people across the Western world – could scarcely not have learned something from World War One. The prospect of a repeat, with modern weapons, was close to unthinkable. And so it should have been.

After Hughes' departure from the prime ministership in early 1923, Australia was led until May 1939 by a trio of genuine peacemakers: S.M. Bruce (Nationalist, 1923–29), who had twice been wounded on the Western Front, and the devout Catholics James Scullin (Labor, 1929–32) and Joseph Lyons (UAP, 1932–39). Scullin and Lyons were pacifists at heart. They took seriously the strictures of the Vatican, which supported appeasement throughout the 1930s, while still criticising the totalitarian regimes in Italy, Germany and the Soviet Union.[112] There was also an active Protestant peace movement in Australia during this period; the Australian Student Christian Movement played a prominent part, as did a number of well-known progressive clerics.[113]

It is important to stress, however, that appeasement was official government policy and enjoyed overwhelming popular support, from citizens spanning all Christian denominations and all major political parties. Both our wartime prime ministers, Robert Menzies (1939–41) and John Curtin (1941–45), had been strong supporters of appeasement until the outbreak of war in Europe.[114] I mean that as praise, not criticism.

### World War Two

On 3 September 1939, Menzies announced that Australia was again at war. The reaction was nothing like that in 1914. There were very few celebrations; certainly, most Church leaders were measured and sombre. But during the war itself, the Churches, like most Australian citizens, supported the national effort against both the Nazis and the Japanese. Any equivocation ceased altogether after the fall of Singapore on 15 February 1942 and the bombing of Darwin four days later.

There was no repeat of the sectarianism of 1914–18. To the contrary, 'the main churches were drawn together by the war'.[115] They also made a much better effort than they had in World War One to provide practical assistance and ministry to the troops in training camps.[116] By war's end, the Australian Churches had done their public image no obvious harm. Indeed, by 1950, rates of regular churchgoing – though *not* overall religious belief – were still at close to their 1901 levels.[117]

Yet the seeds of further trouble had been planted – and, again, it was partly the Churches' fault.

By far the most serious mistake made by the Christian Churches during World War Two – across the West – was failing to challenge the gross excesses employed by governments and the military *on both sides*. The German Churches, hamstrung by fear of Nazi reprisals, and the Vatican, studiously neutral under the new Pope Pius XII, were almost totally supine. But so too, by and large,[118] were the Protestant churches of the Allied powers. They raised barely a whimper against the targeted carpet-bombing of civilians in German and Japanese towns and cities: a strategy that became increasingly ruthless as the war dragged on, and culminated in the dropping of atomic bombs on Hiroshima and Nagasaki in August 1945.[119] By war's end, somewhere around 500,000 Japanese civilians had been killed by American bombing. In Germany, the total death toll from British and American bombing was about the same – possibly even higher. By comparison, around 60,000 British civilians were killed by German bombing.[120]

The issue was raised directly in an extraordinary exchange of letters in mid-1943 between Martin Boyd, the Australian novelist, who was then living in London, and the Archbishop of Canterbury, William Temple. After the fire-bombing of Hamburg in late July – which, over two nights, incinerated around 45,000 civilians and injured many more[121] – Boyd wrote at length to his spiritual leader. 'It is impossible to contend,' Boyd declared, 'that to bring desolation to the countless homes of a great city is in accord with the will of Christ.' He challenged the Churches to take the lead in defining the limits of war: 'Is there no point,' he asked Temple, 'at which the church will withhold its approval?'[122] The Archbishop's reply was brisk: 'The one thing that is certainly wrong is to fight ineffectively.' There would be time for justice and mercy, he wrote, but only when the war was won.[123]

This was, admittedly, a popular sentiment at the time. But it was the duty of the Churches to see further. In the long run, by acceding to what was, at its core, a pagan philosophy – the end justifies the means – they further undermined their own moral authority.

Historians looking back at this aspect of World War Two have not let the Churches off lightly.[124] And, during the decades that followed, the Churches compounded their mistakes.

## The Cold War to Vietnam to 9/11

The threat posed to Christianity by Soviet Communism was very real. But so was the threat posed by nuclear weapons to the very existence of human civilisation. The question was how best to respond to these threats, while remaining consistent with Christian principles. In Australia, throughout the Cold War era (1945–89), neither the Churches nor the major political parties spoke with one voice.

In the main, Coalition governments from Menzies to Fraser backed the Pentagon's policy of maintaining (at least) a 'balance of terror' in the nuclear arms race, and resisting Communist aggression throughout the world with conventional arms. The wars in Korea and Vietnam were fought on that basis. The Menzies Government also attempted, in 1951, to ban the Communist Party in Australia. (The relevant Act of Parliament was declared unconstitutional by the High Court and a subsequent referendum proposal was narrowly defeated.) In the main, all these policies had the strong support of the mainline Protestant Churches and a big majority of Protestant voters.[125] Vocal dissenters were fairly rare – and some of those who did dissent, especially as regards Vietnam, were ostracised.[126]

The Catholic Church in Australia was split, and this led, in turn, to another fateful split in the ALP. The Catholic Social Studies Movement, founded in August 1941, had as its overarching aim 'the creation of a Christian social order by means of large scale action in the social, economic, political and cultural spheres'.[127] Its effective head was a remarkable Catholic layman, B.A. Santamaria. Through the Movement (later the National Civic Council), and its political arm, the Democratic Labor Party (DLP), Santamaria would exercise substantial influence on Australian politics and society for the best part of thirty years. Some of his aims were worthy. But it is hard to escape the conclusion that, with the possible exception of Billy Hughes, he did as much harm to the cause of Christianity in Australia as any other single person.

Santamaria was 'Australia's most high-profile and indomitable Cold War warrior'.[128] In essence he believed (like William Temple) that the end justified the means. On the gravest issues of war and peace, he persistently defied the Vatican. Pope Paul VI, like John XXIII before him, opposed the arms race during the Cold War. Santamaria championed it. He was also an apologist for America's excesses and blunders in Indo-China, including the systematic bombing of civilians, and for Indonesia's annexation of East Timor. Almost anything was worth trying – subversion, false propaganda, racist scaremongering, out-and-out militarism – provided Communism was defeated and the Catholic Church in Australia survived. But not just any Catholic Church – it had to be one in Santamaria's preferred image.

Why did this harm religion in Australia? For one thing, it created a tension between the Catholic laity (who were still disproportionately working class, members of trade unions, and ALP voters) and powerful sections of the Australian Catholic Church hierarchy (those who agreed with Santamaria). A majority of Catholics voted 'No' at the 1951 referendum to ban the Communist Party.[129]

But the pivotal events that accelerated the Secular Juggernaut, in my opinion, were Australian involvement in the Vietnam War and the introduction of conscription. From early 1965, twenty-year-old men were randomly selected for overseas military service (the 'birthday ballot') – this at a time when twenty-year-olds did not even have the right to vote. Arguably this, and the Vietnam War, hit religion even harder than World War One. They radicalised a whole generation, including a new, tertiary-educated political class that became, above all else, anti-*authority*. In the words of Vietnam historian Paul Ham, 'this great movement wrenched Western society from its settled anchorage'.[130]

The Australian Churches – with isolated individual exceptions[131] – did themselves no favours in this period. They largely repeated their mistakes from World War One, except that this time their loyalty was to the United States and the Federal Government, rather than the British Empire. Catholic clergy were almost as united as their Protestant counterparts.[132] Indeed, children in many Catholic schools in the 1960s 'were brought up to support the American intervention in Vietnam and to identify American foreign policy with [their] Catholic faith'.[133]

The rhetoric employed was scarcely less martial than in 1914, and, initially, the cause was popular. The Coalition won a landslide victory in the 1966 federal election on the back of it, Labor leader Arthur Calwell having come out against both Australian involvement and conscription. Dissenters were mocked and traduced. But, as is so often the case with foreign wars, events got out of control and public opinion turned. For the Churches, by 1972, the end result was the same as it had been in

1918: complicity in a war that had come to be regarded by many as a moral and geopolitical catastrophe. They had lost the idealistic Left.

Who was right and who was wrong? Hawks would argue that the peaceniks were misguided, and were proved so decisively in the late 1980s when, under the weight of decades of arms spending, the Soviet economy collapsed. But this is to forget vital facts. The world came within a whisker of nuclear war in October 1962 during the Cuban missile crisis. A holocaust was averted because US President John F. Kennedy and Soviet Premier Nikita Khrushchev – against the advice of their respective military advisers – pulled back from the brink.[134] The Cold War hotted up again in the 1980s when US President Ronald Reagan abandoned 'détente', massively increased US arms spending, and began using inflammatory rhetoric ('The Evil Empire'). There was another extremely close shave on the night of 8–9 November 1983 – the Soviets came within ten minutes of launching their arsenal, by mistake.[135] If the worst had happened then, or in 1962, or at any other time, we would not be here to pontificate on the matter. For whatever reason – Christians would say by the grace of God – the worst did *not* happen. The hawks tend to forget that Pope John Paul II, though a staunch opponent of the Soviet Union, gave his support to the cause of nuclear disarmament;[136] and that President Reagan himself softened during his second term, overruling hardliners in his own administration and responding to Mikhail Gorbachev's overtures for peace.[137]

Some credit must go the peace movement, which, by the mid-1980s, had gathered considerable strength. In Australia, the peace movement of the 1980s drew in a much wider spectrum of people than had been the case in the 1960s. It included adherents from all Christian denominations.[138] But it was mostly a secular movement. Once again, the Churches *en bloc* had missed the chance to take a decisive position on an issue of vital importance, when to do so might have made progressive, peace-loving citizens take another look at the message of Jesus.

Yet another blow to Judaeo-Christianity came with 9/11. It was a ghastly act of terrorism, of course. But in a spirit of vengeance, the United States and its allies, including Australia, declared a vaguely defined 'War on Terror' – a war that US President George W. Bush likened in the early stages to a crusade. Afghanistan was bombed. Then, in March 2003, the 'Coalition of the Willing' invaded Iraq without the approval of the United Nations. The stated grounds for the invasion subsequently proved false, and, in the event, the whole exercise – like Vietnam – became a costly and tragic fiasco.

This time, in Australia, high-profile religious supporters of the war were in a minority.[139] To their great credit, the mainline Churches were near-unanimous in their opposition, both before and after the invasion. But their opinions simply did not matter. The damage to the Churches' heft and standing in the Australian community had long since been done. The Coalition ignored them, and the Left's position was arrived at quite independently. The overall effect of 9/11 and the Iraq War – as well as ongoing Islamic terrorism – has been to make unbelievers of all political colours still more suspicious of *any* deeply felt religion. In the words of Phillip Adams: 'Now the wars within Islam, as intense as the schisms that racked Christianity for centuries, imperil us all.'[140]

# CHAPTER 8

# Sex, gender and self-destruction

The abbreviated test of authentic belief for most churches has little to do with belief in God, but has come to be associated with adherence to repressive sexual values.

Michael Hogan, Australian Catholic historian

The idea that women are fully human is something man-made religions seem to struggle with.

Jane Caro, Australian atheist

I have argued so far that the Churches mostly have themselves to blame for two major causes of the Secular Juggernaut: religious ignorance, and their complicity in the wars of the twentieth century. But we now come to murkier territory. Among some contemporary women, and not a few men, Christian attitudes to issues of sex and gender are said to be a showstopper.

The question is: have the Australian Churches been entirely wrong on these matters since 1788? In other words, can we add sexism and bigotry to the list of their self-destructive sins? Or have the Churches been right to resist the tide of liberal and feminist opinion?

In my view, the answer lies somewhere in between. The statement of Michael Hogan that I have quoted above contains elements of truth, but is incomplete. The statement of Jane Caro is an unfair caricature (though I suspect she exaggerated for effect). It is necessary to examine each relevant issue discretely. What emerges on the Churches' part is a curious mix of outright wrongdoing, obdurate if honest error, and profound wisdom – only some of it causative of secularisation. The same applies to certain other of the Churches' alleged failings.

## Child abuse

Let us deal first with the elephant in the room. It is in a category of its own.

There is now no escaping the dark evil of child sex abuse. The Royal Commission into 'institutional responses' to it, appointed by the Gillard Government in 2012, had yet to report finally when this book went to press. But enough has already been revealed in the course of the commission's hearings – and by other official enquiries – to leave no room for fudging.

This has been a disaster in every way. The moral depravity of so many individual clerics and religious office-holders is bad enough. However, to a greater or lesser extent, such monsters and misfits exist in all organisations where individuals are placed in positions of trust vis-à-vis children. Sporting, scouting and other community groups are also under investigation by the Royal Commission; so too State schools. It is true that within the Catholic Church the pressures placed upon priests by the vow of celibacy has exacerbated the problems. (The rates of offence have been six times worse in the Catholic Church than anywhere else.[1]) But the most indefensible aspect of this wretched, long-running scandal has been the extent of the denial, obfuscation and cover-up.

With honourable individual exceptions, Churches failed to deal forthrightly enough with the culprits or compassionately enough with the victims. They failed to stop further, preventable abuse; they failed to comfort and compensate victims, adequately or at all. For decades, a kind of institutional atheism[2] took hold. The Catholic Church's evident priorities were protecting its own reputation and (once legal claims against it began flooding in during the mid-1990s) minimising financial loss for both it and its insurers. Canny lawyers and spin doctors were allowed to take over.

As journalist Scott Stephens has observed, it was the sacred duty of all Churches to apply *higher* standards than that of the 'corporate executive managing a crisis'. Too many victims and their families 'confronted … a Church intent on pursuing its own legal defence as though there was no divine judge'.[3] For a long time, churches of all denominations behaved little or no better than their secular counterparts.

The best that can be said is that the incidence of sexual abuse *per se* seemed to drop sharply after the 1990s: internal safeguards vastly improved.[4] But the shabby treatment of victims seeking justice continued for another two decades.[5] Only now is a measure of justice being done.

The nadir may have been the routine use by the Catholic Church's Sydney Diocese of the so-called Ellis defence. This argument, upheld by the Court of Appeal of the Supreme Court of New South Wales in 2007, holds that certain entities within the Catholic Church (relevantly, the ones that hold most of its assets) cannot be sued in cases of sexual abuse by clergy. The upshot is that the Church may choose to pay out money to victims – indeed, it has done so many times – but that the victims do not have a *legal* right to sue. One does not have to agree with every word of journalist David Marr's savage assessment of Cardinal George Pell in 'The Prince', Marr's 2013 contribution to *Quarterly Essay*, to be left extremely uneasy by the events described.

All other issues aside, a national enquiry ought to have been held in 2002 when the Anglican Archbishop of Brisbane, Phillip Aspinall, bravely proposed one. Pell argued it was unnecessary and the then prime minister, John Howard, declined Aspinall's request.[6]

Has this calamity been an active cause of secularisation? The question may seem like a no-brainer – 'Duh, of course!' In 2009 Michael Hogan suggested that 'if anything has affected belief and unbelief over the last twenty years, surely it has been the stream of headlines about clergy misconduct'.[7] But, in fact, the answer is not so clear-cut.

Beyond doubt, the Churches *as institutions* have suffered grave reputational harm. They have given their enemies a sword. Few dispute this now, even at the highest levels of the Vatican. For the Catholic Church in particular, the fallout from the scandal may take decades to subside. I agree with Patrick Parkinson, Professor of Law at the University of Sydney and one of Australia's leading commentators in this area: 'in Australia, at least, it may be that the crisis of confidence and trust will not pass until the present generation of leaders, who are tainted by their handling of matters earlier in their careers, have passed the baton on to another generation'.[8]

But has child sexual abuse by clergy actually caused people to renounce God – either the victims, or those who have read about it in the wider community? This is a harder question, and there is no empirical research from Australia of which I am aware. Surprisingly, what little there is from overseas suggests that levels of personal religiosity (as opposed to institutional loyalty) have remained unaffected.[9] In one notable book, Irish cleric Susan Shooter's *How Survivors of Abuse Relate to God*, a case is made that some victims emerge from their dreadful experiences with their faith *enhanced*: they exhibit 'the authentic spirituality of the annihilated soul'.[10] For other victims, of course, the opposite has been the case. In 2013 one middle-aged Australian man gave evidence to the Royal Commission: 'As an 11-year-old I had faith and, more importantly, I wanted to have faith. I have no faith today.'[11]

All such cases are tragic. Even so, as far as Australia is concerned, it is doubtful whether this scandal has been a major operative cause of secularisation. Until the 1990s, the extent of the problem was unknown. Only the victims and the perpetrators knew of it, and then only in individual instances. And within institutional religious settings we are talking of hundreds of cases over decades, not the tens of thousands that would be needed to affect levels of belief nationwide. By the time the scandal broke, first overseas and a little later here, the trend of secularisation was well and truly under way. And even today I get no sense that *existing* believers in any denomination have lost their faith because of the ongoing revelations. As I have said, the evidence from overseas (Ireland in particular) is to the contrary.

The most that can be said with confidence is that unbelievers are now less likely than ever to take heed of the Churches on issues of morality – especially sexual morality. There may also be some switching of allegiances within denominations. The Catholic Church's prospects of making new converts are, in the short term, diminished. But those are quite different things from wholesale secularisation.

## Issues of sex and gender

To what is, I think, a more substantial subject, in terms of explaining the long-term trend toward unbelief. There exists an undeniable tension between, on the one hand, modern, 'progressive' ideas about sex and gender, and, on the other hand, the teachings of the Churches. Some people regard the tension as irreconcilable. In 1999 David Marr published a book that emphasised the subject, *The High Price of Heaven*. Phillip Adams is another to have lambasted the churches on this score:

> The control of sexuality – with emphases on chastity, virginity, celibacy, virgin birthing, adultery, homosexuality and abortion – is frequently paramount. The goings-on in bedrooms take precedence over almost every other aspect of life.[12]

There are a lot of disparate issues (and unstated assumptions) wrapped up in those two sentences. The truth or otherwise of the Virgin Birth is a question of pure theology, about which, for those interested, there is a mountain of careful scholarship.[13] Here I will grapple with the rest of the issues on Adams' list, and a couple of others in the same basket. They are the issues that seem to give today's secular feminist thinkers (men as well as women) the biggest problems with the Christian faith.

Frankly, I do not expect to change many minds. But I feel duty-bound to try to bring some balance – dare I say nuance? – to the discussion. Too many opponents of Christianity seem incapable of doing so, as do too many of its defenders. It is important to understand where the Churches are truly coming from. In large measure their concerns are the protection of women and girls, and fidelity to Scripture (or to the Vatican's binding edicts), not the oppression of the female sex for its own sake. The Churches, for their part, must continue to examine in good conscience whether positions they have taken in the past are still right and defensible.

With an eye to both camps, I would make two overriding points. First, these issues are far from trivial, as libertarians frequently suggest or imply. A society without sexual rules – or, the term I prefer, sexual ideals – would harm women much more than men. But neither are these issues all-important. None of them go to the absolute core of Christianity. People who think they do – Christian and non-Christian – would do well to consider the wise advice of a former Anglican bishop of North Queensland, Dr Ian Shevill:

> The Church has a greater mission than the condemnation of human weakness. It is here to proclaim the divine order. We know that basically the things people are looking for are security, significance and purpose. We know that if they don't find them, they will seek some garish way out.[14]

### Sexual conduct generally

The Christian ideal is chastity outside marriage and monogamy within it. Ludicrous, you think, in this day and age?

It is certainly true that the former ideal – chastity outside marriage – is no longer aspired to, let alone practised, by the vast majority of Australians. The word 'fornication' is scarcely heard nowadays. But, interestingly enough, the latter ideal – embodied, of course, in the Seventh Commandment – *is* still taken seriously. Perhaps as seriously as ever. Breach of the ideal is rarely called adultery these days; 'cheating' is the more common expression. But it is still very much frowned upon, including – perhaps especially – by secular-minded modern women. Up to a point this is right and proper. As we saw in Chapter 2, the *reciprocal* prohibition against adultery was an important point of distinction between Judaeo-Christianity and the patriarchal norms of the classical world.

Problems arise, however, when adultery is considered in isolation. When not understood within the framework of the entire Christian message about marriage, the offence tends to be regarded in shallow, black-and-white terms – it is either too easily dismissed (*It was just sex!*) or too superficially condemned (*How could you do that to me?*). There are usually deep-seated reasons for a spouse's sexual unfaithfulness. To see it as just a breach of contract – or, even more unhelpfully, as an unforgivable blow to the 'innocent' spouse's dignity and pride – is to trivialise not just adultery, but marriage itself. It also trivialises the myriad other sins (on both sides) that are invariably associated with the commission of adultery.

Nevertheless, adultery is still widely regarded as wrong – even outrageous – by *un*believers. To that extent, even today, the Christian message is mainstream. It is not perceived as intolerant or outdated. True, the *reasons* for the traditional Christian prohibition on adultery are often ignored. So are the Christian prescriptions for reducing its likelihood. (I urge a reading of Chapter 5 of Ephesians; see also 1 Corinthians 7:1–7.) Yet I am convinced there would be much less adultery if both husbands and wives genuinely made an effort to put into practice the New Testament vision of the optimal marriage. Catholic theologian Tracey Rowland has argued in favour of a 'sacramental' approach to marital sexuality. 'The [Catholic] Church,' she has emphasised, 'does *not* teach that the only reason for sex is to produce babies.' Pope John Paul II was in fact highly critical of this attitude.[15]

The Christian ideal is that sex within marriage be not merely exclusive but special. As Ronald Conway wrote, ticking off secular libertarians and religious killjoys alike:

> The pornographer and the puritan have always been brothers under the skin; they tear away sex from love, libido from life, sexual union from the ways of the spirit, and then complain bitterly about the sexual deformity of society.[16]

But if adultery still attracts widespread disapproval, the same cannot be said about fornication. Today, the very word would be regarded as quaint, if not offensive, by many sexually active single women. (Single men too.) And yet it cannot be denied that there have been huge downsides to the 'sexual revolution'. The 'post-Pill cheapening of sex into just another contact sport'[17] has undoubtedly harmed women much more than men. An Australian Christian writer, Gordon Menzies, has referred to 'the right-wing side to the sexual revolution, where human bodies become goods in the market place, and where survival of the sexiest promotes injustice and discrimination'.[18] The explosion of online pornography is the ugliest and most obvious manifestation, but there are others, more subtle and insidious.

As Menzies points out, 'there are irreducible differences between the sexual attractiveness of people … so it would be natural to conclude that sexual deregulation has increased the ability of attractive people to exploit unattractive people'. He cites as one example the overwhelming emphasis placed on looks by male users of online dating sites.[19] Others have emphasised demographic trends. In Australia, as in most Western countries, there have been steady falls in both the marriage and birth rates, accompanied by a steady rise in the average age of first-marrieds. Simply, men no longer need to get married in order to have regular sex. They leave marriage till as late as possible. The cruel result for many young women is that marriage and motherhood are delayed for a long time – too often, beyond the point of no return.

The deleterious effects of the sexual revolution on women have united female commentators in Australia as disparate as Germaine Greer (secular Left), Anne Manne (secular centre-Left), Justine Toh (Protestant centre-Left), Melinda Tankard Reist (Catholic centre-Left – though she underplays her religious beliefs), Bettina Arndt (secular centrist, and former 'sex guru'), Tracey Rowland (Catholic traditionalist), Megan Best (Protestant centre-Right) and Angela Shanahan (Catholic Right). Despite their differences, all share a well-founded common concern: that disrespect of women and girls is on the rise, and that the sexual revolution is a central cause.

All that said, the Churches in Australia – Catholic and Protestant – have often handled these issues ineptly. In Chapter 1 I mentioned the sanctimonious treatment of the female convicts, which got things off to a nasty start. More generally, for over 200 years, Christian spokesmen on issues of sexuality have too often tended to exhibit, in Tracey Rowland's nice phrase, 'an unbearably grim demeanour'.[20] Another typical example: shortly before World War One, many Christian bodies were at the forefront of attempts to block the extension of the Federal Government's new maternity allowance to unmarried mothers. It was said that this would be 'condoning immorality'.[21] Yet single mothers and their children were the ones who needed the allowance the most. Charity should have trumped puritanism.

## Divorce

The original marriage laws of all the Australian colonies, passed between 1858 and 1873, were based almost verbatim on the English model, the Divorce and Matrimonial Causes Act of 1857.[22] These laws, in certain respects, were undeniably sexist. Notoriously, a husband could sue for divorce on the ground of a single instance of adultery by his wife; a wife had to prove that her husband's adultery was both aggravated and repeated.[23] This was a clear double standard, without any reasonable basis, Christian or otherwise.

Many Christian feminists of the late nineteenth century not only fought for female suffrage, as we saw in Chapter 4, but also led early attempts to reform the marriage laws. So did some fervent Christian men, including, in New South Wales, the great jurist Sir Alfred Stephen (1802–94), a prominent lay Anglican.[24] Reformers such as these also argued for married women's property rights and a modest extension of the grounds for divorce (on grounds other than adultery – desertion, for example, or physical abuse).

It is true that most male voices within the Churches opposed change, some vociferously so. But on the whole their motives were much less sexual discrimination *per se* than 'concerned paternalism',[25] and, above all, fidelity to their consciences. Catholics were bound by the Vatican's teaching, traceable to the 1184 Council of Verona, that marriage is a sacrament, and hence indissoluble. (Annulments were and are something different.) Protestants were not, of course, so bound, but many who took the Bible seriously could see no conscientious way around Jesus' pronouncements on the subject of divorce. The only ground that Jesus specified explicitly was adultery on the part of a wife (Matthew 19). Yet all Jesus' sayings must be read in context, and it is arguable[26] that this one is not as cut-and-dried as it may appear in isolation. For one thing, most Christians read it as also applying to adultery by a husband – yet it does not say that. For another thing, a literal interpretation of Matthew 19 is hard to square with Mark 10, in which Jesus appears to prohibit divorce entirely. On the former occasion He was answering smart-aleck questions by the Pharisees; on the latter occasion He was fielding honest enquiries by the Disciples. My own view is that Jesus was at pains strongly to discourage divorce, which *always* involves the commission of sin, but that a legalistic approach to the issue is unbiblical. Nevertheless, it is understandable that most clerics and laymen of the nineteenth and early twentieth centuries gave these passages a restrictive interpretation. Many still do today. At any rate, these developments were not, in the late nineteenth century, a cause of secularisation. Christians were divided in their views even then, and it was mostly *Christian* – not secular – men and women who made the initial arguments for reform.

Once women had the vote, it was inevitable that the process would continue. The horrors of the first half of the twentieth century slowed down the reform process, though advances were made at the State level on a piecemeal basis. The impetus for reform resumed after World War Two and culminated in the enactment by the Federal Parliament of the Matrimonial Causes Act of 1959. This was a unification of divorce laws across Australia. It was not especially radical – the principle of fault was maintained – though one provision did arouse controversy: that allowing for five years' separation as a ground for divorce. Prior to 1959 this ground had been available only in Western Australia.[27]

Again, it must be conceded that the Churches led the opposition to this Act. But as in earlier eras, Christian opinion was divided. Modest expansion of the grounds for divorce was not the only issue: also at stake were reforms relating to child custody and maintenance, largely for the benefit of women. Most members of parliament in those days were at least nominally Christian; all had to search their consciences. In the words of a future Liberal prime minister, John Gorton, their task was 'to decide where the greatest injustice really lies'.[28] Australia's first-ever female senator, Dorothy Tangney, was in an especially delicate position. She was both a Western Australian and a practising Catholic. Ultimately she decided, consistently with an earlier statement in 1953, that she should support the Act. Divorce was against her own religious convictions, but since it was on the statute books, she believed 'no man or woman should be at a disadvantage in matrimonial matters simply because of geographical difficulties'.[29]

By far the most fundamental changes to Australian law in this area were effected by the Family Law Act of 1975. It did away with the concept of fault and specified just one ground for divorce: separation for one year. The Churches again were opposed, though not uniformly so. This time, in retrospect, I believe the naysayers were right – not to oppose the entire concept of no-fault divorce necessarily, but to be highly suspicious of the consequences of radical change.

The divorce rate has skyrocketed since 1975, with, overall, lamentable results. Those of libertarian bent might disagree, but there are solid grounds for thinking that the one-year separation period is much too short.[30] The Family Law Act of 1975 *is* part of the Secular Juggernaut – though whether it is a symptom or a cause is hard to say.

### Contraception

It was no coincidence that the Family Law Act was passed in 1975. It was preceded, in the 1960s, by the onset of the so-called sexual revolution. A key event took place on 1 January 1961, when the contraceptive Pill was made legally available in Australia. But attitudes to contraception had been changing for decades before that.

This is another subject on which beliefs and practices among Christians differ markedly. At least at the highest ecclesiastical levels, the split is along Catholic–Protestant lines. Most Protestant Churches permit contraception for the purposes of birth control within marriage. Famously, at the Lambeth Conference of 1930, the Church of England declared that 'each couple must decide for themselves, as in the sight of God, after the most careful and conscientious thought'.[31]

By contrast, the Vatican still prohibits artificial contraception even within marriage, and even in African countries plagued by epidemics of HIV/AIDS. Addressing the latter issue, which centres upon the use (or not) of condoms, Pope Benedict XVI in 2011 issued a post-synodal apostolic exhortation, *Africae Munus*. He remarked:

> Above all, it [AIDS] is an ethical problem. The change of behaviour that it requires – for example, sexual abstinence, rejection of sexual promiscuity, fidelity within marriage – ultimately involves the question of integral development, which demands a global approach and a global response from the Church.[32]

The Vatican's total ban on condoms provokes fury among many Australian unbelievers.[33] I disagree with the ban myself. Many Catholics – including senior churchmen and women – likewise disagree. But it is only fair to point out that the Catholic Church is the single biggest provider of charity and support to AIDs sufferers everywhere. According to a United Nations statement in 2013: 'Statistics from the Vatican in 2012 indicate that Catholic Church-related organizations provide approximately a quarter of all HIV treatment, care, and support throughout the world and run more than 5,000 hospitals, 18,000 dispensaries, and 9,000 orphanages, many involved in AIDS-related activities.'[34]

The Australian experience as regards contraception is instructive on a number of levels. As far as married women are concerned, it is clear that most have exercised self-help since the 1880s, when rudimentary contraceptive devices first became widely available.[35] The birth rate fell appreciably from the 1890s. Initially there was 'stronger regulation of fertility ... among Protestants than Roman Catholics or Lutherans but ... there was little to distinguish them within a decade or two'.[36] This occurred despite the tough stance periodically taken by the Catholic Church. In 1934, for example, an official Catholic publication in Australia stated: 'It is a grave sin to prevent conception by any means whatsoever.' In 1946, in a booklet for couples entering religiously mixed marriages, the following sentence appeared: 'If married people wish to limit the number of their children, the only lawful way is by self-restraint, abstaining from marital relations by mutual consent, either until another child is welcome, *or at least during those times when conception is likely to occur.*'[37] (The words I have italicised were, of course, a reference to the so-called rhythm method. This represented a grudging exception to the general rule.)

Such strictures simply were not followed by a large majority of Catholic women. It was the same in the 1960s, when the Vatican declared its opposition to the Pill. The birth rate in Australia fell sharply after 1961 and Pope Paul VI's hardline encyclical of 1968, *Humanae Vitae*, did not reverse the trend. For example, a survey published in Brisbane in 1978 found that only 24 per cent of lay Catholics under forty were obeying the Church's teachings about artificial contraception.[38] Not only in Australia but across the West, this is 'the first time that the Catholic faithful have ever so consistently scorned a major papal pronouncement'.[39]

Interestingly, this aspect of *Humanae Vitae* came as something of a surprise at the time. In the light of Vatican II there had been expectations of a more liberal ruling; indeed, a committee at the Vatican that had been meeting for five years since 1963 was inclined to recommend reform. But conservatives stepped in at the eleventh hour.[40] In retrospect this was a serious misjudgment. It had bad consequences for the Catholic Church, Christianity in general, and society at large. The Church's authority was undermined even among its own flock and the cause of Christianity much weakened.

Yet, for all that, the Vatican was partly right: the Pill *has* proved a decidedly mixed blessing. It turbo-charged the sexual revolution, with all the unfortunate consequences I have mentioned. A judicious compromise was in order. Like the Protestant Churches, the Vatican ought to have allowed the use of contraception within marriage and otherwise strongly discouraged it. If Christians had delivered this message with a unified and compassionate voice from the 1960s onwards, the course of social history might have been very different. Women – especially young, vulnerable, low-income women – would have benefitted most of all. And by 'women' I include girls beyond the age of puberty.

## Abortion

From one touchy subject to an even touchier one. Feminist writer Anne Summers has recently posed the question: 'Can you be "pro-life" and a feminist?' For Summers the answer is clear: 'I say an emphatic, No.'[41]

*I* say an emphatic 'Yes'. But it depends, of course, on your definition of both terms ('pro-life' and 'feminist'). Most of the early Christian feminists of Australian history whom I discussed in Chapter 4 would have said an emphatic 'Yes'. They would have been aware that abortion was a serious crime, and it would not have crossed their minds that abortion ought not to be a crime. In that sense – the one favoured today by most practising Catholics and Evangelical Protestants in the United States and some in Australia – they were strictly pro-life. If you sincerely believe that a foetus is a fully fledged human being, and a uniquely defenceless one at that, this is a perfectly logical position. In the words of Pope Francis: 'It is not progressive to try to resolve problems by eliminating a human life.'[42]

Modern medical science, it should be said, provides increasing support for that belief. Australia's Megan Best, a leading bioethicist and palliative-care doctor, has outlined the evidence lucidly in her book *Fearfully and Wonderfully Made*.[43] The more we learn about the foetus, the more like a miniature baby it seems. Disciples of science take note.

But there is one complication. In my view, secular feminists exaggerate its importance, while implacably pro-life Christians underplay or ignore it. Whether a foetus is properly regarded as a fully fledged human being or as a potential human being (it is precious either way), it lives inside the mother's body. If the object of the exercise is to save the foetus in as many cases as possible, the most important question is not whether abortion is wrong but how best to encourage pregnant women to go to term. Is the blunt instrument of criminal law the answer?

Some would say it is. But I am dubious, as are many Christians here and overseas. An alternative approach is that recommended by American writer Marcia Pally: 'if one wishes to reduce abortion, one must remove the central financial and emotional reasons to abort'. Abortion must be made unthinkable rather than illegal.[44]

The legal and political reality in Australia is that abortion is effectively available on demand and will not be recriminalised. Recriminalisation did not happen in the United States between 2003 and 2007, when the nominally pro-life Republican Party controlled the presidency, both Houses of Congress, and the Supreme Court. It was scarcely attempted. In Australia, recriminalisation is a complete non-issue and secular feminists should be honest enough to admit it. Instead they are wont to drum up scare campaigns whenever anyone mentions the horribly high incidence of abortion in Australia (around 80,000 to 90,000 per year[45]) or suggests even the most modest restrictions on an unfettered right to abort foetuses. This is another ugly feature of the Secular Juggernaut.

The real issue is, or should be, how to make abortion (in Bill Clinton's phrase) 'safe, legal and rare'. And by 'legal' I do not mean legal in all circumstances. Rather, in the wise words of Mary Ann Glendon, United States Ambassador to the Holy See: 'What is important is that the totality of abortion regulations – that is, all criminal, public health and social welfare laws related to abortion – be in proportion to the importance of the legal value of life, and that, as a whole, they work for the continuation of the pregnancy.'[46]

### Homosexuality and same-sex marriage

The Churches' reputation for bigoted thinking owes much to their stances on these hot-button issues. The question of whether same-sex marriage should be legalised is, in my view, a genuinely vexing one – at least theologically. But the continued condemnation of homosexual acts *per se* is something else. The churches, for the most part, opposed the decriminalisation campaigns of the 1970s and 1980s. This was a bad mistake – albeit largely an honest one – and I have no doubt it has been a not insignificant factor in secularisation.

Personally I shudder when senior contemporary figures in the Churches, such as (Catholic) Archbishop Mark Coleridge of Brisbane, continue to describe homosexuality as 'a warp in the creation'.[47] Sexual fulfilment – within a respectful, monogamous relationship – seems to me a fundamental aspect of God's plan for most human beings. The idea that ingrained homosexual orientation can be removed by therapy – or suppressed for life without damage to a person's physical and mental well-being – is now discredited. In fact, it has been discredited for decades.[48] Many well-meaning (heterosexual) Christians of my acquaintance still cling to this belief, but it is time they gave it up. A certain percentage of people in all societies – probably about 2 or 3 per cent – are born gay. In other words, there are somewhere between 150 and 200 million gay people alive on Earth today. The probability must be that God intends them to have 'a very special social role to perform within the created order, if they are able to negotiate positively the logic of the homosexual condition'.[49] If so, we should all try to help them in that endeavour.

What about the Bible? Speaking for myself, the Scriptural arguments against homosexuality as such are not compelling.[50] It disturbs me when Christians recite them as though they were of cast-iron strength, on a par with the numerous passages that unambiguously denounce greed, say, or idolatry, or even divorce. It is hard to escape the conclusion reached by several American commentators: homosexuality is a 'frontburner issue among evangelicals because they think it is one sin from which they are free'.[51]

It says much for the strength of the religious impulse – or the power of the *overall* Christian (and Muslim and Jewish) messages – that so many gay Australians remain believers. They are frequently patronised or attacked by their fellow religionists, yet do not renounce God. That fact of itself should be food for thought.

What of same-sex marriage? This, to my mind, is a much trickier issue. Legal change is probably inevitable in Australia, because sooner or later the federal Liberal Party caucus will be permitted a conscience vote. But theological truth is not determined by a show of politicians' hands.

A great deal has been written about these issues in recent years, from both a secular and a religious perspective. Let me be honest, if rather lame: at the time of writing, despite careful thought, I have not finally decided where I stand.

The *religious* case for same-sex marriage has been made eloquently by Christians of real stature, including Justice Michael Kirby and Father Frank Brennan in Australia, and Tory Prime Minister David Cameron in Britain.[52] Kirby is absolutely right to insist that 'bullying tactics designed to frighten or shame those who propound differing interpretations of the Bible can have no place in any sincere search for the meaning of written passages'.[53] But, in that spirit, I am bound to say this. Proponents of same-sex marriage frequently overstate their case.

Opposition to it 'is not simply irrational conservative prejudice,'[54] and it is wrong to assert, as some proponents do, that 'the issue only affects gay people'.[55] It affects everyone, because, on any view, marriage is an institution utterly central to human society. Undoubtedly, the State has the right to make civil laws in respect of it. But to the extent that marriage is a *religious* institution – a sacrament – Churches and individual clerics should have the right to refuse to solemnise marriages that they believe, in good conscience, to be contrary to Biblical teachings. This is not 'bigotry' but religious freedom.

As far as Scriptural exegesis is concerned, there is a far stronger case against same-sex marriage than against homosexuality *per se*. Jesus is not recorded as having said anything at all about the latter, but He said a good deal about marriage. Similarly, the handful of glancing references that St Paul made to homosexual acts are reasonably capable of explanation or re-contextualising;[56] but his long and beautiful statements about marriage are not. It is fair to say that both Jesus and Paul did not merely assume that marriage was between a man and a woman; they understood and articulated its very nature in those terms. That said, all the relevant passages are descriptive rather than proscriptive.

There is much to be said for the view of the English Protestant theologian John Milbank: 'it is not a matter of extending the right, nor the teleological good, of marriage to gay people, but rather of redefining the very thing in which marriage consists'.[57] A somewhat more forceful way of putting it is that 'the traditional restriction of marriage to two persons of different sex is not arbitrarily discriminatory'.[58]

Same-sex civil unions sanctioned by the State are a different matter. Like Milbank and many other Christians, I have no difficulty with the idea. But I am well aware that this distinction cuts no ice with a majority of Australians, especially those under forty. Accordingly, for as long as the Churches continue to oppose same-sex marriage, this will only add to their unpopularity. It is another factor in secularisation.

### Female ordination

To complete this survey, it seems necessary to say something about the exclusion of women from the Catholic priesthood and from ministry positions in some Protestant Churches. This is sexism, and personally I find it frustrating. So do many practising Christians of all denominations and both sexes. But, yet again, it is important to understand the reasons for the contrary view. Those who oppose female ordination insist that they are bound in conscience to do so, whether they like it or not.

In the words of a senior theologian at the Vatican, Wojciech Giertych: 'We base ourselves not on human expectations, but ... on the revealed word of God. We are not free to invent the priesthood according to our own customs, according to our own expectations.'[59] The Catechism of the Catholic Church states that only men can receive holy orders because Jesus chose men as his Apostles and the 'apostles did the same when they chose collaborators to succeed them in their ministry'. Catholics also place heavy reliance on the fact that Jesus Himself was a man: since a priest is supposed to serve as an image of Christ, his maleness is essential to that role.[60]

Protestant opponents of female ordination usually base their case on certain passages from Paul's letters in the New Testament. Paul outlined a view of family and church life with men 'at the head'.[61] In practice, the mainline Protestant Churches in Australia have adopted a shifting array of positions. The first woman to be ordained in Australia was the Reverend Winifred Kiek, in 1926, within the Congregational Union of South Australia. The first woman minister in the Methodist Church was the Reverend Margaret Sanders, ordained in 1969.[62] Of the existing 'big three' Churches, the Uniting Church allows female ordination; the Presbyterian Church did so between 1974 and 1991, before reversing its position; and the Anglican Church began to ordain women as priests in 1992 and as bishops in 2008.[63]

The Sydney Diocese of the Anglican Church continues to dissent from the national position, as it does in several other things – a stance that infuriates some people, especially liberal female Anglicans.[64] A prominent and popular Sydney Anglican minister, John Dickson – solidly orthodox on most matters – caused a stir in late 2012 by making a modest, well-reasoned case for allowing women to give sermons.[65] (Not ordination, I stress, just giving sermons.) He was howled down by some even for that. But Sydney Anglicans are exceptional: progressive women with an open mind about God should not judge Protestant Christianity against their standards.

A better model for them may be the Uniting Church. In a long document adopted by its assembly in 1990, *Why Does the Uniting Church Ordain Women to the Ministry of the Word?*, the authors wrote: 'We believe that to deny ordination to a person on the grounds of gender alone is to deny a basic feature of this gospel, which reveals God's love for all human beings without distinction.'[66]

Personally, I agree. And before coming back to the main issue – secularisation – I will give the final word on this issue to the last female

Presbyterian minister in Australia, the Reverend Joy Bartholomew. The daughter of missionaries and a mother of three adult sons (one with Down's syndrome), she presided at the Church of St Andrew in Canberra until her retirement in July 2013. In her view, 'the biblical principle is that women and men should work together to honour God and to bring His will into the world'.[67]

### Sex and gender issues: an overall scorecard

Where does all this leave us? With two questions. First, in which respects did the Churches get things wrong? Second, which stances (whether right or wrong) have been active causes of secularisation?

On the question of correctness (theological or otherwise), views will of course differ. Often – a point worth emphasising again – views differ between and within Churches, making generalisations almost meaningless. (Female ordination and contraception for married couples are good examples: the divide is mostly along Catholic–Protestant lines.) My own opinion is that the mainline Churches have been largely right in their disapproval of the sexual revolution and of abortion on demand. They were wrong to oppose the justified changes to the divorce laws in the late nineteenth century and again in 1959, but right in their misgivings about the Family Law Act of 1975. Their most grievous misjudgments have been in respect of homosexuality *per se*, though the debate about same-sex marriage is a legitimate one.

What of secularisation? Which of these stances have been the most off-putting for people who might otherwise have remained interested in religion – or at least kept an open mind? No doubt many young heterosexual people, men and women, see the Churches' disapproving views on casual sex as hopelessly out of touch, but I doubt this is really a game-changer. Instead, I would point to the ongoing persecution of homosexual people, especially homosexual men, within sections of the various Churches. The Catholic ban on contraception in marriage must also have done much damage over the years, not least because it has been so flagrantly disobeyed by Catholics.

As far as gender questions are concerned, I keep returning to the fact that the majority of practising Christians in Australia (around 60 per cent) are, and have been for a long time, women. If gender issues were at the heart of secularisation, you would expect the percentages to be reversed: the churches would be full of men. It is not so because religiously inclined women do not, on the whole, think in the way that their secular sisters imagine they should. Though some believing women in all eras have disagreed with stances taken by their Churches, a majority have not. And many among the dissenting minority have kept sight of the bigger picture and remained faithful, while fighting for change from within.

## Other ecclesiastical sins and errors

I am almost at the end of the list of charges on the indictment. But, for completeness, there are two others to tackle. Neither, it seems to me, has been a significant cause of secularisation in Australia. But at least arguably they are extra factors in the mix.

### Protestant theology

Since the Reformation, some Catholic theologians have blamed Protestantism itself for the slow decline of religious faith. (See my brief summary of the main differences between Protestantism and Catholicism in Appendix B.) In *The Faith of Australians*, Hans Mol contended that 'secularisation is to some extent the logical outcome of the doctrine of salvation by faith of the individual – bypassing institution or [good] works'. He elaborated:

> The doctrine [of salvation by faith alone] opts for the autonomy of
> the individual – rather than for the shelter of the community and the
> norms which sustain it. Secularisation may be seen as the result of the
> latent, but inevitable dysfunction of this and other Protestant dogmas.[68]

Naturally, as a Protestant, I find this argument unappealing. But it is also unconvincing. True, as Steve Bruce has pointed out, access to religious truth via private reading of the Bible (as opposed to instruction from on high) tends to foster a greater diversity of views. Institutionally, this can lead to 'competing factions and schismatic groups':[69] there are literally thousands of Protestant denominations worldwide, but there is still only one Roman Catholic Church. It is also true that when religion becomes a purely private affair, divorced from charitable involvement in the community, or even from evangelism, a kind of bunker mentality can set in. Sometimes the end result is stagnation.[70] Historically, this has happened more often among smaller Protestant sects.

But there are counter-arguments. One is that the increased pluralism that Protestantism encourages actually *helps* the overall cause of religion. Rodney Stark is one commentator to have advanced this idea: the greater number of 'choices' on offer, he suggests, the more likely it is that everyone will find a religious 'product' suitable for them.[71] For me, this notion smacks too much of free-market economic theory. Of course, freedom of religion is a precious right. But faith is about a sincere seeking for truth, wherever the search leads and whatever the cost, not making a pleasurable choice. To a certain extent institutionalism is necessary and desirable, because it tends to militate against individuals going down paths previously tried and discredited. The accumulated wisdom of centuries is not to be sneezed at.

As an explanation for secularisation, a focus on the differences between Catholic and Protestant theology strikes me as misplaced.

For a start, it is not obvious that Catholic discipline is stricter than Protestant discipline. Rightly or wrongly (I would say wrongly), there are plenty of Protestant denominations, and countless Protestant congregations, in which theological dissent is barely tolerated. (A particular version or reading of the Bible becomes a 'Paper Pope'.) And while, conversely, many other Protestant denominations and congregations tolerate or even encourage open discussion, it is important to remember that the Catholic Church is also far from a homogeneous whole. The Orthodox Church is stiff competition for the Roman Catholic Church, and within both there exist many separate orders (or institutes) with their own aims and preoccupations. Among individual Catholics in Australia, views seem to differ on the whole gamut of theological, moral and sociopolitical issues, at least as much as they do among Protestants. It is a myth that the Catholic Church here was ever a 'monolith, a press button affair in which the Pope or the Cardinal or somebody puts a message on the line and all Catholics obey it'.[72] In Australia today, compare the brand of Catholicism of, say, a member of Opus Dei with that of a Father Bob Maguire or a Kristina Keneally.

It is true that, historically, Catholicism has been strong in many countries where religion was strong. But there are Protestant examples of the same phenomenon – places where many differed among themselves, on points big and small, but where overall levels of belief were still very high. I have in mind not only England, Scotland and Wales in the 200 years or so following the Reformation, but also Germany, the Netherlands and the various Scandinavian countries. Protestants have always formed a sizable majority in the United States (as much as 70 per cent plus), and religious belief has never collapsed there. And in recent years, levels of religious observance have fallen just as steadily in Catholic nations (France, Italy and Spain, for instance) as they have anywhere else.[73]

## The local Churches' lack of Australianness

Another argument is that it took too long for the Churches to develop a uniquely Australian character.[74] This, indeed, was one of *The Bulletin*'s main beefs against them – that they were pale, limp imitations of their British counterparts.

In one sense the whole argument was, and is, bogus. The Christian religion is universal; its fundamental principles transcend national borders. But the practical reality is that all institutions must operate within the system of nation-states. And, up to a point, it is a good and appropriate thing that a national institution reflect the character of its people – as the Church of England used to do magnificently, and to some extent still does.

From the start there were obvious problems for the Church of England in Australia. As time went on these problems were exacerbated, and it is arguable that they were not swiftly enough addressed. Around the time of Federation, the Anglican Dean of Perth proposed that the name 'Australia' be incorporated into the local Church's official title. The idea was not merely rejected at the time – it was not implemented until 1961.[75] For decades into the twentieth century a significant proportion of Anglican clerics continued to be recruited from the Mother Country – especially for senior positions. The problem was less nationality than quality: too many of these men were mediocre, and pompous to boot. In the words of a local, the Reverend R.H. Moore of Fremantle: 'A stranger from abroad not knowing local conditions is bound to come with an exalted idea of his stature.'[76]

Similar issues confronted the Presbyterian Church, though to a lesser degree. By Federation, while many senior positions were still held by Scots, the majority of ministers were Australian-born.[77] The same could not be said of priests and nuns – let alone senior clerics – in the Catholic Church. Until well into the twentieth century many of them continued to be imported, chiefly from Ireland but from numerous other European countries as well.[78] This, however, was necessary, if the Church was to service its remarkable system of parish schools.

Like all the arguments examined in this chapter, this one has some validity – but not much. In the long term, as I suggested in Chapter 5, the multicultural nature of Australia's Churches has actually been a source of underlying strength. In their own time, in fits and starts, each *has* developed a distinctive, non-British character. It is not obvious to me that the process could have happened appreciably faster. In England itself, as we saw in Chapter 3, it took many centuries. The plain fact is that most Australians maintained a sense of loyalty to Britain (or parts thereof) until well into the twentieth century: that loyalty extended to its Churches.

Finally, it is worth remembering that the one early attempt to establish a native Church – the Australian Church of the Reverend Charles Strong – ended in failure. Founded in 1885, and based in Melbourne, it had a small but devoted following before World War One, but thereafter it floundered. The reasons were complex, but one thing is clear: mere nominal Australianness was not enough.

# CHAPTER 9

# Two more belief-killers: scientism and prosperity

Religion is now completely superseded by science.

Richard Dawkins, *The God Delusion*

No one can serve two masters; for a slave will either hate the one and love the other, or be devoted to the one and despise the other. You cannot serve God and wealth.

Matthew 6:24

It is assumed today in some circles – often with unmistakable relish – that the further decline of religion across the West is all but inevitable. In this chapter I will examine that hypothesis, chiefly by reference to two other major factors in secularisation: the phenomenon of scientism, and unprecedented material prosperity. As far as Australia is concerned, I regard these factors as the two most challenging. Why? Because, unlike the others so far considered, they are largely outside the Churches' control. They are insidious.

For Christian readers, it seems necessary to qualify everything that follows. However bleak things may look, God is ultimately sovereign. Accordingly, *nothing* is inevitable. God might, at any time, initiate a religious revival; in any event, human beings have free will. We are capable of learning from previous mistakes and choosing a different course.

To the extent that secularisation can be attributed to past failings of the Churches, all is not lost. It should be within their power – and that of individual believers also – to improve religious education for the young. To think and act more consistently with the Gospel when issues of war and peace next arise for national consideration. To address fully the scandal of child abuse, and, consistently with Scripture, but in the light of contemporary knowledge, to reassess some issues of sex and gender. Sectarianism can be further minimised. A more distinctively Australian Christian identity can, if necessary, be forged.

The difficulty in relation to scientism – and, even more so, prosperity – is that these are states of mind and becoming utterly entrenched in 21st-century Australia. They will be harder to combat. But before discussing these two phenomena, there are others to clear out of the way. They have also been put forward as contributing factors in secularisation, largely outside the Churches' control.[1] While not nearly so important as scientism or prosperity, none is quite dismissible as a red herring.

## Urbanisation

Some suggest that religion flourishes best in small, like-minded communities and that, typically, such communities are rural rather than urban. In modern urbanised societies such as Australia, it is argued, religious solidarity is attacked from both above and below.[2] It is attacked from below by the forces of individualism (the assertion of the right to do one's own thing) and social differentiation. In big cities and towns there is less sense of community. Huge numbers of people move between jobs, marriages, neighbourhoods, even social classes. At the same time, the clustering together of people in urban areas has the effect of increasing the number of lifestyle choices on offer, many of which are incompatible with piety and faith.

Urbanisation, it is argued, can also facilitate attacks on religion from above – by the so-called elites. What happens is that 'those at the centre of society, the carriers of modernisation, missionise the rest, seeking to assimilate them, educating them and socialising them in "respectable" beliefs and practices'.[3] Since the 1960s the trend of elite opinion across the West has been away from the Christian ideal in almost every respect, and, since the voices of the elites have been most powerful in the cities, that is where religion has waned the most. In recent decades that has certainly been true of Australia. By the first half of the twentieth century, country towns were very strong centres of Christianity (and still are). However, the decline of rural industries in the second half of the century – resulting in the gradual migration of the rural population to the cities – has undermined the *relative* strength of the rural churches.[4]

None of these points is invalid. But all of them are deficient, because many of the same points can be made the other way around. If the trend of elite opinion in a big city happens to be in favour of religion – or a particular religion – then religion will take hold faster there (faster, that is, than it might in regions further-flung). We have already seen examples in Part One of this book. In the 30s AD, the Apostles got Christianity started in Jerusalem precisely because it was a crowded urban metropolis. When the Romans brought their new official faith to Britain in the fourth century, it took hold quickest in the cities and towns. When the enclosure movement forced the British working classes into the cities and towns, it was there that vital religious movements such as Methodism sprang up. For many decades after the British colonised Australia, Christianity was strongest in and around Sydney, Hobart, Melbourne and Adelaide – and weakest in the bush. American theorists have argued along the same lines vis-à-vis the United States in the early twentieth century.[5]

In short, urbanisation is not a core reason for secularisation. It is a factor that can speed up the process if the conditions are otherwise ripe.

## Postmodernism

This is another catch-all term frequently bandied about by people saddened and frustrated by the decline of religious belief. But I am not sure that many of them understand what it means. Broadly, when social scientists use the term, they mean one of two things (or sometimes both).[6] First, the notion that the central ideals of the Enlightenment – or modernity – have lost credibility. Second, the observation that in the modern age a person's sense of identity is (or should be) determined by personal choice rather than his or her place in society. In the field of philosophy, the theory's most famous pioneers include Martin Heidegger (1889–1976), Jean-Francois Lyotard (1924–98), Michel Foucault (1926–84), Jean Boudrillard (1929–2007), Jacques Derrida (1930–2004) and Richard Rorty (1931–2007).

The degree to which postmodernist theory has influenced opinion among the broader populace is debatable. I suspect its influence is exaggerated, by both proponents and opponents. But, at any rate, the implications of postmodernism for religion are mixed. On the one hand, it is healthy (if sobering) that some of the more naïvely optimistic aspects of Enlightenment thinking now stand challenged. Christians can and should agree with postmodernists on this much. At the absolute core of Christian theology is the idea that human beings, while having a special place in God's Creation ('a little lower than the angels'), are nevertheless fallen creatures. Left to our own devices, we have a near-infinite capacity for evil. The Enlightenment dream that all the world's ills might be cured by the application of pure reason, and the benevolent use of science and technology, needed to be challenged. To the extent that postmodernism has done this, it is no bad thing. In the words of the man who first used the term, Arnold J. Toynbee, 'Our own Post-Modern Age has been inaugurated by the general war of 1914–1918.'[7]

A related postmodernist idea is that the scientific method is not a reliable – let alone infallible – way of arriving at objective truths. Or, even more broadly, that no human being in any field of endeavour is capable of arriving at objective truth. Why? Because, in the arch words of Australian philosopher James Franklin, 'postmodernism is an attitude ... of unteachable suspicion'.[8] It rejects the very notion of good evidence. Another Australian philosopher, the late David Stove, distilled various versions of it thus: 'We can know things only as they are related to us; under our forms of perception and understanding; and insofar as they fall under our conceptual schemes, etc. So, we cannot know things as they are in themselves.'[9]

Stove called this the Worst Argument in the World, and I am not about to disagree. If everything is relative, on what do we base our lives? If we cannot trust our own senses, where does that leave us? Certainly revelational religion is left high and dry. The Christian religion is based in large part on historical evidence for the life of Jesus: if all that evidence is to be deemed inherently unreliable, then Christianity becomes, at best, just another set of ethical platitudes, debatable at that. There would be similarly grim implications for most other fields of knowledge.

Fortunately, postmodernism has been skilfully rebutted by thinkers in many disparate fields. The attacks on the scientific method have been shown to be especially flimsy.[10] Yet, for all that, I have a sneaking sympathy for any argument that attempts to prick the balloon of contemporary scientific arrogance. It certainly needs pricking (an issue I will come to shortly). In that sense, postmodernists and religionists have something in common.

The second strand of postmodernism – that which focuses on the sources of personal identity – is also a mixed bag for religion. The good part is that the 'post-modern turn is ... a turn away from assuming that modernity, with its typical foci on work as economic activity and on calculation as the acme of reason, will continue to form the matrix for social interaction'.[11] In other words, we are not defined by our jobs or our IQ (or our nationality, our social class, our race, our gender). That is as countercultural an idea as Paul's first-century declaration in Galatians 3:28 ('There is neither Jew nor Gentile, neither slave nor free, nor is there male and female, for you are all one in Christ Jesus'), and a number of Christian thinkers have seen it as a peg on which to hang their hopes of religious revival.[12] Their reasoning is that the fracturing of the materialist worldview might help to get religion reconsidered as, at least, a possible alternative.

So far, to say the least, it does not seem to have worked that way. I suspect the reason is that most citizens across the West are still wedded to a modernist rather than postmodernist worldview. Certainly, you do not often hear the names of Derrida or Foucault or Rorty mentioned in conversation at the office photocopier – let alone at the footy or the beach. And postmodernists themselves are unlikely to embrace the Christian religion as their lifestyle choice. For one thing, it is seen as 'merely one man-made convention among many other alternative conventions'.[13] For another, it is seen as a fun-spoiler, a source of invalid coercion, an odious check on personal freedom.

## The influence of public atheists and anti-religionists

I remarked in the Introduction that proactive atheism has had a revival in the opening years of the 21st century. There seems little doubt that 9/11 was the catalyst. In any event, the names of Richard Dawkins and Christopher Hitchens became well known across the West, at least among the upper-middle classes. Their books debunking Christianity (*The God Delusion* and *God Is Not Great* respectively) sold well and encouraged a stream of copycat authors. The New Atheists, as they were dubbed, also motivated a stream of Christian authors to write books of their own, in an attempt to answer the arguments they had made. (I was one.)

The question is whether either side has had much impact on the views of the population at large. At least in Australia, I believe the answer is 'No'. Both camps have preached mostly to the converted – and a small proportion of the converted at that. Useful oral discussion has proved next to impossible because of lack of opportunity to air the issues properly or incivility in the public square; in the latter respect, the fault has been mainly, but not exclusively, on the atheist side. Tom Frame is right: 'It has become almost a cliché in anti-theistic works to claim that atheists have matured and reached the full stature of humankind while religious believers are intellectually childish and emotionally insecure.'[14]

Of course, it might fairly be pointed out that, historically, it was atheists who endured ridicule and persecution from over-zealous Christians (and other religionists). But the tables have turned.

My overriding point is that the skirmishes over the last decade or so between the New Atheists and their religious protagonists have not only been unilluminating – they have also passed most Australians by.

It has ever been thus. In the second half of the nineteenth century the first prominent 'free thinkers' entered the scene in Australia. In 1879, a young Melbourne journalist named Marcus Clarke penned an article for the *Victorian Review*, 'Civilisation without delusion', that caused a brief stir. It was a rude, all-guns-blazing attack on religious belief, aimed especially at the Christian faith. Clarke predicted that 'the creed which teaches that the intellect should be distrusted will fade away'; he made it crystal-clear he believed it *ought* to fade away. Only then would 'Mankind [be] freed from the terrors of future torments … comprehending that by no amount of prayers can they secure eternal happiness for their souls.'[15] Clarke's brand of slick, sophisticated atheism was something novel in the Australia colonies. Anti-clericism had long been a feature of public debate, and maverick atheists were not unheard of. But this was something else again. It reflected an earnest strain of thinking among the educated urban middle class.

The Australasian Secular Association was founded just three years later, in 1882.[16] It broke up in 1888, but many equivalents have been formed over the years since.[17] Their members and fellow travellers have always been small in number, but, culturally, they have had a not insignificant impact, especially in the last few decades. Likewise nakedly atheist commentators such as Phillip Adams and Peter FitzSimons. Adams has been chipping away at religion since the 1960s. They do not *change* many minds directly, but people of their mindset dominate some important organisations – in the media and tertiary education sectors especially – that might otherwise be more sympathetic to religion and allow for more balanced debate. As things stand, too many act as gate-keepers against Christian voices.

## The demise of Sabbatarianism

Sundays in Australia have long since ceased to be sacred. Laws prohibiting commercial and recreational activities on Sundays began to be wound back in the late nineteenth century, despite the opposition of the institutional Churches. The cause of Sabbatarianism now sounds quaint, even ridiculous, but with the benefit of hindsight one can see that its adherents had a serious point. In the main, opponents of shopping and sport and art gallery attendance on Sundays were not opposed to those activities in and of themselves. Indeed, they understood such activities' attraction. But they also took seriously the Fourth Commandment.

As Tom Frame and others have argued, the gradual relaxation of the laws that encouraged Sunday observance has been a significant cause of secularisation in Australia. Nowadays, the churches and Sunday schools compete with any number of more obviously enjoyable forms of entertainment.[18] Moreover, there seems no prospect whatsoever of a return to the past. To that extent, this factor is irreversible. That said, its importance ought not to be overstated: a prominent Sydney Anglican, Michael Jensen, has recently observed that 'for the most part these days, modern evangelical Christians are completely agnostic on the question of which day the church should gather and whether that day should in some way also be a sacred day of rest'.[19]

In short, if the cause of religion is strong enough, it should not matter whether people are free to do other things on Sundays. Jesus Himself thought Sabbatarianism could be overdone ('the Sabbath was made for man, and not man for the Sabbath'), and St Paul was not fussed by it either.[20]

Having considered these secondary factors, let us now turn to the big two.

## Scientism

Scientism is the widespread belief that science has, or will eventually have, the answers to everything – or to everything that can be known. There is a concomitant notion (sometimes called materialism) that the Universe self-evidently consists of physical matter and nothing else. Everything is essentially mechanical and all matter is unconscious.[21] Hence there is no place for the supernatural; religious belief is 'all but devoid of rationality'; and 'religion and science will never agree'.[22] The American writer Charles Davis once articulated this worldview by likening Christianity to any form of superstition that will 'wither like a leaf before a flame when the scientific attitude is brought to bear on it'.[23]

Let us drill down a little further into this mindset. As far as I can understand, it seems to have taken hold in the late nineteenth century and to be based on two core assumptions. (In his 2012 book *The Science Delusion* the excellent English writer Rupert Sheldrake lists ten assumptions 'that most scientists take for granted', but I believe that mine are the two most important as far as religion is concerned.)

The first is that specific findings of modern science are in direct conflict with statements in the Bible – in particular, the account of Creation in the opening chapters of Genesis. A trio of foundational texts, published in the mid-nineteenth century, in large part gave birth to this assumption: Charles Lyell's three-volume *Principles of Geology* (1830–33), and the two best-known works of Charles Darwin, *On the Origin of Species* (1859) and *The Descent of Man* (1871). Lyell proposed that the age of the Earth was much, much greater than had hitherto been assumed. In Lyell's day the upper estimates were in the hundreds of millions of years; most respectable estimates were in the tens of millions. We now know that the correct figure is approximately 4.56 billion years. Lyell confirmed the theory of uniformitarianism, which holds that the (non-living) Earth was shaped over eons by the steady accumulation of minute changes, brought about by the same processes still in operation today. These ideas were a huge influence on Darwin, who applied them to the living world – even the species *Homo sapiens* itself.

Neither Lyell nor Darwin was an atheist.[24] But the lesson (mis)learned by some of their more influential contemporaries, and by countless millions since, was that science was now irrefutably at odds with the God of the Christian Bible. A God who made the Universe from nothing in the course of six days, before resting on the seventh (Genesis 1–2); a God who placed man 'a little lower than the angels' (Psalm 8:5); a God who made the first woman, Eve, from Adam's rib (Genesis 2:21–23). Above all, a God who takes a personal interest in each and every human being. Some – but by no means all – nineteenth-century clerics made the disastrous error of challenging the very idea of biological evolution. Young-Earth, six-day Creationists were rarer (most emerged in the twentieth century), but they too weighed in. Their argument that the Earth is only 6,000 years old was and is based on a literal reading of the genealogy sections of Genesis (Chapters 5 and 12) and other scattered fragments of Scripture.[25]

Supposedly clear 'contradictions' of the Bible are one thing. But even greater damage has been done to theistic religion in a somewhat less direct way.

The second core assumption underlying scientism is that there is no need to invoke God to explain anything. Before Darwin, one of the strongest and most widely accepted arguments for the existence of God was the appearance of design in the natural world – the so-called teleological argument. This was so despite the posthumous publication in 1779 of David Hume's *Dialogues Concerning Natural*

*Religion*, an attempt to refute the teleological arguments for God. A key Christian text was clergyman William Paley's *Natural Theology or Evidences of the Existence and Attributes of the Deity*, first published in England in 1802 and a best-seller in the first half of the nineteenth century. Its contents were well known throughout the Australian colonies, at least in educated circles. Darwin's discoveries, and others, were alleged to have blown Paley's arguments out of the water: the appearance of design was an illusion.

But the phenomenon of scientism undermined far more than formally argued natural theology. In due course, in sociologist Max Weber's famous expression, it disenchanted the Western world. A 'sophisticated' person today, whether scientifically trained or not, is much less likely than were his forebears to attribute *any* phenomena to God. Weber, writing in 1948, explained this mindset by reference to 'increasing intellectualisation and rationalisation'. He was at pains to stress that this did '*not* … indicate an increased general knowledge of the conditions under which one lives'.[26] In this Weber was surely right – we live in a world of increasing specialisation and sub-specialisation, where most things are left to others. Relatively few people know, for example, how a car works – let alone a microwave oven or a mobile phone.

But Weber was not talking about increased *actual* knowledge of the world on behalf of the broad mass of citizens. Rather, he wrote:

> [Disenchantment] means something else, namely, the knowledge, or the belief, that if one but wished one *could* learn it [that is, some given item of explanatory knowledge] at any time. Hence, it means that principally there are no mysterious incalculable forces that come into play, but rather that one can, in principle, master all things by calculation … One need no longer have recourse to magical means in order to master or implore the spirits, as did the savage, for whom such mysterious powers existed. Technical means and calculations perform the service.[27]

Put to one side, for the moment, the validity of the two assumptions that underlie scientism (that specific findings of modern science are in direct conflict with statements in the Bible, and there is no need to invoke God to explain anything). As Steve Bruce has sagely, if over-cynically, observed: 'the intrinsic merits (or otherwise) of any idea, perspective or ideology are usually only a small part of their success or failure'.[28] What matters is the idea's superficial plausibility.

The causal link between scientism and secularisation appears to me incontrovertible. For a start, there is good evidence that scientists themselves are among the most disenchanted citizens of the West. 'The overwhelming majority of the world's scientists, particularly at senior level, are non-believers.'[29] So asserted Phillip Adams in 2007. Although it depends, in part, on one's exact definition of a scientist, the overall thrust of the assertion is true enough.[30] Granted, this is a relatively recent trend: in various surveys taken during the period 1915–70, less than 30 per cent of American scientists reported having 'no religion'.[31] But there seems no basis for disputing the position today. It is beyond argument that some high-profile contemporary scientists are among the most trenchant critics of religion. Richard Dawkins is far from a lone wolf. An American physicist, Steven Weinberg, is on record as saying: 'Anything that we scientists can do to weaken the hold of religion should be done.'[32] Nevertheless, some theorists of secularisation reject the proposition that scientism is a major cause of irreligion.[33]

Others, however, see it as a deadly factor – if not the deadliest of all.[34] Personally, I lie somewhere in between.

On the one hand, I agree with Tom Frame that scientism is rife in Australia today. Frame reached this (admittedly impressionistic) conclusion after a review of some 500 comments posted on various online blogs. The notion that 'theism is irrational and unreasonable' was, he found, the most commonly expressed opinion of all. And faith in science was the key.[35] Frame's conclusions accord with my own experience since 2008: some of the most vehement atheistic objections to my arguments in *God, Actually*, and in my articles published in online forums, have been along 'scientific' lines.[36] Sometimes the intransigence on display is frightening. In the words of Jane Caro, 'it's just not possible for many people to believe in the supernatural in the age of science; it has become such a psychological imperative they've closed their eyes to everything else'.[37]

This is sobering. But I am less pessimistic than Frame – or, if you prefer, less optimistic than Caro – about the long-term inevitability of religious decline. Certainly, when it comes to combating scientism, I believe that there are decent grounds for hope. Yes, scientism is superficially plausible and deeply entrenched. But ultimately it ought to be combatable with education, for several strong arguments can be brought against it. Not the least powerful, as we saw in Chapter 2, is that the scientific method is itself a product of Judaeo-Christianity. But there are several other arguments. Two in particular persuaded me fifteen years ago that scientism is unsound.

One – the complete answer to any notion that 'science has disproved the Bible' – is that the Bible is not a science textbook; it is a library containing writings by many authors in many genres. The account of Creation in Genesis is poetry, and was never intended to be read literally on all points of detail. To do so – and Christians are often as guilty as atheists in this regard – is to turn the doctrine of Creation into a scientific theory.[38]

A second realisation persuaded me that the essence of scientism is almost certainly false. God *is* needed to explain many things – including many of the discoveries of modern science. The Universe not merely 'is', it is a particular kind of Universe. Happenstance or fluke might be a barely adequate explanation for certain kinds of Universes – random, featureless and dead – but not for the exquisitely ordered and fine-tuned Universe in which we live. If our Universe is a one-off, it must have been designed. The only other rational possibility – the one upon which most of the New Atheists rather desperately fall back – is that there are many, many universes, perhaps an infinite number of them, each with slightly different laws; we just happen to find ourselves in one of the rare few that, fortuitously, sustains self-conscious life.

Today, the most powerful fine-tuning arguments are *not* based on the appearance of design in the natural world. They are based, rather, on the basal laws of physics and chemistry and the so-called constants of nature. These laws and constants are, as it were, wired into the Universe and have remained unchanged since the moment of the Big Bang. They did not evolve in any way explainable by Darwinian theory, which is confined to the realm of terrestrial biology. Grasping this was another crucial breakthrough for me.

Yet I hasten to emphasise that believers in God need not be intimidated by Darwinian evolutionary theory either. Nowadays it is at the root of scientism, and there is no doubt that, historically, its overall effect on religion has been negative. But I am convinced that this is because too many people (atheists and theists alike) know too little about it. Proselytising atheists such as Richard Dawkins get away with murder in ascribing almost everything to a process that is incompletely understood even at the very highest levels of the scientific community.[39] I have explained elsewhere why, in my opinion, the *known* facts of Darwinian evolution – as opposed to the exaggerations and speculations – point *towards*, rather than away from, the existence of God. Evolution itself is a finely tuned process.

Few of the more sophisticated religious thinkers in Australian history have ever thought it necessary to reject evolution in order to defend the

Christian God. From the mid-nineteenth century onwards, after the ground-breaking discoveries of Lyell and Darwin had been popularised, many distinguished Australian clerics accommodated revised theories about the age of the Earth and the evolution of biological organisms. In 1862, preaching in Forbes, the Reverend J.D. Lang explained that 'In the beginning' in Genesis 1:1 means 'in the inconceivably remote past'. In the words of his biographer, Lang 'wanted to show that the revealed word of God in Scripture was entirely accordant with an intelligent view of the works of God in creation'.[40] True, there were also clerics who clung to literalism. But, within a generation or two, good sense had largely prevailed. By 1923, the Anglican Bishop of Gippsland, George Cranswick, could say when delivering the annual Moorhouse Lectures that 'the Kingdom of Science has become the ally of the Kingdom of God'.[41]

Today, most Australian Christians are respectful of science. It is a myth that the majority are young-Earth Creationists or climate change deniers.

That said, it is a shame that more Australian Christians do not take the trouble to educate themselves properly about science. They would then be in a much stronger position to challenge scientism. Put the fine-tuning arguments to one side. The plain fact of the matter is that modern science does not explain nearly as much as most people seem to assume. It does not explain the origin of the Universe or the origin of life on Earth.* It does not explain free will or consciousness or religious faith itself.[42] And it is very hard to see how science could *ever* explain these things. Scientism excludes whole categories of knowledge that are self-evidently acquired by means other than the scientific method: logic, mathematics and philosophy, for instance, to say nothing of ethics and morality. In short, the things that give life meaning.[43]

Sir Gustav Nossal (b. 1931) is one of the most eminent Australian scientists alive today. (His field is research biology – antibody formation and immunological tolerance.) He is also a practising Roman Catholic. He once said, most wisely:

---

\* The Big Bang theory does not purport to explain the initial moment of Creation, the 'how' or the 'why'. It deals with what happened *after* the initial moment of Creation, albeit in its unimaginably early phases. Similarly, Darwinian evolutionary theory does not explain – or purport to explain – the existence of life. It is concerned with the process of diversification of life once life exists.

Science deals with fundamentally repeatable, objective, verifiable observations. It deals with hypotheses of which you can at least say 'this is not patently false'. But the human experience, on the other hand, does not just deal with verifiable facts. The human experience has Shakespeare. It has Beethoven. It has Thomas Aquinas. There is no scientist alive who can tell me how the brain of Shakespeare differs from the brain of the worst scribbler for the tabloid press. This is not yet and may never be in the realm of science.

He continued:

We have to access this huge other area of human experience through other means. Call them the humanities. Theology, of course, is one of the great humanities. A human being struggling to understand the cosmos and to understand his or her own consciousness is not at all antipathetic or opposed to me struggling to understand how cells make antibody molecules.[44]

The key point is that some knowledge lies within the realm of science and some does not. But this does not mean, for the theist, that science must be evaded or downplayed. We saw in Chapter 2 that one of the key findings of modern science – that the Universe had a finite beginning – is spectacularly consistent with a monotheistic view of the world. And the clear theistic implications of the Big Bang theory constitute the tip of the iceberg. As a starting-point, I recommend the books of two distinguished Australian science writers, Paul Davies and the late Charles Birch (1918–2009). A must-read is Davies' *The Goldilocks Enigma: Why is the Universe just right for life?* (2006). (Davies, it should be noted, is not a Christian, at least not in any conventional sense; Birch, on the other hand, was an evangelist.) Other (non-Australian) contemporary authors who have examined this territory in thoroughly readable prose include John Lennox, John D. Barrow, Francis Collins (long-time director of the Human Genome Project), John Polkinghorne and Rupert Sheldrake.

In their reasoned opposition to scientism, these eminent men are now regarded as mavericks. Yet scientism was not an attitude held by the vast majority of Western scientists down the ages – indeed, until the twentieth century, almost all of them were believing Christians.

At the time of Australia's founding, one of most important scientists of all time was at the peak of his powers: Antoine-Laurent Lavoisier

(1743–94), author of the landmark textbook *Elements of Chemistry* (1789). He is often referred to, deservedly, as 'the father of modern chemistry'. Lavoisier was a devout Christian, 'raised in a pious family which had given many priests to the Church'.[45] He held to his beliefs and was executed by guillotine during the French Revolution.[46] Once, writing to an English admirer who had himself been the subject of persecution, Lavoisier wrote: 'You have done a noble thing in upholding revelation and the authenticity of the Holy Scripture.'[47]

Let us bring the argument back to Australia. From the time of the First Fleet, and until the present day, a good number of our own finest scientists and inventors have been serious Christians. Their achievements can be included under the broad rubric of Australia's Judaeo-Christian heritage. I have mentioned a few already in earlier chapters (1 and 4 in particular) but there were dozens of others.

Some were leaders in their fields in Australia.[48] In the nineteenth century, I have in mind the likes of Alexander McLeay (1767–1848), once dubbed 'the father of Australian zoology',[49] and the Reverend W.B. Clarke (1798–1878), often called 'the father of Australian geology'.[50] In the twentieth century, one thinks of figures such as Edward Rennie (1852–1927), long-time professor of chemistry at the University of Adelaide and a leading player in the foundation of the CSIRO,[51] and J.J. Bradfield (1867–1943), the brilliant engineer who designed the Sydney Harbour Bridge.[52] Rennie was a Presbyterian. The other three were Anglicans.

Then there were those on an even higher plane – Australian scientists of genuine *world* eminence. Geologist Alfred Selwyn (1824–1902), *the* critical pioneer of the Australian mining industry, was the son of a clergyman (the Reverend Townsend Selwyn, Canon of Gloucester Cathedral, no less), and a practising Anglican all his life.[53] Botanist Ferdinand von Mueller (1825–96), arguably Australia's most prominent nineteenth-century scientist in any discipline, was a devout Lutheran, in 'constant communication' with the Reverend Hermann Kempe, the pastor of his church.[54] John Tebbutt (1834–1916), whose face appears on the hundred-dollar note, was one of the finest astronomers of the nineteenth century; he was also a committed Anglican, at one time the president of the Windsor branch of the British and Foreign Bible Society.[55] Seismologist and astronomer Edward Pigot (1858–1929) was a Jesuit priest who served for six years as a missionary in China.[56] William Edgeworth David (1858–1934), the leader of the scientific team that accompanied Ernest Shackleton's expedition to the South Pole, was the son of a clergyman and had entered Oxford University intending to take holy orders. Despite his worldwide fame as a scientist, he remained a practising Anglican: late in life he worshipped quietly with his wife at a church in the Blue Mountains of New South Wales.[57]

Theoretical physicist Samuel Bruce McLaren (1876–1916) might have become the greatest Australian scientist ever had he not been killed in action in World War One. He was the son of a Scots Presbyterian missionary to Japan and a practising Presbyterian himself.[58] Neuro-physiologist John Eccles (1903–97), a Nobel Prize winner in 1963 for his work on synapses in the brain, was a sometime Roman Catholic and convinced theist. He believed that 'the human mystery is incredibly demeaned by scientific reductionism' and once described himself as 'a finalist in the sense of believing that there is some Design in the process of biological evolution'.[59]

What conclusions can be drawn here? I do not contend that these men were successful scientists because they believed in God. I do contend that they combined fervent belief in God with extraordinary scientific accomplishment. Another common thread is that nearly all of them were altruistic: they gave back as much to the scientific community as they took from it.

Their lives are one way of challenging – in the Australian context – the furphy of scientism. Of course, other excellent Australian scientists, past and present, have not been believers. But at least until the modern era, very few were out-and-out atheists scornful of religion.

In concluding this section, I feel it is instructive to take a look at the religious views of the greatest ever Australian scientist, Howard Florey (1898–1968). (Some readers may already have been wondering when I was going to come to him.) Sir Robert Menzies once suggested that 'in terms of world well-being, Florey was the most important man ever born in Australia'. It is hard to disagree. Hundreds of millions of people have lived longer and healthier lives as a result of Florey's work. The co-developer of penicillin shared the Nobel Prize in 1945 with colleagues Ernest Chain and Alexander Fleming. It is noteworthy that one of Florey's biographers, R.G. Macfarlane, took the view that it is necessary to understand the work of Fleming, Chain and Florey as part of a 'continuum' from Edward Jenner (1749–1823) to Louis Pasteur (1822–95) to Joseph Lister (1827–1912). All three of those scientific giants – Jenner, Pasteur and Lister – were devout Christians.

Florey himself appears to have been a thoughtful agnostic who leaned towards belief. Another of his biographers, Leonard Bickel, once remarked that 'he [Florey] would have protested at the suggestion that his life's work touched more people on this earth than did the teachings of Jesus Christ'.[60] There appears to be no doubt that Florey was respectful of the religious impulse in others: the colleague with whom he worked most closely, Ernest Chain, was a practising Jew and a deeply religious man.[61] Yet it is difficult to be dogmatic about Florey's own innermost thoughts. For the most part, he stayed silent about them. Another biographer remarked approvingly that 'unlike some contemporary scientists, he was not aggressive in his disbelief'.[62] But 'disbelief' might have been too strong a word.

The adult Florey was not a regular churchgoer. But he was raised in a conventional Christian home in Adelaide and educated at St Peter's (Anglican) College. His family was friendly with Archdeacon Wyndham Clampett, a canon of Adelaide Cathedral and one of the most prominent Anglican clerics in South Australia. As a boy, Florey played with the Clampett children at their father's rectory. One of them, Mollie Clampett, remained a lifelong friend.[63]

What kept the adult Florey away from organised religion? The answer seems clear: his wife of forty years, Ethel Reed. A fellow scientist, she was a genuine, hard-boiled atheist – the sort of person who insists that the human mind is just a 'secretion of the cortical cells of the brain' (her words) and that there is no such thing as morality. The (then) smitten Florey was choosing his words carefully when he wrote to her during their courtship: 'I don't believe in a personal God.' Yet he had the integrity to add: 'But ... I do think there is something ... immeasurably superior to our best thoughts.' He confessed that he envisioned morality as something more than a construct of man: 'If there is no inner incentive then one is only moral because of mutual benefit.'[64] Ethel disagreed, but married Florey anyway. The marriage was unhappy.[65]

Florey survived Ethel, and in June 1967, very late in life, he remarried. This union was extremely happy, but it ended with Florey's death just eight months later. Did he die a believer? There is no cast-iron evidence either way. But, at the very least, he cannot (in life) have forbidden his widow from marking the occasion of his death with religious rites. Florey's funeral service took place at St Nicholas' parish church near his home in Marston, Oxfordshire.[66] There was also a memorial service at Westminster Abbey. The Reverend William Leak said the following prayer, which will be my last word on scientism:

Almighty and eternal God, who hast entrusted the minds of men with the science and skill which can greatly bless or wholly destroy: Grant them also a new stature of spirit to match thy trust.[67]

## Prosperity

We have seen that the Australian census results since 1901 reveal two appreciable drops in religious affiliation. The first came in the aftermath of World War One. The second and much bigger drop, which is still continuing, began in the early 1970s. No doubt a combination of factors has been at play. I suggested in Chapter 7 that the Vietnam War was an important catalyst, not least because of the Australian Churches' support of it. But I am sure that the most important single factor, certainly since the 1980s, has been unprecedented material affluence.

Australians today have *real* incomes more than three times higher than in 1950.[68] The bulk of the working class is richer, in terms of purchasing power, than were most members of the middle class in earlier generations.[69] And as politicians never tire of telling us, we have now enjoyed twenty-three years of uninterrupted economic growth. In October 2014, the global investment bank Credit Suisse reported that Australia is, on one measure (median personal wealth), the richest country in the world. Only 6 per cent of Australians have wealth below US$10,000, compared with 29 per cent in the United States and 70 per cent for the world as a whole.[70]

Now, in at least one respect, this state of affairs is one to be grateful for. Few would wish away the overall rise in life expectancy that has been an important by-product of affluence. The problem is that increased life expectancy has not coincided with any increase in levels of personal happiness or well-being.[71] Nor, as far as I can tell, with any increase in levels of national thankfulness, or civility, or generosity. Rather, as commentators such as Clive Hamilton[72] and Mark Davis[73] have demonstrated, affluence has brought with it numerous unwelcome side effects. Environmental degradation is one, but put that to one side. At the purely human level, working hours have increased, along with levels of job insecurity and credit card debt. Mental illness, binge drinking, drug use, divorce, abortion, the consumption of pornography – all have proliferated. Meanwhile, the birth rate has fallen – and so, even more precipitously, have rates of churchgoing and religious belief.

So much is unarguable. But my task is to demonstrate a relationship of cause and effect. Exactly how, and why, has prosperity in Australia bred irreligion?

\*

For many Christian theologians down the ages, the question would seem simple. It was Jesus Himself who insisted that a man cannot serve two masters, God and Mammon, and St Paul who warned that the love of money is the root of all kinds of evil.[74] In the eighteenth century, John Wesley observed that true religion 'must necessarily produce both industry and frugality, and these cannot but produce riches'. (How right he was as regards Australia! Remember the moral middle class?) But the risk is that religion thus sows the seeds of its own destruction. 'As riches persist,' Wesley added, 'so will pride, anger and love of the world.'[75] One of Wesley's near-contemporaries, the great painter and poet William Blake, put the point more bluntly still: 'Christianity is art and not money. Money is its curse.'

Several modern-day theorists of secularisation have reached broadly similar conclusions. Increasing prosperity, they have found, tends over time to reduce religious commitment.[76]

In 1985, Hans Mol suggested that 'since Australia is affluent, the … perspective of Christianity on events and experiences is obscured by disuse'. Even thirty years ago, thought Mol, religion for the 'average' citizen had become something to be 'dusted off' in times of change or crisis.[77] Roger C. Thompson, writing in 1994, adjudged that economic prosperity since the 1950s had been, in Australia, 'the most corrosive agent in the erosion of Christian belief'.[78]

Yet the strength of the link between prosperity and irreligion is not accepted by all secularisation theorists. Some point to the United States as the most obvious example of a country that is both stupendously wealthy and notably religious. Personally I think the US is a unique case;[79] in any event, it is not the subject of this book. A more interesting argument, as regards Australia, is that we have *always* been obsessed with money – and if nothing has changed in that regard since the early 1800s, the causes of secularisation must lie elsewhere.[80]

One can find, in the relevant literature, several proponents of the first limb of this argument. The Marxist historian Humphrey McQueen contended in 1970 that 'Australia was, and largely is, the frontier of European capitalism'. From the days of the Rum Corps, he maintained, 'colonial culture was dominated by the necessity to make money'.[81] There were economic opportunities available here that had not been available to the lower classes in Britain; hence everyone felt the pressure to get ahead.[82] Henry Parkes himself, writing in 1841 to his sister Sarah in England, made this blunt admission: 'Nothing like getting money; nothing can be done without it. I know the value of money now! Money! Money! Money! Is my watchword in future.'[83] The gold rushes of the 1850s to some extent encouraged this mindset, and the great Depressions of the 1890s and 1930s did not dispel it.

This country's most eminent economic historian of the twentieth century, Keith Hancock, went as far as suggesting that Australians' philosophy had always been essentially acquisitive in character. 'They have said, "Seek ye first a high standard of comfort, and the Kingdom of God shall be added unto you." What they have really wanted is the high standard of comfort.'[84] Ronald Conway, in *The Great Australian Stupor*, deplored 'right-wing attachments in this country [to] squalid "anal" money-grubbing and urban corruption'.[85] He also expressed intense scepticism about big business and the advertising industry, which he regarded as 'the most powerful frame of influence in Australian life'.[86] In the same vein, one of Donald Horne's more acerbic books was entitled, simply, *Money Made Us*.

All these critiques were written before the neo-liberal era. That is what makes them, in retrospect, darkly amusing. True enough, we have always been a commerce-minded country – but back then it was only up to a point. The changes wrought since the 1980s have been of a vastly different order of magnitude. Not even the Global Financial Crisis of 2008–09, or the looming threat of climate change, has checked the worship of money. The attitudes that Hancock and Conway and Horne were bemoaning now look tame indeed.

Conway, for instance, was writing in 1971. He was a deeply religious man, a convert to Catholicism, and at heart a conservative. Indeed, he became a mentor to the young Tony Abbott after Abbott quit training for the priesthood in 1987. When Conway died in 2009, Abbott wrote a kind obituary and lauded *The Great Australian Stupor* for its 'timeless quality' as social commentary.[87] Yet I venture to suggest that Conway would have shuddered at Abbott's – and the nation's – evident priorities on election night in 2013. The prime minister-elect raised a big cheer by declaring that Australia was 'once again open for business!' As though we had ever been closed. Remember those twenty-three years of uninterrupted economic growth.

This completely non-spiritual mindset now permeates almost everything. The hated federal budget of 2014–15 was merely a logical outworking of that mindset. Even most of the criticism of the budget was framed in economic terms. From nations to corporations to individuals, wealth is seen as the measure of everything; *more* wealth (but only for me or my kind) is seen as the answer to everything. Of countless daily manifestations of this attitude, I have rarely seen one sadder than an article about Tasmania published in the *Weekend Australian* on 16 August 2014. The gist of it was that an entire State could be written off as a failure on the basis of selected economic data.[88]

It seems to me self-evident that none of this can possibly be good for religion. Neo-liberalism has coincided with other spiritually destructive phenomena – most notably scientism, and the near-total secularisation of the State education system. But even those phenomena are, I think, secondary to the insidious effects of post-World War Two prosperity. I offer five observations.

### The corruption of the Protestant work ethic

We saw in earlier chapters that the Protestant work ethic was a product of the Reformation and that most middle-class British immigrants of the nineteenth and early twentieth centuries were steeped in it. The basis of this ethic was not the making of money *per se*. The general idea was that people could and should work hard in their chosen field for their own moral betterment and that of society as a whole. Above all, their underlying motive should be the worship of God.

Money should thus be acquired ethically and used wisely: either invested back into the relevant business, to ensure its continuation, or spent philanthropically. There was room for individual and familial enrichment, of course, but this was not the be-all and end-all of the exercise.[89]

When those involved in business and the professions are focused steely-eyed on next year's or next quarter's or next month's bottom line, they cannot be giving much thought to their neighbours or to God – let alone loving them. Likewise when many workers are worried about keeping their jobs. People's time and energies are limited. It takes an enormous amount of effort nowadays to keep earning money at the rate at which we are all constantly encouraged to spend it. Some things have to give, and religion, poorly understood by the younger generations anyway, has become one of those things.

### The enhanced role of the State

As we saw in earlier chapters, the empowerment of the Australian working class – initially through the trade unions – owed much to Christianity. But an unintended consequence was the disempowerment of the Churches.

The Depression of the 1890s convinced the unions that they needed representation in parliament to achieve broad-based social justice – hence the creation, and fast rise, of the ALP. The Great Depression of the 1930s convinced not just the ALP, but all fair-minded people, that the social safety net needed broadening by legislation. The Churches, or some special individuals within them, had done their best during the 1930s, but it had not been enough. When unemployment hit 30 per cent, private charity simply could not cope with the extent of the deprivation.[90]

As I noted in Chapter 5, one of the main features of the making of modern Australia was the gradual erection of a strong social safety net. Few would now wish it gone, or even eroded – as the backlash against the Abbott Government's 2014–15 budget has shown. But a gradual consequence has been a reduced role for the Churches. True, genuine poverty still exists in Australia in isolated pockets – and extensively overseas. But it no longer extends across most of the Australian working class, which is shrinking in any event. This means that there has been a sharp reduction in the frequency with which people truly *need* to interact with the Churches in their daily lives. The State fills most of the gaps.[91]

I hasten to say that this is not a trend peculiar to Australia, or even to the last hundred or so years. The weakening of the Churches' links with the poorer members of the community has occurred across the West over several centuries.[92] But the process has accelerated sharply in Australia since the 1970s. That is why this is such a potent factor in secularisation.

### The postponement of death

One unarguably good by-product of prosperity has been the rise in the life expectancy of the average Australian citizen. A boy born in Australia today can expect to live to the age of eighty years and a girl to eighty-four. At the time of Federation, the equivalent figures were fifty-five and fifty-nine years respectively.[93] In the nineteenth century, the figures were considerably lower still. On most voyages out to Australia there were deaths at sea;[94] in many pioneer families at least one child was stillborn or died in infancy.[95] The deaths of mothers in childbirth, and of young adults of both sexes by illness or misadventure, were also far more common than today. Relatively few people lived much past the Biblical allotment of three score years and ten (Psalm 90:10).

Increased life expectancy has been due primarily to technological advances in modern medicine. The eradication of poverty and (since the 1970s) universal health care have also played a part.

No one would wish it otherwise. But there is no escaping the conclusion that this is another factor in secularisation. When death was a fact of everyday life, people were naturally more conscious of their own mortality – and more inclined to turn their minds to the ultimate questions, including the afterlife. In Chapter 1 we saw that fear of divine judgment was a factor minimising suicide in the early colonies. There is also evidence that many nineteenth-century women actively contemplated the afterlife when they were about to give birth. In the 1840s, a nineteen-year-old married woman named Matilda Murray-Prior was living in outback Queensland when she went into labour. Later she recalled: 'Having neither doctor or nurse, and knowing that I might die before there was any hope of medical assistance, I endeavoured to prepare my mind for leaving this world.'[96]

Christianity teaches 'one's utter dependence upon God to overcome the discontinuity of death'.[97] So do Islam, Hinduism and some other faiths. Of course, death is still a fact of life. But for most Australians today it need not be contemplated, seriously or at all, until old age. In polite conversation the subject is taboo, except in times of sudden tragedy. Then most people lack the necessary language of grief; they must try to console themselves with euphemism and hollow sentiment.

### The distractions of technology

If increased life expectancy has been a good by-product of prosperity – albeit one working against religion – the same cannot be said of some of its other by-products. It seems to me unarguable that modern technology has worked against faith in a number of ways. The fostering of scientism is one. But another, also potent, is sheer distraction.

The beginning of the steep decline in rates of churchgoing in Australia can be traced to a specific event: the introduction of television in 1956. Numbers at evening services straight away fell sharply, and have never recovered.[98] This was not the same thing as unbelief, but, in due course, it fed into the general phenomenon of disenchantment. Likewise, in the 21st century, we have witnessed the widespread use of the Internet, mobile phones, Facebook and other forms of social media, and instant communication. All are antithetical to traditional forms of worship, which require extended periods of quiet, uninterrupted contemplation. It has been argued that some of these technologies, skilfully utilised, may offer an opportunity to reboot religion.[99] Personally, I am dubious.

An obviously negative aspect of modern technology is the opportunity it affords people to engage, more or less anonymously, in harmful activities – gambling on poker machines, for example, or playing violent video games, or accessing hard-core pornography online. Such activities are not only addictive and time-consuming; they corrupt the soul. Efforts to curb them rarely succeed because massive profits are at stake. These are billion-dollar industries. The major political parties are fearful of their power, and the warnings of the Churches have long since ceased to be heeded. (Their campaign in New South Wales in 1956 against the legalisation of poker machines can now be seen as yet another disastrous turning point.[100])

This is another instance where, in recent years, curious political coalitions have developed: opposition to porn and gambling and the like is loudest from the Churches and the secular Left; the 'hardheads' in between are inclined to let everything through to the keeper. Why? Because these industries are 'good for the economy'.[101]

### Acquisitive materialism as a way of life

Where did things go wrong? I agree with Michael Hogan that a vital turning point in Australia was the post-World War Two shift from production to consumption as the key to economic growth. 'The new … dogma', Hogan pointed out, 'was that people must be encouraged to spend and to buy, not to save and to cling to a Protestant or Catholic ascetism.' What gradually emerged was 'a value system centred on hedonism'.[102]

Hogan was writing in 1987, at the beginning of the neo-liberal era. He had not yet witnessed neo-liberalism at full throttle: the obsession with short-term shareholder return, the selling off of public assets, higher and higher executive earnings, and lower and lower income taxes. Nor the emergence of a 24/7 culture, with its inexorable impingement on family life. Nor the commodification of education, especially at the tertiary level. Nor the jettisoning of still-viable industries, or valued social services, for want of government funding. These are in part political judgments – and some readers may be grinding their teeth. But the plain fact is that neo-liberalism does not sit well with basic Christian teachings. The Vatican has said so repeatedly.[103]

So where exactly is the link between acquisitive materialism as a way of life and the decline of religion? To practising Christians, the link may seem obvious. But let me spell it out.

First, there is the argument put by the great English man of letters, Matthew Arnold (1822–88). He coined the term 'philistinism' to describe a certain attitude – that the only things that really matter are those that are clearly part of the economic system.[104] Thus beauty and art and matters of the intellect – and above all, the numinous – are sidelined. Much the same point was made by several nineteenth-century Australian clerics.[105] In 1971, Ronald Conway identified the relevant mindset: 'blank-souled, incurious and rejecting of anything beyond the immediate prize'.[106] In the satirical words of Philip Adams, 'those previously attending church now seek solace in the shopping malls'.[107]

A related but slightly different argument is put by modern-day sociologists of religion: 'The more pleasant this life, the harder it is to concentrate on the next.'[108] Australia in 2015 may be the most materially privileged society in human history. Australians today, this argument runs, worship the various components of their lifestyles: careers, houses, cars, clothes, their bodies, restaurants, holidays, sport, entertainment. They may not be philistines – some, indeed, are highly cultivated – but they live exclusively for the here and now.

There is some truth in both of these lines of argument. But I do not think they encapsulate the whole truth.

As we have seen, despite the massive increase in real wealth that Australians have enjoyed since World War Two, there has been no commensurate increase in happiness. Many Australians do not see themselves as living especially privileged or pleasant lives; rather, they feel overworked and underappreciated – stretched, stressed and insecure.[109] Working-class men, whose job opportunities are becoming increasingly limited, are a case in point.[110]

The problem for the cause of religion is that few such people appear to see it (religion) as a possible answer. On the contrary – and this is the crux of the matter – they are inclined to imagine that the solutions to their problems lie in the material realm. This only exacerbates their sense of dissatisfaction, and produces a state of mind even less receptive to true religion. They become fearful of not 'keeping up', or, what would be an even greater calamity, of losing what they have.[111] And they become covetous of the things they cannot afford.[112] 'As a rule,' observed Clive Hamilton in *Affluenza*, 'no matter how much money people have they feel they need more.'[113]

According to public opinion surveys, this rule applies to people at all socio-economic levels. It is not a cast-iron rule: there is also a cohort of people who express themselves content with their material lot. But many of them fall victim to what is, arguably, an even more poisonous mindset, at least as far as religion is concerned: self-satisfaction, or smugness. They imagine that they fully deserve what they have, as though luck or circumstance – let alone Providence – has no role in human affairs. As commentators such as Hugh Jackson have observed,[114] this may be *the* most deep-seated cause of secularisation.

The very essence of Christianity is that all human beings are, without exception, in need of salvation. The state of your soul is the core issue – not your level of wealth. Accordingly, to the extent that prosperity tends to deflect attention from this issue, it is a killer of belief.

# CHAPTER 10

# What is at stake?

In a sense, I am perhaps less a Christian than I was before the war, but I have been taught very soundly that one must believe in some religion, or sink into the terrible mire of mere selfishness and materialism.

Dr Edward 'Weary' Dunlop, diary entry, 28 January 1943

In the end, to 'regret' religion as such is to regret that humanity ever became more as a species than a collection of especially cunning brutes.

David Bentley Hart

Why does it matter if Christianity – and religion in general – continues to fade away as an operative factor in Australian life? In this final chapter I shall proffer various reasons for concern (other than the ultimate fate of individual souls). It behoves anyone who identifies a problem, however big, to propose solutions, so I shall also make some suggestions as to how the cause of religion might be revived.

## Diminishing knowledge

The first reason for concern is that Australians across the board are becoming increasingly ignorant about things that really matter. Perhaps of greatest concern is the fact that it is otherwise well-educated Australians – those with tertiary degrees – who often seem the most wilfully ignorant. Too many simply do not understand, or want to understand, the fundamentally Christian roots of the West (see Chapter 2), Britain (Chapter 3), and Australia itself (Chapters 1, 4 and 5).

I am talking at this stage not about religious belief, nor even religious knowledge, but basic *historical* knowledge. Some might be tempted to say: 'I'll leave that to the historians.' But such an attitude simply will not do. In every great civilisation in human history, the intellectual elite *at the very least* has had a clear understanding of where they came from. In the greatest civilisation, Christendom, almost every person alive had such an understanding – of the essentials, if not of the fine detail.

The second area of burgeoning contemporary ignorance is religious knowledge. This was my subject in Chapter 6, where I argued that all young Australians deserve the chance to make an informed decision about the most crucial questions of human existence. In a nutshell: is there a God and, if so, what does that God expect of me? No one should try to answer these questions unless and until they have been taught the basics (preferably, rather more than the basics). There is assistance to be derived from 3,000 years of careful scholarship.

If knowledge of what ought to be basic history and basic religious concepts were again to be instilled in schools and at universities,* it is possible that one result would be a modest revival in levels of religious belief. Sheer gratitude, or inquisitiveness, might be the response of some young people. In fact, I am personally confident that this would happen: once the Gospel is heard, even indirectly, its power is strong. But this knowledge should be imparted regardless of the religious consequences.

There is only so long that Australian society can go on living, more or less unknowingly, off Judaeo-Christian capital. If we are to make a clean break from religion, as some people appear to wish, then it should be done deliberately and in full knowledge of all the relevant facts and issues – not sneakily by default.

Let us have a genuine debate. The New Atheists might take as their role model the great German thinker Friedrich Nietzsche (1844–1900). As David Bentley Hart has observed, Nietzsche was 'a man of immense culture who could appreciate the magnitude of the thing against which he had turned his spirit'. Moreover, he 'had the good manners to despise Christianity, in large part, for what it actually was – above all, for its devotion to an ethics of compassion'.[1]

---

* By which I mean instilled in every undergraduate, not merely those taking specialist courses in ancient or modern history.

## Consequences of diminishing faith

Knowledge is one thing. But what will happen to Australia if levels of religious belief continue to decline? It is easy to imagine a time – perhaps the 2021 census – when even nominal identification with Christianity falls below the threshold of 50 per cent. How far further could it fall? To 30 per cent or 20 per cent? To nil – the figure in 1787? When Emperor Constantine converted from paganism in or about AD 312, only about 10 per cent of citizens of the Roman Empire were Christians. But that 10 per cent was fervent, and the figure was already rising exponentially.[2]

Let me come at the issue another way. Go back to the Introduction and the definition I proposed of 'an essentially Christian view of the world'. Then ask yourself this question. What would be the implications for Australia if almost everybody – including those comprising the intellectual elite – genuinely believed in the following:

- The Universe is meaningless. It is uncaused, unplanned, and consists only of inanimate matter. Human beings are just 'chemical scum on a moderate-sized planet'.[3]
- This earthly life is all that there is. What follows death is oblivion. There is no afterlife and (thus) no divine justice to be imposed in it, whether by way of reward or punishment.[4] There is no reunion with loved ones.
- Jesus, if he lived at all, was merely another interesting teacher. (Likewise Mohammad.)

David Bentley Hart, contemplating this prospect for the West, has suggested that what would be lost is, at core, 'the cautery of fear, the balm of hope'.[5] The logical end-point, he says, is nihilism, a situation in which individual will (the capacity to exercise free choice) becomes the ultimate value. In a mild form, this will lead to banality, 'an increasingly insipid or self-absorbed private culture'.[6] Yet even Hart's vision may be insufficiently bleak, for in the honest atheistic worldview there is no such thing as free will; it is an illusion. There is no 'I' who decides anything, just mindless molecules obeying arbitrary physical laws.

But human beings will always live as though free will is real. What happens when few Australians, if any, believe that *God* is real? It is obvious after a moment's thought that none of the suggested 'replacements' for religious faith, whatever their merits, could possibly fill the gaps that would be left. Pantheism, secular humanism, consumerism – all are focused on the here and now. So too, in and of themselves, are even the most worthy of philanthropic causes and worldly pursuits.

Sport, for example, functions as a kind of religion for many Australian men and not a few women. Yet sport is 'precisely the suspension of a serious worldview'.[7] The whole point is to invest significance in something that really does not matter a fig – in this world, let alone the next. I write that as a lifelong lover of sport, as both player and spectator. Take the devoted follower of a football team (any code, but imagine AFL). He arranges his life around the team's schedule, in the same way as a medieval Christian used to arrange his life around the days of the Church year. He invests much of his physical and emotional energy in the cause. His rituals are religious in character: regular fellowship with co-enthusiasts, endless pontification about points of detail, communal singing or chanting, worship of heroes and denunciation of villains. And, always, an eye on the ultimate prize. But in the case of sport the ultimate prize (the premiership, or whatever) is, at its core, meaningless – especially if it can only be achieved vicariously, through the efforts of others.

Even at a purely earthly level, belonging to a church congregation is different in kind to any other form of community involvement. It brings together people of both sexes and all ages. Political, racial and socio-economic barriers are broken down. People must try to get along who have little in common, other than love of God and belief in His promises. In my (admittedly limited) experience in Sydney since 1998, the results can be astonishingly moving.

Occasionally, in recent years, some of the more fair-minded public atheists have recognised that religion does bring societal benefits. While tut-tutting the notion that God exists – indeed, proclaiming that whole debate 'boring' – they are prepared to keep an open mind on secondary matters. British writer Alain de Botton, for instance, has suggested that 'one can be left cold by the doctrines of the Christian Trinity and the Buddhist Fivefold Path, and yet at the same time be interested in the ways in which religions deliver sermons, promote morality, engender a spirit of community, make use of art and architecture, inspire travels, train minds and encourage gratitude at the beauty of spring'.[8]

For the religious believer, this sort of stuff is more pleasant to encounter than the bile of a Dawkins or a FitzSimons. Yet it is still woolly, wishful thinking. The by-products of Christianity were, originally, and for many centuries thereafter, by-products of belief *in the truth* of its central tenets. Granted, some of those by-products have become extremely deep-seated in secular society (the rightness of charity, say, or the wrongness of hypocrisy). Probably they will persist for some time yet, whatever happens to institutional religion and levels of theistic belief. But I doubt they can persist indefinitely. Already, cracks are appearing. Let us look at some aspects of Australian society today.

## Morality and personal conduct

I am not going to argue that in the absence of religion, Australian society would rapidly descend into barbarous and wicked mayhem. In many key respects, believers and unbelievers agree on what is right and wrong. But that is largely because Judaeo-Christian standards, imported in 1788, have remained ubiquitous. Charity and commitment, for example, are still universally considered virtues; dishonesty, adultery and aggressive violence are still widely considered sins.

But the edifice is cracking. Increasingly, 'freedom of the will is our supreme value'.[9] As a result (as I suggested in Chapter 8), Australian public opinion has shifted in some respects as regards the actual content of morality – obvious examples are sex outside marriage, divorce, (non-prescription) drug use, pornography and gambling. These activities are now blithely tolerated, sometimes even encouraged or praised. More serious examples are abortion and euthanasia, practices that were once considered by most Australians as abhorrent. But the shift in opinion is logical in a society 'no longer bound to the obsolete Christian superstition that every life is of equal – which is to say of equally infinite – value'.[10] What comes next? Eugenics? Infanticide? Some may scoff, but infanticide is now being seriously proposed by atheist philosophers such as Peter Singer.[11] It is a chilling throwback to the Graeco-Roman era, when the practice was carried out routinely.

The shifting content of morality is one thing. Where believers and unbelievers differ most starkly is as to morality's ultimate *source*.

Believers say it is external to the Universe: morality is set by God and (in the end) scrupulously policed by God. Unbelievers say that morality is the construct of a given human society; that is, it is set by man and (admittedly most imperfectly) policed by man; we are free, therefore, from any *absolute* moral bonds. In effect we enter into a social contract. In Australia today the situation amounts to this: each citizen 'promises' to 'do the minimum best for others that will allow [him or her] to maximally succeed'.[12] It is a transaction.

The question is: which view of the world, in 21st-century Australia, is more likely to produce virtue and discourage wrongdoing?

Instantly, one confronts the sins of Christians. Since 1788, Australia's institutional Churches have been responsible for some terrible blunders and misdeeds. I have catalogued some of them in earlier chapters. And among prominent individuals of every faith one can cite dire examples of crime, sin and hypocrisy. Australian clerics and evangelists of (once) high standing are not exempt – and it does not stop at sexual abuse.[13]

There are two ways of meeting facts of this kind. The first is theological. Suffice to say that deep thinkers have wrestled for millennia with the phenomenon of human sin – especially among 'religious' people – and how to reconcile it with the existence of a loving God. That is one of the basal issues of Christianity. But the Jesus of the Gospels addressed the issue of religious hypocrisy much better than I can, and, for those interested, there is a mountain of literature on the subject, ancient and modern. Henri Blocher's masterwork *Evil and the Cross* is one particularly powerful treatment.[14] As far as the Churches are concerned, Catholic archbishop Mark Coleridge has summed up the position thus: 'In the end, the moral authority of the Church does not depend upon our own moral excellence. It never has. It depends upon the truth of what we teach.' Above all it depends upon the person of Jesus – 'the magnificence at the heart of the mess'.[15]

The other way of approaching this issue is to attempt a rough calculation of the positive and negative effects of religion at an individual and a societal level.

As far as Australians are concerned, it is unquestionable that there are and always have been many badly behaved believers – and many well-behaved unbelievers. Occasionally one meets a secular saint. But let me nail my colours to the mast. I believe sincerely that, on the whole, Christian believers are rather more likely than unbelievers to abstain from the worst excesses and indulgences. The much-mocked dark-alley test still holds good, at least in Australia in 2015. (That test poses this question: imagine that you are walking home at night and encounter a group of ten men in a dark alley. Would you not be relieved to know they had just come from a Bible study class?) I also believe, with even firmer conviction, that Christian believers are rather more likely than others to go the extra mile in voluntarily doing good. The whole course of Australian history – of world history – points to this. The Christian Golden Rule positively requires it.

A point of clarification about this rule. Many human societies have operated on the basis of a Silver Rule: do *not* do unto others that which you would not want done unto you.[16] Some societies have gone further, framing the rule in positive terms: do unto others that which you would have them do to you. But the Christian Golden Rule goes further still: it commands the doing of good to others with no expectation of reciprocity. 'Love your enemies, do good to those who hate you' (Luke 6:27). It is a magnificent counsel of perfection, which we are all the better for trying, if usually failing, to meet. And at least some Christians will keep trying, for as long as they believe – in the words of Jesus' brother, or cousin – that 'faith without deeds is dead' (James 2:26).[17]

## The legal system

To a related subject, and one close to my heart. In Chapter 3 I lauded the rule of law as one of Britain's most precious gifts to the Australian colonies – and so it was. Yet the rule of law *per se* can be antithetical to individual and communal morality, if it is divorced from its Judaeo-Christian roots. Some of the most evil people and regimes in history have acted in formal compliance with man-made civil laws.

The thrust of the New Testament is that attempted compliance even with *God-made* moral laws is never enough. Why? Because we will always fall short of perfect compliance – far, far short – yet simultaneously overrate our own efforts. In the words of a distinguished American theologian, Albert Barnes, 'All men by nature seek salvation by the law.' In other words, even among sincerely religious people, it is our default position to appeal to our own good deeds or good intentions, when in fact, they are not so very good at all.[18] The result is smug, dishonest legalism.

It follows that compliance with mere *man-made* civil laws is even less of a guarantee of virtue. One of Robert Hughes' most interesting arguments in *The Fatal Shore* was that the rule of law had become, by 1788, 'a supreme ideology, a form of religion ... which began to replace the waning moral power of the Church of England'.[19] Hughes' focus was on the excessively brutal treatment of the convicts, especially the Irish. But his point is relevant more generally, and, in my opinion, applies even more forcefully to Australia today than it did to the young colonies. We seem to be reverting to a strange amalgam of Graeco-Roman and Judaic worldviews: all laws are a construct of man, nothing to get het up about; and compliance with technical rules is what matters.

In legal jargon, this is 'positivism'.[20] In plainer language, it is obeying the letter but not the spirit of written law. No one has articulated the positivists' view better than the late Kerry Packer: 'Of course, I am minimising my tax. Anybody in this country who does not minimise his tax wants his head read.' It would be unfair to single out Packer, who gave more generously to charity than many other men of his kind. My point is that the whole edifice of corporate and commercial law in Australia is now based on such assumptions; they also permeate our attitudes to international human rights law (*Let's interpret our obligations in the narrowest way that is plausibly arguable*). We have largely forgotten the Christian roots of the legal system that the English bequeathed to us.

The future result, I predict, will be more corporate and other scandals of the sort that caused the GFC. There are simply too many overpaid and over-clever CEOs, CFOs, currency traders, bankers, economists, stockbrokers, accountants, big-firm lawyers, PR consultants and other assorted hangers-on. A fair proportion of them survive daily on the very edge of what is legal (if that). Sometimes the powers that be take commercially calculated risks – they knowingly break the law. Media companies, for instance, know when they publish some stories that people will be defamed, probably indefensibly, but calculate that the risk of being sued is worth taking. Most citizens cannot afford to protect their rights against deep-pocket defendants.

But let me give an even starker example of what *must* happen to the legal system if religious belief continues to decline. It is already happening, but things will get worse.

Until quite recently, one of the bedrock features of the rule of law was the duty to tell the truth in court when giving evidence under oath – an oath *sworn to God*. The practice originated in the fourth century under Emperor Constantine (after his conversion to Christianity) and was later incorporated into the Legal Code of Justinian. From that source it was disseminated, primarily through the canon law, to all of European Christendom – including England, and, in due course, Australia.[21]

It is important to understand the basic assumption that underpinned this practice. In these days of moral relativism and affirmations (the secular alternative to the oath), it may seem quaint. But the men who invented the English legal system were Christians. They were also, for the most part, hard-nosed lawyers with an interest in facilitating the strict enforcement of justice. They believed, on strong grounds, that people would *genuinely* be more likely to tell the truth in court if the only certain consequence of not doing so was, in their minds, the blaspheming of God.[22] Today, for many witnesses, oaths must be a meaningless sham. Even a sincerely given affirmation cannot, by its nature, be as solemn an undertaking as an oath.

## The workplace

More than two decades ago, the (now) veteran sociologist Hugh Mackay identified paid work as the new centre of an individual's existence in Australia. Subsequent events have confirmed Mackay's thesis in spades. For most men, and some women too, the workplace is the central social institution, the environment in which adults find their identity.[23]

This might have been no bad thing, had not so many modern workplaces been infected by the amorality of neo-liberalism, or, as the American economist Robert Reich has dubbed it, super-capitalism. It is one thing for billionaires and bankers to be driven by the making of money. But society is demeaned when their priorities and practices are imported into workplaces that should be driven primarily by other values – excellence and integrity (the professions), a love of teaching and learning (schools and universities), patient care (hospitals and nursing homes), public safety and convenience (utilities, transport), taste and creativity (the arts, publishing and journalism). Even the Churches themselves.

The problem is not merely that workplaces generally have become much less congenial places in which to work, because of pernickety managerialism, reduced job security and 24/7 demands. The cancer eating at their heart is essentially moral: people at all levels are judged by their superiors less on the quality of their work and more on their profitability (or expendability). Loyalty is a near-meaningless factor. In organisations of any size, the Protestant work ethic, in which earlier generations were steeped, has been twisted or forgotten. Absent religious revival, combined with a huge shift in political thinking, it is hard to see any end in sight to these galloping trends.

## Government and politics

It is fact of history that democracy has flourished mostly in Christian countries, and, since 1948, in Israel. Attempts to impose democracy in non-Christian countries by fiat or force have failed repeatedly, though India and post-war Japan are exceptions. Thomas Halik has posed the question: 'Can democracy be built in any cultural and moral climate whatever, or does it need a "biosphere" such as the one that was characteristic of Western culture for decades?'[24]

As we saw in Part One, Australian democracy was a product of British Christian values and institutions, upon which our egalitarian ancestors grafted various local add-ons. At the heart of everything was the idea that all persons are made in the image of God and equal in His sight. If that idea fades into inconsequence, what will be the long-term effects?

It is hard to imagine the deliberate jettisoning in Australia of formal democracy itself. Much more likely are attacks by stealth, via measures designed to make it harder for the underclass to cast a vote, or less likely to bother: the imposition of property qualifications at some elections (of city councils, for instance); more complicated registration procedures; non-compulsory voting, and so on. But two other risks are even bigger.

The first is that both sides of politics may continue to head down the paths they have been on for some decades. The Right – neo-liberal on economics, with, for vote-catching purposes, dollops of nationalism, bigotry and anti-intellectualism thrown in. The Left – sincere enough about 'taming and taxing the capitalist monster',[25] if usually too timorous, but dangerously inclined to an open-slather approach on issues of personal and community morality, and increasingly hostile to the Christian religion. On both sides – blanket negativity in opposition; low standards of honesty, candour and probity in government; and utterly cynical electioneering, whereby scaremongering is the norm and campaign promises are either vapid or valueless.

The core problem, I believe, is not that good people do not enter politics. The core problem is that, once in politics, their authenticity is stifled. The average member of Federal Parliament is largely powerless; the same applies, perhaps to a lesser extent, at the State or Territory level. This is the second major risk faced by Australian democracy: that it may become something that is not really *parliamentary* democracy at all, but rule by executive fiat, tempered only by opinion polls. Every few years the electorate has a choice whether to replace one small cadre of leaders and insiders with another. The Rudd Government had the Gang of Four (Kevin Rudd, Julia Gillard, Wayne Swan and Lindsay Tanner); the Abbott Government has gone down a similar route, with power centred in the Prime Minister's Office.[26] Most members of caucus are treated like schoolchildren: you either obey the high command, or rapidly fall from favour.

What does any of this have to do with religion? I shall explain.

Perhaps the worst mistake the Australian Labor Party ever made was to bind its parliamentary members to the so-called Solidarity Pledge – a requirement *always* to vote the party line, on pain of expulsion. In the 1890s the rule made some kind of practical sense, though even then, some principled men objected. Almost invariably they did so on religious grounds. Joseph Cook, a staunch Methodist and future Commonwealth

Liberal Party prime minister, was one of them: he insisted that to take the Pledge would 'narrow and leg-iron the sphere of any candidate' to an unconscionable degree.[27] The ALP still retains this appalling rule. The Liberal Party used to pride itself on a more civilised attitude, but today, in practice, it is no better than Labor. As certain conscience-stricken members found during the Howard years, to depart publicly from the party line – or even to threaten to do so – is to invite career suicide.[28] There is no tolerance for principled dissent.

Edmund Burke, the great Christian conservative, who played such a vital role in Australian history, is famous for many things. One of them is his speech in 1774 to the electors of Bristol on the duties of a member of parliament. He said:

> It ought to be the happiness and glory of a representative to live in the strictest union, the closest correspondence, and the most unreserved communication with his constituents. Their wishes ought to have great weight with him; their opinion, high respect; their business, unremitted attention. It is his duty to sacrifice his repose, his pleasures, his satisfactions, to theirs; and above all, ever, and in all cases, to prefer their interest to his own. But his unbiased opinion, his mature judgment, his enlightened conscience, he ought not to sacrifice to you, *to any man, or to any set of men living.* These he does not derive from your pleasure; no, nor from the law and the constitution. They are a trust from Providence, for the abuse of which he is deeply answerable. Your representative owes you, not his industry only, but his judgment; and he betrays, instead of serving you, if he sacrifices it to your opinion [emphasis mine].[29]

In short: all MPs must be true to themselves and to God; the pull of conscience should trump both public opinion and party discipline. Henry Parkes, the Father of Federation, said much the same thing in 1849, during a speech at a public meeting about the proposed revival of transportation to New South Wales:

> There is a higher loyalty than [that] owed to any monarch – our loyalty to our own nature and to the all-wise God who has planted in us pure and holy sentiments and warmed our being with the love of justice and truth. (Cheers.) To be false to this loyalty would be to abase ourselves before our Creator – to deface the divine impress of humanity which was imprinted on our hearts.[30]

If the major political parties allowed all MPs true freedom of conscience – except, perhaps, on issues of supply and no confidence – I am convinced that politics would become much more honourable and interesting. Funnily enough, the only prominent person I know who has publically advocated this step is the arch-atheist Phillip Adams.[31] It is nonetheless a wise idea. Shifting coalitions would form across party lines, on the merits of particular issues and policies. Debate would be more sincere and eloquent. Members of the public would feel empowered. People might actually join political parties again. I also believe that public policy would more truly reflect public opinion. There would be a move back towards the Christian ideal: more compassionate policies on questions of economics and human rights; more conservative policies on just about everything else. On issues of war and peace, I am optimistic enough to believe that the average man or woman in the street has finally learned the lessons of two world wars, Vietnam and Iraq, even if (probably) too many chicken-hawk national leaders have not. (Remember, in early 2003, the vast majority of Australians were opposed to Australian involvement in any invasion of Iraq not sanctioned by the United Nations.[32])

To allow MPs freedom of conscience would encourage the better angels of their nature. The shemozzle of Tony Abbott's prime ministership is, I believe, explicable in religious terms. By the time this book is published he may already be gone. It seems to me he is a fish out of water, hopelessly conflicted in his own heart, a traditional Catholic who belonged on the right of the ALP – or, ideally, in the old-style DLP. (Bob Hawke has said much the same thing of Treasurer Joe Hockey.) In such a capacity Abbott might have done sterling work for Australia. Instead, in late 1988 – against his own better judgment, but after consultation with his hero-mentor B.A. Santamaria – he joined the Liberal Party,[33] at the very time when it was transitioning from the dutiful party of the moral middle class to the populist party of the super-rich and the go-getting, xenophobic 'aspirationals' and 'tradies'.

Sheer willpower and hard-nosed ambition got Abbott to the top, but no man can suppress his deepest beliefs forever. And Abbott does have (or at least once did have) very deep religious and political beliefs. The problem is that for some years – military issues aside – he has not been true to them. In December 1987, in a heartfelt letter to Santamaria, he complained that the Liberal Party was 'without soul', dominated by 'the more or less simple-minded advocates of the free market' and believers in 'inappropriate economic Ramboism'.[34] Even as a member of John

Howard's cabinet he was generally on the side of social spending.[35] Now, having dragged the Coalition back into power ('I'll do anything to get this job, anything other than sell my arse – but I'd have to give serious thought to it'[36]), he is supposed to be the country's leading spokesman for neo-liberal causes. (Call it economic reform if you like.) That Abbott has failed so utterly in this role is no surprise. In a strange way, it is to his credit.

### Science

I argued in Chapter 9 that scientism has harmed religious belief. This argument is well known. Much less well known is the argument that the decline of religious belief has harmed science – not the scientific method, but the open-minded spirit of enquiry that ought to motivate all scientists, and once did. Rupert Sheldrake has contended that large sections of the scientific community have now closed their minds to the possibility of the supernatural, with the result that certain fields of research are inhibited – consciousness studies, for example, which require thinking way outside the naturalistic square.[37]

Another serious concern is that scientism undermines the notion of truth itself – if our brains are no more than complex lumps of matter, solely the product of mindless evolution, then nothing we think or believe is objectively true. The 'veracity of reason'[38] itself is fatally undermined. Scientists must somehow go about their business on the assumption that what they believe to be true is true, while deep down knowing that there is no such thing as objective truth. G.K. Chesterton, among others, called this 'cognitive suicide'. Nietzsche hit the nail on the head: 'Only if we assume a God who is morally our like can "truth" and the search for truth be at all something meaningful and promising of success.'[39]

## What could be done to revive religion in Australia?

To pose the question in this bald way is almost to trivialise it, but let me wade in. I have argued that the slide towards unbelief in Australia has had various deep-seated causes. It follows that any solutions must address those causes, or such of them as can be addressed. Realistically, my suggestion that politicians be allowed far greater freedom of conscience stands no chance of being adopted by the hard-headed power brokers in the major parties. Moreover, for the foreseeable future, technological progress and material prosperity will remain the norms in Australia – and few would wish them away.

Feasible solutions lie in three areas: righting rightable wrongs, tackling ignorance (which includes tackling scientism), and championing issues about which large numbers of secular Australians rightly feel strongly. What follows is a personal wish list: a plea to Christians, and others religiously inclined, to fight for the cause of theistic belief.

### Righting rightable wrongs

Some aspects of the status quo are satisfactory, such as the commitment of all religious bodies to worthy charitable causes, here and overseas. Many individual congregations are thriving. But the Churches have some bridges to mend.

I have two specific things in mind. The first relates to the ongoing Royal Commission on Institutional Responses to Child Sexual Abuse. For a certainty, its findings will be damning and its recommendations onerous. All the Churches involved – and most obviously the Catholic Church – should throw self-interested caution to the wind. Do not wait for a lambasting by the commission and then grudgingly respond at a snail's pace. To the extent possible, and to the extent it has not already been done – act immediately.

If monetary compensation is still an issue for some complainants, err on the side of generosity. If a personal apology is the issue, give one fulsomely. It ought to be a no-brainer. This scandal might not have been a major active cause of secularisation, but serving the ends of justice, now and forever, may be a small but significant part of the process of renewal. In any event, justice should be done and then some.

Here is another suggestion: put an end to the centuries of hateful prejudice against men and women of homosexual orientation. This would *not* mean endorsing gay marriage or gay adoption – they are distinct and genuinely complicated issues – nor countenancing salaciousness and promiscuity. It would mean ceasing to shame and stigmatise people purely on the basis of their physiology, by doing away with the cruel and humiliating pretence that they should live a celibate life from youth to the grave. In short, renounce the teaching that homosexual acts are immoral in and of themselves.

I realise there are tenable Scriptural arguments for the old view. Nevertheless, it is casting a very long bow to say that those arguments are obviously superior to the counter-arguments. Personally, I think the counter-arguments are the stronger; in any event, if there are two reasonably arguable positions, the one that ought to prevail is the one that promotes love and joy and human dignity (and accords with the objective findings of modern science). That is plain common sense.

The analogy is not exact, but Christians of earlier eras found it in their hearts to rethink the Scriptural arguments in support of slavery. So too the arguments for a geocentric view of the Universe. At a purely literal level, those arguments were also tenable. But sensible clerics found a way around them and should do so again. As English author Francis Spufford has written, homosexuality is a rare example of 'a soluble problem of conflicted desire … a lucky subset of a much larger class of insoluble ones'.[40] So let us at least tackle the soluble one. As things stand, homosexual people comprise around 2 per cent of the Australian population and are twice less likely to be Christians than heterosexuals.[41] (The only surprise is that they are not five or ten times less likely.)

A generous, eloquent, humble announcement by the major Australian Churches on this issue could have astounding power. We saw in Chapter 5 that when, in the 1960s and 1970s, the Churches reached out to Indigenous people on issues such as land rights, their receptivity to the Gospel escalated enormously. The effect on homosexual people of a similar turnaround might be comparable. The allegiance of roughly the same proportion of the Australian population is at stake.

## Tackling ignorance

The only cure for ignorance is the systematic imparting of knowledge. This begins with the teaching of the young at school. Thus:

- The one-third of Australian schoolchildren who currently attend Church schools must all be taught properly and thoroughly and *passionately* about religion, from Kindergarten to Year 12 – something that simply does not happen at the moment, especially in high-fee, notionally Protestant schools. A token period per week is pathetic. The Churches have no excuse here. Concerns about maximising income streams and league table rankings should be of secondary importance. These are either Church schools or they are not. If the people who administer them and teach at them are not seriously interested in furthering the cause of religion, as a top priority, they should be replaced by people who are. This, for me, is *the* litmus test issue for the Australian Churches. Do they care enough to make their schools 'antechambers' again?
- The remaining two-thirds of Australian children who currently attend State schools should also be taught about religion. I refer here not to systematic doctrinal instruction, but the imparting of historical and

religious *knowledge*, as part of the compulsory examinable curriculum. By all means retain the current Scripture classes, and the chaplaincy service, but they are manifestly inadequate on their own. The key is to give young Australians a more accurate understanding of their country's historical roots and cultural heritage, and a decent chance of making an *informed* decision about religion. Somehow, Australian politicians and educationalists must be persuaded that this is a fair thing, whatever their own beliefs may be.

- In all schools, and ideally in universities too, the teaching of science should include sophisticated instruction on the history and philosophy of science, and its Judaeo-Christian roots.

I am under no illusions as to the difficulties that would be involved in implementing these measures, especially the second. Strong resistance would be encountered from aggressive secularists and others with vested interests in the status quo. Nevertheless, the effort should be made. Either that, or the Churches might just as well admit that the overall cause is hopeless. The demographic trends will become irreversible.

### Effective evangelism

What of evangelising to adults – inside church and outside? How should the Churches go about it? Of two general principles I am utterly convinced.

The first is that there is no future for Christianity – or any other theistic religion – in offering up a wishy-washy form of humanism. Christianity teaches many wise truths about the world – not least about the primacy of love, the reality of evil, and the potentially beneficial by-products of suffering. But ultimately it stands or falls on its basal *supernatural* claims. Attempts by ultra-liberal theologians to win over unbelievers by downplaying or sidelining those claims – such as those made by the Englishman John A.T. Robinson in the 1960s, or the American Episcopalian bishop John Shelby Spong in the 1980s and 1990s – have got nowhere. Even books such as Francis Spufford's *Unapologetic*, while well-meaning and full of useful insights, are most unlikely to make a dent in secularism and ignorance. The challenge is to convince people that the startling, the amazing, the apparently 'foolish' (St Paul's word in 1 Corinthians 1:18) really is *true*. It is only that realisation that is life-changing.

The most effective Christian evangelists have never shied away from orthodox theism. Among leading clerics in Australia, Protestant and Catholic alike, that rule certainly holds good. The likes of, say, John Bede Polding and J.D. Lang in the nineteenth century, or Daniel Mannix and Howard Mowll (Anglican Archbishop of Sydney, 1933–58) in the twentieth, may have differed on many second- and third-level issues. But not on the absolute essentials. Likewise among world figures of the highest eminence, giants of the modern era as disparate in style and emphasis as Billy Graham, Martin Luther King, Desmond Tutu and Pope John Paul II.

It remains to be seen whether Pope Francis will rise to those heights. But if he does, it will *not* be because he jettisons the essentials of the Christian faith in a quest for secular relevance. As many contemporary experts on Catholicism have explained, Francis is not unorthodox in his theology. He simply chooses to accentuate the positive.[42] He is patently a man of high intellect, deep humility and mischievous humour – a better communicator, perhaps a better showman, than many of his predecessors. But he is no heretic on, say, the Virgin Birth, or the physical resurrection of Christ, or the miracles of the New Testament, or even women priests – let alone my three bare-minimum criteria of an essentially Christian view of the world. On all those things and more, he is rock-solid. If it were otherwise, he would not have been elected Pope. The same applies to the new Archbishop of Canterbury, Justin Welby, another promisingly attractive figure.

The second general principle of which I am convinced is that, to the extent feasible, all Christian denominations should work together. Ecumenicism – or 'visible unity'[43] – is as important now as it has ever been. As we saw in Chapters 4 and 5, the Australian Churches, and, even more so, Australian lay Christians, have a reasonable record in this regard. They should strive to build upon it. This does not mean suppressing debate about genuine differences, but conducting such debate respectfully while striving for common ground and confronting the real enemy: unbelief. The same principle should apply vis-à-vis other religions. God, if He exists, is the God of all.[44] Religionists of all kinds must not allow secularists to win by default, by presenting an unedifying spectacle of discord and demagoguery.

### Issues to champion

The question is how to make an impact on the 90 per cent of the adult population who no longer go to church.

I see little point in wasting energy on issues of mere symbolism or tokenism. Thus, for example, if federal MPs voted to do away with the saying of the Lord's Prayer in the House of Representatives and the Senate, it would be sad, but little more. It may even be preferable that unbelievers and hypocrites do not continue to utter hollow platitudes.[45]

Far more important are what the Churches do about the really momentous issues facing Australia and the world today. The Churches have a choice. They can behave like weathervanes, following the opinions of an irreligious majority, or a powerful secular elite, and avoid giving offence. Or they can take firm, principled stands, issue by issue, consistent with the teachings of Christ. The former course would be the easier, but it would also lead to irrelevance. The latter course would not only be brave and right; in the long run, it would also offer the best prospects for evangelism. To encourage thinking unbelievers in Australia to take another look at religion, it will be necessary to think big and aim high. In the words of Tom Frame, 'a religion which disturbs individuals and disrupts society never evokes disinterest or indifference'.[46]

Christians cannot hope to please everyone. Indeed, true Christianity has become incompatible with some of the most stridently held beliefs of both the Right and the Left of politics. Those mired in monetary greed or permissive nihilism are probably already lost to the Churches anyway. But there are still plenty of decent citizens who – perhaps without fully realising it – are *already* thinking along Christian lines. It depends which causes are the most important to them.

In my judgment, good people are there to be won on both the Right and the Left – but almost certainly more on the Left, because there the Churches are coming from a lower base. Most of the well-meaning idealists in Australia – those who are not already Christians – are of the Left. They want to believe in something and they want their leaders to believe in something, beyond material enrichment.

### War

The Churches, indeed all Christians, should henceforth become the strongest anti-war voices in Australia. There are reasons for confidence that a corner has already been turned in this regard – and not before time, given the horrific blunders of the twentieth century, canvassed in Chapter 7. If pacifism is too much to hope for, and possibly undesirable anyway, the least we can expect is that just war principles be scrupulously and fearlessly insisted upon. The Churches should not be discouraged by their failure in 2002–03 to alter the course of events vis-à-vis Iraq. Next time other world leaders might listen.

Personally I do not see this as an ideological issue. Given the turbulent situation in the world and the destructive power of modern weapons, it is about respect for human life and plain common sense – even self-preservation. As a guiding principle I again fall back on the practical wisdom of Henry Parkes. Reacting in 1885 to an unholy scramble in New South Wales to send troops to the Sudan, when not even Britain herself had asked for any, he said (as reported in the local press):

> It was not the men who idly and lightly entered into war who were the best friends either of individuals or of communities, but it was the men who looked with a clear insight into the future, who weighed the probabilities on each side of every great question, and would prepare for the worst calamity, and labour to the utmost of their power to produce the greatest good. (Applause.)[47]

### Societal restraint

On the domestic front, the Churches should speak up stoutly in defence of old-fashioned decency and decorum. There need not be a return to hectoring wowserism. But wealthy corporate interests, and libertarians across the ideological spectrum, need to be challenged at every step on issues such as pornography, gambling, advertising, the sexualisation of children, alcohol consumption, recreational drug use, excessive credit card debt, obscenity, prostitution, family law reform, and anti-social working hours and conditions.

Perhaps the biggest sleeper issue is abortion. As discussed in Chapter 8, few would advocate a repeal of the *legal* right to choose. But there is room for the Churches to reventilate the *moral* issues, much more candidly than has been the case for decades, and in the light of the latest medical science. If the Churches do not do this, no one else will, for the issue is political dynamite. Yet no normally sensitive person should be happy with the status quo: 80,000 to 90,000 abortions per year. Even within a secular feminist's worldview – and certainly a Christian feminist's – there should be room for mature discussion on such measures as compulsory counselling, parental and spousal notification, the encouragement and facilitation of adoption, full freedom of conscience for pro-life doctors, and (at least arguably) a formal ban on late-term abortions. Perhaps above all, as Pope Francis has argued, Christians should be far less judgmental about single mothers. If a young woman has made a decision in favour of life she should be praised and assisted, not vilified and shunned.

If this national conversation could be conducted in the right spirit (admittedly a big 'if'), I am convinced it would be a beneficial thing – not only for the sake of unborn babies and their mothers, but for all citizens with a social conscience. There might well be flow-on effects for the general cause of religion.

### Foreign aid, the treatment of refugees and asylum seekers, and climate change

I have bracketed these three issues together because there are common elements. Each is pertinent to Australia's international reputation and sense of collective decency – our preparedness (or not) to set aside selfish, short-term tribalism and consider 'the brotherhood of man'. The major Churches, for the most part, have honourable records on each.[48] But their efforts could still be more vocal and focused.

These are global issues of the gravest consequence. Let me set the context.

Foreign aid is something quite distinct from private charity. It involves the voluntary transfer of resources by sovereign national governments. In 2013, the total sum involved worldwide was in the region of $160 billion, of which Australia contributed around $5 billion, mostly to developing countries in the Indo-Pacific region. The Abbott Government has twice cut the foreign aid budget by a large amount: by 2016–17 it will have fallen to a derisory 0.22 per cent of gross national income. The OECD target is 0.7 per cent.[49] Britain met the target in 2013.

A refugee, according to the official United Nations definition, is a 'person who, owing to a *well-founded* fear of being persecuted for reasons of race, religion, nationality, membership of a particular social group, or political opinion, is outside the country of his nationality, and is unable to or, owing to such fear, is unwilling to avail himself of the protection of that country' (emphasis mine).[50] Until a request for refuge has been accepted by the receiving country, the person making the request is referred to as an 'asylum seeker'. Every refugee was once an asylum seeker and every asylum seeker has a legal right to make a claim. There are approximately 15 million refugees in the world and 1 million asylum seekers. Australia deals with only a very small fraction of the world's asylum seeker claims and resettles 13,750 refugees each year, mostly from Afghanistan, Iran, Sri Lanka and Iraq. Notoriously, all asylum seekers who arrive in Australia by boat and without a visa (including children) are kept in offshore mandatory detention centres and are ineligible for resettlement in Australia, *even if their claim for refugee status is upheld*. (Historically, most such claims *have* been upheld.[51]) The stated purpose of these policies – which are unique to Australia – is to deter asylum seekers from arriving in Australia.[52]

Climate change is the term used to refer to the predicted long-term effects of the emission into the Earth's atmosphere of man-made greenhouse gases (mainly carbon dioxide). One predicted effect is a rise over coming decades in average global temperatures of anywhere between 2 degrees Celsius and 6 degrees Celsius. The likely flow-on effects – disrupted weather patterns, sea-level rises, increased incidence of wildfires, species extinctions, crop failures, and so on – are widely debated. But the overall picture is somewhere between serious and completely catastrophic, unless – and perhaps even if – drastic action is taken. Australia generates about 1.5 per cent of global greenhouse gas emissions. On a per capita basis we are one of the world's largest polluters.[53]

Christian attitudes to these issues should be shaped by certain core Biblical principles. One, peculiarly relevant to affluent and peaceful Australia, is this: from those to whom much is given, much will be expected (Luke 12:48). Another is the overriding duty to love one's neighbour as oneself (the Second Commandment of Jesus). Asylum seekers become our neighbours when and if – and by whatever means of transport – they arrive in Australia. But in a globalised world, there is a strong case for saying that everyone is our neighbour – certainly those people overseas who are directly affected by our actions here. The giving or withdrawal of foreign aid is such an action. So is the emission of greenhouse gases. Indeed, there is a sense in which the serious tackling of climate change by rich Western countries would be an invaluable form of foreign aid. All studies suggest that it will be people in Third World countries who suffer the most from flooding, drought, famine and so forth.

When it comes to climate change – and the environment more generally – a third core Biblical principle looms large. At stake is not merely the well-being of the human race, but the finely balanced ecosystem of the Earth itself. The Earth is not mankind's to harm or destroy. 'The Earth is the Lord's, and everything in it' (Psalm 24:1; see also Deuteronomy 10:4). We have a duty of stewardship over Creation (see Genesis 1:28), a duty owed ultimately to God Himself. This duty trumps amorphous and convenient notions of national interest. In the words of novelist Tim Winton: 'it's a sacramental mission'.[54]

Cynical sceptics may be muttering: *All this assumes that foreign aid 'works', that asylum seekers are 'genuine', and that climate change is real.* None of these assumptions, it is claimed, is adequately proven. But how much proof do such people need? What kind of proof would be adequate? The lay citizen has a choice. He can believe what he wants to believe, or he can inform himself about the views of qualified experts and listen to public figures who merit trust. Frankly, when it comes to all three of these issues, I see no good reason to trust ambitious, poll-driven politicians or those with a hefty financial stake in maintaining the status quo. On foreign aid and asylum seekers, I trust people who have devoted their lives to the poor and persecuted of the Third World, often at major personal cost. On climate change, I trust the vast majority of the world's qualified scientists (as to the technical aspects of the question) and most of the world's religious leaders (as to the moral aspects).

The Catholic Church has shown strong moral leadership on these issues. On refugees and asylum seekers, the relevant teachings are conveniently laid out in a document entitled *Refugees: A Challenge to Solidarity*, issued by the Vatican through two of its Pontifical Councils (Cor Unum and Pastoral Care of Migrants and Itinerant People). This document should be read in full. It makes nonsense of the supposedly 'Christian' justifications that have been proffered from time to time for Australia's policies since 2001.[55] It states:

> The first point of reference should *not* be the interests of the State, or national security, but the human person, so that the need to live in community, a basic requirement of the very nature of human beings, will be safeguarded.[56]

Likewise, on climate change, the Vatican has been forthright. In September 2014, in an address delivered to the UN Climate Change Summit in New York, the Vatican Secretary of State, Cardinal Pietro Parolin, made some very bold remarks. Stressing 'a moral imperative to act', the Cardinal said:

> A principal element which has emerged from the more than thirty years of study on the phenomenon of global warming is the increasing awareness that the entire international community is part of one interdependent human family. The decisions and behaviours of one of the members of this family have profound consequences for the others; there are no political frontiers, barriers or walls behind which we can

hide to protect one member from another against the effects of global warming. There is no room for the globalisation of indifference, the economy of exclusion or the throwaway culture so often denounced by Pope Francis.

The Cardinal concluded by calling for a huge paradigm shift: 'The ethical motivations behind every complex political decision must be clear. At present, this means consolidating a profound and far-sighted revision of models of development and lifestyles, in order to correct their numerous dysfunctions and deviations.'[57]

Anyone inclined to disregard or distrust reliable sources such as these should question their own motives. In Australia, the Churches must implore that there be candour. Church leaders should take every opportunity to stare down relevant politicians and decision-makers, and ask the toughest *moral* questions. Lay Christians should ask the same questions of people of their acquaintance – both fellow Christians and interested non-Christians.

On foreign aid: why is it that the world's poorest and most vulnerable people should be among the first to suffer when cuts, necessary or otherwise, are made to the federal budget? Is it because they are not Australian voters? Is it because most Australian voters will decide how they vote on the basis of other issues? Tellingly, the Abbott Government's first round of cuts to foreign aid was among the very few cuts disclosed to Australian voters *before* the September 2013 federal election (albeit just a few days before). Most of its budget cuts – including many that Abbott and others had promised before the election would *not* be made – were kept under wraps until the government's first budget was handed down in May 2014.

On asylum seekers and refugees: why do you back the policies of deterrence? Is it *truly* because you wish to prevent people from risking their lives by boarding unseaworthy boats? Or is that just a convenient excuse? Would you know or care if the very same people instead languished for years in a refugee camp, or drowned while on a boat heading for a country other than Australia, or died in the country from which they wished to flee? If all boat journeys to Christmas Island could somehow be rendered safe, would you then welcome all the asylum seekers who came? Would you then be prepared to accept that each individual claim for refugee status should be treated on its individual merits? Few supporters of strict deterrence of asylum seekers seemed to care about safety issues when SIEV X sank during the 2001 election campaign with the loss of 353 lives. Indeed, then and for years thereafter, to suggest that Australian surveillance authorities might possibly have done more to prevent the tragedy was to bring down a barrage of criticism on one's head.[58]

Now, some even pricklier questions. Are you in favour of Australia resettling many more 'genuine' refugees than we do at present? If not, why not – given that the boats have been 'stopped'? Why, at the very least, should conditions in offshore detention centres not be made more humane? Why should children be incarcerated? If most asylum seekers to Australia were white-skinned – fleers from Zimbabwe or South Africa, say – would your attitude to all these issues be the same?

On climate change: are you basing your position on a thorough, honest and dispassionate consideration of the evidence? Even if you genuinely believe that climate change is not a real threat, have you considered the possibility that you may be wrong? Given the potentially catastrophic consequences for the human race and the planet if you *are* wrong, why are you not in favour of meaningful precautionary action? Is it because any such action would, in the short term, cost you money? Is it because taking such action might cost you votes? Is it because opposing the taking of such action might win you votes? Is your advanced age a factor? Is it the case that you, personally, will not have to live with the worst consequences of climate change, when and if it happens? If you are in a position of power and influence, and you believe in God, have you considered how you will answer to Him?

## The economy – a grand gesture?

To everything I have said in the previous section, it may be objected: *These fine thoughts are all very well, but 'at the present time' Australia cannot afford to spend more money on foreign aid or asylum seekers or in combatting climate change. If anything, we should be spending even less on these indulgences. We have a 'budget emergency'!*

Do we? As I pointed out in Chapter 9, Australia, per capita, is one of the richest societies in human history. There are already vast sums of money in government and private coffers. Yet levels of government and private debt are indeed dangerously high, and prudence would seem to dictate that something be done to rein them in.

The Churches *must* enter this debate and emphasise the moral issues. As far as personal spending and indebtedness is concerned, they should embark on a crusade against 'affluenza'. Let us hear much more from them publicly about the importance of thrift and self-restraint, and gratitude for the benefits that Providence has already bestowed. As far as government debt is concerned, they should not be afraid to mention the unmentionable. Obvious options are to come down much harder on tax avoiders and evaders, and to raise taxes on those who can afford to pay more – perhaps much more. (In the decades after World War Two, during the Menzies era, personal income tax rates in Australia were as high as 75 per cent. Society did not collapse. Indeed, many people now look back on those years with great fondness.) Another option is to reprioritise government spending. Are the current priorities right and proper? In further cutting foreign aid in 2014, the Abbott Government admitted that it did so to fund yet more military commitments in Iraq.[59] We are about to spend tens of *billions* of dollars on submarines and fighter jets.

These are the bare minimum things that the Churches could do. But if they really want to influence this debate, and make a practical difference, a far harder thing may be called for. The Churches could volunteer to share the financial sacrifice, in order to get the federal budget back into the black. Many atheists rail against the so-called purple economy – the sizable assets of the Churches, the generous tax concessions they receive. Well, the atheists have a point. What a wonderful way to disarm them, and to demonstrate genuine piety and patriotism, by *giving* some of this wealth back to Australia at a time of need! It is only money, after all.

Could it be done by land sales alone? I do not have access to the relevant data. Perhaps the Churches themselves would need to cut their budgets, to make do with less. To the extent that their day-to-day operations might thus be affected, individual clerics and parishioners would have to step up, by providing their services at reduced pay or by volunteering or by reaching into their own pockets. None of this would be easy, but that is the point. And make no mistake: such things can be done, on a grand scale, if the spirit is willing. As we saw in Chapter 6, when colonial governments withdrew State aid in the 1870s and 1880s, the Catholic Church responded by greatly expanding its system of parish schools. The key was *voluntarism*: teachers worked for next to nothing, other than board and keep.

Perhaps I am a dreamer. But religion is at a crossroads in this country. Certainly, if Christianity is to survive as a significant force, let alone to flourish again, those who care must act, and act soon; otherwise, the label 'Post-God Nation' will become increasingly apt.

As things stand, genuinely observant Christians comprise about 10 per cent of the Australian population – about the same as in the Roman Empire at the time of Constantine's conversion. History proves that this is a sufficient base on which to build great things, and we have many advantages that the early Christians lacked until the fourth century, not least freedom of religion. On the other hand, there are now huge and insidious obstacles to overcome. Who will prevail – the voices for God, or the voices for the substitute gods, those the Romans worshipped as Venus (sex and romance), Mars (war) and Plutus (wealth)? Since Australians have free will, the decision is up to us.

Why should Australians choose God? Let me answer that question, and finish this book, by painting a picture of two possible futures for this country – one dystopian, the other utopian.

The first is a future in which present trends continue. That may not lead to suddenly obvious disaster, but it will lead to something bleak and unedifying. A country in which the mainstream Churches keep emptying, and extremists are the only religious voices to be heard. In which most citizens do not appreciate their heritage, adequately or at all. In which scientists close their minds to the deepest questions. In which 'economic growth' remains the guiding lodestar for the powers that be. In which 'national security' is sought through the curtailing of precious freedoms, the stockpiling of weapons, and the waging of yet more wars (until the all-encompassing global war that would be the end of everything). In which charity is left to government – grudgingly by some, self-righteously by others. In which most people retreat to their own private lives, seeking ephemeral solace in whatever diverts them from introspection. In which paid work becomes, even more than it is already, a thing to endure not enjoy. In which the purpose of education is largely if not entirely vocational. In which politics remain a soulless, low-rent contest between apparatchiks of the plutocratic Right and the selectively moral Left. In which the downtrodden and dispossessed have no realistic hope for anything better. In which the social costs of nihilism and inequality – violent crime, abortion, drug use, pornography, mental illness, gambling, obscenity, racism, environmental damage and the rest – continue to proliferate, even if lucky people manage to insulate themselves from their worst effects. In which euthanasia and same-sex marriage are legalised, and we move on to the next round of libertarian demands.

Above all, I envisage a future in which many, if not most, Australians – however wealthy and otherwise fortunate – sense that something is missing from their lives. Kerry Packer once confessed to Phillip Adams: 'That's what I've got inside me, a big black hole.'[60]

My utopian dream is of a different Australia. One in which most people experience what David Bentley Hart calls 'the cautery of fear, the balm of hope'. Fear of the adverse judgment of a stern but all-wise God, who demonstrated in Jesus how the perfect life should be lived. Hope that by trusting in Jesus and trying – however imperfectly – to emulate His example, there is a purpose to life beyond self-advancement in the here and now. Spouses would cherish each other. Children would grow up expecting less, being grateful for what they have, and honouring their parents. Scientists would better understand the limits of their expertise and the moral dangers inherent in so much of their work. The media would be respectful of religious faith, because most journalists would know something about it. The wealthy would take to heart the fundamental Biblical lesson that they have what they have not because they 'deserve' it, but by the grace of God: it is He who gives them the ability to produce wealth (Deuteronomy 8:17–18). The budget would be balanced in no time, because it would be done, in large part, *voluntarily* by the sanctified – and otherwise fairly. People would rejoin not merely churches but charities, community groups and political parties. Estimable leaders might emerge again from, for the ALP, the cream of the Christian working class, and, for the Liberal Party, the uppermost ranks of the moral middle class.

Imagine if Australia were looked upon by the world not merely as the luckiest country on Earth, but also as the most righteous. A truly Christian beacon of faith, hope and love. In the words engraved on the pedestal of the Statue of Liberty:

'Keep, ancient lands, your storied pomp!' cries she
With silent lips. 'Give me your tired, your poor,
Your huddled masses yearning to breathe free,
The wretched refuse of your teeming shore.
Send these, the homeless, tempest-tost to me,
I lift my lamp beside the golden door!'

That would be real, deserved 'national security'. But I said this was a utopian vision.

# Biographical sketches

Various key figures in Australian history and culture are mentioned in the main text. What follows is by way of supplement, with a focus on their religious lives (or, in the case of clerics, their *secular* achievements). The names are arranged alphabetically, by surname. Most of the subjects are founding fathers, judges and writers. For those wanting more detail on the religious beliefs of Australia's prime ministers, see my book *In God They Trust?*

## John Batman (1801–39)

The co-founder of Melbourne seems to have been a likeable rogue with a consciousness of his own sinfulness. He realised to the end his need for salvation. Born and raised in Parramatta, in western Sydney, his father, William Batman, was an emancipated convict who became a fruit vendor. William also became an extremely devout Christian. His spiritual adviser was the Reverend Samuel Marsden, and, under Marsden's influence, William ensured that all his children were brought up 'in strictly religious principles, of the evangelical order'. The whole Batman family attended St John's Church in Parramatta every Sunday – an Anglican service in the morning and (after 1816) a Methodist service in the evening conducted by the Reverend Samuel Leigh. John went to a day school in Parramatta and also to a Wesleyan Sunday school next door to his home, where he mixed freely with Aboriginal children.

In 1821, as a young man, John Batman ventured to Van Diemen's Land with his brother. He worked extremely hard as a farmer and pioneer land-holder, mixed well in local society (high and low), and in due course became close to George Arthur, the evangelical lieutenant-governor. But Batman was never a puritan like Arthur. Handsome, strong and gregarious, fond of drink and women, he died young of syphilis. But he also sustained a (mostly) happy marriage, to an Irishwoman named Eliza Callaghan, and raised seven daughters with her – all of whom were baptised.

Main source: C.P. Billot, *The Story of John Batman and the Founding of Melbourne* (Hyland House, 1979)


### Geoffrey Blainey (b. 1930)

Blainey has been justly described as the 'most prolific, wide-ranging, inventive, and, in the 1980s and 1990s, most controversial of Australia's living historians'. Yet the qualifying word 'living' was scarcely necessary. Blainey stands favourable comparison with any historian since 1788. His books *The Rush That Never Ended* (1963) and *The Tyranny of Distance* (1966) were classics of careful, readable, original scholarship. And Blainey is a polymath. I doubt whether anybody knows more than he does about the history of Australia, and his knowledge of human history as a whole is prodigious as well. Also among his thirty-odd books are titles such as *The Causes of War*; *The Great Seesaw: A new view of the Western World, 1750–2000*; and *A Short History of the World*.

All this makes Blainey's views on religion interesting at the very least. He himself is of the Wesleyan Methodist tradition. In 2011 he published a 600-page book, *A Short History of Christianity*, notable for its ecumenicism, its tolerance towards other faiths, and, especially, its historical rather than theological approach to the subject. Blainey concluded that 'of all the known people of the world, living or dead, Jesus is the most influential'. Moreover, 'by the standard of the times, his life is astonishingly documented'.


### James Bonwick (1817–1906)

Bonwick arrived in the colonies in 1840 and lived mostly in Victoria. He was a prolific writer of books about Australian history and society – over fifty in all – and conducted a great deal of original research and document-archiving. This was an essential, if imperfect, resource for later generations of historians. Bonwick also authored many of the textbooks used in colonial schools. The subjects covered went well beyond history: astronomy, geography, grammar, anthropology and trade were among the others, at a time when it was difficult to obtain suitable books locally. Bonwick was an intensely religiously man and his wife Esther (nee Beddow) was the daughter of a Baptist clergyman.

Main source: *Australian Dictionary of Biography*

## Martin Boyd (1893–1972)

A member of a phenomenally distinguished artistic family, Boyd is one of the great Australian novelists. His masterpiece, *Lucinda Brayford* (1946), was an attempt to depict aspects of both Australian and English life in the decades before and after World War One. Boyd himself lived in both countries. During the writing of *Lucinda Brayford* he derived great solace from almost nightly attendance at Evensong, at the sublime King's College Chapel in Cambridge.

Religion was vital to Boyd's make-up. As a young man he had contemplated joining the clergy – perhaps even becoming a monk. He had been influenced a great deal by his mother Minnie, a Low Church Anglican with 'uncompromising eternal values'. Her favourite Bible verse was Philippians 4:8: 'Finally, brethren, whatsoever things are true, whatsoever things are honest, whatsoever things are just, whatsoever things are pure, whatsoever things are lovely, whatsoever things are of good report; if there be any virtue, and if there be any praise, think on these things' (KJV). This verse resonated with Boyd. Another powerful influence on him as a boy was his headmaster at Trinity College in Kew, Canon George Merrick Long. Later in life, Boyd would write that 'next to my parents, I owe more to [him] than anyone else in the world'. Boyd treasured 'above all the sense of spiritual values which he [Long] implanted in us'.

At the age of forty-five, in the first of two autobiographies (*A Simple Flame*), Boyd wrote: 'I believe that for the western world the most potent spiritual truths [are] still enshrined in the Christian religion.' Unlike his mother, Boyd much preferred a High Anglican style of worship. In later middle age it appears that his worldview morphed into a kind of soft Christian humanism. Certainly, he became distrustful of dogma. But near the end of his life, in his second autobiography (*Day of My Delight*), he reaffirmed his religious faith.

Main source: Brenda Niall, *Martin Boyd* (Oxford University Press, 1977)

## Christopher Brennan (1870–1932)

Brennan was a tortured genius who wrestled with faith all his life. Indeed, according to one biographer, he decided to 'go in for verse' (Brennan's famous quip) in order to pursue a 'spiritual quest for an absolute which he believed could be found through poetry'.

The quest was needed because, while a young man at Sydney University studying logic, philosophy and classics, Brennan had lost his childhood faith. His Irish-born parents were solid Catholics, and their precocious teenage son had been educated at Jesuit schools (St Aloysius and St Ignatius Colleges in Sydney). There had even been expectations he would become a priest. That idea was abandoned, but Brennan's enquiring mind was not satisfied by logic and philosophy either. He spent decades as a 'seeker for Eden', and it shows in some of his most moving poems. Late in life, in or around 1925, he began a gradual return to the Catholic fold.

Main sources: *Australian Dictionary of Biography*; Australian Poetry Library

## (Francis) Gerard Brennan (b. 1928)

Brennan was the first Catholic to hold the office of chief justice of the High Court of Australia. Appointed by Prime Minister Paul Keating, he served in that position from April 1995 to May 1998.

Brennan is a devout Catholic. He grew up in what he later described as a loving Catholic household, attending the Range Convent School, St Joseph's Christian Brothers' College in Rockhampton, and Downlands College in Toowoomba. His son Frank Brennan is a well-known Jesuit priest and author. In the words of two joint biographers: 'In many respects, Brennan embodied the tension that is at the heart of the judicial oath. He believed that it was a primary function of law to protect minorities and the disadvantaged, and his decisions struggled to achieve this result.'

Main source: Website of the High Court of Australia

## C.M.H. (Manning) Clark (1915–91)

Clark's six-volume *History of Australia*, published between 1962 and 1981, is an indispensable if flawed masterpiece. For all the gorgeous rhetoric it contains, it was the end result of decades of hard yakka: the discovery and compilation of thousands of primacy-source documents. In any assessment of Clark, his inspiring example as a teacher of the bright, up-and-coming Australian elite – at Geelong Grammar, Melbourne University and the Australian National University – must also be weighed in the scales. As a tutor and lecturer, Clark had the precious knack of inspiring the young. Interestingly, 'his language was that of a high churchman, with numerous Biblical allusions'.

Nowadays Clark is esteemed by the Left and disdained by the Right. This is partly the result of his disconcertingly naïve book, *Meeting Soviet Man* (1960), and partly of his identification, later in life, with two iconic and controversial Labor prime ministers – Gough Whitlam and Paul Keating. But, as Guy Rundle (among others) has pointed out, some of Clark's most virulent early critics were from the Left.

It is vital to understand that Clark was a product of Australia's small colonial upper-middle class and never, in any meaningful sense, a Marxist. His father, the Reverend C.H.W. (Charles) Clark, was a minister of the Church of England. A tolerant High Church Anglican, he served in various clerical roles in New South Wales and Victoria between 1906 and 1951. His wife Catherine (nee Hope) could boast even more impressive Christian credentials. She was 'a damsel of noble family' and a 'formidable and unswerving adherent of her religion': her great-great grandfather was none other than the Reverend Samuel Marsden; her parents, the Hopes, were members of a leading colonial family.

Manning Clark himself was educated at Melbourne Church of England Grammar School, Melbourne University's Trinity College and then Balliol College at Oxford. His own faith waxed and waned – to put it mildly – but he long derived a kind of hopeful comfort from the rites of the Catholic Church. Late in life 'the solemn rituals of the mass – the consecration of the host, the customary greetings of peace, and the soaring voices of the choir – washed Clark's fear of death away, allowing him to feel "tender towards everyone" and to believe that there might be "mercy" and "forgiveness" after all.'

Main source: Stephen Holt, *Manning Clark and Australian History 1915–1963* (University of Queensland Press, 1982)

## David Collins (1756–1810)

The first Judge-Advocate of New South Wales was a man in the best traditions of *noblesse oblige* High Anglicanism. A tolerant ecumenicist who 'believed the same great Creator of the universe was worshipped alike by Protestant and Catholic', he had once told his father that 'nature intended and fashioned me to ascend the pulpit'.

Though not a trained lawyer, Collins was decent and capable, close to Governors Arthur Phillip and John Hunter and intensely loyal to them. Later he became Lieutenant-Governor of Van Diemen's Land. He adopted a stern but fair attitude to the convicts, variously referring to them as 'the people' and 'servants of the Crown' who enjoyed the 'protection of British laws'. His sudden death in 1810 was a huge loss and had fateful consequences for the history of Van Diemen's Land.

Main source: *Australian Dictionary of Biography*


## Bruce Dawe (b. 1930)

Most Australians have read at least a few of Bruce Dawe's poems. His collections sell very well and his work has now been studied by two generations of school students. It is renowned for its accessibility: Dawe may well be the most popular poet we have ever had. I mean that in the best of ways. The man has a brilliant knack for snapshotting 'ordinary' people, events, moments, thoughts.

Dawe has been a practising Catholic since 1954. Raised in various towns on the outskirts of Melbourne, largely by a Protestant mother, he became sceptical about religion as a teenager. Then, initially via contact with an inspirational teacher who was also a Methodist lay preacher, he began taking a serious interest. Through a combination of influences – a university crush on a beautiful and intelligent Catholic woman, reading *Lives of the Saints* and contemplation of apostolic succession – he went over to the Church of Rome. In 1997 he stated candidly: 'I'm a traditionalist in religion. That makes me a conservative.' But he said in the same interview that he believes in 'a fun-loving god … [who] had a sufficient sense of humour to create us'. That sort of whimsical wisdom is the hallmark of his poetry.

Main source: Transcript of interview with R. Hughes, 8 July 1997, for the Australian Biography Project


## William Patrick (Bill) Deane (b. 1931)

A justice of the High Court from 1982 to 1995, and governor-general from 1996 to 2001, Deane is one of Australia's most distinguished living statesmen. He is descended from Irish settlers who came to the Australian colonies from Tipperary in 1851, in the wake of the great potato famine. As a boy growing up in Canberra, he was close to Canberra's first parish priest, Monsignor Patrick Haydon. He served as an altar boy and received his primary school education from the nuns of St Christopher's Convent in Manuka. His secondary schooling was at St Joseph's College in Sydney, where he was greatly influenced by Brother Ligouri (Reginald O'Hearn), known to all as 'Lig'. As a young man, Deane was briefly a member of the DLP: he had joined at the urging of poet James McAuley but soon became disillusioned. His brand of Catholicism, while heartfelt, has always been ecumenical in flavour: he was an admirer of the great reformist Anglican Ernest Burgmann and came to champion 'the modern, universal Church', made up of Christians of all denominations.

As governor-general, Deane, with his wife Helen (also a Catholic), championed social justice issues including multiculturalism, Indigenous rights, refugees and homelessness. A consistent theme of Deane's public and private utterances was that Australia's moral worth as a nation could best be judged by our treatment of the most disadvantaged human beings (both inside and outside Australia). He drew this teaching directly from Chapter 25 of Matthew's Gospel; other critical texts for Deane were the parables of the Good Samaritan and the Rich Man, and the letter of James. Notably, Deane defended the Churches against suggestions they should stay silent as regards 'political' issues: 'The very suggestion that church leaders aren't qualified to talk about the disadvantaged,' he once said, 'is an insult to the people who are asked to swallow it.'

Main source: Tony Stephens, *Sir William Deane: The things that matter* (Hodder, 2002)

## Edward 'Weary' Dunlop (1907–93)

During his captivity on the Burma–Thailand railway, Weary Dunlop tended to men racked by starvation, cholera, dysentery, ulcers and all manner of other ailments and injuries. He witnessed disgusting inhumanity, yet somehow reached the end of his life without hate in his heart. Why? Because, he once said, the experience of helping POWs in the camps was life-affirming. 'I understood what it would mean to love your neighbour more than yourself.'

Dunlop's diaries from that time make riveting reading. When they were first published, in 1986, he dedicated them to POWs everywhere and quoted Scripture: 'I pray that "They shall hunger no more, neither shall they thirst any more; neither shall the sun light on them nor any heat"' (Revelation 7:16). The choice of a Biblical quotation reflected Dunlop's heritage: he was from a long line of Scots Presbyterians on his father's side. His great-grandfather, the Reverend Walter Dunlop, had been a well-known minister at Dumfries, and his father, James ('Wattie') Dunlop, followed in this tradition. Weary's mother Alice had been raised an Anglican, but she adjusted after marriage to her husband's Non-conformism. Both were teetotallers and Sunday school teachers, and thoroughly Calvinist in their thinking, though for reasons of geography (they lived in rural Victoria) the Dunlop family worshipped in the local Methodist church. Weary's older brother Alan commented late in life that their parents' early lessons in Christian morality were well learned. The values imparted by Wattie and Alice 'remained with us,' he wrote, 'inspiring us to seek to be of service to our day and age'. Weary certainly lived this ethic: apart from his legendary conduct as a POW, he played rugby union for Australia, became an eminent surgeon, and devoted himself to many charitable causes.

What of his inner life? It appears that, as a teenager, he decided that he had an open mind about the 'heaven and hell approach to life'. Certainly he was less strict about observing the Sabbath than his parents wished, and, once he became an adult, drifted away from orthodox Christianity. He came to believe, for example, that 'faith comes in varied and extraordinary guises' and that 'there are as many ways to God as there are faiths and religions'. He flirted with aspects of Eastern religion, in particular the Buddhist notion that all men are equal in the face of suffering and death. As all that suggests, he was anything but irreligious. He once said: 'I do not want to remove that mustard seed of faith from anyone else.'

One of his closest confidants as a POW was a Catholic priest named Father Bourke, who became a lifelong friend. Bourke once described Weary as a man of 'Christ-like virtues' – and as 'a man with a definite belief in God, perhaps without any precise affiliation'. The evidence bears Bourke out. In 1940, shortly after enlisting to serve in World War Two, Weary spent a good deal of time in Jerusalem. The old Russian church on the Mount of Olives became one of his havens, where he could enjoy 'a great detachment and sense of peace'. A few years later, as a POW, Weary was reduced to tearing up Bibles: he used the paper to make cigarettes for others. But before doing so he 'methodically memorised anything he wanted to remember' – principally the Sermon on the Mount – and attended many services conducted by the padres, both Protestant and Catholic. On Easter Saturday 1943, some hundreds of men attended the Anglican service, conducted in the evening by candlelight. Of those, about sixty took Communion.

Weary wrote in his diary: 'The theme of the address was suffering, the cross and the empty tomb.' He added with remarkable grace: 'The suffering of which we had experienced something, only a little of that endured by millions of others.'

Main sources: Sue Ebury, *Weary: The life of Sir Edward Dunlop* (Penguin, 1994); E.E. Dunlop, *The War Diaries of Weary Dunlop, Java and the Burma–Thailand Railway 1942–1945* (Nelson, 1986)

## Herbert Vere Evatt (1951–60)

The youngest-ever High Court judge, a key player in the establishment of the United Nations, and Federal Labor Opposition Leader from 1953 to 1960, Evatt was a leading figure in mid-twentieth century Australian history. He was raised by a devout Anglican mother. Though he himself was not a conventionally observant Christian, he had 'absorbed his mother's receptiveness to a coherent, embracing harmony'. He voluntarily attended church services from time to time and 'acknowledged the wisdom of God's judgment, a respectful belief in a supreme arbiter who bestowed ultimate justice and order'.

Source: Peter Crockett, *Evatt, A life* (Oxford University Press, 1993)

## John Forrest (1847–1918)

Forrest was probably the most important Western Australian ever, and a key founding father. But for his efforts, it is unlikely that Western Australia would have joined the Federation as an original State.

His parents, William and Margaret Forrest, were lower middle-class Scots who arrived in the fledgling colony in December 1842. Back in Scotland they had been practising Presbyterians, but in their new surroundings they adapted their religion to the Church of England. William became a churchwarden, and both he and his wife raised their ten children with pious habits. In the evenings, at their home near Bunbury, there were readings by candlelight of the Bible or *Pilgrim's Progress*, and at the age of twelve John was sent to Bishop Hale's School in Perth. The headmaster, Canon G.H. Sweeting, instilled in his boys a blend of 'patriotic Anglicanism [and] benevolent imperialism'. He had a big influence on Forrest, as did one of Forrest's best friends at the school, Septimus Burt (1847–1919), a member of one of the colony's 'six hungry families' (see Chapter 5). Indeed, as far as the law and Anglicanism are concerned, the Burts were probably *the* most notable family. (Septimus

Burt later served in Forrest's government as the first Attorney-General of Western Australia.)

Though Forrest was never as devout or as scholarly an Anglican as Burt, he often quoted Scripture and was stolidly faithful after his own fashion. And his faith mattered to him. Before entering politics he carved out a career as Surveyor-General of Western Australia, leading expeditions into the interior in 1869, 1870 and 1874. His achievement was a negative one, but nonetheless important: he established beyond doubt that vast tracts of Western Australia and South Australia were waterless wastelands unfit for colonisation. A biographer, Frank Crowley, has suggested that Forrest's upbringing was crucial: 'from his parents he had inherited a sound constitution and a firm respect for the Sabbath. He always tried to avoid travelling on Sundays, which was most necessary for the well-being of his men, and he placed great reliance on Divine Providence.'

Main source: Frank Crowley, *Big John Forrest 1847–1918: A founding father of the Commonwealth of Australia* (University of Western Australia Press, 2000)


## Miles Franklin (1879–1954)

Like her near-contemporary Henry Handel Richardson, Stella Maria Sarah Miles Franklin often wrote under a male pseudonym. Her first and most famous novel, *My Brilliant Career* (1901), could not find an Australian publisher, but with help from Henry Lawson, she secured one in stuffy old England. Given Franklin's status as an ardent Australian nationalist and feminist, this was more than ironic.

She was a fascinating religious type. A child of the squattocracy, she was raised in rural New South Wales (at Brindabella, near the Snowy Mountains) by parents who were no more than nominally Anglican. Her father, indeed, became a rationalist. But her maternal grandmother was a pious woman: she played from *Hymns Ancient and Modern* in her home, and frequently urged young Stella to pray.

Not surprisingly, this combination of influences produced conflicting thoughts. From an early age Stella was a quester – 'dissatisfied with God' but not prepared to give Him up. During a rationalist phase she wrote an essay entitled 'A dialogue: An infidel and a religionist'. But at other times, out in the bush, she felt a sense of transcendence. In May 1894, aged fifteen, she opted to be confirmed as an Anglican. But her spiritual quest continued in adulthood.

An independent woman of sophisticated learning and high intelligence, it seems that Franklin would have *preferred* to reject God and the Churches – but could never quite do it. In the words of her biographer Jill Roe, 'something of the old church teachings lurked in her mind'. Through the influence of a close friend and fellow-feminist, Vida Goldstein, she became interested for a while in Christian Science. She was generally suspicious of the large institutional Churches, because of their conservative teachings on sexuality, but approved of reformist Protestant clerics such as Ernest Burgmann. Practical charity was what she looked for, as 'more acceptable to God, more in accordance with my view of Christianity'. It would appear that, in old age, she feared death. Her precise state of mind at the end must now be unknowable, but at any rate she was cremated with Anglican rites.

Main source: Jill Roe, *Her Brilliant Career: The life of Stella Miles Franklin* (Belknap Press, 2009)


## Helen Garner (b. 1942)

Garner is not normally associated with Christianity. Yet, as a number of critics have noted, several of her books feature explicitly Christian characters and themes. *Cosmo Cosmolino* (1992) is the most obvious one. Tellingly, after it was published, there was a backlash. Garner recalled: 'people in the literary world recoiled. They were saying that "Helen Garner's found God." I think some were embarrassed – you know the way that Australians can be very embarrassed about things that are not rational?'

Sources: Romana Koval, 'Rewind to Ms Garner's Angels', *Sydney Morning Herald*, 21 April 2012; Elaine Lindsay, 'The dark. The light. Helen Garner and the city', *Women-Church: An Australian journal of feminist studies in religion*, No. 27, Spring 2000


## Mary Gaudron (b. 1943)

Gaudron was the first woman to be appointed to the High Court of Australia. She served from 1987 to 2003. Raised in Moree, in outback New South Wales, by working-class parents, she was educated in the Catholic school system: a little convent primary school in Moree East, followed by St Ursula's Catholic High School in Armidale. Her pious and dedicated mother, Bonnie, who was a convert to Catholicism, took seriously the solemn promise she had made to raise her children in the faith.

Source: Pamela Burton, *Moree to Mabo: The Mary Gaudron story* (UWA Publishing, 2010)

## George Gipps (1791–1847)

The Governor of New South Wales in the formative period 1837–46, Gipps was the son of an English clergyman. As a boy in Canterbury he had been a schoolmate of William Grant Broughton, who later served as the Anglican Bishop of Australia (and subsequently Sydney). In his own right, according to biographer Peter Cochrane, Gipps 'was the epitome of moral earnestness with his devotion to temperance, his disapproval of gambling, his homebody inclinations and his insistence on daily prayers for the entire Government House retinue'.

Main source: Peter Cochrane, *Colonial Ambition: Foundations of Australian democracy* (Melbourne University Press, 2006)


## Murray Gleeson (b. 1938)

Gleeson was the first Catholic to become chief justice of the Supreme Court of New South Wales. He served in that position for a decade, from 1988 to 1998, before his appointment as chief justice of the High Court of Australia, a position he occupied with steely honour until 2008.

Gleeson was no mere nominal Catholic: his faith was an important, lifelong influence. As a three-year-old he was asked by his grandfather what he wanted to be when he grew up. 'I'm going to be the Pope,' was young Murray's reply. He was educated exclusively in the Catholic system and did not encounter a lay teacher until university. But Gleeson's Catholicism was not of the social justice variety. He was a black-letter lawyer in the tradition of Owen Dixon, and a political conservative – but a conservative in the mould of Edmund Burke rather than that of the modern-day Liberal Party. Gleeson's religion mattered in the same way as it did for Burke.

Main sources: Michael Pelly, *Murray Gleeson – The smiler* (The Federation Press, 2014); Brian Davies, 'A life on the Bench – and at the Bar: A conversation with Murray Gleeson, former chief justice of the High Court', *The Catholic Weekly*


## Germaine Greer (b. 1939)

Australia's most important feminist thinker, and author of the truly ground-breaking book *The Female Eunuch* (1970), grew up in Victoria in the 1950s and spent her formative years at Star of the Sea College in Gardendale (then known as Elsternwick), Victoria. Established in 1883 by the Irish Presentation Sisters, it was and still is an important convent school. Greer has acknowledged more than once the debt she owes to her teachers. They broadened her horizons. 'If it hadn't been for the nuns,' she once said, 'I might well have gone to a secretarial college, had streaks put in my hair and married a stockbroker.'

It is true that she has criticised the quality of the teaching she received at Star of the Sea concerning the formal proofs of God. Yet it seems that even on that score her mind may not be altogether closed; or, if it is now closed, that she rather regrets the fact. 'If I'd been taught by the Jesuits,' she once wrote wistfully, 'I'd probably still be a Catholic.'

It fascinates me that Greer, in later life, has become more socially conservative on a number of issues. She has observed, for example, that 'marriage made more sense when it was indissoluble. It's the woman trying to cope with the strains of a one-parent family who will suffer most from the relaxation of the divorce laws.'

Main sources: Rosemary Forgan and Jackie Bennett (eds), *There's Something About a Convent Girl* (Virago, 1991); Edmund Campion, *Australian Catholics* (Penguin, 1987)

## Samuel Walker Griffith (1845–1920)

Griffith, the first chief justice of the High Court of Australia and the principal draftsman of the Constitution, was the son of a Welsh Congregationalist pastor, the Reverend Edward Griffith. In the 1840s and early 1850s, the Reverend led congregations in Merthyr Tydfil and Portishead, and Wiveliscombe (in Somerset). He and his family immigrated to Queensland in 1853 at the invitation of the Colonial Missionary Society. In 1860, after stints at Ipswich, and Maitland (in New South Wales), he took up a posting in Brisbane, where he stayed until his retirement in 1888. The Reverend's status as the leader of the Congregational Church in Brisbane was useful when his brilliant young adult son was a rising barrister: it got him invitations to functions at Government House, though Griffith himself felt his father's religious Non-conformism was a social handicap.

Griffith was steeped from birth not merely in 'religion' but in the Non-conformist culture of upright conduct and rigorous self-improvement. His mother, Mary Griffith (nee Walker), shared her husband's Evangelicalism and piety, urging her son on numerous occasions not to be 'ashamed of Christ!' Griffith received a Greek New Testament for his fourth birthday, and, as a child, was expected to read the Bible daily. He did so, along with every book in his father's library by the age of seven. He received his formal education at various small church schools in Brisbane, Maitland and Sydney before enrolling at Sydney University at the age of fifteen.

His mother also urged him to 'choose a wife, dear Sam, who would train your children for Heaven'. Griffith complied, marrying Julia Thomson in June 1870 with Presbyterian rites. This proved a happy, stable union, a grand base for Griffith's prodigious achievements.

What were Griffith's own religious views? John Hirst has suggested that 'religion did not mean much to him', and it is true that his passions were the classics and the law. He did not devote his life to Christ as his parents had wished. Yet until old age he continued to read the Bible and attend church – Anglican services rather than those of the dissenters – and was a prominent Freemason. He was also the first Australian translator of Dante's *Inferno*.

Main source: Roger B. Joyce, *Samuel Walker Griffith* (University of Queensland Press, 1984)


## Keith Hancock (1898–1988)

In the era before World War Two, Keith Hancock was regarded as Australia's most distinguished historian. There is still a case for saying that he was our finest ever. His *Survey of British Commonwealth Affairs* (1937–42) was monumental, and his popular book *Australia* (1930) highly influential – in a long-term and not merely short-term way. Decades before it became conventional wisdom, Hancock 'attacked ... three pillars of the Australian settlement – protection, state socialism and the White Australia policy – which he saw as together working for stagnation'. A true liberal rather than a socialist or conservative, he anticipated much of the Whitlam–Fraser–Hawke–Keating agenda.

Hancock was yet another son of a clergyman – in his case, indeed, an archdeacon. It was once written of the Reverend William Hancock (1863–1955) that 'probably no man ever rendered greater service to the Church [of England] in Victoria'. His famous son was not quite so devout, at least in his younger years: much of Hancock's historical work emphasised economic themes. Even so, one biographer adjudged that 'Christianity remained a primal influence, and [later in life] he gradually returned to it'.

Main Source: *Australian Dictionary of Biography*

## Gwen Harwood (1920–95)

Harwood was a highly distinguished Australian poet, but it was perhaps as a letter-writer that her talents shone most brightly. Gregory Kratzmann's 500-page compilation of her correspondence was a revelation to me. The contents justified the assertion on the dust-jacket: '[they] present a strong claim that Gwen Harwood be considered this country's greatest letter-writer'.

One of the reasons the letters are so captivating is that Harwood was steeped not only in the written word but also in both music and religion. As a teenager in Brisbane she was the assistant organist at All Saints' Church in Wickham Terrace – the city's oldest Anglo-Catholic congregation – and fell in love with the curate. She became a communicant, and, a few years afterwards, entered the Convent of the Poor Clares at Toowong as a novice. She left six months later, but the experience was formative.

Kratzmann suggests in an editorial aside that Harwood was 'not in any conventional sense a believer', but that was putting things too extremely. True, after moving to Hobart in 1945 with her husband, she ceased for many years to be a churchgoer. The demands of domesticity and writing swamped her; in her own words, she waged an inner war 'against God and the suburbs'. But she always exhibited a reverence for Scripture (especially the book of Job) and an appreciation of the fundamental *seriousness* of Christianity. In one letter in late 1954, she remarked on a 'hideous' range of Christmas cards that she had seen on display in a *Christian* bookshop in Hobart: 'in little compartments marked FLORAL CHRISTMAS, SNOW GLITTER CHRISTMAS, DICKENS CHRISTMAS, HUMEROUS CHRISTMAS, MASCULINE CHRISTMAS, JUVENILE CHRISTMAS ... it's true they have a RELIGIOUS CHRISTMAS but it hardly cancels out the general effect'. Marvellous!

Several of Harwood's correspondents – James McAuley among them – were staunch believers. She also kept in touch with various friends from All Saints' in Brisbane, and finally, in 1985, resumed churchgoing – at All Saints' in Hobart (also Anglo-Catholic). Though often irritated by the forms of modern liturgy and sometimes scathing of individual clerics and parishioners (once she referred to the Catholic Archbishop of Tasmania, G.C. Young, as a 'repulsive trap-mouthed cleric'), she enjoyed the sense of community and served at one time as secretary of the parish council. Near the end of her life Harwood wrote in one of her letters this tantalising sentence: 'It amazes me that I have so much trouble with the resurrection of the body when I have none at all about the Assumption.' Make of that what you will.

Main source: Gregory Kratzmann, *A Steady Storm of Correspondence: Selected letters of Gwen Harwood 1943–1995* (University of Queensland Press, 2001)

## Bill Hayden (b. 1933)

Hayden variously served as federal treasurer (1975), Federal Labor Opposition Leader (1977–83), federal minister for trade and foreign affairs (1983–88) and governor-general (1989–96). He may have been the best, most thoughtful prime minister Australia never had.

Religion-wise, his story is compelling. He was the first governor-general to take an affirmation rather than an oath. But he had grown up steeped in Irish Catholicism, and, as a teenager, harboured ideas of becoming a priest. He lost his faith as a young man in the most tragic circumstances imaginable. His five-year-old daughter, Michaela, was hit by a car and killed while walking to Sunday school. She had been sick with a cold for several days and Hayden had asked her whether she would like to miss it that day and go with him for a drive instead. The little girl had insisted that she did not want to miss Sunday school. Hayden, understandably, could never see religion in the same way again. Even so, he admitted to his biographer, John Stubbs, a reverence for the Catholic Mass. He also confessed that 'church people keep coming up when I reflect on my life'.

Main source: John Stubbs, *Hayden* (William Heinemann Australia, 1989)

## Robert Herbert (1831–1905)

Herbert was the first premier of Queensland, and his religious connections were responsible for his initial arrival in the colony in 1859. He came as private secretary to Governor George Bowen, and had obtained that position because he and Bowen were at Eton together. Indeed, they had lived in the same manse and shared a housemaster, the Reverend Edward Coleridge, a son of Samuel Taylor Coleridge. The Reverend – obviously with some success – encouraged all his boys into public service. In Queensland, Herbert counted two leading Anglicans among his closest friends: the Reverend John Tomlinson, founder of All Saints' Anglican Church, and the Reverend Bowyer Edward Shaw. They all rowed together!

Main source: Bruce Knox, *The Queensland Years of Robert Herbert, Premier: Letters and papers* (University of Queensland Press, 1977)

## Henry Bournes Higgins (1851–1929)

Higgins – long-time justice of the High Court and responsible for the seminal *Harvester* basic wage decision of 1907 – was the second son of an Irish Protestant (Wesleyan) minister, the Reverend John Higgins, and his pious and dutiful wife Anne. Higgins spent his first eighteen years in Ireland, where he attended a Wesleyan school in Dublin (George Bernard Shaw was a co-pupil) and imbibed his family's 'homely' religiosity. One of his favourite childhood books was Prideaux's *Connexion of the Old and New Testaments*. In 1870 the family immigrated to Victoria, where the Reverend Higgins worked as an itinerant preacher.

As a young man at Melbourne University, Higgins undertook a study of comparative religion under a noted professor, W.E. Hearn. His Wesleyan faith was shaken: he could no longer accept 'his father's brand of innocent devotion'. In particular, he became disturbed by the orthodox Christian concept of eternal Hell. His biographer, John Rickard, adjudged that 'though he came close to agnosticism, he seems to have retained some sort of religious faith'.

My own view is that Higgins undoubtedly retained belief in a Creator God. It is possible that he became a deist, though he continued to worship regularly, with his wife Mary Alice, in the Church of England (St George's at Malvern) and to pray habitually that 'God's Kingdom may come'. At any rate religion was in his blood. Apart from his parents, one of his brothers, John, was a devout Baptist; another, George, became a Quaker, and his sister Ina a Christian Scientist.

Main sources: John Rickard, *H.B. Higgins: The rebel as judge* (George Allen & Unwin, 1984); *Australian Dictionary of Biography*

## A.D. Hope (1907–2000)

There is a strong case that Hope was – at least until Les Murray – the best-known Australian poet internationally. He was also an eminent and influential literary critic and a pioneering academic: foundation professor of English at ANU, and an early advocate of the (then unfashionable) notion that Australian literature was worth studying as a fully fledged tertiary subject.

Hope is yet another eminent Australian whose father was a Protestant clergyman – the Reverend Percival Hope served as a Presbyterian minister at various parishes in New South Wales and Tasmania. A.D. Hope always remained fondly proud of that heritage and deeply fascinated by metaphysical questions. One of his tutors at Oxford was none other than C.S. Lewis. Hope was not as sure in his faith as Lewis, not by a long shot, but he never shied away from tackling the biggest existential questions. Biographer Mark O'Connor has argued that 'it was the nature of the universe that he sought hardest to grasp in verse'.

Main source: *Australian Dictionary of Biography*

## John Hunter (1737–1821)

Arthur Phillip's 'deputy' on the First Fleet, and the second governor of the infant New South Wales (1795–1800), Hunter was a man of sincere faith. Indeed, in several respects, he was not your typical 'sea-dog'. Born in the port town of Leith, near Edinburgh on the Firth of Forth, his father William was a sea captain in the merchant service. But his mother Helen (nee Drummond) was a woman of some breeding. She was the niece of George Drummond, an important lord provost of Edinburgh, responsible for the construction of the 'New' Town in the 1760s.

As a boy in Leith, John was groomed by his parents for the ministry of the Church of Scotland. But his mother died when he was ten, and he was sent to live with his paternal uncle in the English market town of King's Lynn, Norfolk. There he attended the school attached to St Margaret's Anglican Church and studied classics and divinity. His mentor as a teenager was Dr Charles Burney, a teacher and family friend. Eleven years older than Hunter, Burney was a well-connected man of talent and sensibility. He was a pianist, composer, church organist and music historian; he was also a friend of Sir Joseph Banks. Before settling on the sea as his true vocation, Hunter studied theology at the University of Aberdeen and seriously considered entering the ministry.

All his life he remained a firm Christian; at times he could be 'more parsonical than the parsons'. I am baffled by biographer Robert Barnes' assessment that Hunter was 'not deeply religious'. He attended church every Sunday, professed belief in 'the holy scriptures of truth' and 'wrote and spoke of Christ as his Saviour'. It is hard to classify him by denomination: 'his initial Presbyterian inclinations became blurred'. In old age, after retiring from the Royal Navy, he regularly attended the Anglican Church of St John in Hackney (in north-east London). He was buried in the churchyard there.

Main sources: Arthur Hoyle, *The Life of John Hunter: Navigator, governor, admiral* (Mulini Press, 2001); Robert Barnes, *An Unlikely Leader: The life and times of Captain John Hunter* (Sydney University Press, 2009)

## Reverend Richard Johnson (1753–1827)

Johnson was the Anglican chaplain on the First Fleet. He thought himself a failure in the colony, and returned to England in 1800 a disappointed man. But he was too hard on himself. The work he did in comforting the early colony – through the legal ceremonies of marriage, baptism, burial and the like – was probably more important than he realised. Similarly, his visitations to the sick. Even his sermons seem to have struck a chord, at least those given on special occasions. In June 1790 news came through of King George III's recovery from a bad illness. Watkin Tench recorded that 'a general thanksgiving to Almighty God … was ordered to be offered up' and that Johnson preached with 'gratitude and solemnity'. By December of the following year, 1791, divine service was being performed every Sunday, in either Sydney or Parramatta.

Johnson also saw himself as 'half a farmer', and in that capacity he did vital work for the early colony. As a naval officer of the First Fleet he was granted two acres of land by Governor Phillip early on, but there is a case, in retrospect, that the grant ought to have been much bigger. Unlike many of the other grantees, Johnson knew what he was doing. In the first two seasons (1788–89 and 1789–90) he produced sorely needed crops of wheat, barley and oats, and after being granted 100 acres at Petersham in 1791, his output soared. He was the first person in the colony to grow citrus fruits (cannily, he had acquired the seeds in Rio de Janeiro on the journey out) and one of the first to see his allocation of sheep, goats, pigs and fowls increase very considerably. By the time he returned to England in 1800 his farms at Petersham ('Canterbury Vale') and Kissing Point were thriving concerns.

Main source: Neil K. Macintosh, *Richard Johnson, Chaplain to the Colony of New South Wales: His life and times 1755–1827* (Pilgrim International, 1978)

## Thomas Keneally (b. 1935)

Keneally – author of *The Chant of Jimmie Blacksmith* (1972), *Schindler's Ark* (1982), and literally dozens of other books – is a rival to Patrick White as Australia's greatest ever novelist. It is fairly well known that he entered St Patrick's Seminary at Manly, Sydney, when a very young man, to train for the Catholic priesthood. Far less known are the events that led up to his decision to do so. They were related by Keneally himself in an evocative and revealing book of childhood memoirs.

The whole story is told with a masterly, light touch, but what emerges is that Irish-Catholicism was central to his upbringing, both inside and outside the family home. He attended a Christian Brothers school, St Patrick's at Strathfield, and went to Mass regularly. At one stage he was taking Communion four or five days a week and for years he carried around in his jacket pocket a book of poetry by Gerard Manley Hopkins – his 'poet-hero-Jesuit'. A Father McGlade later introduced him to the work of W.H. Auden and Graham Greene. Keneally and his mates often argued about the existence and nature of God, and a close family friend named Rose Frawley became a nun. So did a pretty but phlegmatic girl from nearby Santa Sabina College, Bernadette Curran, the long-time object of Keneally's intense, unrequited love. Once, to try to impress her, he entered the Newman Society essay competition and won second place. His final interview for the seminary was conducted by Archbishop Norman Gilroy himself.

Keneally's grounding in Catholicism was, therefore, thorough and heartfelt. And it has stayed with him. Though ordained a deacon, he did not become a priest: celibacy, institutionalism and a reaction against dogma eventually put him off. But he has maintained a broad, ecumenical form of Christian faith. In 2006 he told an interviewer: 'Sometimes it's as if the God of the nice-little-churches withdraws and you are left with God the unutterable, God the unspeakable, God the indefinable and I think it is quite possible that God evades all the nets of our definitions … I love words and live by them, but there are some realities that slip through our web of words.'

Main source: Thomas Keneally, *Homebush Boy* (Minerva, 1995)


## Michael Kirby (b. 1939)

Kirby was a justice of the High Court of Australia from 1996 to 2009, and, before that, from 1984, the President of the Court of Appeal of the Supreme Court of New South Wales. His whole life has been one of dedicated public and private service. Whether as a student, campus politician, solicitor, barrister, law reform commissioner, judge, conference delegate, AIDS campaigner, writer, public speaker, or human rights advocate, Kirby gave (and still gives) 100 per cent.

It is not sufficiently well known that one of the biggest influences on him has been his lifelong Christian faith. Time and again he has referred to its sustaining, consoling power. His beloved father Don was a conservative Anglican, and, as a little boy in the mid-1940s, he attended Sunday school at St Andrew's Church in Strathfield. Kirby belongs to the old-fashioned liberal Anglican tradition. His religion is Christ-centred. He recalls 'the kindly face' of Jesus in the coloured illustrations of his boyhood Bible. 'The foundation of … all of the great religions … is love,' he insists. 'Love for the vulnerable, the poor and those sick of body and heart.'

Main sources: Michael Kirby, *A private life: fragments, memories, friends* (Allen & Unwin, 2011); Daryl Dellora, *Michael Kirby: Law, love and life* (Viking, 2012)

## Reverend John Dunmore Lang (1799–1878)

Lang, the 'father' of Presbyterianism in Australia, made a phenomenal contribution to this country as both cleric and politician. He arrived in Sydney in May 1823 and died there in August 1878. Viewed through the secular lens of the twenty-first century, his greatness may be almost impossible to understand. His anti-Catholicism, though not unusual for the time, looks especially ugly. But even that was a product of over-zealous Protestant idealism.

Lang believed that 'there is no realm of life exempt from obligation of service to God'; he once said that 'all my political opinions were taken from the Scriptures'. Today he would be anathema to the culture warriors of both the postmodern Left and the neo-liberal Right. On the one hand, he was highly conservative – to the point of priggishness – on matters of private morals; on the other hand, he was an outspoken progressive on issues of economic justice. Even in the nineteenth century 'he was undoubtedly the most acclaimed and most denounced man of his time'. Yet people saw his exceptional qualities. Between 1843 and 1864 he stood for election to parliament seven times – and never lost. His base, Scots Church in Sydney, was 'perhaps as large and wealthy as all other Presbyterian congregations in the colony put together'.

Some might say he was a populist, and it is true that he generally disapproved of both the convicts and the wealthy pastoralists (the 'squattocracy'). On such questions as the extension of the franchise and trial by jury, he championed the cause of the middle classes, especially the lower-middle classes – the craftsmen, builders, shopkeepers, small farmers, and country printers and journalists who did much to make Australia great. On some momentous issues he bucked popular opinion, and history mostly proved him right. He was a strong supporter of Irish Home Rule. He welcomed the discovery of gold (many did not) as likely to promote greater political freedom and democracy. He was unusually friendly to the Chinese immigrants, admiring them as 'quiet, peaceful, industrious and law-abiding'. He was an outspoken opponent of British involvement in the Crimean War, denouncing it early on as 'manifestly immoral'.

Perhaps Lang's most lasting contribution – outside the affairs of the Presbyterian Church – was in shaping the map of Australia. He represented the fledgling settlements of both Port Phillip (Melbourne) and Moreton Bay (Brisbane) in the New South Wales Parliament, and, in the words of Russel Ward, 'probably did more than any other single man to secure separation and self-government for both Victoria and Queensland'. He was also a very early advocate of the Federation of the colonies – and even of republicanism.

Main source: D.W.A. Baker, *Days of Wrath: A life of John Dunmore Lang* (Melbourne University Press, 1985)

### Henry Lawson (1867–1922)

Lawson has been 'claimed' by both Christian and secular apologists, and it is easy enough to see why. The evidence cuts both ways. He was not a regular churchgoer and, at various stages of his life, an alcoholic or near to it. Much of his published work is laced with anti-clericism.

Yet he also exhibited strong admiration for the Salvation Army. Both versions of his poem 'Booth's Drum' were tributes to the Army's founder, General William Booth, and the worldwide work of its noblest adherents, including those in Australia. The second version of this poem contains a tantalising couplet, in which the narrator (Lawson himself?) discloses: 'That I was saved one strenuous night/In old North Sydney years ago'. In similar vein, Lawson once wrote a note to his publisher, George Robertson, defending himself against allegations of blasphemy. In it he asserted: 'I never wrote or said a blasphemous thing in my life, nor thought one as far as Christ and Christianity is concerned.' But to further complicate matters he added this qualifying phrase: 'heathen though I may be as my old Norse fathers were'. (Lawson's father was a Norwegian who, according to Lawson, 'went in a good deal for what we used to call "spiritualism"'.)

The ambiguity of Lawson's beliefs is demonstrated in a splendid 1898 poem, 'The Christ of the Never'. The narrator dismisses professional churchmen who mouth lofty sentiments without having any real affinity for their flock – those 'who feel not, who know not – but preach'. To me this poem is not anti-religious. Rather, in John Dickson's fine phrase, it is 'a song of praise to the ideal of Jesus'. The unnamed hero of the poem is a grizzled, itinerant lay preacher who does understand his flock. He is a 'Plain spokesman where spokesman is needed/Rough link twixt the bushman and God'. Lawson based him on a real-life person, Peter McLaughlin.

Main source: Australian Poetry Library

## John Macarthur (1767–1834)

To put it mildly, Macarthur had many character flaws. But apart from his wife, the saintly Elizabeth, no one did more than he to bolster the New South Wales economy in its early decades.

During his first period of exile in England, Macarthur showed off his own samples of merino wool, and, in 1803, presented to the British government a 'Statement of the improvement and progress of the breed of fine woolled sheep in New South Wales'. On the strength of it he received a huge grant of land and a wide-ranging brief to return to New South Wales and develop a local wool industry. For various reasons the project stalled, but after the Reverend Samuel Marsden's breakthrough in 1811 – when Macarthur himself was in England during his second exile – interest in Australian wool exports increased. Perhaps the key development came in 1819–20, when Macarthur (by then back in Sydney) convinced visiting commissioner J.T. Bigge that wool was central to the colony's future. Bigge reported accordingly to his masters in London, and various government policies were adjusted to that end. Governor Thomas Brisbane began to implement them after his arrival in 1821. Of course, local producers such as Macarthur still had to produce the goods. And they did.

What of religion? Macarthur himself was scarcely a pious man. Ruthless and ill-tempered, he was driven less by greed than by a fierce sense of 'honour', almost Graeco-Roman in its nature and scope. Though formally a High Anglican, and 'serene and puritanical in his domestic life', his deepest religious views remain somewhat obscure. In 1811, the Reverend Henry Fulton claimed that Macarthur had used deistical arguments in a discussion about divine revelation, and asserted that the chief uses of 'religion' were political.

Main source: Michael Duffy, *Man of Honour: John Macarthur: Duellist, rebel, founding father* (Macmillan, 2003)

## Dorothea Mackellar (1885–1968)

Mackellar wrote what is perhaps Australia's best-known and best-loved poem, 'My Country'. ('I love a sunburnt country/A land of sweeping plains …') But she herself regarded a different poem, 'Colour', as one of her finest. It was read aloud at her funeral service at Sydney's St Mark's Anglican Church, in Darling Point. The concluding verse is as follows: 'Thanks be to God, Who gave this gift of colour/Which who shall seek shall find/Thanks be to God, Who gives me strength to hold it/Though I were stricken blind.'

Mackellar (who never married) came from a privileged upper-middle class family of quiet, believing Anglicans. Her father, Charles Mackellar, was a distinguished physician who served in the New South Wales Parliament. Her brother, Keith Mackellar, was killed in action during the Boer War in 1900: his grief-stricken parents commissioned a stained-glass window at St James' Church in King Street featuring the image of St George with Keith's face. St James remains a bastion of High Church Anglicanism in Sydney. At a service there during Lent 2014, the minister remarked: 'Dorothea is close to us here at St James', for the image of her brother Keith oversees our activities.'

Main source: Australian Poetry Library

## Lachlan Macquarie (1762–1824)

Some Christian historians have underrated Macquarie's faith. Roger C. Thompson has suggested it 'had little spiritual content' and Hugh Jackson that it amounted only to a 'generalised belief in God'. That may have been true in the decade or so following his first wife's death. When Jane Macquarie (nee Jarvis) died in India in July 1796, her bereaved husband grieved for some years thereafter, apparently 'gain[ing] no solace from precepts of religion'. By early middle age Macquarie 'believed that an august God presided over each individual's destiny, but consigned to the realm of mystery why this just and unearthly being made visible so few signs of His presence and providence'.

However, Macquarie's faith strengthened appreciably after his remarriage in November 1807. Elizabeth Macquarie (nee Campbell) had a passionate Protestant faith. In the words of John Ritchie, 'Christianity provided the bedrock of her values and the Jesus of the New Testament moulded her vision.' Among the key Biblical texts she marked for remembrance were these from Isaiah: 'relieve the oppressed' and 'make intercession for transgressors'.

It also needs to be borne in mind that Macquarie and Elizabeth were brought even closer together by recurrent tragedy in their private life. Their infant daughter Jane died of consumption in December 1808 and Elizabeth subsequently suffered six miscarriages. When she fell pregnant again in Sydney, in the winter of 1813, Macquarie made this entry in his private journal: 'May the Almighty Ruler of all events grant that our mutual fervent prayers and most earnest wishes to have offspring may at length be realised – and thereby complete our Earthly happiness.' In the event, on 28 March 1814, they were blessed with a healthy baby boy, who was named after his father.

Main source: John Ritchie, *Lachlan Macquarie: A biography* (Melbourne University Press, 1986)

## Reverend Samuel Marsden (1765–1838)

Despite Marsden's faults, credit must be given where it is due. Beyond his role in the Anglican Church, two further contributions to Australia stand out.

The first was in agriculture. Like Reverend Richard Johnson, Marsden came from a rustic background in West Yorkshire. He was exceptionally strong of physique – the surviving portraits show a stout, bull-like figure – and the Protestant work ethic had been instilled in him in childhood. His father was a butcher and farm labourer and his uncle a blacksmith. Marsden was nothing if not industrious. Notoriously, despite his position as chaplain, he accepted generous land grants from the governors and bought a lot of extra land from other settlers. By 1805 he owned some 1700 acres near Parramatta and, with the help of much convict labour, was farming it productively. His crops included wheat, maize and hops; he also kept livestock in large numbers. Governor King rated Marsden 'the best practical farmer in the colony'.

Marsden's speciality was sheep husbandry, and it was arguably in this field that he made his most momentous contribution to Australia. For a more than a decade after 1795 he conducted experiments in cross-breeding, with the aim of producing sheep with a high-quality fleece, adapted to local conditions. Finally, during a visit to England in 1807–08, he was able to present a sample of his wool to an expert firm of manufacturers. It 'produced a cloth at least equal, and in the opinion of the manufacturers, superior, to that of the best French looms'. Marsden was ecstatic. He had a suit cut from the cloth, which he wore to a function at which he was presented to George III. His Majesty was impressed, asked that a coat of his own be made from the same material, and gave Marsden a present from his own stud of five merino ewes.

By then, Marsden was on a kind of crusade for the local wool industry. In 1811, back in Parramatta, he sent the first commercial shipment of wool to England – 4,000 to 5,000 pounds, dispatched on the *Admiral Gambier*. It fetched a high price, and excited a jealous John Macarthur into action. Marsden's words proved prophetic: 'This will be the beginning of the commerce of this new World.' In the 1820s wool became the colony's biggest export (until then it had been whale oil), and large-scale sheep-grazing its most lucrative occupation. In due course, the consequences were enormous.

Marsden, with justification, has been criticised for avarice. He once tried to defend himself by citing the example of St Paul ('The one who is unwilling to work shall not eat'), but the comparison was ludicrous. Marsden, unlike Paul, revelled in his prosperity – and to an unseemly degree. By 1830 he owned 11,650 acres. But it is fair also to acknowledge Marsden's public-spirited side. Apart from his pioneering efforts for the wool industry, he 'gave back' to the community in other (secular) ways. In 1798, with surgeon Thomas Arndell, he made a useful report to Governor John Hunter on the overall state of agriculture in the colony. From 1822, upon its inception, he served as a senior vice-president of the Agricultural Society of New South Wales.

Marsden's other great contribution to public life was as a missionary. After 1801 he had the local superintendence of the London Missionary Society (established 1795). He was also involved in the affairs of the Church Missionary Society for Africa and the East (established 1799) and the British and Foreign Bible Society (established 1804). In New South Wales his efforts among the Indigenous peoples were a failure. Indeed, he eventually formed 'such a conviction of the Aborigines' innate depravity as to exclude the notion of their civilization and conversion'. To be fair to Marsden, he felt intense guilt over this in old age ('From us they have suffered infinite loss … we have much to answer for on their account to the judge of all the earth'). And – the other side of the ledger – his missionary work succeeded spectacularly in New Zealand. He travelled there seven times between 1814 and 1837 and formed a genuine love for the Maori. Thousands were converted, with consequences that were both spiritual and geopolitical. According to biographer A.T. Yarwood, 'the missionary activities which he promoted paved the way for established government and organized European settlement [in New Zealand] soon after his death.' In a real sense, Marsden was *the* pioneer of Anzac.

Main source: A.T. Yarwood, *Samuel Marsden: The great survivor* (Melbourne University Press, 1977)

## General John Monash (1865–1931)

Monash's religious life-story is a fascinating one. His paternal grandfather, Baer-Loebel Monasch, was a Prussian Jew from the town of Krotoschin (now Krotoszyn in Poland). A bookbinder turned printer–publisher by trade, Monasch specialised in scholarly editions of the Torah in both the German and Hebrew languages, and harboured an ambition that his sons might become Jewish scholars. (That did not happen, though his daughter married Heinrich Graetz of Breslau University, a distinguished nineteenth-century historian who wrote a classic eleven-volume history of the Jews.)

Louis Monasch, the second son of the family, immigrated to Australia in 1853–54, at the height of the gold rushes. Louis dropped the 'c' in his surname, set up business as a wholesale merchant in Melbourne, and became a British citizen. In 1863, while visiting Germany, he married a Jewish woman, Bertha Manesse. The couple were not strictly orthodox, but neither were they unmindful of their religious heritage; one biographer has described them as 'enlightened' or 'liberated' Jews. In any event, they moved in Jewish circles in Melbourne society, and their beloved son John, born in June 1865, was schooled thoroughly in Judaism. During his boyhood he went to synagogue on Saturdays and was prepared for his bar mitzvah by the Reverend Isadore Myers. (One of the presents that John received on the big day was a signed copy of his Uncle Heinrich's eleven-volume magnum opus – in a French translation!) At that point John was told by his father that 'he was of an age when he was answerable to God'. Encouraged by his devout cousin, Albert, John kept going to synagogue until his early twenties. But this influence was counterbalanced by his weekday education at various State and private schools, including St Stephen's Church of England school in Richmond and the redoubtable Scotch College (Presbyterian), at which some thirty Jewish students were excused from prayers.

At Melbourne University, the young Monash went to meetings of the Wesley Church Moral Improvement Society and to lectures given by Thomas Walker, the founder of the Australasian Secular Association. Monash was impressed by William Winwood Reade's book *Martyrdom of*

*Man* (1872), a kind of substitute bible for secularists, and briefly became a 'free thinker'. Part of it was youthful bravado, a rebellion against his Jewish heritage. In one letter, to his brother Leo, Monash declared he was 'an infidel of the very blackest type, an atheist and a materialist'. But this was a passing phase. By 1885 he was courting a pious Jewish woman named Eva Blaschki, who demanded that he 'come clean' on religion. In a thoughtful letter to her, Monash denied any suggestion that he was 'without faith, without belief in the Supreme'. While he claimed to reject the 'ancient conception of God' – including miraculous intervention in human affairs – he believed in a deity and accepted 'wholly and unreservedly the moral teachings of the Bible'.

For most of his adult life Monash was not a practising Jew. Once, in 1924, he referred to himself as a 'cultural Jew'. But after the Allied victory in World War One, in which he played such an important part, it was understandable that he was feted by the Jewish communities of both England and Australia. Monash observed Yom Kippur after 1920 and accepted many requests from the Australian Jewish community to participate in public functions. In 1921, for example, he agreed to preside at meetings of welcome for the Chief Rabbi of the British Empire, J.H. Hertz. He joined the board of management of the St Kilda Jewish congregation and took up the Zionist cause, becoming, in 1927, the national president of the Australian Zionist Federation, albeit as a figurehead.

Main sources: Geoffrey Serle, *John Monash: A biography* (Melbourne University Press, 1998); Roland Perry, *Monash: The outsider who won a war* (Random House, 2007)


## Les Murray (b. 1938)

There are obvious similarities between Murray and Bruce Dawe. Both are eminent and commercially successful poets, though Murray is probably the more famous, both here and overseas. As a long-time literary editor of *Quadrant* he was highly influential in elite conservative circles, but his appeal as a poet is broad and his verse has been translated into numerous languages.

Like Dawe, Murray is a practising Catholic who, as a young man, converted from Protestantism (Free Kirk Presbyterianism, in Murray's case). His work is more self-consciously 'religious' than Dawe's: he is on record as saying that 'he sees his writing as helping to define, in cultural and spiritual terms, what it means to be Australian'.

Main source: Australian Poetry Library

## Evan Nepean (1752–1822)

The principal organiser of the First Fleet 'behind the scenes', Nepean is one of the most underappreciated figures in Australian history. There is no room for serious argument about his High Anglican beliefs. In later life he established a branch of the British and Foreign Bible Society in India, and his youngest son, also named Evan, rose to high office in the Church of England: he became a Chaplain in Ordinary to Queen Victoria and was buried in Westminster Abbey.

Main source: *Australian Dictionary of Biography*


## Ruth Park (1917–2010)

There are intriguing parallels between Park and Gwen Harwood. Born just a few years apart, they both juggled the demands of marriage and motherhood to become extremely distinguished writers in more than one genre.

In the 1960s and 1970s, Park wrote the *Muddle-Headed Wombat* series of children's books. Utterly charming, they have delighted millions of Australians ever since. But Park was also a serious novelist. Her most acclaimed book, *The Harp in the South* (1948), was translated into thirty-seven languages. Along with its sequel, *Poor Man's Orange* (1949), it paints a vivid portrait of working-class Irish-Catholic life in the slums of inner Sydney. Though she was born and raised in New Zealand, it was a milieu that Park came to know well. After migrating to Australia in 1942 she lived for some years in the (then) down-at-heel suburb of Surry Hills. Park's fiction has been described, with Frank Hardy's, as 'Catholic realist'. But that does not do her full justice. Frequently she conveyed a sense of the fantastical – the 'wondrous strange' – peeping in on the mundane.

Educated at a small Catholic college, where (such was her family's poverty) the nuns lent her clothes to wear, Park remained deeply influenced by Catholicism until well into middle age. Her work resonated and sparkled because of it. (In another novel, *Serpent's Delight* (1953), the life of a middle-class family is transformed when its youngest member – a small girl – sees a vision of the Blessed Virgin.) It appears that Park's personal faith waned around the time of her husband's sudden death in 1967, which she said 'nearly killed her'. At any rate, she later turned to Zen Buddhism, and sought training from spiritual teachers in San Francisco and Japan. Evidently this was another step on her spiritual journey: she was always a compassionate, enquiring seeker.

One question especially fascinated her: what is the ultimate source of a writer's inspiration? Her rather mystical suggestion, advanced late in life, was this: 'Some sorcery in the subconscious.'

Main source: Marion Halligan, 'Some sorcery in the subconscious', in Joy Hooten (ed.), *Ruth Park: A celebration* (Friends of the National Library of Australia, 1996)


## Henry Parkes (1815–96)

Parkes' religious beliefs make an interesting study. It has been asserted that he was never deeply committed to Christianity, and, in a conventional sense, that is probably a fair comment. He was certainly a worse-than-average sinner. But his life simply cannot be understood without reference to religion: in the words of Roger C. Thompson, 'he had imbibed an identity between Protestantism and social progress'. Once, on the hustings in 1869, he identified Protestantism with 'the freedom of man and the progress of the world'. Parkes also knew his Bible and studied it to a timetable; frequently he peppered his everyday speech with Biblical expressions. A favourite, after he had reminded an audience that he had risen from humble origins, was this one of Jesus': 'Go thou and do likewise' (Luke 10:37, (KJV)).

This was all fair enough, for Parkes was indeed the son of yeoman parents and had a solid grounding in the Christian faith. As a child he was educated at the (Anglican) parish school in the village of Stoneleigh, Warwickshire, attached to the Church of St Mary. He went to church every Sunday as a boy, possibly in deference to his mother, and as a teenager and a young man in Birmingham was a regular worshipper at the New Meeting House in Carr's Lane. This was a huge and influential church, 'the chief centre of Midland congregationalism'. The long-time preacher there, John Angell James, was a severe Calvinist and a remarkable man. Parkes never became deeply immersed in Congregationalism, nor was he personally close to James, but he taught for a while in the Sunday school at the nearby village of Yardley.

After that phase of his life, and certainly in Australia, his formal religious observance was sporadic. But there can be no question he maintained a sharp consciousness of his own sin and believed in a Creator God who would pass judgment on his soul. Two snippets bear mention from late in his life. Once, after passing an especially pleasant few hours at home, he wrote in his private diary: 'And with God's blessing I may have many [more] such mornings.' In October 1893 he drafted and swore an affidavit that began in these terms: 'In the name of the all-wise God before whom I must soon appear ...'

Main sources: A.W. Martin, *Henry Parkes: A biography* (Melbourne University Press, 1980); Robert Travers, *The Grand Old Man of Australian Politics: The life and times of Sir Henry Parkes* (Kangaroo Press, 2000)

## Banjo Paterson (1864–1941)

Paterson defies easy religious categorisation. In contrast to Henry Lawson, who was raised in poverty and struggled to earn a living, Paterson came from a wealthy grazing family and worked as a solicitor until the age of forty. By the end of his life he was a scion of the Australian Club. His religious roots were Presbyterian, and when he married, in 1903, the service was conducted according to Presbyterian rites. So was his funeral service.

Paterson's most famous ballads – 'The Man from Snowy River', 'Clancy of the Overflow', 'The Geebung Polo Club', 'The Man from Ironbark', 'How the Favourite Beat Us', 'Saltbush Bill' – are not overtly religious. Nor are they 'protest' poems, like many of Lawson's. Rather, they are a romantic celebration of certain values – courage, independence, mateship, irony, horsemanship – which can be interpreted in almost any way one wants. 'Waltzing Matilda' is rather darker, but, again, not overtly religious.

There are, however, some references to God in the lesser-known works. These prove that Paterson's religious knowledge was deep. 'A Bush Christening' is one such poem, though the tone is light. In both 'Over the Range' and 'Lost' the narrator assumes that there is life after death. 'Sunrise on the Coast' explores notions of Creation.

'Only a Jockey' is about the accidental death of a fourteen-year-old boy. It concludes with these wistful lines, indicative, perhaps, of a certain scepticism on Paterson's part:

Knew he God's name? In his brutal profanity,
That name was an oath – out of many but one –
What did he get from our famed Christianity?
Where has his soul – if he had any – gone?
Fourteen years old, and what was he taught of it?
What did he know of God's infinite grace?
Draw the dark curtain of shame o'er the thought of it,
Draw the shroud over the jockey-boy's face.

Main source: Australian Poetry Library

## Charles Pearson (1830–94)

Pearson was a highly influential historian, educationalist and journalist in the pre-Federation era. One admiring biographer described him as 'the outstanding intellectual of the Australian colonies ... [combining] Puritan determination in carrying out reforms with a gentle manner and a scrupulous respect for the traditional rules and courtesies of public debate'. His book *National Life and Character: A forecast* (1893) was a best-seller – a rough equivalent of, say, Donald Horne's *The Lucky Country* in 1964. One of Pearson's themes was prescient: 'he concluded that in English-speaking and European countries the state would increasingly take over the traditional roles of family and church ... Most people would live out meaningless lives in huge, orderly, dull cities.'

Pearson was the first Headmaster of Presbyterian Ladies' College in Melbourne and a progressive Christian voice. His father, the Reverend John Norman Pearson, had been a principal of the Church Missionary College at Islington in London.

Main source: *Australian Dictionary of Biography*

## Arthur Phillip (1738–1814)

Phillip's religious views have long been the subject of debate. There is an absence of decisive evidence, and it is fair to say, as Hugh Jackson has done, that his 'opinions on the more ultimate religious issues remain a mystery'. Thomas Keneally's verdict – that he was an 'agnostic', a 'colourless secular saint' – represents today's conventional wisdom. But I am far from convinced, and contrary views have been expressed.

B.H. Fletcher, writing in 1967, thought him 'a not untypical member of the contemporary Church of England into which he had been baptised'. That seems to me right. Certainly Phillip was no Evangelical Christian, or the record would show it. During his five years at Port Jackson he prioritised practical survival over the building of a church. But religious formalities were observed in the colony, and, looking at the whole sweep of Phillip's life, it is clear that he and his parents, and both his wives, respected the Church of England as a civilising moral institution. Certainly, they conformed to its rituals, and to that extent Phillip must be counted a High Anglican.

As an infant he was baptised at All Hallows Church in Bread Street, central London. His first marriage, in 1763, to a widow sixteen years his senior, was solemnised at the Church of St Augustine in

Watling Street. There were no children of the marriage and the couple formally separated in 1769, though they never divorced. The first Mrs Phillip died in 1792 and Phillip remarried in May 1794, in Bath, soon after his return to England. It seems likely that Phillip and his second wife, Isabella Whitehouse, were at least occasional churchgoers in Bath, where they lived together contentedly until his death in August 1814. Phillip's funeral was conducted in the small country church of St Nicholas in nearby Bathampton and his remains were buried near the church porch, in those days a mark of high respect (because everyone entering the church would be reminded of the deceased's life). At her own request, Isabella Phillip was buried beside her late husband. On 9 July 2014, a special service was held at Westminster Abbey marking the bicentenary of Phillip's death. A memorial was dedicated to him on the floor of the nave of the abbey close to the graves of the Unknown Soldier and David Livingstone (and not far from that of Isaac Newton).

Whatever stance one takes as to Phillip's personal religious views, any fair-minded Christian would endorse the sentiments of Captain John Fortescue in 1789: 'I do think God Almighty made Phillip on purpose for the Place.'

Main source: George Mackaness, *Admiral Arthur Phillip: Founder of New South Wales* (Angus & Robertson, 1937)


## John Hubert Plunkett (1802–69)

Plunkett – Solicitor-General and later Attorney-General under Governor Richard Bourke, and the draftsman of the seminal Church Act of 1836 – is one of the best examples in Australian history of a man whose worldview was shaped by the twin influences I canvassed in Chapter 3: Christianity and the rule of (British) law.

He was born in Roscommon, Ireland, into a family that was aristocratic but not wealthy. The Plunketts were practising Catholics with a 'firm allegiance to God and church'. (Indeed, they were descendants of Oliver Plunkett, the fifteenth-century Archbishop of Armagh, who, in 1461, had been hanged, drawn and quartered for treason.) The young John Plunkett took a career in the law, and, during his early life in Ireland, became involved in the movement for Catholic emancipation. Shortly before coming to Sydney in 1832 to take up the position of solicitor-general, he married a young woman, Maria Charlotte McDonoughan, who had been schooled in Paris by nuns. In

Sydney, Plunkett's closest friend was Father John Joseph Therry; he was also a firm backer of Caroline Chisholm.

Main sources: John N. Molony, *An Architect of Freedom: John Hubert Plunkett in New South Wales 1832–1869* (Australian National University Press, 1973); *Australian Dictionary of Biography*

## Pedro Fernandez de Quiros (1565–1614)

Described by Manning Clark as 'one of the flowers of the Catholic reformation', de Quiros was once something of a cult figure among Australian Catholics. In the early twentieth century the Australian Catholic Truth Society issued tens of thousands of copies of a pamphlet entitled (inaccurately) *The Discovery of Australia by de Quiros*, and in 1964 James McAuley published an epic poem, *Captain Quiros*, in which the hero was depicted as a Catholic martyr. A novel by John Toohey, *Quiros*, was published as recently as 2002.

It is not hard to understand the man's mystique. Like Ferdinand Magellan, de Quiros was a genuinely devout man. He had served the like-minded Alvaro de Mendana on an ill-fated voyage to the Pacific in 1595 to 1596, but that experience did not deter him. In 1598 he returned to Spain and petitioned King Phillip III to support another voyage. For de Quiros it was 'a mission ... evangelical as well as geographical'. In 1600 he went to Rome and sought the backing of the Pope, Clement VIII, on the ground that Terra Australis might be populated by 'millions of heathen souls, ripe for salvation'. Eventually, in March 1603, his zeal paid off. He was authorised to return to Peru to organise another expedition for the purpose of finding Terra Australis and claiming it for Spain and the Catholic Church. A party of 160 men on three ships left Callao in December 1605.

Of course, de Quiros never reached Terra Australis. But he honestly believed he had in May 1606, when his fleet landed on the largest of the group of islands now known as Vanuatu (formerly New Hebrides). De Quiros named it *Australia del Espiritu Santo* (the Southern Land of the Holy Spirit) and claimed it for the Holy Catholic Church and His Most Christian Majesty, King Phillip III of Spain. He also declared his intention to establish a colony there, to be called Nova Jerusalem. Nothing came of that, but the island is still called Espiritu Santo and is a frequent destination for Australian tourists.

Main source: Manning Clark, *A History of Australia*, Volume I (Melbourne University Press, 1980)

# Dr William Redfern (1774–1833)

Redfern was a committed Protestant Christian; so was his wife Sarah (nee Wills). Not much is known of their married life, or how they worshipped, but from 1814 Redfern served on the Committee of the Society for the Promotion of Christian Knowledge and Benevolence, an organisation dominated by Non-conformists and Evangelicals. Its functions were later taken over by the Benevolent Society of New South Wales, created in May 1818 at the initiative of the Colonial Auxiliary Bible Society. Redfern was its honorary medical officer. And it was not coincidental, we may be sure, that his apprentice at the Rum Hospital, Henry Cowper, was a son of the Reverend William Cowper, the chief instigator of the Benevolent Society. These were the families who kept New South Wales going in those profoundly challenging times.

Sarah Redfern lived until 1875. Twice widowed, she was a truly admirable pioneer woman. A collection of her letters was published after her death. The editor wrote: 'In printing these letters, which were quite unknown to me till the grave had closed over the beloved writer, I do so in the hope, with God's blessing, that they may be the means of urging so many whom she dearly loved to prepare for Eternity, the warm desire of her own heart, and the daily subject of her earnest prayers. One hour each week, in the company or with the help of a Christian friend, was devoted by her to earnest prayer in behalf of all whom she loved.'

Main source: Edward Ford, *The Life and Work of William Redfern* (Australasian Medical Publishing, 1953)


# Henry Handel Richardson (1870–1946)

Ethel Florence Lindesay Richardson, who wrote under a male pseudonym throughout her career, was Australia's first great novelist of either sex. To this day she is still in the top flight. Her finest works were *Maurice Guest* (1908), *The Getting of Wisdom* (1910), and (her masterpiece) *The Fortunes of Richard Mahony* (1930).

Richardson was not a conventionally religious person but she was well educated in Christianity and believed fervidly in the afterlife. Indeed, the latter preoccupation dominated her thinking for decades, especially after the death of her beloved husband, John George Robertson, in 1933. In several respects she took after her father, Walter Richardson, a free-thinking doctor who (to the family's shame) died of syphilis in 1879. Dr Richardson had rebelled against the 'fierce retributive' Protestantism of his Irish youth and gradually moved away from formal religion. But he never lost interest in metaphysics. To the contrary, he was immersed in all the great religious–intellectual issues of the day, including the search for the historical Jesus. His copy of the Bible was copiously annotated and his library well-stocked with various works of theology. Late in his life – like many seekers of that era – he became attracted to spiritualism. In 1869 he was the first president of the Victorian Association of Progressive Spiritualists, a position later held by Alfred Deakin.

The doctor's famous daughter, only nine when he died, revealed in her childhood memoir (*Myself When Young*) that her father's influence had been very strong. As an impressionable teenager she read many of the books he had left behind in his library, and she treasured a copy of *Pilgrim's Progress* that he had given to her. This 'encouraged a vision of life as an arduous journey, beset with sin and huge challenges, to a celestial end'. At Presbyterian Ladies' College in Melbourne, to which she was sent as a boarder in 1883, she won prizes for Bible study and participated in daily prayers. Half a century later, she remarked in all sincerity that her 'principal debt [to PLC] ... was a sound knowledge of the Bible'. Even so, like her father, she had moved away from formal religion. She also left Australia to live in Europe, becoming a member of the London Spiritualist Alliance. One biographer thought that 'Spiritualism supplanted rather than complemented orthodox belief'. Yet to the very end she believed strongly in life after death.

Main source: Michael Ackland, *Henry Handel Richardson: A life* (Cambridge University Press, 2004)


## George Robertson (1860–1933)

Robertson is a little-recognised giant of Australian cultural and intellectual history. According to one biographer, he 'considered booksellers to be as much engaged in educational work as headmasters and university professors and regarded bookshops as cultural centres'. In its early years, Angus & Robertson supported the likes of Banjo Paterson (who was a close friend of Robertson), Henry Lawson, C.J. Dennis and Ethel Turner (author of *Seven Little Australians*). It also published C.E.W. Bean's epic *Official History of Australia in the War of 1914–18*, and, later in the twentieth century, authors of the calibre of Jon Cleary, Ruth Park and Judith Wright.

Robertson was steeped in religion. His father, the Reverend John Robertson, had been a minister of the Unitarian Church at Gosfield, near Halstead in Essex. George's wife was an active worker for the Presbyterian Church in Australia, as was his daughter Bessie, who married a clergyman's son. Robertson himself, though a sporadic churchgoer, was on friendly terms with several clerics. He ensured that Angus & Robertson published many religious books, including school textbooks of a religious flavour (the Australasian Catholic School Series among others) and some interesting works of Australian theology (a rarity then as now). These were among his most profitable titles.

Main source: Jennifer Alison, *Doing Something for Australia: George Robertson and the early years of Angus and Robertson, Publishers, 1888–1900* (Bibliographical Society of Australia and New Zealand, 2009)

## George William Rusden (1819–1903)

Rusden was a ground-breaking colonial historian, a rival to Charles Pearson, best known for his controversial three-volume *History of Australia*, published in 1883. It set pens and tongues racing at the time. Rusden had fingers in many other pies: farming, local government, education reform, the University of Melbourne, billiards (he was reputedly the 'finest player in the colony'), Shakespeare appreciation, China. Though a political conservative in most things, and a lover of all things English ('a walking Westminster Abbey', wrote one obituarist), he also had a deep knowledge of Indigenous peoples and was a steely advocate on their behalf.

To use a resonant old term, Rusden was a Renaissance man. He was also an ardent, pious Anglican. His father, the Reverend George Keylock Rusden, had kept a private school in Surrey for more than two decades before migrating to New South Wales in 1834. Thereafter he served for many years as chaplain at St Peter's in East Maitland. His illustrious son maintained a close, lifelong association with the Church of England.

Main source: *Australian Dictionary of Biography*

## John Shaw Neilson (1872–1942)

Shaw Neilson is not as well known as he ought to be. Of Scottish–Gaelic heritage, he endured an impoverished upbringing in rural South Australia (two of his sisters died young of tuberculosis) and got only a rudimentary education. He never married, had poor eyesight, and laboured for most of his life as an itinerant bushman. Yet somehow he wrote disarmingly lovely lyric poems ('Song Be Delicate', for one) comparable with those of the best of the French Symbolists. It was a kind of miracle: almost certainly, Shaw Neilson was unacquainted with their work.

He was a deeply religious man, if not, in later life, in an orthodox sense. As a boy his chief reading was the Bible and the poetry of Robert Burns. His mother was a 'bleak Presbyterian', his sister Maggie a Salvationist. These influences are evident in his most profound poems, which are quiet, wistful celebrations – of the beauteous fragility of nature, the infinite consolations of love, the simple virtues of humility and piety.

Professor A.R. Chisholm compared Shaw Neilson's vision with that of St Francis of Assisi. Some poems are overtly Christian. They are like reading the Sermon on the Mount – or the philosophy of Søren Kierkegaard – adapted in sweet verse to early twentieth-century Australia. My favourites are 'Canticle of the Sun', 'The Gentle Water Bird', 'Schoolgirls Hastening', 'Surely God Was a Lover' and (see the lines quoted at the beginning of Chapter 2) the magnificent 'He Was the Christ'.

Main source: A.R. Chisholm (ed.), *The Poems of Shaw Neilson* (Angus & Robertson, 1973)

## William Charles Wentworth (1790–1872)

A renowned explorer, publisher and statesman, W.C. Wentworth was perhaps the best-known anti-clericist in early New South Wales. He regularly lambasted individual ecclesiastics and whole denominations: Manning Clark described him as 'a recoiler from the Judaic-Christian whine about human depravity and unworthiness'.

But almost certainly Wentworth was *not* an atheist. At any rate he was not a *public* atheist. The motto on his family coat of arms was 'In God is Everything' and Wentworth himself was thoroughly steeped in Christianity. In 1823, in his celebrated poem 'Australasia', he wrote in Biblical terms of the moment a decade earlier when he, Blaxland and Lawson first crossed the Blue Mountains: 'the beauteous landscape grew,/Op'ning like Canaan on rapt Israel's view'. After the death of John Macarthur in 1834, Wentworth lamented that 'I little thought when I last saw him that we were to meet no more in this world'. In the 1830s and 1840s Wentworth and his family were regular attenders at St James' Anglican Church in Sydney; his daughter Laura was especially devout. It appears that Wentworth struggled to share her fervent faith and even stopped going to services in the 1850s. But he continued to read the Bible at home and there is good evidence that he retained a belief in God and an afterlife. Late in his life he said publicly that he admired 'the great Christian code'.

Main source: Andrew Tink, *William Charles Wentworth: Australia's Greatest Native Son* (Allen & Unwin, 2009)

## Patrick White (1912–90)

Australia's only winner of the Nobel Prize for Literature, in 1973, White was raised as an Anglican. But until his late thirties he was, by his own admission, a believer only in a 'conventional, infantile sense'. Then, around Christmas 1951, he had a personal religious experience. He slipped over while walking in his garden in a thunderstorm, and found himself rolling around in a patch of mud, cursing God. Somehow, by the end of that process, he had become a believer: he realised he had faith in what he was cursing. In June 1952 he wrote to a friend: 'You may be surprised to hear I started going to church six months ago ... I am quite convinced.'

Much of Patrick White's body of work was an attempt to convey a sense of the numinous. Although he came to believe that any vision of God is only ever 'half-glimpsed, even by the most devout believers', he did his best. The character of Sam Parker in *The Tree of Man* (1955) undergoes a similar experience to White's own. *Voss* (1957) is based on the real-life story of Ludwig Leichhardt, the tragic German-Lutheran explorer I mentioned in Chapter 4. In *Riders in the Chariot* (1961) the central character, Ruth Godbold, is a sympathetically portrayed Evangelical, yet the book's underlying message is that 'all faiths, whether religious, humanistic, instructive, or the creative artist's act of praise, are in fact one'. *The Vivisector* (1970) also explores religious themes. In the year of its release White explained to a friend: 'I suppose what I am increasingly intent on trying to do in my books is to give professed unbelievers glimpses of their own unprofessed faith.' (I have included this line at the beginning of the book.)

White himself was far from an orthodox Christian. He was never comfortable with the Anglican scene in Sydney, especially during the era of Archbishop Howard Mowll, a muscular Evangelical of no-nonsense style. The 1959 Billy Graham crusade did not impress him at all – he thought it vulgar – and the Anglo-Catholic parish of Christ

Church St Laurence, where he worshipped for a time, did not satisfy him either. Like many a great artist, White was a cantankerous soul. 'The dogma of any religious sect', he once wrote, 'seem to me ridiculous and presumptuous. Faith is something between the person and God, and must vary in forms accordingly.'

But White did not throw out the baby (God) with what he saw as the bathwater. He focused on the big picture. In a letter of 15 June 1954, he made this wise remark as regards the New Testament: 'I have to take on trust some of the obscurer details … which are not sufficiently important to interfere with the goodness and rightness and immensity of the whole.' He always remained sure that 'there is a design behind the haphazardness'. He believed in an afterlife. During his twilight years he refused to take Holy Communion – but for principled reasons. 'If I refuse the offer,' he wrote to a friend, 'it is because I cannot see myself as a true Christian … I am a <u>believer</u>, but not the kind most "Christians" would accept.' The underlining was White's own.

Main source: David Marr (ed.), *Patrick White Letters* (Random House Australia, 1994)


## Ronald Wilson (1922–2005)

Wilson became President of the Human Rights Commission of Australia in 1990 and authored the *Bringing Them Home Report* in 1997. He had served previously as Solicitor-General of Western Australia and as a High Court judge. His life was one of distinguished private and public service.

Born into a struggling family in Geraldton, Western Australia, he was forced to leave school at fourteen and work his way up. Religion-wise, he began life as a Presbyterian before joining the Uniting Church on its formation in 1977. He held a range of senior positions in both bodies, including Moderator of Assembly, Presbyterian Church in Western Australia (1965); Moderator, West Australian Synod, Uniting Church in Australia (1977–1979); President of the Assembly, Uniting Church in Australia (1988–91), the first layperson to hold that post; and President of the Australian Chapter of the World Conference on Religion and Peace (1991–96).

One senior legal colleague, Robert Nicholson, maintained that Christianity 'permeated [Wilson's] entire outlook and activities. If there is one single element which explains and knits together his views, involvements and achievements, it was his Christian view of what should be justice in the world. Within the church, he spoke in Christian terms. Outside the church, he spoke in terms of justice and human rights. But in reality, for him, they were indivisible.'

Main source: Antonio Buti, *Sir Ronald Wilson: A matter of conscience* (University of Western Australia Press, 2007)

## Tim Winton (b. 1960)

Winton can lay claim to be being one of the best-loved West Australians ever. A highly esteemed novelist and short-story writer for both adults and children, his work has been adapted for radio, stage and screen. He is also widely known for his passionate environmental advocacy. Like Tom Keneally and Les Murray, he is a National Living Treasure. Yet Winton's active Christian faith has tended to be underplayed, except within Australia's religious community. This despite the fact that – to use religious broadcaster Rachael Kohn's nice expression – 'it's there in his writing, sometimes just a glimmer, other times a full-throated hymn'. I suspect that a goodly portion of Winton's readers simply do not notice the subtler Biblical allusions, at least not at a conscious level. On the other hand, his popularity has not suffered from the occasional use of nakedly Christian images and themes. In the short story 'The Turning' (2004), for instance, a recently converted wife screams out about Jesus as her husband beats her: 'He's every f___ing thing you aren't!'

Winton's parents were converts to the (Evangelical) Church of Christ in the 1960s and raised their children accordingly. 'We went to church three times on Sunday,' Winton once recalled. 'We went to Sunday school in the morning, then church at eleven and then we went back at 7.30 at night. It was a pretty gentle form of fundamentalism; it wasn't all fire and brimstone.' As a teenager, Winton read a great deal of theology, mostly of left-wing Protestant slant (John Howard Yoder, Jim Wallis). But as he got older his faith became less intellectual and more ecumenical: 'part of me is irrepressibly Protestant and anti-clerical and anti-institutional, and another part of me is strangely Catholic'. He now belongs to an Anglican parish near his home in Fremantle.

Main source: Interview with Rachael Kohn on ABC Radio's *The Spirit of Things*, 26 December 2004

# Key theological differences between Catholicism and Protestantism

Although any summary is fraught with danger, I feel I must attempt one. Traditionally, Protestants cited four slogans: 'Christ alone', 'the Bible alone', 'faith alone' and 'grace alone'. In essence, they rejected the following glosses or add-ons insisted upon by the Roman Church:

- Priests were essential 'mediators' between God and man – Mass could not be conducted nor Eucharist (Holy Communion) taken unless a priest 'acted in the person of Christ'.
- Transubstantiation – during the Eucharist, the bread and wine were changed (in substance if not in physical form) into the actual body and blood of Christ, thereby 'renewing' Christ's atoning sacrifice on the Cross.
- The Bible could not be read and interpreted unaided – the Roman Catholic Church was the final arbiter of its meaning.
- Salvation depended upon *both* trust in Christ ('faith') *and* the individual believer's response to Christ, as evidenced by good conduct ('works') – salvation was a gradual process, which might even continue after death (in purgatory), rather than a once-and-for-all event.

- The seven sacraments (baptism, confirmation, Eucharist, penance, anointing of the sick, holy orders, matrimony) were, as applicable, essential for salvation.
- Mary, the mother of Jesus, was also the mother of all Christians, and could and did act as a 'mediatrix' between Christ and man.

Although I have used the past tense, to emphasise that this was the position in 1788 (and until well into the twentieth century), some of these differences still exist. I say 'some' not 'all' differences, because the 'test of salvation' – surely the most crucial issue – has been broadened substantially by the Catholic Church since Vatican II in the 1960s. As to that issue, see the Joint Declaration on the Doctrine of Justification by the Lutheran World Federation and the Catholic Church (1999), adopted by the World Methodist Conference in 2006.

Main source: Ray Galea, *Nothing in My Hand I Bring: Understanding the differences between Roman Catholic and Protestant beliefs* (Matthias Media, 2007)

# ENDNOTES

## Introduction

1. Judith Ireland, 'Time to scrap Lord's Prayer in parliament: Greens', *Sydney Morning Herald*, 14 January 2014.

2. See George Weigel, 'The challenge of Pope Benedict XVI – can it be heard in these Christophobic times?' *Religion and Ethics*, ABC, 12 February 2013, available online at www.abc.net.au/religion/articles/2013/02/12/3688691.htm. Weigel attributes the term 'Christophobia' to a prominent international scholar of constitutional law, Joseph Weiler.

3. 'Say a little prayer for the Greens', *The Australian*, editorial, 16 January 2014.

4. Ian Turner, *The Australian Dream: A collection of anticipations about Australia from Captain Cook to the present day* (Sun Books, 1968), p. ix.

5. Manning Clark, 'What do we want to be and what should we believe?' *The Bulletin*, Special Bicentennial Edition, 26 January 1988, p. 11.

6. See Stephen Holt, *Manning Clark and Australian History 1915–1963* (University of Queensland Press, 1982), pp. 149, 153.

7. Mark Peel and Christina Twomey, *A History of Australia* (Palgrave Macmillan, 2011), p. 54.

8. Warren Bonett (ed.), *The Australian Book of Atheism* (Scribe, 2010), p. 1.

9. Peter Jensen, *The Future of Jesus: Does He have a place in our world?* (Matthias Media, 2008), p. 11.

10. Russel Ward, *Australia Since the Coming of Man* (Lansdowne Press, 1982), p. 40; Robert Hughes, *The Fatal Shore: A history of the transportation of convicts to Australia 1787–1868* (Pan Books edition, 1987; first published by Harvill Secker, 1987), p. 66ff.

11. David Hill, *1788: The brutal truth of the First Fleet* (William Heinemann Australia, 2009), p. 25.

12. Hughes, *The Fatal Shore*, p. 27.

13. Hill, *1788*, p. 7.

14. Ward, *Australia Since the Coming of Man*, p. 38; Mollie Gillen, *The Founders of Australia: A biographical dictionary of the First Fleet* (Library of Australian History, 1989), p. xv.

15. Hill, *1788*, p. 9. See also Hughes, *The Fatal Shore*, pp. 37–9.

16. Gordon Hay, 'Biography of John Howard', from the website of the John Howard Society of Canada, www.johnhoward.ca/about/biography/index.php.

17. Quoted in John Singleton, 'At the roots of Methodism: Wesley fought for prison reform', 10 September 1999, available at archive.wfn.org/1999/09/msg00113.html.

18. A.T. Yarwood, *Samuel Marsden: The great survivor* (Melbourne University Press, 1996; first published in 1977), p. 13. See also Neil K. Macintosh, *Richard Johnson, Chaplain to the Colony of New South Wales: His life and times 1755–1827* (Pilgrim International, 1978), pp. 21–22.

19. Quoted in Hughes, *The Fatal Shore*, p. 39.

20. Gavin Souter, *A Company of Heralds: A century and a half of Australian publishing by John Fairfax Limited and its predecessors 1831–1981* (Melbourne University Press, 1981), p. 11.

21. Ibid., pp. 15 and 26 (McGarvie), 32 (Mansfield), 54–7 (West) and 94 (Curnow). To be precise, McGarvie was the 'leader writer' of the *Sydney Herald*, the paper which Fairfax bought in 1841 (in partnership with Charles Kemp) and later renamed. The editor of the *Sydney Morning Herald* in the years 1873–86 (i.e. between West and Curnow) was Robert Garran, a prominent lay Congregationalist and outstanding constitutional lawyer.

22. Helen Irving, 'Australia's foundations definitely and deliberately were not Christian', *Sydney Morning Herald*, 9 June 2004.

23. Ward, *Australia Since the Coming of Man*, p. 7.

24. Patrick O'Farrell, *The Catholic Church and Community in Australia: A history* (Nelson, 1977), p. 17. See also Michael Duffy, *Man of Honour: John Macarthur: Duellist, rebel, founding father* (Pan Macmillan, 2003), p. 115.

25. Ronald Conway, *The Great Australian Stupor: An interpretation of the Australian way of life* (Sun Books, 1971), p. 187.

26. Tom Frame, *Losing My Religion: Unbelief in Australia* (UNSW Press, 2009). For a more positive view of the influence of Christianity on Australia, see Stuart Piggin, *Spirit of a Nation: The story of Australia's Christian heritage* (Strand Publishing, 2004). Piggin's book, however, focuses on Evangelical Protestant Christianity.

27. See, for example, Hugh Jackson, *Australians and the Christian God: An historical study* (Mosaic Press, 2013), p. 211 ('at no time in the period from 1860 to the present did the collective consciousness of Australians become deeply imbued with belief in the truth of the Christian religion').

28. Elizabeth Farrelly, 'All I want for Chrissie is tolerance – for our ways', *Sydney Morning Herald*, 28 November 2013, p. 22.

29. Roger C. Thompson, *Religion in Australia: A history* (Oxford University Press, 1994), p. 9; Hughes, *The Fatal Shore*, p. 323.

30. Thompson, *Religion in Australia*, p. 44; Jackson, *Australians and the Christian God*, pp. 86–90.

31. Roy Morgan Research, cited in Tracey Joyner, 'Christians set to become a minority in Australia', *The Satellite*, 17 April 2014.

32. See mccrindle.com.au/the-mccrindle-blog/church_attendance_in_australia_infographic.

33. Steve Bruce, *God is Dead: Secularization in the West* (Blackwell Publishing, 2002), pp. 3, 43.

34. Muriel Porter, *The New Puritans: The rise of fundamentalism in the Anglican Church* (Melbourne University Press, 2006), p. 66.

35. See Christopher Akehurst, 'The Decline of the suburban church', *Quadrant*, December 2013, pp. 51–56.

36. Terry Allen, 'Evaluating Billy Graham 50 years on', available online at www.christianfaith.com/resources/evaluating-billy-graham-50-years-on.

37. Jenny Hocking, *Gough Whitlam: A moment in history* (The Miegunyah Press, 2008), p. 155. In 1967 Whitlam met Billy Graham in person. It was a chance encounter at the White House: Whitlam, in his capacity as federal opposition leader, had been received by US President Lyndon B. Johnson, and Graham was on the grounds for another function.

38. Phillip Adams, *Adams vs. God: The rematch* (Melbourne University Press, 2007), p. ix.

39. Thomas Wells, 'Why I am not an atheist', *The Philosopher's Beard*, 24 April 2014, available online at www.philosophersbeard.org/2014/04/why-i-am-not-atheist.html.

40. Frame, *Losing My Religion*, pp. 18–22.

41. Hans Mol, *The Faith of Australians* (Allen & Unwin, 1985), p. 133. See also Frame, *Losing My Religion*, pp. 98ff; Bruce, *God is Dead*, p. 71 (citing Grace Davie's work in Britain since 1945).

42. See Bruce, *God is Dead*, pp. 186ff.

43. Mol, *The Faith of Australians*, p. 135.

44. Quoted in Edmund Campion, 'The privatisation of religion', *The Bulletin*, Special Bicentenary edition, 26 January 1988, p. 156.

45. See, for example, Michael McKernan, *Australian Churches at War: Attitudes and activities of the major Churches 1914–18* (Southwood Press, 1980), p. 21. See also Bruce, *God is Dead*, p. 48.

46. In 1992, Hugh Mackay and two other social researchers interviewed some dozens of middle-class Australians in small groups. The subject was religion. 'The prevailing view was deism of an anaemic and uncertain kind.' See Jackson, *Australians and the Christian God*, p. 212.

47. See C. FitzSimons Allison, *The Cruelty of Heresy: An affirmation of Christian orthodoxy* (Morehouse Publishing, 1994), p. 156 (discussing a similar definition proposed by the US writers Charles Glock and Rodney Stark in their 1968 book *American Piety*).

48. Allison, *The Cruelty of Heresy*, p. 157.

49. Mol, *The Faith of Australians*, p. 131.

50. Quoted in Bruce, *God is Dead*, p. 55.

51. Frame, *Losing My Religion*, p. 294.

52. Diarmaid MacCulloch, *A History of Christianity: The first three thousand years* (Penguin Books, 2010), p. 11.

53. Geoffrey Blainey, *A Shorter History of Australia* (William Heinemann Australia, 1994), p. 220–21.

54. Thomas Carlyle, *On Heroes, Hero-Worship, and the Heroic in History* (1840), available online at www2.hn.psu.edu/faculty/jmanis/carlyle/heroes.pdf.

55. See Michael Hogan, *The Sectarian Strand: Religion in Australian history* (Penguin, 1987), p. 81. See also Raymond Apple, *The Jewish Way: Jews and Judaism in Australia* (The Great Synagogue, 2002), p. 30.

56. See Frame, *Losing My Religion*, pp. 118–19.

57. Ibid., p. 6.

58. Ibid., pp. 5–6.

59. Quoted in John Marsden (ed.), *This I Believe* (Random House, 1996), p. 166.

60. Two Roy Morgan opinion surveys in late 2013 put the figure for non-Christian religions slightly higher, at 8.3 per cent.

61. Farrelly, 'All I want for Chrissie is tolerance', p. 23.

**Chapter 1: The survival of colonial Australia**

1. Hogan, *The Sectarian Strand*, p. 9.

2. Duffy, *Man of Honour*, p. 115 (see note 24 to the Introduction).

3. See Ian Breward, *Australia: 'The most Godless place under heaven'?* (Beacon Press, 1988).

4. Gideon Goosen, *Australian Theologies: Themes and methodologies into the third millennium* (St Pauls Publications, 2000), p. 101.

5. Gordon Briscoe and Len Smith (eds.), *The Aboriginal Population Revisited: 70,000 years to the present* (Aboriginal Studies Press, 2002); Per Axelsson and Peter Sköld (eds.), *Indigenous Peoples and Demography: The complex relation between identity and statistics* (Berghahn Books, 2011), pp. 15–16.

6. Hughes, *The Fatal Shore*, p. 17 (see note 10 to the Introduction).

7. Goosen, *Australian Theologies*, p. 97.

8. Prue Vines, *Law and Justice in Australia: Foundations of the legal system* (2nd edition, Oxford University Press, 2009), p. 133.

9. W.E.H. Stanner, quoted in Robert Kenny, *The Lamb Enters the Dreaming: Nathanael Pepper and the ruptured world* (Scribe, 2007), pp. 155, 352.

10. Christine Nicholls, '"Dreamtime" and '"The Dreaming": Who dreamed up these terms?', *Our Languages*, 29 January 2014, available online at www.ourlanguages. net.au/news/national/item/1007-%E2%80%98dreamtime%E2%80%99-and-%E2%80%98the-dreaming%E2%80%99-who-dreamed-up-these-terms?.html.

11. Goosen, *Australian Theologies*, pp. 106–11.

12. Tim Flannery (ed.), Introduction to *Watkin Tench: 1788* (Text edition, 2009, first published 1789 as *A Narrative of the Expedition to Botany Bay*), p. 2.

13. John Moore, *The First Fleet Marines 1786–1792* (University of Queensland Press, 1987), p. 257. See also the entry on Dawes in the *Australian Dictionary of Biography* ('He [Dawes] was of the company of the humane and deeply religious reformers of his day.')

14. Flannery (ed.), *Watkin Tench*, p. 249.

15. Ibid., pp. 249–52.

16. Ibid., p. 250.

17. Macintosh, *Richard Johnson*, p. 49 (see note 18 to the Introduction).

18. Frame, *Losing My Religion*, p. 41.

19. Commemoration Service in Honour of Admiral Arthur Phillip, Mary le Bow Church, London, 4 March 2013, available online at britain-australia.org.uk/uploads/Arthur_ Phillip_Service_2013.pdf.

20. Moore, *The First Fleet Marines*, p. 93.

21. Flannery (ed.), *Watkin Tench*, p. 45.

22. Hogan, *The Sectarian Strand*, p. 10.

23. Yarwood, *Samuel Marsden*, p. 33 (see note 18 to the Introduction).

24. Ibid., p. 60; Macintosh, *Richard Johnson*, p. 58.

25. Yarwood, *Samuel Marsden*, p. 35; Jackson, *Australians and the Christian God*, p. 37 (see note 27 to the Introduction).

26. Yarwood, *Samuel Marsden*, p. 33.

27. Jackson, *Australians and the Christian God*, p. 36.

28. Hogan, *The Sectarian Strand*, p. 11.

29. Of the leaders of New South Wales between Phillip and Macquarie, the least Christian in their attitudes were Lieutenant-Governors Francis Grose (1793–94) and Joseph Foveaux (1808–09). Grose was positively 'anti-religious', decreeing that church services should begin at 6 a.m. on Sundays and last no longer than 45 minutes. He did not attend church himself, quarrelled constantly with the chaplain, and in other respects was a poor role model for believers. He sanctioned the trade in rum which made New South Wales infamous, and cancelled Phillip's order for equal rations. Foveaux did at least complete the building of St Phillip's Church in York Street, and later provided useful assistance to Macquarie. But while the commander on Norfolk Island he had run a sadistic regime. His own head gaoler once remarked: 'Major Foveaux was one of them hardened and determined men who believe in the lash more than the Bible.' Governors King and Bligh, though reasonably effective administrators, were not godly men either: they made lavish reciprocal land grants to each other. King had two sons by a convict mistress and acquired a reputation for heavy drinking. Bligh's foul-mouthed and short-tempered behaviour was notorious. To the extent that they helped the chaplains it was more from duty than conviction.

30. Moore, *The First Fleet Marines*, p. 286. According to Moore, the reputation of the Marines has suffered unfairly for two reasons: the 'incorrigibility' of their commander, Major

Robert Ross, and the misbehaviour of their successors, the New South Wales Corps. The latter body consisted, in large part, of deserters from London's Savoy Military Prison and defaulters who joined up to escape court martial for earlier offences. In the blunt words of Robert Hughes: 'most of them were scum'. While that verdict may be harsh, the record shows that some among them were unusually grasping, and few were practising Christians. Their generally amoral influence continued until 1809, when most members of the Corps were recalled to England following the illegal deposal of Governor William Bligh (in the infamous 'Rum Rebellion'). The Marine Corps, by contrast, was a fine body of men. There were strict criteria for recruitment, in terms of physical fitness and the possession of trade skills, and emphasis was placed on further education after recruitment (of both the Marines and their children). Importantly, also, most of the Marines who came on the First Fleet – all except the officers – were permitted to bring their wives and children. This was another civilising influence. Given all these circumstances, it is not surprising that they were more religiously inclined. See also Jackson, *Australians and the Christian God*, p. 37.

31. In September 1796, the London Missionary Society had dispatched a party to Tahiti on a ship called the *Duff*. Most of those on board were Congregationalists, with a sprinkling of Presbyterians, Methodists and Anglicans. They encountered violent rebellion from the Tahitian natives and eleven of the missionaries, some with their families, made their way to Sydney on the first available ship. On their arrival on 14 May 1798, they were immediately made welcome by Governor John Hunter and Rev. Samuel Marsden. At least three, Rowland Hassall, William Henry and James Cover, stayed in New South Wales for extended periods. In July 1800 Henry and Cover established a congregation at Kissing Point; later known as St Anne's, Ryde, it was the third Church founded in the colony. Hassall became an energetic itinerant preacher and a close associate of Marsden. In February 1810, seven more missionaries arrived from Tahiti and were dispersed into the community.

32. Rev. James Cameron, *Centenary History of the Presbyterian Church in New South Wales* (Angus & Robertson, 1905), pp. 2–3.

33. There was a handful of Jews on the First Fleet – estimates range from four to sixteen – and on most subsequent ships that arrived in the colony. As was the case for the various Christian denominations, the religious aspect of Judaism in the early colony was tied directly to Britain. The Chief Rabbi in England called the shots. But it is important to recognise that the Jewish community in Australia (as elsewhere) never identified itself solely by religion. In the words of Rabbi John S. Levi: 'Judaism is neither a religion nor a faith … it is a sense of extended family or peoplehood.' Orthodox (that is, practising) Jews were always a minority within a minority. At first, like Catholics, they were not able to worship in public. One of the first to show religious initiative was Joseph Marcus, a German-born Jew who began conducting informal, private services in or about 1817. The first Jewish burial ground was allotted in 1820 (with the cooperation of the Anglican chaplain, William Cowper), but it was not until 1828 that a free settler, Philip Joseph Cohen, was authorised by the Chief Rabbi of England to hold services and conduct marriages. The first rabbi in New South Wales was Aaron Levy, a member of the London Beth Din (rabbinical court); the first officially accredited minister was Michael Rose, in 1835. Numbers grew slowly but steadily. By their own tradition Jews did not seek converts (this had been a condition of their re-entry to England imposed by Oliver Cromwell in the 1650s) but by 1830 there were around 400 Jews in the colony and by 1845 around 800. By 1850 Jews comprised about 0.5 per cent of the population, a figure which has stayed more or less constant to this day.

34. Brian H. Fletcher, 'Christianity and free society in New South Wales 1788–1840', *Journal of the Royal Australian Historical Society*, 1 December 2000, available online at www.thefreelibrary.com/Christianity+and+free+society+in+New+South+Wales+1788–1840.-a067872416.

35. Ibid.

36. See generally Victor Isaacs and Rod Kirkpatrick, *Two Hundred Years of Sydney Newspapers: A short history* (Rural Press, 2003).

37. Quoted in Fletcher, 'Christianity and free society in New South Wales'.

38. Hogan, *The Sectarian Strand*, p. 46.

39. Thomas Keneally, *Australians: Origins to Eureka* (Allen & Unwin, 2009), p. 365. See also C.M.H. (Manning) Clark, *A History of Australia*, Volume II (Melbourne University Press, 1981), p. 89.

40. Fletcher, 'Christianity and free society in New South Wales'; Peter Cochrane, *Colonial Ambition: Foundations of Australian democracy*,(Melbourne University Press, 2006).

41. Keneally, *Australians*, p. 304.

42. Edmund Campion, *Australian Catholics* (Penguin, 1987), pp. 4–6.

43. Ibid., p. 4.

44. Stephen Judd and Kenneth Cable, *Sydney Anglicans* (Anglican Information Office, 2010), p. 21.

45. Hill, *1788*, p. 56 (see note 11 to the Introduction).

46. Hogan, *The Sectarian Strand*, p. 11. Ironically, the first Roman Catholic ceremony was conducted in New South Wales just four days later. A French scientific expedition to the South Seas commanded by Jean-Francois La Pérouse had stopped at Botany Bay on 26 January 1788 – the very day Phillip landed at Port Jackson – and stayed for several weeks. On 17 February one of their party died and was buried with Catholic rites. Both the departed (Louis Receveur) and the man who conducted his obsequies (Jean-André Mongez) were priests.

47. Quoted in Helen Heney, *Australia's Founding Mothers* (Nelson, 1978), p. 103.

48. Campion, *Australian Catholics*, pp. 10–11; Hughes, *The Fatal Shore*, p. 190; Vivienne Parsons, 'Dixon, James (1758–1840)', *Australian Dictionary of Biography* (Melbourne University Press, 1966), accessed online at adb.anu.edu.au/biography/dixon-james-1980/text2401.

49. Parsons, 'James Dixon', *ADB*.

50. Hogan, *The Sectarian Strand*, pp. 24, 31; Vivienne Parsons, 'O'Flynn, Jeremiah Francis (1788–1831)', *Australian Dictionary of Biography* (Melbourne University Press, 1967), accessed online at adb.anu.edu.au/biography/oflynn-jeremiah-francis-2521/text3413.

51. Campion, *Australian Catholics*, pp. 4–6.

52. Ibid., p.13.

53. Ibid., p. 9.

54. Conolly soon went to Van Diemen's Land, where he died in 1839. Therry stayed in Sydney and threw himself unstintingly into his work. Though not a disrespectful man, he was prepared to criticise the authorities for their favouritism towards the Church of England, and in 1826 was replaced as official chaplain by Father Daniel Power. But at all times Therry remained a highly influential Catholic figure. Reinstated as an official chaplain in 1837, he served two long stints in Van Diemen's Land and a short one in Port Phillip before returning to Sydney in 1854. He died in 1864, 'an heroic figure', much loved by the populace, if not by everyone in the Protestant establishment or the Catholic Church hierarchy.

55. Hogan, *The Sectarian Strand*, pp. 24–25.

56. Quoted in ibid., p. 20.

57. Quoted in Jackson, *Australians and the Christian God*, p. 40.

58. Quoted in Ibid., p. 42.

59. Hughes, *The Fatal Shore*, p. 154.

60. Margaret Spufford, quoted in Bruce, *God is Dead*, p. 48.

61. Bruce, *God is Dead*, pp. 57–59.

62. Allan M. Grocott, *Convicts, Clergymen and Churches: Attitudes of convicts and ex-convicts towards the Churches and clergy in NSW from 1788 to 1851* (Sydney University Press, 1980), pp. 14–15; Jackson, *Australians and the Christian God*, p. 65; Breward, *Australia: 'The most Godless place under Heaven'?*, pp. 1–2.

63. Quoted in Grocott, *Convicts, Clergymen and Churches*, pp. 77–78.

64. See Jackson, *Australians and the Christian God*, p. 65.

65. Hughes, *The Fatal Shore*, p. 467. See also p. 175.

66. Brian Fletcher, 'Anglicanism and the shaping of Australian society', in Bruce Kaye (ed.), *Anglicanism in Australia: A history* (Melbourne University Press, 2002), p. 297. As to Catholicism, see also Hogan, *The Sectarian Strand*, p. 26; Keneally, *Australians*, p. 304; Campion, *Australian Catholics*, pp. 4–6.

67. See Jackson, *Australians and the Christian God*, p. 48.

68. Thompson, *Religion in Australia*, p. 9 (see note 29 to the Introduction).

69. Hughes, *The Fatal Shore*, pp. 222, 379.

70. Moore, *The First Fleet Marines*, p. 66.

71. Ibid., p. 65.

72. Hill, *1788*, p. 108.

73. Moore, *The First Fleet Marines*, p. 278.

74. Flannery (ed.), *Watkin Tench*, pp. 68–69; see also Moore, *The First Fleet Marines*, pp. 101–02.

75. Hughes, *The Fatal Shore*, p. 102.

76. Keneally, *Australians*, p. 119.

77. Flannery (ed.), *Watkin Tench*, pp. 165–66.

78. Hughes, *The Fatal Shore*, pp. 129, 135.

79. Jackson, *Australians and the Christian God*, p. 63.

80. Quoted in Hughes, *The Fatal Shore*, p. 222.

81. Ibid., p. 467.

82. Ibid., pp. 130, 200.

83. Ibid., pp. 134–35.

84. Ibid., p. 130.

85. Ibid., p. 202.

86. Ibid., pp. 477–79.

87. Quoted in Introduction to Alfred Tetens, *Among the Savages of the South Seas: Memoirs of Micronesia, 1862–1868* (Stanford University Press edition, 1958), p. xxiv.

88. Gillen, *The Founders of Australia*, p. xxiii (see note 14 to the Introduction).

89. F.P. Lock, *Edmund Burke, Volume II: 1784–97* (Oxford University Press, 2009), pp. 24–25. See also Cassandra Pybus, 'First Fleet follies', *Weekend Australian*, 1 October 2008 (an unfavourable review of David Hill's book *1788*.

90. Quoted in Peter J. Stanlis, *Edmund Burke and the Natural Law* (Transaction Publishers, 1958), p. x.

91. Lock, *Edmund Burke*, pp. 24–25. See also Hughes, *The Fatal Shore*, p. 64; Philip D. Curtin, *The Image of Africa: British Ideas and Action 1780–1850*, Volume I (University of Wisconsin Press, 1964), pp. 94–95.

92. Harold B. Carter, *Sir Joseph Banks 1743–1820* (British Museum (Natural History), 1988), p. 546. See also Curtin, *The Image of Africa*, p. 95.

93. Hughes, *The Fatal Shore*, p. 57.

94. Hill, *1788*, p. 19.

95. Manning Clark, *A History of Australia*, Volume II (Melbourne University Press, 1980), p. 46.

96. MacCulloch, *A History of Christianity*, p. 875 (see note 52 to the Introduction).

97. See John Gascoigne, *Joseph Banks and the Enlightenment: Useful knowledge and polite culture* (Cambridge University Press, 2003), pp. 52–54.

98. Carter, *Sir Joseph Banks*, pp. 23ff. See also on 'the Chain of Creation', J.C. Beaglehole, (ed.), *The Endeavour Journal of Sir Joseph Banks 1768–1771* (Angus & Robertson, 1962), Volume I, p. 94 and Volume II, p. 20.

99. Andrew Tink, 'Arthur Phillip', in David Clune and Ken Turner, *The Governors of New South Wales 1788–2010* (The Federation Press, 2009), pp. 42–43. But compare Hughes, *The Fatal Shore*, p. 83 (forty-eight deaths, though still a low figure).

100. Hill, *1788*, p. 118.

101. Tink, 'Arthur Phillip', pp. 41–43.

102. Hill, *1788*, p. 283; R.J. Ryan (ed.), *The Second Fleet Convicts* (Australian Documents Library, 1982), p. xii.

103. Michael Pembroke, *Arthur Phillip: Sailor, mercenary, governor, spy* (Hardie Grant Books, 2013), p. 138.

104. Tink, 'Arthur Phillip', p. 32.

105. Hill, *1788*, p. 85 (Nepean was 'the most important single figure in the organisation of the venture').

106. Keneally, *Australians*, p. 189.

107. Ibid., p. 57.

108. Ibid., p. 56.

109. Hill, *1788*, p. 276.

110. Keneally, *Australians*, pp. 124, 201; Hill, *1788*, p. 283.

111. Hill, *1788*, pp. 129–31.

112. Tink, 'Arthur Phillip', p. 51; Robert Barnes, *An Unlikely Leader: The life and times of Captain John Hunter* (Sydney University Press, 2009), pp. 82–83.

113. Flannery (ed.), *Watkin Tench*, p. 36.

114. Geoffrey Blainey, foreword to Barnes, *An Unlikely Leader*, p. v.

115. Phillip gave the order and Hunter obeyed. He departed on the *Sirius* on 2 October 1788 and arrived at the Cape in quick time, on New Year's Day 1789. Disregarding Phillip's suggestion to sail west (back the way they had come), Hunter backed his own judgment and opted for a much longer easterly route, around Cape Horn. This took advantage of the prevailing winds (the 'Roaring Forties') and cut weeks off the voyage. Yet on the outward journey he contended with frigid weather, a serious leak in the ship, icebergs at Cape Horn, and an outbreak of scurvy among the crew. The return journey was also a trial. Four crew members deserted at the Cape; the wind alternated between flaccid calm and blustery gales. But eventually, on 9 May 1789, the *Sirius* arrived back in Sydney with precious supplies of food (principally flour and salt).

116. John Hunter, *An Historical Journal of the Transactions at Port Jackson and Norfolk Island* (University of Sydney Library digital text, 2003; first published by John Stockdale, London, 1793), p. 105, available online at adc.library.usyd.edu.au/data-2/hunhist.pdf.

117. Hughes, *The Fatal Shore*, p. 97.

118. Flannery (ed.), *Watkin Tench*, p. 77. See also p. 68.

119. Heney, *Australia's Founding Mothers*, p. 73; Hogan, *The Sectarian Strand*, p. 12.

120. Hill, *1788*, p. 167.

121. Patricia Grimshaw, Marilyn Lake, Ann McGrath and Marion Quartly, *Creating a Nation* (McPhee Gribble Publishers, 1994), p. 42.

122. Keneally, *Australians*, pp. 96–97.

123. Vines, *Law and Justice in Australia*, p. 161; see also (on the *Kable* case) pp. 4–5, 159–61. The correctness of the decision in *Kable* was confirmed by the Supreme Court of New South Wales in *R. v. Farrell* (1831) 1 Legge 5.

124. Hughes, *The Fatal Shore*, p. 467. Hughes also referred to an incident at the infamous Macquarie Harbour prison, when a convicted murderer named Trennam stabbed a fellow prisoner. Trennam 'explained' that he was tired of life and wanted to die. Asked why he did he not simply drown himself, Trennam replied: 'Oh, the case is quite different. If I kill myself I shall immediately descend to the bottomless pit, but if I kill another I would be sent to Hobart Town and tried for my life; if found guilty the parson would attend me, and then I would be sure of going to Heaven.'

125. Quoted in Grocott, *Convicts, Clergymen and Churches*, pp. 60-61.

126. Clifford Tolchard, *The Humble Adventurer: The life and times of James Ruse* (Lansdowne Press, 1965), p. 132.

127. Margaret Steven, 'Campbell, Robert (1769–1846)', *Australian Dictionary of Biography* (Melbourne University Press, 1966), accessed online at adb.anu.edu.au/biography/campbell-robert-1876/text2197. According to Steven, 'For many years Campbell was associated with the London Missionary Society which acknowledged his "constant kindness and effective acts of friendship shewn towards our Society and its concerns". The Society's missionary activity in the Pacific was early blended with speculative trading and Campbell acted for it as agent, banker and supplier at half his usual commission.'

128. From an article by Brian J. McKinlay, *Geelong Advertiser, available online at* firstfleetfellowship.org.au/stories/john-white.

129. Gillian Hull, 'From convicts to founding fathers – three notable Sydney doctors', *Journal of the Royal Australian Society of Medicine*, July 2001; vol. 94, no. 7, pp. 358–361, at p. 358.

130. Ibid.

131. Edward Ford, *The Life and Work of William Redfern* (Australasian Medical Publishing Company, 1953), p. 1.

132. Ibid., pp. 21–24.

133. Edward Ford, 'Redfern, William (1774–1833)', *Australian Dictionary of Biography* (Melbourne University Press, 1967), accessed online at adb.anu.edu.au/biography/redfern-william-2580/text3533.

134. Hughes, *The Fatal Shore*, p. 357. See also Ward, *Australia Since the Coming of Man*, p. 65.

135. See, for example, Humphrey McQueen, *A New Britannia* (Penguin, 1971), pp. 129–33ff.

136. The bad reputation of the female convicts and emancipists was based largely on one thing. The sexual mores in the early colony were lax by the highest Christian standards and – significantly – by later Victorian standards. Sex outside marriage was commonplace. In Helen Heney's words, 'low-born mistresses were the accepted thing, and poverty exacted the common law marriage'. But by the standards of the Georgian era none of this was unusual. The move to 'anti-sensualism' came later, in the mid-nineteenth century – first among the middle classes, and later among the working classes.

137. L.L. Robson, *The Convict Settlers of Australia* (Melbourne University Press, 2nd edition, 1994; first published 1965), p. 8.

138. Hughes, *The Fatal Shore*, pp. 71–72.

139. Hill, *1788*, p. 62.

140. Quoted in Keneally, *Australians*, p. 119.

141. Moore, *The First Fleet Marines*, p. 175.

142. Letter from Hunter to Viscount Sydney, 1797, quoted at www.fellowshipfirstfleeters.org.au/storie6.html.

143. John Hirst, *Sense and Nonsense in Australian History* (Black Inc., 2009), pp. 43, 108.

144. Robson, *The Convict Settlers of Australia*, p. 129.

145. Ward, *Australia Since the Coming of Man*, p. 65 (see note 10 to the Introduction).

146. Moore, *The First Fleet Marines*, p. 66.

147. Jackson, *Australians and the Christian God*, p. 42.

148. Quoted in J.W. Franklin, *Corrupting the Youth: A history of philosophy in Australia* (Macleay Press, 2003), p.213.

149. B.K. Hyams and B. Bessant, *Schools for the People? An introduction to the history of State education in Australia* (Longman, 1972), pp. 5–6.

150. Grimshaw et al., *Creating a Nation*, p. 70. See also Hogan, *The Sectarian Strand*, p. 36.

151. Hyams and Bessant, *Schools for the People?*, pp. 6–8.

152. Ibid., p. 12.

153. Hogan, *The Sectarian Strand*, p. 50.

154. Mol, *The Faith of Australians*, p. 84.

155. Hyams and Bessant, *Schools for the People?*, p. 2.

156. Ibid., pp. 9–10.

157. See generally M.H. Ellis, *Lachlan Macquarie: His life, adventures and times* (HarperCollins, 2010, first published 1947); John Ritchie, *Lachlan Macquarie: A biography* (Melbourne University Press, 1986).

158. Quoted in A.G.L. Shaw, *The Story of Australia* (4th edition, Faber & Faber, 1972), p. 46.

159. Heney, *Australia's Founding Mothers*, p. 246.

160. Guy Rundle, *50 People Who Stuffed Up Australia* (Hardie Grant, 2013), p. 95. Rundle aptly described Macquarie as 'a man who … made the place a model for the latest ideas of enlightened government and liberalism, a belief in reform, and that the individual was not a body to be punished and broken into order, but a soul to be reshaped and directed'.

161. Luke Slattery, *The First Dismissal: How Governor Macquarie invented an idea of Australia, a convict built it and Britain tried to tear it down* (Penguin Specials, 2014), p. 41.

162. Ritchie, *Lachlan Macquarie*, p. 134.

163. Quoted in Grimshaw et al., *Creating a Nation*, p. 56.

164. Barnes, *An Unlikely Leader*, p. 282.

165. Peter G. Bolt, *The Indispensable Parson: William Cowper (1778–1858): The life and influence of Australia's first parish clergyman*, Bolt Publishing Services, 2011, p. 179; K.J. Cable, 'Cartwright, Robert (1771–1856)', *Australian Dictionary of Biography* (Melbourne University Press, 1966), accessed online at adb.anu.edu.au/biography/cartwright-robert-1882/text2211.

166. See J.H.L. Cumpston, *Charles Sturt: His life and journeys of exploration* (Georgian House, 1951), pp. 51, 164. Cumpston concluded: 'His leadership was humane – the life-long friendship and respect shown by those who shared all risks with him is evidence enough. His faith in God was real and steadfast, his belief in Divine protection was not affectation – "not to myself do I accord any credit".' See also Shaw, *The Story of Australia*, pp. 69–71, Ward, *Australia Since the Coming of Man*, p. 73.

167. See generally Ivan Rudolph, *Eyre: The forgotten explorer* (HarperCollins, 2013). See also Hughes, *The Fatal Shore*, p. 311 (Eyre was a man of 'unquestionable decency and candour').

168. Keneally, *Australians*, p. 302; Shaw, *The Story of Australia*, pp. 62–63. But compare Miriam Estensen, *Matthew Flinders: The life of Matthew Flinders* (Allen & Unwin, 2003), p. 478 (attributing to Flinders a 'casual attitude' to religion).

169. Quoted in James Boyce, *1835: The founding of Melbourne & the conquest of Australia* (Black Inc., 2011), p. 150.

170. Quoted in Cumpston, pp. 145–46.

171. Quoted in Hirst, *Sense and Nonsense in Australian History*, p. 189.

172. Jill Conway, 'Macarthur, Elizabeth (1766–1850)', *Australian Dictionary of Biography* (Melbourne University Press, 1967), accessed online at adb.anu.edu.au/biography/macarthur-elizabeth-2387/text3147.

173. Ibid.

174. Ibid. And see generally Duffy, *Man of Honour*.

175. Heney, *Australia's Founding Mothers*, p. 77.

176. Duffy, *Man of Honour*, pp. 16–17.

177. Quoted in Keneally, *Australians*, p. 251.

178. Quoted in Heney, *Australia's Founding Mothers*, p. 121.

179. Quoted in Duffy, *Man of Honour*, p. 76. See also Manning Clark, *A History of Australia*, Volume II, pp. 20–21 ('Happily she knew that she and all mankind were under the superintendence of an Almighty Ruler').

180. Quoted in the entry about Elizabeth Macarthur on the website *Influential Australian Christians*, at atributetoaustralianchristians.wordpress.com/2010/10/28/elizabeth-macarthur.

181. Conway, 'Elizabeth Macarthur', *ADB*.

182. Quoted in Heney, *Australia's Founding Mothers*, p. 203.

183. Quoted in the entry about Elizabeth Macarthur on atributetoaustralianchristians. wordpress.com/2010/10/28/elizabeth-macarthur.

184. Hirst, *Sense and Nonsense in Australian History*, p. 127.

185. Breward, *Australia: 'The most Godless place under heaven'?*, p. 9.

186. See www.stvincents.com.au/index.php?option=com_content&task=view&id=132&Itemid=160.

187. See, for example, Margaret Kiddle, *Caroline Chisholm* (Melbourne University Press, 1950); Carole Walker, *A Saviour of Living Cargoes: The life and work of Caroline Chisholm* (Connor Court, 2011). Englishmen Eneas Mackenzie and Samuel Sidney wrote admiring biographies of Chisholm in the nineteenth century.

188. Quoted in Shaw, *The Story of Australia*, p. 94.

189. Walker, *A Saviour of Living Cargoes*, p. 36.

190. Ward, *Australia Since the Coming of Man*, p. 96.

191. Walker, *A Saviour of Living Cargoes*, pp. 13–14.

192. Ibid., p.16.

193. Judith Iltis, 'Chisholm, Caroline (1808–1877)', *Australian Dictionary of Biography* (Melbourne University Press, 1966), accessed online at adb.anu.edu.au/biography/chisholm-caroline-1894/text2231.

194. Quoted in Campion, *Australian Catholics*, p. 24.

195. Iltis, 'Caroline Chisholm', *ADB*.

196. Ibid.

197. Grimshaw et al., *Creating a Nation*, pp. 107–11.

198. Ibid., p. 89.

199. Adams, *Adams vs. God*, p. 144.

200. Compare Hirst, *Sense and Nonsense in Australian History*, pp. 80ff, esp at p. 91.

201. Quoted in Keneally, *Australians*, p. 405. See generally pp. 405–14.

202. Ward, *Australia Since the Coming of Man*, p. 93.
203. Boyce, *1835*, p. 173.
204. Ibid., p. 170.
205. Niel Gunson (ed.), *Australian Reminiscences and Papers of L. E. Threlkeld, Missionary to the Aborigines, 1824–1859* (Australian Institute of Aboriginal Studies, 1974), pp. 14, 95, 178.
206. Quoted in Boyce, *1835*, p. 169.
207. John Harris, *One Blood: 200 years of Aboriginal encounter with Christianity – a story of hope* (2nd edition, Albatross Books, 1994), pp. 27–28. See also Noel Pearson, 'A Rightful Place: Race, recognition and a more complete Commonwealth', *Quarterly Essay* 55, pp. 9–10.
208. Harris, *One Blood*, p. 49.
209. What can be said of George Arthur? In the words of a generally admiring biographer, A.G.L. Shaw, he 'showed neither wisdom nor understanding in his attitude [to Aboriginals] and, though hampered by past abuses, he adopted the policy demanded by popular opinion'. In the end, Shaw thought, '[Arthur] turned to "conciliation" only when extermination was almost complete.' The same could be said of the Rev. William Bedford, who was involved in decision-making as a member of Arthur's Aborigines Committee. Even the trusted Methodist missionary who 'saved' the lives of the last Indigenous survivors, George Augustus Robinson (1791–1866), emerges as a morally compromised figure. The few hundred souls whom he persuaded to surrender, late in 1831, were led to believe they would one day return to their homeland. Many died in detention and the dwindling group of survivors was dispatched, between 1832 and 1835, to indefinite exile on Flinders Island. From a Christian perspective, are there any points to be made in mitigation? It would be nice to be able to say, as Arthur and others publicly did, that it was all the fault of convicts, ex-convicts and bushrangers – i.e., dastardly, un-Christian types. It is true that such people did most of the actual killing. Even so, the argument is unsatisfactory. For the most part, the killers were not acting on their own behalf. Some formed part of an official police force and almost all were doing the bidding of 'respectable' free settlers. The Anglican Church accepted land grants from these men. The powers that be cannot escape so lightly. The best that can be said is this. *First*, the primary culprits – the white, male settlers who took the land and became rich in the process – were in no sense representative Christians. Mostly they were nominal Anglicans; a few evidently went through the motions of religious observance. But that is all. These were not missionaries but tough, amoral adventurers. *Second*, without Arthur and Robinson, the story would have been even worse. By the late 1820s a total, immediate wipe-out was imminent. In November 1828 Arthur at least directed that 'defenceless women and children be invariably spared' and in August 1830 that 'no violence or restraint be used against friendly Aborigines'. Yet the settlers resented, and largely ignored, even modest restrictions of this kind. *Third*, neither the settlers' nor Arthur's conduct was sanctioned by the British authorities – secular or religious. To the contrary, as word filtered back to London of the reality of the situation, they expressed their stern disapproval. In April 1830 the British Government issued a despatch recommending that settlers be prosecuted for the murder of natives. The 1830–31 report of the Church Missionary Society in London condemned the extent to which 'the ancient proprietors have been deprived forcibly and without compensation'. *Fourth*, lone voices of Christian conscience on the island did, occasionally, speak up. For example, the chief justice, Sir John Pedder, questioned the legality of the exile plan on the basis that Indigenous peoples were human beings – and British subjects. He proposed a treaty, but was blocked by Arthur. *Fifth*, it seems tolerably clear that Arthur laboured under a guilty conscience. He admitted as much in a January 1828 memo ('I cannot divest myself of

the consideration that all aggression originated with the white inhabitants'), and, later in the 1830s, he was a strong advocate of a treaty with the Kulin people of Port Phillip. In an extraordinary letter to his friend John Montague, written on the voyage back to England in 1836–37, he made a general confession: 'No one has more reason to cast himself unreservedly upon the providence of God than I have. Although I have deserved nothing but wrath, yet His mercy and goodness have always protected me, and if I were not to resign myself altogether to Him, my equal in ingratitude could not be found on the face of the Earth … What I now most desire is to give glory to God and what I now most highly lament is that I have hitherto been such an unprofitable servant to Him.' *Sixth*, and finally, there were clerics who came later to Tasmania who did something to atone for past wrongs. Significant numbers of 'half-caste' Aboriginals continued to live on islands in the Bass Strait, but by the 1870s they were under increasing pressure from white settlers to cede even this territory. To their credit, the Churches stood up for the beleaguered Aboriginal people, and, in 1881, Cape Barren Island was set aside for them. It was a tiny token, but it provided a lifeline. Some 130 years later, the 2011 census recorded a resident population of Aboriginal people in Tasmania of 19,625 – the vast majority on the main island. Moreover, on 10 May 2005, the Tasmanian Government released Crown lands on Cape Barren Island to be overseen by the local Aboriginal association. This was the first official 'return' of Crown land to an Aboriginal community in Tasmanian history. See generally A.G.L. Shaw, 'Arthur, Sir George (1784–1854)', *Australian Dictionary of Biography* (Melbourne University Press, 1966), accessed online at adb.anu.edu.au/biography/arthur-sir-george-1721/text1883; James Boyce, *God's Own Country? The Anglican Church and Tasmanian Aborigines* (Social Action and Research Centre, Anglicare Tasmania, 2001); James Boyce, *Van Diemen's Land* (Black Inc., 2008).

210. Paul Eckert, 'A drought of the Word of God: A Bible translator makes a plea from his heart', *Eternity*, October 2014, p. 7.

211. Threlkeld's principal publication was *An Australian Grammar … of the Language, as Spoken by the Aborigines … of Hunter's River*, published in Sydney in 1834 by the Society for Promoting Christian Knowledge. His other works included *Aboriginal Mission, New South Wales* (1825); *Specimens of a Dialect, of the Aborigines of New South Wales, Being the First Attempt to Form Their Speech Into a Written Language* (1827); *A Statement Chiefly Relating to the Formation and Abandonment of a Mission to the Aborigines* (1828); *An Australian Spelling Book, in the Language as Spoken by the Aborigines, in the Vicinity of Hunter's River* (1836); and *A Key to the Structure of the Aboriginal Language* (1850). Threlkeld's main linguistic writings were rearranged and edited by Dr John Fraser in 1892.

212. Eckert, 'A drought of the Word of God', p. 7.

213. See Boyce, *God's Own Country?*, p. 37.

214. Robert Kenny, *The Lamb Enters the Dreaming: Nathanael Pepper and the ruptured world* (Scribe, 2007), p. 30.

215. Quoted at www.aboriginalheritage.org/history/history.

216. Quoted in Kenny, *the Lamb Enters the Dreaming*, p. 63.

217. Quoted in Grimshaw et al., *Creating a Nation*, p. 135.

218. Pearson, *A Rightful Place*, p. 24.

219. Quoted in Robert Grieve Black, *The Story of Australia* (2012), p. 12.

220. Pearson, *A Rightful Place*, p. 26.

221. Ibid., p. 25.

222. Keneally, *Australians*, p. 332.

223. Quoted in Mike Seccombe, 'Grudging Howard's regretful speech', *Sydney Morning Herald*, 27 August 1999.

**Chapter 2: An enduring legacy to the West**

1.  Tamas Pataki, 'Soothsaying in schools? Reflections on the SRI debate', *Religion and Ethics*, ABC, 1 June 2011, available on line at www.abc.net.au/religion/articles/2011/06/01/3232609.htm. For an excellent (though necessarily brief) article in reply, see John Dickson, 'Best of 2011: Historical facts against atheist delusions', *Religion and Ethics*, ABC, 9 January 2012, available online at www.abc.net.au/religion/articles/2011/06/15/3244185.htm.

2.  See generally John Dickson, *Jesus: A Short Life* (Lion Hudson, 2008), pp. 7–14.

3.  Allison, *The Cruelty of Heresy*, p. 70 (see note 47 to the Introduction).

4.  See David M. Scholer (ed.), *Social Distinctives of the Christians in the First Century: Pivotal essays by E.A. Judge* (Hendrickon Publishers, 2008), Chapters 1 and 5.

5.  E.A. Judge, 'The Biblical shape of modern culture' in *The First Christians in the Roman World: Augustan and New Testament Essays*, ed. by James R. Harrison (Mohr Siebeck, 2008), p. 717.

6.  Bruce, *God is Dead*, p. 5 (see note 33 to the Introduction).

7.  See generally Vishal Mangalwadi, *The Book That Made Your World: How the Bible created the soul of Western civilization* (Thomas Nelson, 2011); Rodney Stark, *The Victory of Reason: How Christianity led to freedom, capitalism and Western success* (Random House, 2005).

8.  John Bright, *A History of Israel* (4th edition, Westminster John Know Press, 2000), p. 133.

9.  See note 55 to the Introduction.

10. Bright, *A History of Israel*, p. 76.

11. Ibid., pp. 44, 47, 68, 73–83, 92–94, 101–03.

12. Ibid., pp. 107–27, esp at 123 (date of the Exodus), 139–41.

13. Ibid., p. 145. See also John Dickson, 'Historical facts against atheist delusions', rebutting the so-called 'minimalist' argument that monotheism was a late post-Exilic development in Hebrew history.

14. Bright, *A History of Israel*, pp. 159–60.

15. Ibid., pp. 129–33, 137–43.

16. Ibid., pp. 143, 162.

17. Ibid., p. 343.

18. Ibid., p. 432.

19. Robert Winston, *The Story of God* (Bantam Books, 2005), p. 160.

20. MacCulloch, *A History of Christianity*, p. 43 (see note 52 to the Introduction).

21. See Benjamin Isaac, *The Near East under Roman Rule: Selected papers* (Brill, 1998).

22. MacCulloch, *A History of Christianity*, pp. 23–24.

23. Allison, *The Cruelty of Heresy*, p. 120.

24. Bright, *A History of Israel*, pp. 450–51.

25. See generally Allison, *The Cruelty of Heresy*; Alister E. McGrath, *Christian Theology: An introduction* (4th edition, Blackwell Publishing, 2007).

26. David Bentley Hart, *Atheist Delusions: The Christian revolution and its fashionable enemies* (Yale University Press, 2009), p. 221.

27. Ibid., pp. 222–23.

28. Rebecca Newberger Goldstein, 'What's in a Name? Rivalries and the birth of modern science' in Bill Bryson (ed.), *Seeing Further: The Story of Science & The Royal Society* (Harper Press, 2011), p.116; Mangalwadi, *The Book That Made Your World*, p. 227.

29. Michael Hart, *The 100: A ranking of the most influential persons in history* (Simon & Schuster, 1993), pp. 99–102.

30. Ibid., p. 69.

31. Ibid., pp. 450–55.

32. Goldstein, 'What's in a Name', pp. 113, 122.

33. Bruce, *God is Dead*, p. 6.

34. See, for example, John D. Barrow, *The World Within the World* (Oxford University Press, 1988); Peter Harrison, *The Bible, Protestantism and the Rise of Natural Science* (Cambridge University Press, 1998); E.A. Burtt, *The Metaphysical Foundations of Modern Physical Science* (Prometheus Books, 1999); Rodney Stark, *For the Glory of God: How monotheism led to reformations, science, witch-hunts, and the end of slavery* (Princeton University Press, 2003).

35. Stark, *For the Glory of God*, pp. 198–99.

36. Mangalwadi, *The Book That Made Your World*, pp. 70, 222, 238.

37. Ibid., pp. 92–100.

38. Jim Rawson, 'Why and How Christianity Changed Humanity' (Campus Crusade Australia, August 2010), p. 2, available online at www.transformingmelbourne.org/component/k2/item/download/17. See also Philip Ball, 'Making Stuff: From Bacon to Bakelite' in Bryson, *Seeing Further*, p. 298.

39. Mangalwadi, *The Book That Made Your World*, p. 238.

40. Judge, 'The Biblical Shape of Modern Culture', pp. 723–24.

41. Quoted in Paul Davies, *The Goldilocks Enigma: Why Is the Universe Just Right for Life?* (Allen Lane, 2006), p. 7.

42. See John C. Lennox, *God's Undertaker: Has science buried God?* (Lion Hudson, 2009), pp. 20, 50–51; Bruce, *God is Dead*, p. 6.

43. Mangalwadi, *The Book That Made Your World*, p. 208ff.

44. Quoted in Lennox, *God's Undertaker*, p. 24.

45. Quoted in Lennox, *God's Undertaker*, p. 21.

46. Quoted in Rawson, 'Why and How Christianity Changed Humanity', p. 5; Hart, *The 100*, p. 248–53 (re Descartes).

47. Quoted in Grant R. Jeffrey, *Creation: Remarkable evidence of God's design* (WaterBrook Press, 2003), p. 85; re Newton's pre-eminence, Pierre-Simon Laplace, quoted in Hart, *The 100*, p. 14.

48. Mangalwadi, *The Book That Made Your World*, p. 236.

49. Lennox, *God's Undertaker*, pp. 21–22.

50. See Dickson, 'Historical facts against atheist delusions'.

51. Lennox, *God's Undertaker*, pp. 67–68.

52. Gregory Benford, 'Time: the winged chariot', in Bryson, *Seeing Further*, p. 448.

53. Lennox, *God's Undertaker*, pp. 68–69.

54. See, for example, Peter Harrison, 'Christianity and the rise of western science', Religion and Ethics, ABC, 8 May 2012, available online at www.abc.net.au/religion/articles/2012/05/08/3498202.htm

55. E.H. Carr, *What Is History?* (2nd edition, Penguin Books, 1990 reprint), p. 109.

56. Judge, 'The Biblical Shape of Modern Culture', p. 721.

57. Carr, *What Is History?*, p. 110.

58. Ibid., p. 109–11.

59. MacCulloch, *A History of Christianity*, pp. 9, 158–59.

60. Judge, 'The Biblical Shape of Modern Culture', pp. 721, 726–27.

61. Ibid., p. 727.

62. Mangalwadi, *The Book That Made Your World*, pp. 335–36.

63. Judge, 'The Biblical Shape of Modern Culture', p. 727.

64. Quoted in Tim Keller, *Every Good Endeavor: Connecting your work to God's work* (Dutton, 2012), p. 216.

65. Francis Collins, *The Language of God* (Free Press, 2007), p. 205.

66. Martin Luther King, 'The American Dream' (1965), reproduced in Clayborne Carson and Peter Holloran (eds.), *A Knock at Midnight: Inspiration from the great sermons of Martin Luther King, Jr.* (Abacus, 2000), p. 12.
67. Mangalwadi, *The Book That Made Your World*, p. 191.
68. Bruce, *God is Dead*, p. 11; Keller, *Every Good Endeavor*, p. 208.
69. See Gary Ferngren, '"Honour the Image of God": The Incarnation and early Christian philanthropy', *Religion and Ethics*, ABC, 15 July 2014, available online at www.abc.net.au/religion/articles/2014/07/15/4046472.htm.
70. See generally on the Fall, James Boyce, *Born Bad: Original Sin and the making of the Western World* (Penguin, 2014). Boyce is an Australian.
71. MacCulloch, *A History of Christianity*, p. 112ff.
72. See David M. Scholer (ed.), *Social Distinctives*, Chapters 1 and 5.
73. Edwin Judge, 'The Social Identity of the First Christians', in ibid., p. 134.
74. MacCulloch, *A History of Christianity*, pp. 118–19; Mangalwadi, *The Book That Made Your World*, p. 277.
75. MacCulloch, *A History of Christianity*, p. 118.
76. Mangalwadi, *The Book That Made Your World*, p. 65.
77. Sir Edward Gibbon, *The Christians and the Fall of Rome* (Penguin Books – Great Ideas, 2004), ed. by David Womersley, pp. 2–3 (an extract from Gibbon's epic work *The History of the Decline and Fall of the Roman Empire*, Volume I, first published 1776). See also Mangalwadi, *The Book That Made Your World*, p. 304.
78. Ernst Troeltsch, quoted in Rebecca S. Tropp and Mark Lewis Taylor (eds.), *Reconstructing Christian Theology* (Fortress Press, 1994), p. 314.
79. See generally John Dickson, *Humilitas: A lost key to life, love and leadership* (Zondervan, 2011). For a neat summary of the historical arguments see Dickson's piece 'How Christian humility upended the world', *Religion and Ethics*, ABC, 27 October 2011, available online at www.abc.net.au/religion/articles/2011/10/27/3349673.htm.
80. Bruce, *God is Dead*, p. 11.
81. Keller, *Every Good Endeavor*, p. 21.
82. Ibid., pp. 68–74. But compare Bruce, *God is Dead*, pp. 7–8.
83. Mangalwadi, *The Book That Made Your World*, pp. 150ff.
84. Ibid., p. 349.
85. Ibid., pp. 114, 260–61.
86. See MacCulloch, *A History of Christianity*, pp. 866–73, esp at p. 871.
87. Quoted in Tink, 'Arthur Phillip', p. 34.
88. MacCulloch, *A History of Christianity*, pp. 866–67.
89. Michel Onfray, *The Atheist Manifesto: The case against Christianity, Judaism and Islam* (Melbourne University Press, 2007), pp. 49–50.
90. Warwick O. Fairfax, *The Triple Abyss: Towards a modern synthesis* (Geoffrey Bles. Ltd, 1965), p. 233. Warwick O. Fairfax was a grandson of John Fairfax, the founder of *The Sydney Morning Herald*.
91. Quoted in Keller, *Every Good Endeavor*, p. 46.
92. See Rawson, 'Why and How Christianity Changed Humanity', p. 9.
93. Judge, 'The Biblical Shape of Modern Culture', p. 731.
94. Ibid., p. 728.
95. See Tracey Rowland, 'Saint John Paul II: Doctor of Incarnate Love', *Religion and Ethics*, ABC, 26 April 2014, available online at www.abc.net.au/religion/articles/2014/04/26/3992516.htm.

96. Quoted in Judge, 'The Biblical Shape of Modern Culture', p. 728.
97. Rawson, 'Why and How Christianity Changed Humanity', p. 15.
98. Epictetus, quoted in Keller, *Every Good Endeavor*, p. 46.
99. Keller, *Every Good Endeavor*, pp. 33–43.
100. Quoted in Judge, 'The Biblical Shape of Modern Culture', p. 731; see also Keller, *Every Good Endeavor*, pp. 44–47.
101. See Ferngren, 'Honour the Image of God'.
102. Peter O'Brien, quoted in Keller, *Every Good Endeavor*, p. 216.
103. Geoffrey Blainey, *A Short History of Christianity* (Viking, 2011), pp. 68–69.
104. Quoted in Ferngren, 'Honour the Image of God'.
105. Mangalwadi, *The Book That Made Your World*, p. 306.
106. Ibid., pp. 301, 307.
107. Cf. Keller, *Every Good Endeavor*, p. 47.
108. Judge, 'The Biblical Shape of Modern Culture', p. 731. See also Frame, *Losing My Religion*, pp. 127–29 (note 26 to the Introduction).
109. See the summary of Hayes' thinking in Barnes, *An Unlikely Leader*, pp. 41–42 (see note 112 to Chapter 1).

## Chapter 3: Britain's debt to Judaeo-Christianity

1. MacCulloch, *A History of Christianity*, p. 164 (see note 52 to the Introduction).
2. See Peter Ackroyd, *The History of England, Volume I: Foundation* (Macmillan, 2011), p. 36.
3. For an intriguing argument that Constantine's conversion took place in AD 309/10, rather than 312, see the article by Jona Lendering and Bill Thayer entitled 'Common Errors (40): Constantine's conversion' at rambambashi.wordpress.com/about/.
4. Ackroyd, *Foundation*, p. 35.
5. Winston Churchill, *A History of the English Speaking Peoples, Volume I: The Birth of Britain* (Cassell 4th cheap edition, 1971, first published 1956), p. 50.
6. Ibid., pp. 63–64. See also Ackroyd, *Foundation*, pp. 56–57.
7. MacCulloch, *A History of Christianity*, p. 340.
8. Ibid., pp. 339–40.
9. Ackroyd, *Foundation*, p. 59.
10. MacCulloch, *A History of Christianity*, p. 341.
11. See Ackroyd, *Foundation*, pp. 58–59, 371 (re schools). See also Churchill, *The Birth of Britain*, pp. 69–70.
12. Neil Oliver, *Vikings: A history* (Phoenix, 2013), pp. 234–36; Ackroyd, *Foundation*, pp. 64–65.
13. Ackroyd, *Foundation*, pp. 68–69.
14. Ibid., p. 70. See also Oliver, *The Vikings*, pp. 313–14.
15. Ackroyd, *Foundation*, p. 83; see also Churchill, *The Birth of Britain*, pp. 108–09.
16. Ackroyd, *Foundation*, p. 91.
17. See David Bates, 'William I (known as William the Conqueror)' in *Oxford Dictionary of National Biography* (Oxford University Press, 2004).
18. MacCulloch, *A History of Christianity*, pp. 552–53.
19. Roger Scruton, *England: An elegy* (Pimlico, 2001), p. 121.
20. *Taylor's case* (1676) 1 Vent 293. This decision was followed by English courts in a string of later cases including *The King v. Williams* (1797) 26 Howell's State Trials 653, the indictment of the publisher of Thomas Paine's 'Age of Reason' for blasphemy.
21. *Taylor's case* (1676) 1 Vent 293.
22. Heney, *Australia's Founding Mothers*, pp. 54–55 (see note 47 to Chapter 1).

23. Quoted in Graham McLennan, 'The Hand of God: His story of Australia' (2012), p. 16, available online at www.chr.org.au/documents/11.-The-Hand-of-God/The_Hand_of_God.pdf.

24. Quoted in Richard Ely, *Unto God and Caesar: Religious issues in the emerging Commonwealth, 1891–1906* (Melbourne University Press, 1976), p. 94.

25. *Reg. v. Ramsey and Foote* (1883) 48 L.T. (N.S.) 733.

26. Ackroyd, *Foundation*, pp. 102–03.

27. Ibid., p. 59.

28. Quoted in Vines, *Law and Justice in Australia*, p. 52 (see note 8 to Chapter 1).

29. Churchill, *The Birth of Britain*, p. 158.

30. J.P. Somerville, quoted in Vines, *Law and Justice in Australia*, p. 91. See also pp. 92–93.

31. Vines, *Law and Justice in Australia*, pp. 60–61.

32. Quoted in Vines, *Law and Justice in Australia*, p. 61.

33. Ibid.

34. Vines, *Law and Justice in Australia*, pp. 45–46; Churchill, *The Birth of Britain*, pp. 171–73.

35. Ian Barker, *Sorely Tried: Democracy and trial by jury in New South Wales* (Francis Forbes Lectures, 2002), p. 28.

36. Vines, *Law and Justice in Australia*, pp. 47–48.

37. Churchill, *The Birth of Britain*, p. 205. See also Ackroyd, *Foundation*, pp. 171–73.

38. J.P. Somerville, quoted in Vines, *Law and Justice in Australia*, p. 97.

39. Vines, *Law and Justice in Australia*, p. 38.

40. Maitland, *Equity* (2nd edition, 1936), p. 23.

41. Vines, *Law and Justice in Australia*, p. 55.

42. M. Chesterman, quoted in Vines, *Law and Justice in Australia*, p. 57.

43. Brian Davies, 'A life on the Bench – and at the Bar: A conversation with Murray Gleeson, former chief justice of the High Court', *Catholic Weekly*, 19 October 2008.

44. Robert Bolt, *A Man for All Seasons* (A & C Black, 2013), p. 50.

45. MacCulloch, *A History of Christianity*, p. 627.

46. Ibid., p. 630.

47. Richard Dawkins, 'Why I want all our children to read the King James Bible', *Guardian*, 20 May 2012, available online at www.theguardian.com/science/2012/may/19/richard-dawkins-king-james-bible.

48. Hart, *The 100*, p. 469 (see note 29 to Chapter 2).

49. Muriel Porter, *The New Puritans: The rise of fundamentalism in the Anglican Church* (Melbourne University Publishing, 2006), p. 19.

50. Manning Clark, *A History of Australia*, Volume VI (Melbourne University Press, 1987), p. 280.

51. Scruton, *England*, p. 87.

52. MacCulloch, *A History of Christianity*, p. 649.

53. Conway, *The Great Australian Stupor*, p. 10 (see note 25 to the Introduction).

54. Judd and Cable, *Sydney Anglicans*, p. 3 (see note 44 to Chapter 1).

55. MacCulloch, *A History of Christianity*, pp. 748–49.

56. Judd and Cable, *Sydney Anglicans*, p. 3.

57. 'John Wesley (1703–1791): The Methodist Minister', at abolition.e2bn.org/index.php.

58. Jackson, *Australians and the Christian God*, p. 50 (see note 27 to the Introduction).

59. MacCulloch, *A History of Christianity*, p. 753.

60. Ibid., p. 7.

61. Ibid., pp. 313–14.

62. See Donnchadh Ó Corráin, 'Vikings in Ireland and Scotland in the Ninth Century', O'Donnell Lecture, University of Oxford, 8 May 1997, esp. at p. 25 ('when and how the Vikings conquered and occupied the Isles is unknown, perhaps unknowable').

63. See Oliver, *The Vikings*, pp. 292, 300–07.

64. MacCulloch, *A History of Christianity*, p. 638.

65. Ibid., pp. 330–33; Churchill, *The Birth of Britain*, pp. 56–57.

66. MacCulloch, *A History of Christianity*, pp. 332–33.

67. Hart, *The 100*, p. 218.

68. MacCulloch, *A History of Christianity*, p. 734.

69. Hughes, *The Fatal Shore*, p. 182 (see note 10 to the Introduction).

70. Quoted in Hughes, *The Fatal Shore*, p. 182.

71. See, for example, as regards the mixed motives of the Spanish, Miriam Estensen, *Terra Australis Incognita: The Spanish quest for the mysterious Great South Land* (Allen & Unwin, 2006).

72. Holt, *Manning Clark and Australian History*, pp. 147–49 (see note 6 to the Introduction).

73. Quoted in McLennan, 'The Hand of God', p. 1.

74. Edward Gaylord Bourne, 'Historical Introduction', in Emma Helen Blair (ed.), *The Philippine Islands: 1493–1803*, Volume I (Harvard, 1903). In 1529, by the Treaty of Zaragoza, the Papal Line was extended to the other side of the globe – the so-called anti-meridian. Henceforth, in this hemisphere, any newly-discovered territory to the *east* of the Papal Line would be Spain's; any to the *west* would be Portugal's. There was, however, an ongoing problem. Spain and Portugal could not agree on how to fix the exact location of the Papal Line. (For reasons which need not concern us, they calculated it from different points in the Cape Verde Islands.) In the hemisphere containing the Great South Land, the Spanish fixed the Papal Line at longitude 135 degrees east (the 135 meridian) and the Portuguese at longitude 129 degrees east (the 129 meridian). In time, the Spanish view prevailed, but no one forgot the Portuguese view either. The Papal Line has played a not insignificant role in Australian history – and geography. The original western border of New South Wales, declared by the British in 1786, was fixed at the 135 meridian – probably to minimise possible conflict with Portugal regarding the 'disputed area' between the 129 and 135 meridians, parts of which Portugal still occupied (East Timor and Macau). But by 1829 Britain was not kowtowing to anyone. When fixing the border between New South Wales and the new colony of Western Australia, it adopted the 129 meridian. That remains the eastern border of Western Australia today – a charming reminder of the Papacy's geopolitical power in times long past.

75. Manning Clark, *A History of Australia*, Volume I, p. 25. See generally Jan Ernst Heeres, *The Part Borne by the Dutch in the Discovery of Australia, 1606–1765* (BiblioBazaar, 2008).

76. See generally Heeres, *The Part Borne by the Dutch*.

77. Clark, *A History of Australia*, Volume I, p. 23.

78. See generally Jack E. Patterson, *Fonseca: Building the New World: How a controversial Spanish bishop helped find and settle an empire in the Americas* (Create Space Independent Publishing Platform, 2010).

79. Clark, *A History of Australia*, Volume I, p. 12.

80. Ibid., p. 13.

81. Hughes, *The Fatal Shore*, p. 45.

82. J.C. Beaglehole, *The Life of Captain James Cook* (Stanford University Press edition, 1992, first published 1974 by A. & C. Black Ltd), p. 109.

83. Clark, *A History of Australia*, Volume I, pp. 43–44.

84. See Beaglehole, *James Cook*, pp. 99–100.

85. Transcript of sealed instructions given to Lieutenant James Cook, 30 June 1768, available online at www.foundingdocs.gov.au/resources/transcripts/nsw1_doc_1768.pdf.

86. Clark, *A History of Australia*, Volume I, p. 49 (note 31); Hughes, *The Fatal Shore*, p. 53.

87. Shaw, *The Story of Australia*, pp. 32–33 (see note 158 to Chapter 1).

88. Hughes, *The Fatal Shore*, p. 49.

89. Clark, *A History of Australia*, Volume I, p. 44.

90. Beaglehole, *James Cook*, p. 698.

91. Ward, *Australia Since the Coming of Man*, pp. 31, 34 (see note 10 to the Introduction).

92. See Clark, *A History of Australia*, Volume I, pp. 45–46.

93. Matthew Verschuur, 'Captain Cook and the Bible', *The Protector*, 20 June 2005, available online at www.bibleprotector.com/archive_files/CAPTAIN_COOK_AND_THE_BIBLE.pdf.

94. Frank McLynn, *James Cook: Master of the seas* (Yale University Press, 2011), p. 111.

95. Guy Rundle, *50 People Who Stuffed Up Australia*, pp. 19–20 (see note 160 to Chapter 1).

96. Quoted in Dan O'Sullivan, *In Search of Captain Cook: Exploring the man through his own words* (I.B. Tauris, 2008), p.180.

97. Beaglehole, *James Cook*, pp. 1–6.

98. Ibid., p. 7.

99. John Gascoigne, *Captain Cook: Voyager between two worlds* (Bloomsbury Academic, 2008), p. 17.

100. Rob Mundle, *Cook: From sailor to legend* (ABC Books, 2013), pp. 15, 17–18; Beaglehole, *James Cook*, p. 706.

101. Quoted in Beaglehole, *James Cook*, p. 520.

102. See the entry on Cook at atributetoaustralianchristians.wordpress.com/2012/11/17/james-cook/. See also Beaglehole, *James Cook*, p. 246.

103. Peter Gardner, 'Cook's Stepney (now named Tower Hamlets)', *Cook's Log*, vol. 6, no. 3 (1983), p. 206, available online at www.captaincooksociety.com/home/detail/cook-s-stepney-now-named-tower-hamlets.

104. Beaglehole, *James Cook*, p. 695.

105. W.H. Fitchett, *The New World of the South* (John Murray, 1917), p. 70.

106. Ibid.

107. Quoted in O'Sullivan, *In Search of Captain Cook*, p. 180. See also Clark, *A History of Australia*, Volume I, p. 45.

108. McLennan, 'The Hand of God', p. 2.

109. Quoted in Beaglehole, *James Cook*, p. 150. See also p. 707.

110. Beaglehole, *James Cook*, pp. 247, 610.

111. Ibid., p. 614.

112. Quoted in O'Sullivan, *In Search of Captain Cook*, p. 182.

113. Quoted in Beaglehole, *James Cook*, p. 507.

114. O'Sullivan, *In Search of Captain Cook*, pp. 180–83.

115. Alan W. Smith, 'False trails and fallacies 1 – James Cook: Freemason? Freethinker?', *Cook's Log*, vol. 20, no. 3 (1997), p. 1401, available online at www.captaincooksociety.com/home/detail/false-trails-and-fallacies-1-james-cook-freethinker-freemason.

**Chapter 4: Passage to Federation**

1. Hughes, *The Fatal Shore*, p. 283.

2. Ward, *Australia Since the Coming of Man*, p. 79.

3. Hughes, *The Fatal Shore*, pp. 490–91. See generally John V. Barry, 'Maconochie, Alexander (1787–1860)', *Australian Dictionary of Biography* (Melbourne University Press,

1967), accessed online at adb.anu.edu.au/biography/maconochie-alexander-2417/text3207.

4. W.B. Ullathorne, *The Catholic Mission in Australasia* (Rockcliff & Duckworth, 1837), pp. iv–v.

5. John Reynolds, 'West, John (1809–1873)', *Australian Dictionary of Biography* (Melbourne University Press, 1967) accessed online at adb.anu.edu.au/biography/west-john-2784/text3965.

6. Hughes, *The Fatal Shore*, p. 546. See also John H. Cullen, 'Willson, Robert William (1794–1866)', *Australian Dictionary of Biography* (Melbourne University Press 1967), accessed online at adb.anu.edu.au/biography/willson-robert-william-2800/text3995. Willson was also a pioneer in reform of conditions for the housing and treatment of the insane. Many more Irish convicts were sent to Van Diemen's Land after 1840 (about 10,000). This was a direct result of the cessation of transportation to New South Wales and the Irish Potato Famine of 1845–49. Although leading Catholics such as Willson fought against transportation, one of its incidental effects after 1840 was the strengthening of Catholicism in that colony. Only some of the new arrivals were Mass attenders, but almost all were 'religious' in a broad sense. For such people, 'the sacred infused almost every aspect of everyday life'. Boyce, *Van Diemen's Land*, p. 226.

7. Boyce, *Van Diemen's Land*, pp. 237–38. See also Hughes, *The Fatal Shore*, pp. 266–69, 530–31.

8. Boyce, *Van Diemen's Land*, p. 242.

9. Shaw, *The Story of Australia*, p. 116.

10. Boyce, *Van Diemen's Land*, p. 240.

11. Donald Horne, *10 Steps to a More Tolerant Australia* (Penguin Books, 2003), p. 81.

12. See John Hirst, *Sense and Nonsense in Australian History*, p. 12.

13. Tony Abbott, *Battlelines* (Melbourne University Publishing, 2009), p. 162. See also David Marr, 'Political animal: The making of Tony Abbott', *Quarterly Essay* 47, August 2012, p. 40.

14. Fletcher, 'Anglicanism and the Shaping of Australian Society', p. 295 (see note 66 to Chapter 1).

15. David Stoneman, 'Richard Bourke: For the honour of God and the good of man', *Journal of Religious History*, vol. 38, no. 3, September 2014, p. 341.

16. *The Colonist*, 25 August 1836.

17. Stoneman, 'Richard Bourke', p. 344.

18. Quoted in Frank Bongiorno, 'Richard Bourke' in Clune and Turner, *The Governors of New South Wales*, p. 180 (see note 99 to Chapter 1). See further Stoneman, 'Richard Bourke', pp. 347–51.

19. Quoted in Stoneman, 'Richard Bourke', pp. 350–51.

20. John N. Molony, *An Architect of Freedom: John Hubert Plunkett in New South Wales 1832–1869* (Australian National University Press, 1973), p. 9.

21. Ibid., p. 264.

22. Bede Nairn, *Civilising Capitalism: The labor movement in New South Wales 1870–1900* (Australian National University Press, 1973), p. 2.

23. Stoneman, 'Richard Bourke', p. 346.

24. Bruce, *God is Dead*, pp. 10–11 (see note 33 to the Introduction).

25. Regrettably, there have been many instances of petty rivalry among Australian Church leaders since 1836. In 1847 the Anglican bishop of Sydney, William Grant Broughton, complained at length when his Catholic counterpart, John Bede Polding, was granted formal precedence over him. (Polding was an *arch*bishop.) The governor of the day,

Charles FitzRoy, was justifiably irritated: 'these alterations in precedence [should not cause] mortification to any sensible mind'. There was a similar example of unseemly sectarian bickering on the very day of Federation, 1 January 1901. A grand procession from the Sydney Domain was boycotted by Catholic, Presbyterian and Wesleyan Church leaders because of squabbles over precedence. Catholics also boycotted the swearing-in ceremony at Centennial Park and the official Commonwealth banquet that evening. On the occasion of the Pope's first ever visit to Australia, in 1970, a Christian ecumenical service was held at Sydney Town Hall. The Anglican archbishop of Sydney, Marcus Loane, refused to attend.

26. John Hirst, *Sense and Nonsense in Australian History*, pp. 302–04.
27. Breward, *Australia: 'The Most Godless Place Under Heaven'?*, p. 10.
28. Hogan, *The Sectarian Strand*, p. 110.
29. Quoted in Bruce Knox (ed.), *The Queensland Years of Robert Herbert Premier: Letters and papers* (University of Queensland Press, 1977), p. 133.
30. Everard Leske, *For Faith and Freedom: The Story of Lutherans and Lutheranism in Australia, 1838–1996* (Openbook Publishers, 1996), pp. 81–82, 85.
31. The early history of Western Australia was in some ways similar to that of New South Wales. Sheer survival was a challenge, and the first governor, James Stirling (1791–1865), was a capable and honourable career naval man in the mould of Arthur Phillip. Also like Phillip, he was a phlegmatic High Anglican with no great interest in religion. But the Anglican Church soon achieved dominance – key early figures were Stirling's successor as governor in 1839, John Hutt (1795–1880); the Reverend John Wollaston (1790–1856), who arrived in 1840 and saw out his life in the colony; and the first Anglican bishop of Perth, Matthew Hale (1811–95). Hutt was yet another member of William Wilberforce's Clapham Sect. Hale was a direct descendant of Sir Matthew Hale, the seventeenth-century lord chief justice of England, the man who had declared that Christianity was 'part and parcel' of the law of England: see Chapter 3. In Perth, Bishop Hale started a school for boys in 1858 that, ever since, has educated many of Western Australia's most prominent citizens. And yet, despite the strength of the Anglican Church, Churches of other denominations also existed and achieved acceptance in that colony. Hutt, like Bourke in New South Wales and Herbert in Queensland, was an ecumenicist. Two important pre-Federation figures in Western Australia, Governor Frederick Weld (1823–91) and the gold-miner/politician William Marmion (1845–96), were proud Catholics. Marmion's sudden death on 4 July 1896 caused widespread grief. More people attended his funeral than any other funeral in the colony to that time.
32. Shaw, *The Story of Australia*, p. 86.
33. Nairn, *Civilising Capitalism*, p. 1.
34. Boyce, *1835*, p. xiii.
35. Ibid., pp. 37, 129. Peter Cochrane, in his magisterial book *Colonial Ambition: Foundations of Australian democracy* (Melbourne University Press, 2006), nominated James Stephen as the key behind-the-scenes figure in the Colonial Office: 'He was an extraordinary figure in the empire's constitutional evolution … Devotion to his faith made his work a mission, first for the cause of slave emancipation, then for colonial self-government.' See also Manning Clark, *A History of Australia*, Volume II, p. 83.
36. Boyce, *1835*, p. 132.
37. Quoted in ibid., p. 36.
38. Quoted in ibid., p. 40. See also p. 134.
39. Ibid., p. 61ff.

40. Ibid., p. 132. See also Kenny, *The Lamb Enters the Dreaming*, p. 78 (see note 215 to Chapter 1); Ann Galbally, *Redmond Barry: An Anglo-Irish Australian* (Melbourne University Press, 1995), p. 53.

41. Boyce, *1835*, p. 246.

42. Quoted in H.W. Nunn, *A Short History of the Anglican Church in Victoria 1847–1947* (Editorial Committee of the Centenary Celebrations, Melbourne Diocese, 1947), p. 66.

43. Galbally, *Redmond Barry*, p. 52.

44. Shaw, *The Story of Australia*, p. 119.

45. Boyce, *1835*, pp. 86–90ff.

46. Ibid., p. 122.

47. Ibid., p, 180.

48. I should note that the history of South Australia – like that of all the colonies – was not free from tragedy as regards the Indigenous population. See generally Robert Foster and Amanda Nettelbeck, *Out of the Silence: The history and memory of South Australia's frontier wars* (Wakefield Press, 2012).

49. Douglas Pike, *Paradise of Dissent: South Australia, 1829–1857* (Cambridge University Press, 1967).

50. Hogan, *The Sectarian Strand*, p. 40.

51. Quoted in Sally O'Neill, *George Fife Angas* (Oxford University Press, 1972), p. 12.

52. Ward, *Australia Since the Coming of Man*, p. 80.

53. Leske, *For Faith and Freedom* (see note 30 above).

54. Percival Serle, 'Ridley, John', *Dictionary of Australian Biography* (Angus & Robertson, 1949).

55. Ibid. See also Michael Page and Robert Ingpen, *Turning Points in the Making of Australia* (Rigby, 1980), p. 25.

56. Ward, *Australia Since the Coming of Man*, p. 124.

57. Todd, the son of a London grocer, was a man of simple piety. He was a founder in 1859 of the Brougham Place Congregational Church, North Adelaide, and, in 1865, of the Stow Memorial Congregational Church in Adelaide, at which he and his family were regular worshippers. The town of Alice Springs was named after his wife. See G.W. Symes, 'Todd, Sir Charles (1826–1910)', *Australian Dictionary of Biography* (Melbourne University Press, 1976), accessed online at adb.anu.edu.au/biography/todd-sir-charles-4727/text7843.

58. Page and Ingpen, *Turning Points*, p. 43.

59. Jackson, *Australians and the Christian God*, p. 66 (see note 27 to the Introduction).

60. See Alan Powell, *Patrician Democrat: The political life of Charles Cowper 1843–1870* (Melbourne University Press, 1977). Powell mounted a persuasive argument that Cowper's background in the Evangelical wing of the Sydney Anglican Church helped him politically: he was able, better than many of his peers, to empathise with the middle classes, even those at the lower socioeconomic end.

61. See generally Peter Cochrane, *Colonial Ambition: Foundations of Australian democracy* (Melbourne University Press, 2006).

62. Ibid., p. 296.

63. Blainey, *A Shorter History of Australia*, p. 72.

64. Quoted in Keneally, *Australians*, p. 506.

65. Quoted in A.W. Martin, *Henry Parkes: A biography* (Melbourne University Press, 1980), p. 79.

66. Keneally, *Australians*, pp. 508–09.

67. Judd and Cable, *Sydney Anglicans*, p. 63 (see note 44 to Chapter 1).

68. Ibid., p. 63; Jackson, *Australians and the Christian God*, pp. 49, 51–54.

69. Jackson, *Australians and the Christian God*, pp. 49–51. See also Souter, *A Company of Heralds*, p. 6 (note 20 to the Introduction).

70. Page and Ingpen, *Turning Points*, pp. 47–48.

71. Valerie Yule, 'McColl, Hugh (1819–1885)', *Australian Dictionary of Biography* (Melbourne University Press, 1974), accessed online at adb.anu.edu.au/biography/mccoll-hugh-4067/text6487.

72. It is vital to stress that H.V. McKay was no mere accumulator of wealth. Though a hard taskmaster, he had a generous, charitable and philanthropic streak. When he died in 1926 he left a large trust fund, which helped to pay for the establishment of the Royal Flying Doctor Service by the Rev. John Flynn. During his lifetime, McKay had been a strong supporter of Flynn's Australian Inland Mission, created in 1912 to minister to the spiritual, social and medical needs of people in the outback.

73. *The Advertiser* (Adelaide), 22 November 1915, pp. 7, 10, available online at oa.anu.edu.au/obituary/barr-smith-robert-63. See also Dirk Van Dissel, 'Barr Smith, Robert (1824–1915)', *Australian Dictionary of Biography* (Melbourne University Press, 1976), accessed online at adb.anu.edu.au/biography/barr-smith-robert-63/text7591.

74. Quoted at adelaidia.sa.gov.au/people/robert-barr-smith.

75. *The Advertiser* (Adelaide), 22 November 1915.

76. Ibid.

77. 'A Grand Old Man', *The West Australian*, 10 October 1913, p. 5.

78. Hirst, *Sense and Nonsense in Australian History*, p. 145ff.

79. Blainey, *A Shorter History of Australia*, p. 96.

80. Robert D. Lindner, '3 Australian Evangelicals in politics in the Victorian Age: The cases of J.D. Lang, W.G. Spence, and J.S.T. McGowen', *Lucas: An Evangelical history*, no. 13, June 1992, p. 45.

81. Coral Lansbury and Bede Nairn, 'Spence, William Guthrie (1846–1926)', *Australian Dictionary of Biography* (Melbourne University Press, 1976), accessed online at adb.anu.edu.au/biography/spence-william-guthrie-4628/text7623.

82. Quoted in Lindner, '3 Australian Evangelicals', p. 50.

83. Ibid., p. 49.

84. McQueen, *A New Britannia*, pp. 196–97. *Looking Backward from 2000* was serialised in the *Worker* newspaper in 1890 and widely read throughout Australia. It became a sort of bible of the Labor movement. Edward Bellamy, the son of a Baptist minister, envisaged a socialist utopia being peaceably created in the twentieth century.

85. Hirst, *Sense and Nonsense in Australian History*, p. 17.

86. Quoted in Mol, *The Faith of Australians*, p. 209.

87. Quoted in J. Vernon Radcliffe, 'James Keir Hardie', *The British Labour Party*, Volume III (1948), available online at www.labourhistory.org.uk.

88. Quoted in Lucy Taksa, 'James Sinclair Taylor McGowen' in David Clune and Ken Turner (eds.), *The Premiers of New South Wales 1856–2005*, Volume II (The Federation Press, 2006), p. 110.

89. Taksa, 'James Sinclair Taylor McGowen', pp. 99–100; Lindner, '3 Australian Evangelicals', p. 53.

90. Lindner, '3 Australian Evangelicals', p. 55.

91. Quoted in ibid., p. 57.

92. See Thompson, *Religion in Australia*, pp. 25–28 (see note 29 to the Introduction).

93. Nairn, *Civilising Capitalism*, pp. 50, 193–94.

94. Table entitled 'Annual rate of population growth and sex ratio, Australia, 1810–2009', available online at adsri.anu.edu.au/demo-stats.aust.

95. Hill, *1788*, pp. 69–70; Hughes, *The Fatal Shore*, p. 132.

96. Hughes, ibid., p. 133.

97. Yarwood, *Samuel Marsden*, pp. 119–20 (see note 18 to the Introduction). See also Grimshaw et al., *Creating a Nation*, p. 116.

98. Australian National Church Life Survey (2011), available online at www.ncls.org.au/default.aspx?sitemapid=6988.

99. See Mol, *The Faith of Australians*, p. 71.

100. Ibid., p. 68.

101. Ibid.

102. Grimshaw et al., *Creating a Nation*, p. 91 (see note 121 to the Introduction). See generally Mary Eberstadt, 'How the West really lost God', *Policy Review*, No. 143, June and July 2007.

103. See C.R. Badger, 'Moorhouse, James (1826–1915)', *Australian Dictionary of Biography* (Melbourne University Press, 1974), accessed online at adb.anu.edu.au/biography/moorhouse-james-4238/text6841.

104. Grimshaw et al., *Creating a Nation*, p. 118.

105. Martin, *Henry Parkes*, p. 14.

106. Ibid., pp. 14–15; see also Robert Travers, *The Grand Old Man of Australian Politics: The life and times of Sir Henry Parkes* (Kangaroo Press, 2000), p. 19.

107. Martin, *Henry Parkes*, p. 14.

108. Ibid., p. 158.

109. Ibid., p. 251. See also Travers, *The Grand Old Man*, p. 170.

110. Martin, *Henry Parkes*, p. 295.

111. Quoted in ibid., p. 159. See also pp. 191, 295.

112. Ibid., p. 257.

113. Ibid., p. 159.

114. See generally Hilary M. Carey, *Believing in Australia: A cultural history of religions* (Allen & Unwin, 1996), pp. 135–39. One of Carey's sharpest points is that 'clergy wives of all denominations could, in the right circumstances, exert real dominion'. She was referring to dominion over, not merely the relevant congregation, but the whole geographical area in which her husband's parish was situated. This was especially true in rural regions.

115. Jo Piazza, *If Nuns Ruled the World: Ten sisters on a mission* (Open Road Media, 2014).

116. See generally George O'Neill, *The Life of Mary of the Cross* (Pellegrini & Co., 1931); Anne Henderson, *Mary MacKillop's Sisters: A life unveiled* (HarperCollins, 2010).

117. Campion, *Australian Catholics*, p. 48.

118. Osmund Thorpe, 'MacKillop, Mary Helen (1842–1909)', *Australian Dictionary of Biography* (Melbourne University Press, 1974), accessed online at adb.anu.edu.au/biography/MacKillop-mary-helen-4112/text6575.

119. Quoted in Henderson, *Mary MacKillop's Sisters*, p. 309. Keating gave a speech at the launch of Henderson's book, on 18 February 1997.

120. Campion, *Australian Catholics*, pp. 45–50.

121. See www.maryMacKillop.org.au/_uploads/rsfil/001156_dcae.pdf.

122. Ward, *Australia Since the Coming of Man*, p. 151.

123. Ibid., p. 152.

124. Mark Davis, *The Land of Plenty: Australia in the 2000s* (Melbourne University Press, 2008), p. 2.

125. Hirst, *Sense and Nonsense in Australian History*, pp. 52–53.

126. Ward, *Australia Since the Coming of Man*, p. 150.

127. Carey, *Believing in Australia*, p. 134.

128. Ross Fitzgerald and Trevor L. Jordan, *Under the Influence: A history of alcohol in Australia* (ABC Books, 2009), p. 162.

129. Quoted in *The Encyclopaedia of Women and Leadership in Twentieth-Century Australia*, available online at www.womenaustralia.info/leaders/biogs/WLE0774b.htm.

130. I should mention that in 1884 Spence published a novel entitled *An Agnostic's Progress from the Known to the Unknown*. Whether it reflected a crisis of faith on her own part late in life is unclear.

131. See generally Audrey Oldfield, *Woman Suffrage in Australia: A gift or a struggle?* (Cambridge University Press, 1992). I have also relied on the entries in respect of each of the women listed in the *Australian Dictionary of Biography*.

132. Helen Jones, 'Lake, Serena (1842–1902)', *Australian Dictionary of Biography* (Melbourne University Press, 2005), accessed online at adb.anu.edu.au/biography/lake-serena-13037/text23573. Further examples: Margaret McLean founded the Women's Christian Temperance Union of Victoria with the object of 'doing all that women can do, when inspired by the love of Christ'. Bessie Harrison Lee entitled a book of memoirs *One of God's Lamplighters*.

133. Janice N. Brownfoot, 'Dugdale, Henrietta Augusta (1827–1918)', *Australian Dictionary of Biography* (Melbourne University Press, 1972), accessed online at adb.anu.edu.au/biography/dugdale-henrietta-augusta-3452/text5269.

134. Scott's maternal grandfather was the Reverend George Keylock Rusden, chaplain at St Peter's Anglican Church in East Maitland. After her mother suffered a nervous breakdown, Scott lived at Rusden's parsonage and Rusden and his wife became her surrogate parents. Scott was also close to her maternal aunt, Rose Selwyn, whose husband, the Rev. E.A. Selwyn, was a future Dean of Newcastle. Judith A. Allen, *Rose Scott: Vision and revision in feminism* (Oxford University Press, 1994), pp. 43–44, 101–02.

135. Thompson, *Religion in Australia*, pp. 40–41. For example, in Western Australia in the 1890s, Premier John Forrest saw support for women's suffrage as politically expedient for his government. Forrest believed that women would vote conservatively, thus countering the goldfields' vote for Labor.

136. Quoted in Fitzgerald, *Under the Influence*, p. 160. See also p. 164.

137. Hirst, *Sense and Nonsense in Australian History*, p. 205. See also p. 8.

138. Ibid., p. 200–01.

139. Richard G. Ely, *Unto God and Caesar: Religious issues in the emerging Commonwealth 1891–1906* (Melbourne University Press, 1976), pp. 7–9.

140. Ibid., pp. 9–11. See also Thompson, *Religion in Australia*, pp. 42–43.

141. Ely, *Unto God and Caesar*, p. 13ff.

142. Ibid., p. 31.

143. Carolyn Maree Evans, *Legal Protection of Religious Freedom in Australia* (The Federation Press, 2012), p.70.

144. Ely, *Unto God and Caesar*, pp. 34, 49, 54, 130.

145. McLennan, 'The Hand of God', p. 11 (see note 23 to Chapter 3).

146. Frame, *Losing My Religion*, p. 57.

147. Ely *Unto God and Caesar*, p. 74.

148. Ibid.

149. Ibid., p. 38.

150. Quoted in Ely, *Unto God and Caesar*, p. 109.

## Chapter 5: The making of modern Australia

1.  Quoted in Gavin Souter, *Lion and Kangaroo. Australia: 1901–1919, The rise of a nation* (Fontana Books, 1978), p. 40.
2.  Jackson, *Australians and the Christian God*, p. 154ff (see note 27 to the Introduction).
3.  In a comprehensive survey of religious attitudes conducted in 1966, around 70 per cent of people in all age groups affirmed either that they 'knew God existed and had no doubts about it' or that 'while they had doubts, [they] felt that they believed in God'. The former were more prevalent than the latter. Mol, *The Faith of Australians*, p. 78 (see note 41 to the Introduction).
4.  *Ex parte H.V. McKay* (1907) 2 CAR 1.
5.  *R v. Barger* (1908) 6 CLR 41. The High Court decided the case on technical issues of Constitutional law. It did not overturn Higgins' views about the method of calculating the basic wage.
6.  Quoted in John Rickard, *H.B. Higgins: The rebel as judge* (George Allen & Unwin, 1984), p. 309.
7.  See Souter, *Lion and Kangaroo*, pp. 104–05.
8.  Grimshaw et al., *Creating a Nation*, pp. 200–01 (see note 121 to Chapter 1).
9.  See Rickard, *H.B. Higgins*, pp. 173–74. See also pp. 78–79.
10. See, for example, Gerard Henderson, 'Failed policy strong on sentiment', *Sydney Morning Herald*, 18 December 2007, available online at www.smh.com.au/news/opinion/failed-policy-strong-on-sentiment/2007/12/17/1197740178864.html.
11. Rickard, 'Higgins, Henry Bournes', *Australian Dictionary of Biography* (Melbourne University Press, 1983), accessed online at adb.anu.edu.au/biography/higgins-henry-bournes-6662.
12. Tony Stephens, *Sir William Deane: The things that matter* (Hodder, 2002), p. 96.
13. Quoted in Roger B. Joyce, *Samuel Walker Griffith* (University of Queensland Press, 1984), p. 147.
14. Joyce, *Samuel Walker Griffith*, p. 151.
15. Ibid., p. 245.
16. Archbishop Donaldson was the son of Stuart Donaldson, the first premier of New South Wales, and Amelia Donaldson (nee Cowper), daughter of the Rev. William Cowper.
17. Joyce, *Samuel Walker Griffith*, p. 357.
18. Susan Margarey and Kerrie Round, *Roma the First: A biography of Dame Roma Mitchell* (Wakefield Press, 2007), pp. 17, 67, 272.
19. Philip Ayres, *Owen Dixon* (The Miegunyah Press, 2003), p. 55. See also pp. 190, 201-02.
20. Quoted in Stephens, *Sir William Deane*, p. 104.
21. For two rather different perspectives on the White Australia Policy, see David Walker, *Anxious Nation: Australia and the rise of Asia, 1850–1939* (University of Queensland Press, 1999); Keith Windschuttle, *The White Australia Policy: Race and shame in the History Wars* (Macleay Press, 2004). For a short overview of the various factors at play, see Manning Clark, *A Short History of Australia*, pp. 216–19; Mungo MacCallum, 'Australian story: Kevin Rudd and the lucky country', *Quarterly Essay* 36, 2009, pp. 24–25.
22. Al Gabay, *The Mystic Life of Alfred Deakin* (Cambridge University Press, 1992), p. 175.
23. As to each of the prime ministers, see Roy Williams, *In God They Trust? The religious beliefs of Australia's prime ministers 1903–2013* (Bible Society of Australia, 2013), pp. 92–99 (Joe and Enid Lyons), 120–38 (Menzies), 171–81 (Fraser). As to Hasluck, see the main text.
24. See generally Judith Brett, *Australian Liberals and the Moral Middle Class: From Alfred Deakin to John Howard* (Cambridge University Press, 2003).
25. Quoted in Cameron Hazelhurst, *Menzies Observed* (George Allen & Unwin, 1979), p. 283.
26. Williams, *In God They Trust?*, pp.122–23.

27. As to each of the prime ministers, see Williams, *In God They Trust?*, pp. 54–62 (Fisher), 70–78 (Hughes), and 231–52 (Rudd). William Guy Higgs (1862–1951), a long-time Labor senator and MHR from Queensland, and federal treasurer in 1915–16, was raised an Anglican but became in later life a passionate Christian Scientist. Francis Gwynne (Frank) Tudor (1866–1922), federal Labor Opposition leader from 1916 to 1922 and one of the most principled and effective opponents of conscription during World War One, was a Congregationalist deacon and Sunday school teacher. Francis Daniel (Frank) Crean (1916–2008), federal Labor treasurer in 1973–74, was a deeply religious Presbyterian who came to worship in the Uniting Church. Kim Christian Beazley (b. 1948), federal Labor Opposition Leader from 1996 to 2001 and again from 2005 to 2006, was raised by a passionately Protestant father active in the Moral Rearmament Movement and is himself a believing Anglican.

28. As to each of the prime ministers, see Williams, *In God They Trust?*, pp. 87–91 (Scullin), 92–99 (Lyons), 110–19 (Chifley), and 193–208 (Keating). E.G. ('Ted') Theodore (1884–1950) was federal Labor treasurer from 1931 to 1933. A practising Catholic, he was the son of a Rumanian immigrant and the grandson of a priest of the Orthodox Church. His mother had converted from Methodism to Catholicism. Arthur Augustus Calwell (1896–1973), federal Labor Opposition leader from 1960 to 1967, was a devout Catholic and papal knight. In 1965 he had the guts to oppose Australia's involvement in the Vietnam War at the height of its popularity. Bill Shorten (b. 1967), Labor Opposition leader since October 2013, was schooled at by the Jesuits at Xavier College in Melbourne. In a speech to the Australian Christian Lobby in October 2014, he described himself as a believing Christian and referred to his 'local priest' at St Thomas' Catholic Church in Moonee Ponds.

29. As to H.V. Evatt and Bill Hayden, see Appendix A. As to each of the prime ministers, see Williams, *In God They Trust?*, pp. 45–48 (Watson), 100–109 (Curtin), 161–70 (Whitlam), 182–92 (Hawke) and 253–61 (Gillard). Matthew Charlton (1866–1948), federal Labor Opposition leader from 1922 to 1928, was a coalminer by trade and a Baptist by denomination. He attended Sunday school as a boy and was married (in 1899) in a Baptist Church, but, beyond that, there is little on the public record regarding his inner life. Wayne Swan (b. 1954), federal Labor treasurer from 2007 to 2013, described himself in 2008 as a 'non-practising Christian'.

30. Hogan, *The Sectarian Strand*, p. 128.

31. Conway, *The Great Australian Stupor*, p. 197.

32. Peter Kurti, 'The forgotten freedom: Threats to religious liberty in Australia', CIS Policy Monograph 139 (Centre for Independent Studies, 2014), p. 4.

33. Judd and Cable, *Sydney Anglicans*, p. 196.

34. Ibid., pp. 199–203. See also Thompson, *Religion in Australia*, pp. 72–73.

35. See generally Don Wright, *Alan Walker: Conscience of the Nation* (Openbook, 1997).

36. Quoted at www.flyingdoctor.org.au/About-Us/Our-History/The-John-Flynn-Story/.

37. Thompson, *Religion in Australia*, p. 34ff. See also Judd and Cable, *Sydney Anglicans*, pp. 184–85.

38. See generally Renate Howe, *A Century of Influence: The Australian Student Christian Movement 1896–1996* (University of New South Wales Press, 2009). Notable members of the ASCM have included H.V. Evatt, Bob Hawke, Brian Howe (a minister in the Methodist and Uniting Churches, and Paul Keating's deputy prime minister in the period 1991–95) and Kevin Rudd.

39. C.R. Badger, *The Reverend Charles Strong and the Australian Church* (Abacada Press, 1971).

40. Peter Hempenstall, *The Meddlesome Priest: A life of Ernest Burgmann* (Allen & Unwin, 1993), p. 149.

41. T.P. Boland, 'Duhig, Sir James (1871–1965)', *Australian Dictionary of Biography* (Melbourne University Press, 1981), accessed online at adb.anu.edu.au/biography/duhig-sir-james-6034/text10315.

42. Other progressive Protestant clerics in the twentieth century were the Rev. John Thomas Lawton (1878–1944), a remarkable Presbyterian educationalist in Melbourne; John Hope (1891–1971), the long-time Anglo-Catholic rector of Sydney's Christ Church St Laurence; F. Oswald Barnett (1883–1972), a Melbourne-based lay Methodist who campaigned vigorously for slum reform; the Rev. Stephen Yarnold (1903–78), another Victorian Presbyterian active in social causes (he was chaplain at Pentridge Gaol from 1963 to 1970 and a close friend of federal ALP leader Arthur Calwell); and the Rev. Keith Dowding (1911–2008), a maverick Presbyterian in Western Australia who maintained close ties with the left of the ALP. His son Peter Dowding was a Labor premier of that State. When Dowding Senior died in 2008 the *West Australian* called him, justly, a 'tireless social crusader'.

43. Carey, *Believing in Australia*, p. 111.

44. Ibid., p. 125.

45. See the website of the National Council of Women of Australia, at www.ncwa.org.au/Index.asp?pagename=About+Us&site=1&siteid=6553.

46. Carey, *Believing in Australia*, p. 131.

47. Campion, 'The privatisation of religion', p. 156 (see note 44 to the Introduction).

48. Keith Dunstan, quoted in Hogan, *The Sectarian Strand*, p. 153.

49. For example, temperance and gambling were central issues at the New South Wales State elections of 1904 and 1907. The Liberal government of Joseph Carruthers, an Anglican, won both times on the strength of the Protestant vote. This was far from unprecedented. One nineteenth-century premier of South Australia, a staunch Methodist named John Colton (1876–77), campaigned on a full suite of 'wowser' policies. These included the locking-up of children's swings on Saturday nights, so as to protect the Sabbath.

50. Thompson, *Religion in Australia*, pp. 59, 85; Hogan, *The Sectarian Strand*, p. 236.

51. Fitzgerald and Jordan, *Under the Influence*, p. 145 (see note 128 to Chapter 4).

52. Ibid., p. 176.

53. Carey, *Believing in Australia*, p. 100.

54. Conway, *The Great Australian Stupor*, p. 187.

55. Ibid., p. 52.

56. Quoted in Bruce Knox, *The Queensland Years of Robert Herbert* (see note 56 to Chapter 5), p. 15.

57. Admittedly, as Ross Fitzgerald and Trevor Jordan have observed, any call for total prohibition of alcohol sometimes required a convoluted reading of Scripture: 'Even though there was no specific injunction against alcohol in the Bible, temperance advocates sometimes explained away the references to alcohol by insisting that the Bible referred to two types of wine. The good wine that St Paul recommended to Timothy was unfermented, and the bad wine that Solomon declared a "mocker" was fermented. At other times, they insisted that alcohol was against the spirit of the Scriptures, if not the letter. Christ could not promote drink or anything else which could cause a brother to stumble.' See Fitzgerald and Jordan, *Under the Influence*, p. 153.

58. Ibid., p. 173ff.

59. Campion, 'The privatisation of religion', p. 156.

60. As 'Tracey' put it in June 2014, in the comments thread following an article on the ABC's Religion and Ethics website: 'I think in Australia most Christians ... believe ... in the right to be homophobic.'

61. Mol, *The Faith of Australians*, pp. 159–61. See also Gary D. Bouma and Beverley R. Dixon, *The Religious Factor in Australian Life* (MARC Australia, World Vision in association with the ZADOK Centre for Christianity and Society, 1986).

62. Marion Maddox, *God Under Howard: The rise of the religious right in Australian politics* (Allen & Unwin, 2005), pp. 140–44.

63. Mol, *The Faith of Australians*, pp. 160–61.

64. Christopher Hitchens, *God is Not Great: How religion poisons everything* (Allen & Unwin, 2007), p. 56.

65. Thompson, *Religion in Australia*, p. 54.

66. Ibid., pp. 79–80. See also Ward, *Australia Since the Coming of Man*, pp. 184–85.

67. Souter, *Lion and Kangaroo*, p. 303.

68. Ibid., p. 25.

69. See Joanna Cruickshank, 'Darwin, race and religion in Australia', *Religion and Ethics*, ABC, 11 April 2011, available online at www.abc.net.au/religion/articles/2011/04/11/3187793.htm.

70. Ernest Gribble (1868–1957) was a courageous, well-meaning eccentric. According to one biographer, 'his theology was a mix of High Church Anglicanism and muscular Christianity'. By today's standards he was paternalistic and authoritarian, but he cared passionately about Aboriginal people and lived and worked with them for sixty years at sites in Queensland and Western Australia. He wrote three important books: *Forty Years with the Aborigines* (1930), *The Problem of the Australian Aboriginal* (1932) and *A Despised Race: The vanishing Aboriginals of Australia* (1933). See Christine Halse, 'Gribble, Ernest Richard Bulmer (Ernie) (1868–1957)', *Australian Dictionary of Biography* (Melbourne University Press, 1996), accessed online at adb.anu.edu.au/biography/gribble-ernest-richard-bulmer-ernie-10367/text18363.

71. Quoted in Noel Loos, *White Christ Black Cross: The emergence of a Black Church* (Aboriginal Studies Press, 2007), p. 100.

72. See Keith Windschuttle, *The Fabrication of Aboriginal History, Volume III, The stolen generations, 1881–2008* (Macleay Press, 2009).

73. See Chapter 3 of the Human Rights Commission's Social Justice Report 1998, available online at https://www.humanrights.gov.au/publications/social-justice-report-1998-chapter-3-church-responses. See also Davis, *Land of Plenty*, p. 67.

74. W.E.H. Stanner, 'Howitt, Alfred William (1830–1908)', *Australian Dictionary of Biography* (Melbourne University Press, 1972), accessed online at adb.anu.edu.au/biography/howitt-alfred-william-510/text6037.

75. Dean Ashenden, 'The Strange Career of the Australian Conscience', 10 June 2010, available online at insidestory.org.au/the-strange-career-of-the-australian-conscience (re Spencer and Gillen).

76. Howitt came from a devout Anglican–Quaker family: his father, William, had authored a book, *Colonization and Christianity* (1838), condemning Europeans for their treatment of native peoples. Fison was a Wesleyan Methodist minister of unusual kindliness and intelligence. Gillen was a feisty Irishman, given to anti-clericism but steeped in Catholic doctrine and tradition. To his mates he was known as His Catholic Majesty, the Pontiff, the Amir of Alice Springs. As for Baldwin Spencer – perhaps the most important figure of the four – it is true that he abandoned conventional religion as a young man. But his father had been 'a pillar of Manchester Congregationalism'. Spencer inherited a quintessentially English-Protestant worldview, upon which (as a scientist specialising in biology) he grafted the popular Darwinian assumptions of his age. I would argue that his essential decency was the product of the former (English Protestantism); to the extent

that he looked down on Indigenous peoples, and believed them a doomed 'throwback' race, it was the insidious influence of social Darwinism which was to blame. See the *ADB* entries on each man.

77. Elkin was a voluminous writer. Perhaps his three most important publications were *The Australian Aborigines: How to understand them* (1938), *Aboriginal Men of High Degree* (1946), in which his respect for the tribal elders is evident, and *Citizenship for the Aborigines* (1944), an important forerunner to the 1967 referendum.

78. Peter Bindon, 'A Century of Effort: Contributions to the study of Aboriginal ethnology and linguistics by Pallottine missionaries in North West Western Australia', *Nelen Yubu*, Issue 78, 2001/2002, available online at catholic-church.org/apostolic-groups/catholic_life/biographies.html.

79. Barry Hill, quoted in Hirst, *Sense and Nonsense in Australian History*, p. 100.

80. Quoted in Hirst, *Sense and Nonsense in Australian History*, p. 66.

81. Quoted in Robert Manne, 'Pearson's gamble, Stanner's dream', *The Monthly*, August 2007.

82. Hirst, *Sense and Nonsense in Australian History*, p. 66.

83. Dean Ashenden, 'My Hero', meanjin.com.au/articles/post/my-hero/.

84. Ibid.

85. For example, Stanner worked as a speechwriter for Bertram Stevens (1889–1973), a strict teetotal Methodist (and one-time lay preacher), when Stevens was premier of New South Wales in the 1930s. In 1935 Stanner accompanied Father Peter Docherty to the Northern Territory to establish a Catholic mission at Port Keats (now Wadeye), a place to which he (Stanner) returned many times. For what it is worth, Stanner's wedding in 1962 took place at St Philip's Anglican Church in Sydney. See D.J. Mulvaney, 'Stanner, William Edward (Bill) (1905–1981)', *Australian Dictionary of Biography* (Melbourne University Press, 2012), accessed online at adb.anu.edu.au/biography/stanner-william-edward-bill-15541/text26753.

86. See generally Noel Loos, *White Christ Black Cross* (note 71 above). See also Hirst, *Sense and Nonsense in Australian History*, p. 101 ('Aboriginals today are more devoted to Christianity than settler Australians').

87. See Rainbow Spirit Elders, *Rainbow Spirit Theology: Towards an Australian Aboriginal theology* (HarperCollins Religious, 1997). As to its roots in the 1840s, see Boyce, *God's Own Country*, p. 41.

88. Paul Eckert, 'A drought of the word of God', *Eternity*, October 2014, p. 7.

89. Gideon Goosen, *Australian Theologies*, pp. 89–131. See also Thompson, *Religion in Australia*, pp. 130–31.

90. Goosen, *Australian Theologies*, p. 96.

91. Ibid., p. 100.

92. Ibid., pp. 105–06.

93. Quoted in Tony Stephens, *Sir William Deane*, p. 246. See also Campion, *Australian Catholics*, p. 243.

94. Quoted in Thompson, *Religion in Australia*, pp. 28–29.

95. Quoted in Yarwood, *Samuel Marsden*, pp. 238–39.

96. Harris, *One Blood*, p. 4 (see note 207 to Chapter 1).

97. Jackson, *Australians and the Christian God*, p. 53.

98. In Hilary Carey's *Believing in Australia* there is a striking table at pp. 77–81. It lists 44 'select' missions and mission schools established before 1900. All major Christian denominations are well represented.

99. Jan Kociumbas, 'Noble, James (1876–1941)', *Australian Dictionary of Biography* (Melbourne University Press, 1988), accessed online at adb.anu.edu.au/biography/noble-james-7853/text13641.

100. Philip Jones, 'Unaipon, David (1872–1967)', *Australian Dictionary of Biography* (Melbourne University Press, 1990), accessed online at adb.anu.edu.au/biography/unaipon-david-8898/text15631.

101. Richard Broome, 'Nicholls, Sir Douglas Ralph (Doug) (1906–1988)', *Australian Dictionary of Biography* (Melbourne University Press, 2012), accessed online at adb.anu.edu.au/biography/nicholls-sir-douglas-ralph-doug-14920/text26109.

102. Geoffrey Bolton, 'Paul Hasluck: An intellectual in Australian Politics', public lecture for the National Archives of Australia, 19 May 2004, available online at www.naa.gov.au/Images/Bolton_tcm16–35759.pdf.

103. Scott Bennett, 'The 1967 Aborigines Referendum', paper prepared for the Australian Bureau of Statistics, available online at www.abs.gov.au/AUSSTATS/abs@.nsf/Previousproducts/1301.0Feature%20Article12004. See generally Bain Attwood and Andrew Marcus, *The 1967 Referendum: Race, power and the Australian Constitution* (Aboriginal Studies Press, 2nd edition, 2007).

104. See www.creativespirits.info/aboriginalculture/history/australian-1967-referendum.

105. Thompson, *Religion in Australia*, p. 128.

106. Quoted at indigenousrights.net.au/land_rights/campaigning_for_land_rights,_1963–68.

107. The text of the booklet is reproduced in full at www.nma.gov.au/indigenous/resources/documents/land_rights_of_australian_aborigines,_frank_engel,_1965/page_8.

108. The text of His Holiness' address can be read in full at www.vatican.va/holy_father/john_paul_ii/speeches/1986/november/documents/hf_jp-ii_spe_19861129_aborigeni-alice-springs-australia_en.html.

109. See Franklin, *Corrupting the Youth*, pp. 388–98 (see note 148 to Chapter 1). But compare Frank Brennan, *Acting on Conscience: How can we responsibly mix law, religion and politics?* (UQP, 2007), pp. 166–72. Brennan sought to defend his father (and Justices Deane and Gaudron) from suggestions that Catholicism had informed the *Mabo* judgments. I still do not quite understand why Brennan felt the need to do so: the suggestion ought to have been worn like a badge of honour, at least by the two practising Catholics, Brennan and Deane. The nature of Justice Gaudron's Catholicism at the time *Mabo* was decided is less clear to me.

110. Franklin, *Corrupting the Youth*, p. 388.

111. Maddox, *God Under Howard*, p. 143.

112. In 1995 the Minister for Aboriginal Affairs in the Keating Government, Robert Tickner, prohibited the construction of a bridge to Hindmarsh Island (near Goolwa, South Australia) intended to service a proposed marina. Women of the local Ngarrindjeri people insisted that the site was sacred; proponents of the bridge alleged that the women's claims had been 'fabricated'. After concerted pressure from senior federal Liberal politicians and from anti-land rights groups across Australia, egged on by sections of the right-wing media, the South Australian Liberal government appointed a Royal Commission. It found in favour of the developers. But the hearing and its outcome amounted to a sad, sacrilegious farce, for reasons cogently explained by Marion Maddox in her book *God Under Howard*. The commission purported to investigate, not merely the genuineness of the women's beliefs, but their *intrinsic validity*. 'The beliefs said to constitute the "women's business",' it held, 'are not supported by any form of logic.' As Maddox observed: 'The harder questions of which religious beliefs *are* supported by logic, and what kinds of logic

it is reasonable to look for in support of religious truth, the commission left unexplored.' Of course, the broader aim of the whole exercise was political: to paint the Indigenous women as 'liars' and the Keating Government and its supporters as stooges or dupes being played by dodgy Indigenous activists. After the March 1996 federal election, the Liberal Party's campaign director, Andrew Robb, explained with apparent insouciance: 'We rode it very hard. It was a clear wedge issue for Labor.' Several Christian bodies, including the South Australian Synod of the Uniting Church, condemned this flagrant and utterly cynical attack on religious dignity and freedom.

113. See generally Maddox, *God Under Howard*, pp. 130ff, 188, 214.
114. Maddox, *God Under Howard*, pp. 143–44.
115. See Brennan, *Acting on Conscience*, pp. 5–11.
116. Thompson, *Religion in Australia*, p. 130.
117. Professor Andrew Markus, *Mapping Social Cohesion 2013: National report* (Scanlon Foundation and Monash University), p. 38.
118. Australian Bureau of Statistics, available online at www.abs.gov.au/ausstats/abs@.nsf/ Lookup/BEF8BD30A177EC39CA257C4400238EED.
119. Bruce, *God is Dead*, p. 220.
120. Campion, *Australian Catholics*, p. 180.
121. Ibid., p. 176.
122. Conversation with the author in 2013.
123. Campion, *Australian Catholics*, p. 183.
124. Ibid., p. 184.
125. In a survey of Australian historians in universities taken in 1987, 48% of 124 respondents said that they were atheists. A further 12% said that they were agnostics. See Malcolm Campbell and Mark Hutchinson, 'After Serle, before the Bicentenary: A survey of academic historians', *Australian Historical Association Bulletin*, no. 62, May 1990, p. 19.
126. Rundle, *The 50 people who stuffed up Australia*, p. 107.
127. Holt, *Manning Clark and Australian History*, p. 160 (see note 6 to the Introduction).
128. Ibid., p. 133.
129. Quoted in ibid., p. 116.
130. Quoted in David Marr (ed.), *Patrick White Letters* (Random House Australia, 1994), p. 363.
131. From an interview with Danielle Wood for *Island* magazine, no. 98, Spring, 2004.
132. Quoted in Marsden, *This I Believe*, p. 279 (see note 59 to the Introduction).

## Chapter 6: Ignorance

1. Frank Crowley, *Big John Forrest 1847–1918: A founding father of the Commonwealth of Australia* (University of Western Australia Press, 2000), pp. 157–58.
2. Quoted in Crowley, *Big John Forrest*, p. 128.
3. Pew Research, U.S. Religious Knowledge Survey (2010), available online at www. pewforum.org/2010/09/28/u-s-religious-knowledge-survey/.
4. Adams, *Adams vs. God*, p. xxiv (see note 38 to the Introduction).
5. Mol, *The Faith of Australians*, p. 64 (see note 41 to the Introduction).
6. Christian Research Association, 'Bible engagement among young Australians: Patterns and social drivers' (2010), report available online at www.cra.org.au/Bible_ Engagement_Report.pdf.
7. · John Dickson, 'The irreligious assault on the historicity of Jesus', *Religion and Ethics*, ABC, 24 December 2012, available online at www.abc.net.au/religion/ articles/2012/12/24/3660194.htm.

8. Richard Dawkins, *The God Delusion* (Bantam Press, 2006), p. 97.

9. See John Dickson, 'I'll eat my Bible if Jesus didn't exist', *The Drum*, 21 October 2014, available online at www.abc.net.au/news/2014–10–17/dickson-ill-eat-a-page-from-my-bible-if-jesus-didnt-exist/5820620.

10. John Dickson, 'Nativity naivety: Andrew Bolt tries his hand at Biblical criticism', *Religion and Ethics*, ABC, 16 March 2012.

11. Marion Maddox, *Taking God to School: The end of Australia's egalitarian education?* (Allen & Unwin, 2014), p. 143.

12. Conway, *The Great Australian Stupor*, p. 212 (see note 25 to the Introduction).

13. Judd and Cable, *Sydney Anglicans*, p. 127 (see note 44 to Chapter 1).

14. Mol, *The Faith of Australians*, p. 221.

15. Davis, *Land of Plenty*, p. 76 (see note 124 to Chapter 4).

16. Jackson, *Australians and the Christian God*, pp. 162–63 (see note 27 to the Introduction).

17. Bruce, *God is Dead*, p. 100 (see note 33 to the Introduction).

18. Maddox, *Taking God to School*, p. 87.

19. Quoted in Samuel Lewis Goldberg and Francis Barrymore Smith (eds), *Australian Cultural History* (Cambridge University Press, 1988), p. 12.

20. www.smh.com.au/federal-politics/political-news/education-review-overhaul-of-bloated-national-curriculum-widely-supported-20141012–114zkz.html#ixzz3IvEtmmHS.

21. See Maddox, *Taking God to School*, p. 124ff (re the role in Victoria of Access Ministries).

22. Ibid., pp. 152–53.

23. Jennifer Buckingham, 'The rise of religious schools', CIS Policy Monograph 111 (Centre for Independent Studies, 2010), p. 15.

24. Conway, *The Great Australian Stupor*, p. 47.

25. Maddox, *Taking God to School*, pp. 113–15; Buckingham, ibid., pp. 9–10.

26. Maddox, *Taking God to School*, p. xviii.

27. Ibid., pp. 1–28, 93–98.

28. See David Hastie, 'Liberty and Equality: Australia's history of schooling that Marion Maddox doesn't tell', *Religion and Ethics*, ABC, 5 May 2014, available online at www.abc.net.au/religion/articles/2014/05/05/3998022.htm.

29. Ibid.

30. Ibid.

31. Sacred Congregation for Catholic Education, *The Religious Dimension of Education in a Catholic School: Guidelines for reflection and renewal* (1988).

32. National Catholic Education Commission, *Religious Education in Dialogue: Curriculum around Australia* (2008), p. 100.

33. Ward, *Australia Since the Coming of Man*, p. 125 (see note 10 to the Introduction).

34. Annette Patterson, 'Shaping the specialist: Initial teacher training for English specialists in Australia', in Jeanne Gerlach, Annette Patterson and Robin Peel (eds.), *Questions of English: Aesthetics, democracy and the formation of subject* (Routledge, 2002), pp. 288–89. See also the website of the Fellowship of First Fleeters, http://www.fellowshipfirstfleeters.org.au/index.html, entry for Isabella Rosson.

35. Hogan, *The Sectarian Strand*, p. 50.

36. Yarwood, *Samuel Marsden*, p. 107 (see note 18 to the Introduction); Hyams and Bessant, *Schools for the People?*, p. 6 (see note 149 to Chapter 1).

37. McLennan, 'The Hand of God', p. 4 (see note 23 to Chapter 3).

38. Heney, *Australia's Founding Mothers*, pp. 178–79 (see note 47 to Chapter 1); Yarwood, *Samuel Marsden*, pp. 73–74.

39. Quoted in Yarwood, *Samuel Marsden*, p. 87.

40. Ibid., p. 107.

41. Hyams and Bessant, *Schools for the People?*, pp. 14–15.

42. V.W.E. Goodin, 'Taber, Thomas (1763–1842)', *Australian Dictionary of Biography* (Melbourne University Press, 1967), accessed online at adb.anu.edu.au/biography/taber-thomas-2714/text3819.

43. Ibid. Two prominent teachers of this period bear special mention, the Rev. Henry Fulton (1766–1836), the ex-convict whom I introduced in Chapter 1, and Laurence Hynes Halloran (1765–1831). Fulton opened a school in July 1814, in Castlereagh Street in Sydney, at which he instructed 'young gentlemen' in classics, modern languages and 'such Parts of the Mathematics, both in Theory and Practice, as may suit the Taste of the Scholar'. It was, perhaps, Australia's first overtly 'posh' school. Halloran, also an Irishman, was no less colourful a character. He had recanted from Catholicism as a young man and harboured thereafter an ambition to obtain orders in the Established Church. Though subsequently awarded a doctorate in divinity from King's College, Aberdeen, his clerical dream never came true. Indeed, he was transported to Sydney in 1818 for forgery, having faked a document in the name of an English MP, in connection with an attempt to accredit himself as a curate! This did not prevent him from opening Sydney's first grammar school in 1820. Though a hapless administrator and businessman, and a vexatious litigant, he earned a reputation as a highly gifted teacher.

44. Hyams and Bessant, *Schools for the People?*, pp. 11–12.

45. Yarwood, *Samuel Marsden*, p. 137.

46. Quoted in Thompson, *Religion in Australia*, p. 8 (see note 29 to the Introduction).

47. Heney, *Australia's Founding Mothers*, p. 252.

48. Ritchie, *Lachlan Macquarie*, p. 132.

49. Grimshaw et al., *Creating a Nation*, p. 62.

50. Hyams and Bessant, *Schools for the People?*, p. 10.

51. Heney, *Australia's Founding Mothers*, p. 252, Ritchie, *Lachlan Macquarie*, p. 181.

52. V.W.E. Goodin, 'Reddall, Thomas (1780–1838)', *Australian Dictionary of Biography* (Melbourne University Press, 1967), accessed online at adb.anu.edu.au/biography/reddall-thomas-2579/text3531.

53. Neil Gunson, 'Hassall, Thomas (1794–1868)', *Australian Dictionary of Biography* (Melbourne University Press, 1966), accessed online at adb.anu.edu.au/biography/hassall-thomas-2167/text2779.

54. Ibid. See also Yarwood, *Samuel Marsden*, p. 201.

55. Heney, *Australia's Founding Mothers*, p. 225.

56. Judd and Cable, *Sydney Anglicans*, p. 8.

57. Ibid., pp. 8–9.

58. Manning Clark, *A History of Australia*, Volume II, pp. 32–33; see also the website of Catholic Australia www.catholicaustralia.com.au/church-in-australia/history.

59. D.W.A. Baker, 'Lang, John Dunmore (1799–1878)', *Australian Dictionary of Biography* (Melbourne University Press, 1967), accessed online at adb.anu.edu.au/biography/lang-john-dunmore-2326/text2953.

60. Judd and Cable, *Sydney Anglicans*, pp. 9–10. See also Ross Border, 'Scott, Thomas Hobbes (1783–1860)', *Australian Dictionary of Biography* (Melbourne University Press, 1967), accessed online at adb.anu.edu.au/biography/scott-thomas-hobbes-2645/text3685; Clark, *A History of Australia*, Volume II, pp. 94–95.

61. Clark, *A History of Australia*, Volume II, p. 68 ('with more parsons and teachers the lower orders would live soberly and quietly').

62. Judd and Cable, *Sydney Anglicans*, pp. 10, 27.

63. V.W.E. Goodin, 'Cape, William Timothy (1806–1863)', *Australian Dictionary of Biography* (Melbourne University Press, 1966), accessed online at adb.anu.edu.au/biography/cape-william-timothy-2234/text2207.

64. Hogan, *The Sectarian Strand*, p. 53.

65. Judd and Cable, *Sydney Anglicans*, p. 26.

66. Ibid., pp. 26–27.

67. Hogan, *The Sectarian Strand*, pp. 74, 77.

68. D.W.A. Baker, *Days of Wrath: A life of John Dunmore Lang* (Melbourne University Press, 1985), p. 443.

69. Hogan, *The Sectarian Strand*, p. 53.

70. Ibid., pp. 51–52. See also Jackson, *Australians and the Christian God*, p. 59; Thompson, *Religion in Australia*, p. 12.

71. Judd and Cable, *Sydney Anglicans*, pp. 39–40; Thompson, *Religion in Australia*, p. 13; Hogan, *The Sectarian Strand*, pp. 53–54.

72. Thompson, *Religion in Australia*, p. 13; Hogan, *The Sectarian Strand*, pp. 54–55. The Attorney-General, J.H. Plunkett, the architect of the Church Act of 1836, entered into the spirit of things by adopting an attitude of pragmatic open-mindedness. It is a great pity that more men in authority did not follow his example. Simultaneously, Plunkett supported State aid to religious schools, and, in the period 1848–66, sat on the National Schools Board. In short, he tried to make the dual system work. In Plunkett's mind, *secular* education included the truths of natural religion, God, the afterlife, and the Ten Commandments. See Molony, *Architect of Freedom*, p. 279ff (see note 20 to chapter 4).

73. Hogan, *The Sectarian Strand*, p. 55.

74. Ibid., p. 55. See also Thompson, *Religion in Australia*, p. 15; Ward, *Australia Since the Coming of Man*, p. 125.

75. Hogan, *The Sectarian Strand*, p. 60.

76. Gwyneth M. Dow, *George Higinbotham: Church and State* (Sir Isaac Pitman & Sons Ltd., 1964), p. 53.

77. Judd and Cable, *Sydney Anglicans*, pp. 97–99.

78. Martin, *Henry Parkes*, p. 311.

79. Judd and Cable, *Sydney Anglicans*, p 99; Thompson, *Religion in Australia*, p. 20.

80. Travers, *The Grand Old Man of Australian Politics*, p. 160 (see note 106 to Chapter 4).

81. Campion, *Australian Catholics*, p. 34.

82. Ibid.

83. Quoted in Dow, *George Higinbotham*, p. 96; see also Hogan, *The Sectarian Strand*, p. 90; Judd and Cable, *Sydney Anglicans*, pp. 102–03.

84. Blainey, *A Shorter History of Australia*, p. 211.

85. Hastie, 'Liberty and Equality', p. 3. (To be clear, David Hastie himself listed this as the second of three major factors in the establishment of State schools in the nineteenth century.)

86. Mol, *The Faith of Australians*, pp. 203–04.

87. Judd and Cable, *Sydney Anglicans*, p. 103.

88. Quoted in Gwyneth Dow, 'Higinbotham, George (1826–1892)', *Australian Dictionary of Biography* (Melbourne University Press, 1972), accessed online at adb.anu.edu.au/biography/higinbotham-george-3766/text5939.

89. Dow, *George Higinbotham*, p. vi.

90. Ibid., p. 7.

91. Ibid., pp. 7–8.

92. Ibid., p. 8.

93. Ibid., pp. 11–12.

94. Ibid., pp. 69–72.

95. Ibid., p. 80.

96. Ibid., p. 100. See generally Denis Grundy, *Secular, Compulsory and Free: The Education Act of 1872* (Melbourne University Press, 1972).

97. Dow, *George Higinbotham*, pp. 57–64.

98. Ibid., p. 116.

99. Ibid., p. 150.

100. Ibid., p. 148.

101. Ibid., p. 100.

102. Ibid., p. 112.

103. Quoted in ibid., p. 134.

104. See Thompson, *Religion in Australia*, pp. 18–19.

105. Judd and Cable, *Sydney Anglicans*, p. 101.

106. Ibid., p. 104. See also Martin, *Henry Parkes*, pp. 306ff.

107. A.E. Cahill, 'Vaughan, Roger William Bede (1834–1883)', *Australian Dictionary of Biography* (Melbourne University Press, 1976), accessed online at adb.anu.edu.au/biography/vaughan-roger-william-bede-4773/text7941.

108. See Williams, *In God They Trust?*, p. 32.

109. Judd and Cable, *Sydney Anglicans*, pp. 101–04.

110. Ibid., p. 105.

111. Thompson, *Religion in Australia*, p. 32.

112. Quoted in Dow, *George Higinbotham*, p. 157.

113. Campion, *Australian Catholics*, p. 34.

114. Maddox, *Taking God to School*, p. 41.

115. Judd and Cable, *Sydney Anglicans*, pp. 129–30; Martin, *Henry Parkes*, pp. 310–11, Maddox, *Taking God to School*, pp. 33–34 (re Queensland), p. 54 (re right of entry granted to clergy in New South Wales and Tasmania).

116. Judd and Cable, *Sydney Anglicans*, p. 130.

117. Manning Clark, quoted in Conway, *The Great Australian Stupor*, p. 47.

118. By 1900 there were some dozens of Catholic orders with a presence in Australia. A full list appears as Table 4.1 in Hilary Carey's book *Believing in Australia*. In terms of education, the most important Catholic orders were the Irish Jesuits (who offered schools for the more well-to-do), and the Christian Brothers and the Sisters of St Joseph (who catered for the poor). The main object of all Catholic schools was succinctly stated by Brother H.B. O'Hagan, at the opening of a school in Balmain in 1887: 'Our main object shall ever be to teach our pupils to value above all things their eternal salvation, and to secure this by faithfully and steadfastly adhering to the faith of their fathers.'

119. See Hogan, *The Sectarian Strand*, pp. 95–100.

120. Campion, *Australian Catholics*, p. 141. Campion added (p. 146) that the 'the single most influential document in Australian Catholic history' was the so-called 'Green Catechism' issued in 1885. It was used in all Catholic schools throughout Australia for the next 80 years. Revised just once, in 1936, it consisted of four main sections— the creed, commandments, sacraments and prayers. The material was set out concisely in question-and-answer format.

121. Hogan, *The Sectarian Strand*, p. 115.

122. Ibid. See also Mol, *The Faith of Australians*, p. 107.

123. Hogan, *The Sectarian Strand*, p. 116.

124. Quoted in Mol, *The Faith of Australians*, p. 108.

125. Mol, *The Faith of Australians*, p. 128. See also Hogan, *The Sectarian Strand*, pp. 98ff.

126. Ward, *Australia Since the Coming of Man*, p. 117.

127. D.J. Murphy, *T.J. Ryan: A political biography* (University of Queensland Press, 1990), p. 41; Maddox, *Taking God to School*, p. 123.

128. Maddox, *Taking God to School*, pp. 123–24.

129. Judd and Cable, *Sydney Anglicans*, p. 59–60 (re Sydney).

130. See Paul Oslington, 'Australian universities and religion: Tales of horror and hope', *The Conversation*, 26 February 2014, available online at theconversation.com/australian-universities-and-religion-tales-of-horror-and-hope-23245.

131. Jackson, *Australians and the Christian God*, p. 205.

132. Maddox, *Taking God to School*, pp. 148–49.

133. Mol, *The Faith of Australians*, pp. 128–29.

134. Frame, *Losing My Religion*, p. 292.

135. Mol, *The Faith of Australians*, p. 116.

136. Ibid., pp. 121–22.

137. Conway, *The Great Australian Stupor*, pp. 96–97.

138. Campion, *Australian Catholics*, p. 235.

## Chapter 7: War and nationalism

1. See Frank Brennan, *Acting on Conscience: How can we responsibly mix law, religion and politics?* (University of Queensland Press, 2007), p. 101.

2. The Vatican's official position as regards the Iraq War was implacable opposition – both before and after the invasion. As Pope John Paul II pointedly reminded US President George W. Bush, in an address on 4 June 2004: 'You are very familiar with the unequivocal position of the Holy See in this regard, expressed in numerous documents, through direct and indirect contacts, and in the many diplomatic efforts which have been made since you visited me, first at Castelgandolfo on 23 July 2001, and again in this Apostolic Palace on 28 May 2002.'

3. Statement Against Military Action in Iraq, World Council of Churches Executive Committee, Geneva, 18–21 February 2003.

4. In 2003 some individual Australian clerics initially hedged their bets about Iraq, including, in Sydney, Cardinal George Pell and Anglican Archbishop Peter Jensen. Nevertheless, shortly after hostilities began, Jensen said that he 'remained unpersuaded'. Pell waited longer to clarify his position, but later insisted that 'I never publicly endorsed the Iraq war'. One of the very few prominent clerics in Australia who did publicly endorse the invasion of Iraq was Bishop Tom Frame, then senior Anglican chaplain to the Australian Defence Force. Frame justified his stance on Christian principles of just war. But only 15 months later, Frame recanted and apologised. He made a formal announcement on Palm Sunday 2004 and later published an article in the *Melbourne Anglican* entitled 'Forgive me, I was wrong on Iraq'. The article, which should be read in full, concluded as follows: 'On March 18 last year – two days before the war began – I addressed students in the united faculty of theology at The University of Melbourne. In reply to the question: "Is the proposed war against Iraq just, or just another war?" I said: "We are, as yet, unable to say with complete confidence. The final determination cannot be made until we are acquainted with the information now known by the Government, when we have seen the extent of the WMD that the 'coalition of the willing' alleges Iraq maintains, and when the full human cost of war has been calculated." I am now able to answer that question: it was just another war. Looking back on the events of the past 18 months I continue to seek God's forgiveness

for my complicity in creating a world in which this sort of action was ever considered by anyone to be necessary. Even so, come Lord Jesus.' See Brennan, *Acting on Conscience*, pp. 11, 109–11.

5. Let there be no mistake about the malevolent folly of the Iraq War. To millions in Australia and around the world, it appeared unwise from the start even on legal, military and geopolitical grounds. Ultimately it proved calamitous: hundreds of thousands dead, infrastructure ruined, Islamic terrorism and sectarian violence exacerbated, trust in America undermined, trillions of dollars wasted. It soon transpired that Saddam Hussein's (secular) regime did not possess *any* weapons of mass destruction (let alone an imminent nuclear weapons 'capability'), the stated pretext for the invasion.

6. Thompson, *Religion in Australia*, p. 96 (see note 29 to the Introduction).

7. Frame, *Losing My Religion*, p. 62 (see note 26 to the Introduction).

8. Ward, *Australia Since the Coming of Man*, p. 185 (see note 10 to the Introduction).

9. Conway, *The Great Australian Stupor*, p. 45 (see note 25 to the Introduction).

10. Joan Beaumont, *Broken Nation: Australians in the Great War* (Allen & Unwin, 2013).

11. Stephen Holt, *A Short History of Manning Clark* (Allen & Unwin, 1999), p. 162.

12. This is one of the chapter headings in Jane Caro, Antony Loewenstein, Simon Smart and Rachel Woodlock, *For God's Sake: An atheist, a Jew, a Christian & a Muslim debate religion* (Pan Macmillan Australia, 2013).

13. Adams, *Adams vs. God*, p. 237 (see note 38 to the Introduction).

14. I wrote in *God, Actually*: 'Ever since the Treaty of Westphalia in 1648, which entrenched the system of sovereign nation states, most wars have not been waged even notionally for purposes "religious". National leaders have had no difficulty in finding other reasons to fight – especially in more recent times. As the English agnostic John Humphrys has justly written, "the bloodiest century in the history of mankind [the twentieth century AD] can be blamed on many things but religion comes some way down the list".'

15. Karen Armstrong, *Fields of Blood: Religion and the history of violence* (Bodley Head, 2014). See also the contributions of Australians Rachel Woodlock and Simon Smart in Caro et al., *For God's Sake*, pp. 147–52, 160–64 – between them, they effectively rebut the argument that 'religion causes most of the conflict in the world'.

16. Peter Hitchens, *The Rage Against God: How atheism led me to faith* (Zondervan, 2010), p. 127.

17. Perhaps the clearest statement of the Australian Government's true reasons for participating in the invasion of Iraq in 2003 has come from, of all people, Tony Abbott. In his 2008 book, *Battlelines*, Abbott offered this glib one-liner: 'With eyes wide open, the [Howard] government committed Australian forces ... because that's what being a reliable ally means' (p. 76). This sentence at least had the virtue of (possibly unintended) candour: it was always clear that the government's decision to go to war in Iraq was about pleasing the Bush administration. The supposed existence of WMDs was the Americans' pre-war pretext. If the Americans had advanced a different pre-war pretext (true or false), then, on the basis of Abbott's testimony, the government would still have done as it did, in order to prove that Australia was a 'reliable ally'. Eighty pages later in *Battlelines*, Abbott reverted to the post-invasion 'script': 'It was to liberate other people, to advance everyone's interests and to uphold universal values that the "coalition of the willing" went to war in Iraq. If it's possible to engage in an altruistic war, this was it' (p. 158). The mind boggles – especially in light of Abbott's Catholicism and the Vatican's stance throughout (see note 2 above). John Howard himself told me in a 2012 interview that he received no Christian opposition from within the Liberal Party caucus in the lead-up to the invasion – 'none whatsoever'. It seems, then, that Catholics within the caucus, including Abbott, regarded themselves as free to ignore the Vatican's strictures.

18. See generally Roland H. Bainton, *Christian Attitudes Toward War and Peace: A historical survey and critical re-evaluation* (Abingdon Press, 1960); Mark Evans (ed.), *Just War Theory: A reappraisal* (Edinburgh University Press, 2005).

19. See the superb twin articles by Stanley Hauerwas, 'Man of war: Why C.S. Lewis was not a pacifist' and 'Telling the truth about the sacrifices of war', published on the website of *Religion and Ethics*, ABC, on 24 August 2012 and 24 April 2013 respectively. Hauerwas argued, audaciously but convincingly, that C.S. Lewis *ought* to have been a pacifist.

20. Hauerwas, 'Man of war', p. 6.

21. For a strident local example see Paul Kelly, 'It was a war we had to fight in', *The Australian*, 6 August 2014.

22. See Jensen, *The Future of Jesus*, p. 78, referring to Col Stringer's much-read book *800 Horsemen*. See also Apple, *The Jewish Way*, pp. 24, 61.

23. See Nicholson Baker, *Human Smoke: The beginnings of World War Two, the end of civilization*: (Simon & Schuster, 2008). This book was alternately lauded and castigated by professional reviewers, but, to my mind, the facts laid out in the primary source documents speak for themselves.

24. Quoted in Baker, *Human Smoke*, p. 456.

25. It is hard to disagree with this assessment: 'For the professing Christian, of all the questions that arise out of the study of the Third Reich and the Holocaust the most terrible are these: What were the Churches doing? How could such a monstrous crime be committed in the heart of Christendom by baptized Roman Catholics, Protestants, and Eastern Orthodox who were never rebuked, let alone excommunicated? Where were the Christians?' – Franklin H. Littell, 'Foreword' in Aime Bonifas, *Prisoner 20-801: A French national in the Nazi labor camps* (Southern Illinois University Press, 1987), p. vii.

26. James Carroll, *House of War: The Pentagon and the disastrous rise of American power* (Scribe, 2006), p. 9. See generally on 'total surrender' pp. 5–12.

27. Hitchens, *The Rage Against God*, p. 66.

28. Australia took some Jewish refugees (including 15,000 in the three years from 1938), but not nearly as many as we could have or should have. At the Evian Conference of July 1938, the Australian delegate, T.W. White, made this remark: 'It will no doubt be appreciated also that as we have no real racial problem, we are not desirous of importing one by encouraging any scheme of large-scale foreign migration … I hope that the conference will find a solution of this tragic world problem.'

29. See Baker, *Human Smoke*, passim.

30. See generally David Engel, *The Holocaust: The Third Reich and the Jews* (Pearson, 1999), esp. pp. 47–48.

31. Walter F. Mondale, 'Evian and Geneva', *New York Times*, 28 July 1979.

32. Apple, *The Jewish Way*, pp. 59–61.

33. See, for example, Tony Stephens, *The Last Anzacs* (Fremantle Press, 2009). One of Stephens' subjects, Tom Epps (1897–1997), a survivor of both the Dardanelles campaign and the Western Front, drew this lesson: 'I was brainless, but I'm not sorry I went. It taught me how stupid the politicians and military can be. They were boneheads. The 1914–18 war was mass murder. Ninety-nine per cent of war is stupid.'

34. The Australian soldiers who fought in Papua and New Guinea largely had one man to thank for the kindnesses extended to them by the fuzzy-wuzzy angels: Sir Hubert Murray, the administrator there in the period 1908–40. Murray was a benevolent and much-loved figure who won the confidence and gratitude of the local population. One biographer described him as 'quiet and pleasant voiced, a good scholar with a fine brain, a sincere Christian who as a Roman Catholic could say, "As an administrator I draw no

distinction between the different Churches; they are all working for the same general end, and all deserve government sympathy and support."' The Papuans paid Murray this tribute: 'During all these years we have seen your good works and all the helpful things you have done. When we have come to speak to you, you have not closed your ears, nor have you frowned on us, but have received us, and listened to us and taken action for us. We have seen all the good things you have done, and our happiness is great because of you. Therefore we all beg of you not to leave us, but stay here as our governor for years to come. For we know you and how you have led us into the ways of your laws, treating white people and ourselves just the same. We know that you love us well, and we are full of love for you our governor.' See Shaw, *A History of Australia*, pp. 245–46 and the entry on Murray in the *Australian Dictionary of Biography*.

35. Ward, *Australia Since the Coming of Man*, p. 166.
36. Quoted in Campion, *Australian Catholics*, p. 140.
37. Hitchens, *The Rage Against God*, p. 80.
38. It is important to note that, *legally*, Australia in 1914–19 could not authorise the declaration of war or the making of peace with a foreign power. We could not even declare ourselves neutral, without calling into question our status as a dependency of Britain – albeit a self-governing one. See Souter, *Lion and Kangaroo*, pp. 29–30, 211 (see note 1 to Chapter 5).
39. Quoted in Souter, *Lion and Kangaroo*, p. 165.
40. Ibid.
41. Souter, *Lion and Kangaroo*, pp. 165–66. It helps to understand the full sequence of events. In November 1910, federal Parliament went into a recess that lasted ten months. There was an Imperial Conference in London in May–June 1911, and an Australian parliamentary delegation attended the coronation of King George V at Westminster Abbey on 22 June 1911. Near the end of his time in London, Fisher provoked uproar back home in Australia. He was quoted as having remarked to an English interviewer named W.T. Stead: 'We are not an Empire. No end of mischief has arisen through the use of that word.' Fisher insisted Australia was an 'independent, self-governing community' and that 'there is no necessity to say that we will or will not take part in England's wars'. In August 1911, back in Australia, Fisher felt obliged to 'clarify' his position – hence the comments quoted in the main text. Even then, many Empire loyalists were not satisfied.
42. Quoted in McQueen, *A New Britannia*, p. 80 (see note 135 to Chapter 1). Deakin wrote *The Federal Story* over the period 1898–1900, though it was not published until 1944.
43. Souter, *Lion and Kangaroo*, p. 64.
44. Pro-British defenders of the Boer War (1899–1902) claimed it was about 'liberty' for the so-called Uitlanders – British settlers in Transvaal (mostly gold-miners) who were denied the right to vote by the local Boer government. But the real issue was who should control southern Africa. The British had two colonies there (the Cape Colony and Natal). The Boers, who were descendants of Dutch and German settlers, had established their own two states, the South African Republic (also known as Transvaal) and the Orange Free State. In Australia, in the words of Gavin Souter, 'opposition to the war was rationally strong but numerically weak'. It came from *The Bulletin*, small sections of the nascent ALP (including a young Billy Hughes) and a few other isolated voices. The Protestant Churches overwhelmingly supported the British cause. The Catholic Church was divided, but for political rather than theological reasons: the Boers' desire for independence was compared by some with the cause of Ireland. Very few commentators got to the heart of the issue: the evil of war itself. Notable exceptions were the Rev. Professor John Rintoul, Master of Ormond College at Melbourne University

(Presbyterian), and the Rev. Charles Strong of the Australian Church. See Souter, *Lion and Kangaroo*, pp. 62–63; McQueen, *A New Britannia*, pp. 32–34; Thompson, *Religion in Australia*, p. 48 (re Rintoul and Strong).

45. Quoted in Souter, *Lion and Kangaroo*, p. 65.
46. Thompson, *Religion in Australia*, p. 52; Souter, *Lion and Kangaroo*, p. 115.
47. Australia at Federation had three territorial possessions: Norfolk Island, Lord Howe Island and Macquarie Island. This 'Lilliputian Empire' of our own was enlarged in March 1902 when we assumed control of British New Guinea. See Souter, *Lion and Kangaroo*, p. 184.
48. Souter, *Lion and Kangaroo*, p. 113.
49. Ibid., pp. 109ff.
50. Ibid., pp. 113–14. Japan was then a British ally, though Australia was *never* comfortable about her ambitions.
51. See generally Hirst, *Sense and Nonsense in Australian History*, pp. 211–13; McQueen, *A New Britannia*, pp. 84–85.
52. Ibid.
53. Souter, *Lion and Kangaroo*, pp. 135ff.
54. Ibid., p. 143.
55. Ibid., p. 147.
56. 'The Old, Old Story' (1913).
57. Speech at Horsham, Victoria, on 1 August 1914, quoted at www.abc.net.au/news/2014-08-04/world-war-i-australian-reaction-to-outbreak-of-conflict/5603588.
58. House of Representatives, 3 August 1914, quoted at www.abc.net.au/news/2014-08-04/world-war-i-australian-reaction-to-outbreak-of-conflict/5603588. On 31 July, during a speech on the hustings at Colac in Victoria, Fisher had said: 'Should the worst happen after everything has been done that honour will permit, Australians will stand beside our own, to help and defend her, to our last man and our last shilling.'
59. David Day, *Andrew Fisher: Prime Minister of Australia* (Fourth Estate, 2008), p. 350.
60. See Philip Jenkins, 'The last crusade: The First World War and the birth of modern Islam', *Religion and Ethics*, ABC, 5 August 2014, available online at www.abc.net.au/religion/articles/2014/08/05/4027679.htm.
61. On 1 November 1914, Pope Benedict XV issued an encyclical, *Ad Beatissimi Apostolorum* (Appealing for Peace). His Holiness described 'the spectacle presented by Europe' as being 'perhaps the saddest and most mournful spectacle of which there is any record'. He cited passages from the Gospels – including Matthew 24:6–7, Luke 2:14 and 6:20–2, and John 13:34 and 15:12 – in pleading for a negotiated peace.
62. There were heroes among the World War One chaplains. To name but three: Father John Fahey, a Catholic from Western Australia, who, at his own insistence, landed with the troops at Gallipoli on the first day; the Rev. Andrew Gillison, a Presbyterian from Victoria, who was killed at Gallipoli in August 1915 trying to rescue an injured Digger; and Captain Rev. S.E. Maxted, an Anglican from New South Wales who acted for many hours as a stretcher-bearer at Fromelles and was blown up by a shell after having sat down to rest. See McKernan, *Australian Churches at War*, pp. 50, 51–52, 59 (see note 45 to the Introduction).
63. Conway, *The Great Australian Stupor*, p. 41; see also McKernan, *Australian Churches at War*, pp. 129–31 – this was the hopeful view of some of the AIF chaplains.
64. See Bill Gammage, *The Broken Years: Australian soldiers in the Great War* (Australian National University Press, 1974).
65. McKernan, *Australian Churches at War*, pp. 134–35.

66. Frame, *Losing My Religion*, p. 62.

67. Quoted in McKernan, *Australian Churches at War*, p. 131.

68. See Carey, *Believing in Australia*, pp. 111ff (see note 114 to Chapter 4).

69. Quoted in Kevin Phillips, *American Theocracy* (Viking, 2005).

70. There were very few anti-war dissidents among Protestant clergy in 1914–18. I have mentioned in the main text two brave Presbyterians from Queensland, the Revs Gibson and Wilson. Among the small number of others who were like-minded was the Rev. B. Linden Webb, a Methodist from Hay, New South Wales. In 1915 Webb published a short book, *The Religious Significance of the War*, putting the pacifist case. The Rev. Charles Strong of the Australian Church also adopted a pacifist stance, as did a Sydney-based Congregationalist minister, the Rev. Albert Rivett.

71. Nationalism itself is a perversion of the Old Testament idea of the Chosen People. The English historian E.H. Carr regarded this as an important factor in the rise of modern nationalism. See Carr, *What Is History?*, p. 67.

72. McKernan, *Australian Churches at War*, p. 2. For a contrary view, at least as regards one denomination, see Judd and Cable, *Sydney Anglicans*, pp. 186–88.

73. Quoted in McKernan, *Australian Churches at War*, p. 33.

74. Ibid., p. 35. See also MacCulloch, *A History of Christianity*, p. 916. Belgium had been created in the 1830s specifically to accommodate the faith of its Roman Catholic inhabitants.

75. See McKernan, *Australian Churches at War*, p. 154.

76. Hauerwas, 'The sacrifices of war', p. 3.

77. McKernan, *Australian Churches at War*, pp. 173–74.

78. See Patrick J. Buchanan, *Churchill, Hitler and 'the Unnecessary War': How Britain lost its Empire and the West lost the world* (Crown Publishers, 2008), pp. 77–81, 84, 322, 390–91, 398–99. Estimates vary considerably on the exact number of German civilians who died between November 1918 and June 1919 as a result of the British naval blockade, but the point is made.

79. Quoted in ibid., p. 79.

80. MacCulloch, *A History of Christianity*, p. 813. See also p. 915.

81. McKernan, *Australian Churches at War*, pp. 149–51.

82. Ibid., p. 153. This was part of the text of a 'manifesto' issued on polling day 1917 by nine pacifist-minded ministers of religion across Australia.

83. Ibid., pp. 136–37.

84. Quoted in McKernan, *Australian Churches at War*, p. 26.

85. Campion, *Australian Catholics*, p. 71.

86. McKernan, *Australian Churches at War*, p. 73.

87. Ibid., pp. 93–99.

88. Quoted in Souter, *Lion and Kangaroo*, p. 246. The bushman was none other than John Shaw Neilson, the great Australian poet.

89. Frame, *Losing My Religion*, p. 293.

90. Beaumont, *Broken Nation*, pp. 234–35; cf. Thompson, *Religion in Australia*, p. 60.

91. *Ad Beatissimi Apostolorum* (1914).

92. Quoted in McKernan, *Australian Churches at War*, pp. 122–23. I emphasise the word 'questioning'. Mannix never expressed a firm view one way or the other on the justice of the war itself.

93. Beaumont, *Broken Nation*, pp. 224–26. Despite the near unanimity of Australian Protestant Church leaders in favour of the 'Yes' case, a few notable opponents of conscription were committed Protestants, such as Frank Tudor, the leader of the federal

ALP after 1916. Tudor was a Congregationalist. Others included the South Australian State Labor MPs Robert Richards and Norman Makin (Methodists). See Thompson, *Religion in Australia*, pp. 60–61.

94. Quoted in McKernan, *Australian Churches at War*, p. 80.

95. McKernan, *Australian Churches at War*, p. 85.

96. German Catholics were uniquely vulnerable. An infamous case was that of Charles Jerger, a priest of the Passionist order, who, quite unjustly, was interned and ultimately deported. See Gerard Henderson, 'The deportation of Charles Jerger', *Labour History* no. 31, November 1976, pp. 61–78.

97. Quoted in Hogan, *The Sectarian Strand*, p. 187 (see note 55 to the Introduction).

98. Thompson, *Religion in Australia*, p. 61. See also Campion, *Australian Catholics*, p. 86; Souter, *Lion and Kangaroo*, p. 256.

99. Souter, *Lion and Kangaroo*, pp. 254–55; Thompson, *Religion in Australia*, p. 60; Beaumont, *Broken Nation*, pp. 228–29.

100. Shaw, *The Story of Australia*, p. 226.

101. Quoted in Campion, *Australian Catholics*, p. 83.

102. See Hirst, *Sense and Nonsense in Australian History*, pp. 214–15.

103. Quoted in Souter, *Lion and Kangaroo*, pp. 281–82.

104. Campion, *Australian Catholics*, p. 86.

105. Lindner, '3 Australian Evangelicals', p. 59 (see note 80 to Chapter 4).

106. Hirst, *Sense and Nonsense in Australian History*, p. 17.

107. This is the thrust of Paul Keating's argument against the excessive sanctification of Gallipoli. See Gabrielle Chan, 'Paul Keating describes First World War as "devoid of virtue"', *Guardian Australia*, 11 November 2013, available online at www.theguardian.com/world/2013/nov/11/paul-keating-describes-first-world-war-as-a-war-devoid-of-any-virtue.

108. See Grimshaw et al., *Creating a Nation*, pp. 218, 235. Making the point that tens of thousands of Australian women died in childbirth before and after 1915, yet their sacrifice for the nation was not sanctified.

109. Fletcher, 'Anglicanism and the shaping of Australian society', p. 306 (see note 66 to Chapter 1).

110. Mark McKenna, 'Patriot Act', *Australian Literary Review*, 6 June 2007, p. 3.

111. See Ken Inglis, *Sacred Places: War memorials in the Australian landscape* (3rd edition, Melbourne University Press, 2008).

112. See Pope Pius XI's trio of encyclicals against Italian Fascism (*Non abbiamo bisogno* [1931]); German Nazism (*Mit brennender Sorge* [1937]; and atheistic Communism (*Divini redemptoris* [1937]).

113. Thompson, *Religion in Australia*, p. 90. Bishop Ernest Burgmann was a key figure, though once the war began he did not adopt a pacifist stance.

114. See generally Christopher Waters, *Australia and Appeasement: Imperial foreign policy and the origins of World War II* (I.B. Taurus, 2012). An invaluable book.

115. Hogan, *the Sectarian Strand*, p. 227. For example, Catholic Archbishops Gilroy (Sydney) and Duhig (Brisbane) argued throughout that World War Two was a just war.

116. Judd and Cable, *Sydney Anglicans*, pp. 240–42.

117. Thompson, *Religion in Australia*, p. 95. In 1950, according to a Gallup poll, 47 per cent of Australians went to church at least once a month.

118. A few brave Protestant clerics criticised the Allies' excesses during World War Two, such as night bombing of civilian populations. One of the most outspoken was Englishman George Bell, the Bishop of Chichester, a close friend of Dietrich Bonhoeffer. Bell enraged

Winston Churchill so much that he lost any chance he might have had of becoming the Archbishop of Canterbury. See MacCulloch, *A History of Christianity*, p. 949; see also on Bell, Baker, *Human Smoke*, pp. 90–91, 309, 329, 332.

119. See generally Carroll, *House of War*, pp. 40–102.

120. See Matthew White, *Source List and Detailed Death Tolls for the Primary Megadeaths of the Twentieth Century*, available online at necrometrics.com/20c5m.htm.

121. 'The bombing of Hamburg in 1943', www.historylearningsite.co.uk/hamburg_bombing_1943.htm.

122. Quoted in Brenda Niall, *Martin Boyd* (Oxford University Press, 1977), p. 135.

123. Ibid., p. 136.

124. See, for example, A.C. Grayling, *Among the Dead Cities: The history and moral legacy of the WWII bombing of civilians in Germany and Japan* (Bloomsbury, 2006).

125. Thompson, *Religion in Australia*, pp. 100–01.

126. Ibid., pp. 123–24.

127. Quoted in Thompson, *Religion in Australia*, p. 102.

128. Brian Costar and Paul Strangio, 'B.A. Santamaria: "A true believer"?', *History Australia*, vol. 1, no. 2 (2004), p. 270, available online at researchbank.swinburne.edu.au/vital/access/services/.../swin.../SOURCE1.

129. Thompson, *Religion in Australia*, p. 101.

130. Paul Ham, *Vietnam: The Australian war* (HarperCollins, 2007), p. 277.

131. See Thompson, *Religion in Australia*, pp. 123–24.

132. Ibid., pp. 120–21. See also Hogan, *The Sectarian Strand*, pp. 263–65.

133. Val Noone, quoted in Thompson, *Religion in Australia*, p. 121.

134. See Ernest R. May and Philip D. Zelikow (eds), *The Kennedy Tapes: Inside the White House during the Cuban Missile Crisis* (The Belknap Press, 1997); Carroll, *House of War*, pp. 278–84.

135. See Nathan Bennett Jones, 'Operation RYAN, Able Archer 83, and miscalculation: The war scare of 1983', paper delivered at the International Graduate Conference on the Cold War, University of California, Santa Barbara, April 2008, available online at www.wilsoncenter.org/index.cfm?topic_id=1409&fuseaction=topics.item&news_id=400459.

136. Carroll, *House of War*, pp. 378–80, 578–79.

137. Ibid., pp. 381–418.

138. Hogan, *The Sectarian Strand*, p. 265.

139. See notes 1–4 above.

140. Adams, *Adams vs. God*, p. xvii.

## Chapter 8: Sex, gender and self-destruction

1. Patrick Parkinson, 'Restoring faith: Child sexual abuse and the Catholic Church', *Religion and Ethics*, ABC, 15 November 2012, available online at www.abc.net.au/religion/articles/2012/11/15/3633611.htm.

2. Scott Stephens, 'The Religion of the Humble? Cardinal Pell and the peril of institutional atheism', *Religion and Ethics*, ABC, 28 March 2014, available online at www.abc.net.au/religion/articles/2014/03/28/3973715.htm.

3. Ibid.

4. See Patrick Parkinson, 'Child sexual abuse and the Churches: A story of moral failure? – part two', *Religion and Ethics*, ABC, 25 October 2013, available online at www.abc.net.au/religion/articles/2013/10/25/3877072.htm.

5. Ibid.

6. David Marr, 'The prince: Faith, abuse and George Pell', *Quarterly Essay 51*, 2013, pp. 66–67.

7. Michael Hogan, 'Is Australia losing its religion?', *Australian Review of Public Affairs* (November 2009), available online at www.australianreview.net/digest/2009/11/hogan1.html (a review of Tom Frame's book *Losing My Religion*).

8. Parkinson, 'Child sexual abuse and the Churches'.

9. Susie Donnelly and Tom Inglis, 'The media and the Catholic Church in Ireland: Reporting clerical child sex abuse,' *Journal of Contemporary Religion*, vol. 25, no. 1, January 2010, pp. 1–19.

10. Susan Shooter, *How Survivors of Abuse Relate to God* (Ashgate, 2012).

11. Quoted in Dan Box, 'Catholic Church less than the sum of its many parts', *Weekend Australian*, 21–22 December 2013, p. 16.

12. Adams, *Adams vs. God*, p. xix (see note 38 to the Introduction).

13. See, for example, Robert J. Gromacki, *The Virgin Birth: Doctrine of Deity* (Baker Book House, 1981); Andrew Lincoln, *Born of a Virgin?* (Eerdmans, 2013).

14. Quoted in Conway, *The Great Australian Stupor*, p. 190 (see note 25 to the Introduction).

15. Tracey Rowland, 'Catholics and the media: Grim-reapers need not apply', *Religion and Ethics*, ABC, 15 March 2012, available online at www.abc.net.au/religion/articles/2012/03/15/3454158.htm.

16. Conway, *The Great Australian Stupor*, p. 138.

17. George Weigel, 'Paul VI was right after all: *Humanae Vitae*, 45 years on', *Religion and Ethics*, ABC, 31 July 2013, available online at www.abc.net.au/religion/articles/2013/07/31/3815554.htm.

18. Gordon Menzies, 'The survival of the sexiest: Where has the sexual revolution gotten us?', *Religion and Ethics*, ABC, 10 October 2012, available online at www.abc.net.au/religion/articles/2012/10/10/3607967.htm.

19. Ibid.

20. Rowland, 'Catholics and the media' (see note 15 above).

21. Grimshaw et al., *Creating a Nation*, pp. 206–07 (see note 121 to Chapter 1).

22. Until that landmark piece of legislation, civil divorce had been permitted by Act of Parliament only *on a case-by-case basis*. For centuries the question of divorce had rarely arisen: generally it was of concern only to men and women of the upper classes, who had a stake in large amounts of property and often married for dynastic reasons. For the rest, if celebrated at all, marriage was, until the mid-eighteenth century, an informal affair. It was not until 1757 in England that the law required marriages to be celebrated by a clergyman in front of witnesses and a form of legal registration. See generally Henry Finlay, *To Have But Not to Hold: A history of attitudes to marriage and divorce in Australia 1858–1975* (The Federation Press, 2005).

23. Ibid., pp. 50–55.

24. Martha Rutledge, 'Stephen, Sir Alfred (1802–1894)', *Australian Dictionary of Biography* (Melbourne University Press, 1976), accessed online at adb.anu.edu.au/biography/stephen-sir-alfred-1291/text7645. It must be conceded that, as Sydney Anglicans went, Stephen was exceptional. A proposal in New South Wales in 1886 to allow divorce for desertion, drunkenness and repeated assault was opposed by most Anglican clergy and briefly defeated – but the measures became law in 1892. See Judd and Cable, *Sydney Anglicans*, p. 147.

25. Margaret Harrison, 'Book Review', *Melbourne University Law Review*, vol. 30, 2006, p. 599. This was a review of Finlay's *To Have But Not to Hold*.

26. See, for example, Gerry W. Webb, 'A liberating view of divorce and remarriage (a Biblical response to traditionalism)' (2003), available online at members.shaw.ca/homechristian/docs/articles/divorce.htm.

27. Finlay, *To Have But Not to Hold*, pp. 222–23.

28. Quoted in Alan Trengove, *John Grey Gorton: An informal biography* (Cassell Australia, 1969), p. 150.

29. See 'Tangney, Dame Dorothy Margaret (1907-1985)', *The Biographical Dictionary of the Australian Senate, Volume III: 1962–1983* (University of New South Wales Press, 2010), pp. 457–463, available online at biography.senate.gov.au/index.php/tangney-dorothy-margaret/.

30. This argument was made strongly at the time by Christians of all denominations, both in parliament and out. An amendment to the Bill in 1975 requiring a two-year period, where one of the parties did not consent to divorce, failed by just one vote in the House of Representatives. The proposal made good sense. It tends to be women, especially low-income women, who suffer the greatest hardship as a result of a divorce they have not initiated.

31. MacCulloch, *A History of Christianity*, p. 972 (see note 52 to the Introduction).

32. Quoted in John Westen, 'At UN Vatican reaffirms stance against condoms for HIV/AIDS prevention – analysis', *Life Site News*, 25 November 2011, available online at www.lifesitenews.com/news/at-un-vatican-reaffirms-stance-against-condoms-for-hiv-aids-prevention-anal.

33. See, for example, Caro et al., *For God's Sake*, pp. 119, 228, 236, 260 (see note 12 to Chapter 7).

34. UNAIDS Press Statement, Geneva, 14 March 2013.

35. Anne Summers, *Damned Whores and God's Police: The colonization of women in Australia* (Penguin Books, 1975), pp. 319–20.

36. Grimshaw et al., *Creating a Nation*, pp. 194–95.

37. Campion, *Australian Catholics*, p. 108 (see note 42 to Chapter 1).

38. Ibid., p. 221. See also Grimshaw et al., *Creating a Nation*, p. 271; Ward, *Australia Since the Coming of Man*, p. 223 (see note 10 to the Introduction).

39. MacCulloch, *A History of Christianity*, p. 973.

40. Ibid.

41. Anne Summers, 'There is no such thing as a pro-life feminist', *Sydney Morning Herald*, 22 January 2012, available online at www.smh.com.au/federal-politics/political-opinion/there-is-no-such-thing-as-a-prolife-feminist-20120121-1qba0.html. Summers failed to note that Melinda Tankard Reist was on record as saying she does not favour the recriminalisation of abortion in Australia.

42. Quoted in Greg Sheridan, 'Pope's orthodox doctrine captures the world', *Weekend Australian*, 21–22 December 2013, p. 20.

43. Megan Best, *Fearfully and Wonderfully Made: Ethics and the beginning of human life* (Matthias Media, 2012).

44. Marcia Pally, 'The politics of the "new evangelicals": Rethinking abortion and gay marriage', *Religion and Ethics*, ABC, 9 February 2013.

45. Department of Health and Ageing, answer to Senate Question Number 325 asked on notice on 31 January 2005, by Senator Ron Boswell; A. Chan and L.C. Sage, 'Estimating Australia's abortion rates 1985–2003', *Medical Journal of Australia*, vol. 182, no. 9 (2005), pp. 447–452.

46. Quoted in Frank Brennan, 'How the Catholic Church can better promote a culture of life', *Religion and Ethics*, ABC, 19 March 2013, available online at www.abc.net.au/religion/articles/20, 13/03/19/3718903.htm.

47. Quoted in Frank Brennan, 'Why the Church needs to rethink same-sex marriage', *Religion and Ethics*, ABC, 10 July 2013, available online at www.abc.net.au/religion/

articles/2013/03/19/3718903.htm. Archbishop Coleridge made his remark in April 2013 on ABC television's *Q & A* programme.

48. See generally Simon LeVay, *Queer Science: The use and abuse of research into homosexuality* (MIT Press, 1996); Michael Kirby, 'The 1973 deletion of homosexuality as a psychiatric disorder: 30 years on', *Australian & New Zealand Journal of Psychiatry*, vol. 37 no. 6, pp. 18–31, 674–677.

49. John Milbank, 'Gay marriage and the future of human sexuality', *Religion and Ethics*, ABC, 13 March 2012, available online at www.abc.net.au/religion/ articles/2012/03/13/3452229.htm.

50. See Nigel Wright (ed.), *Five Uneasy Pieces: Essays on Scripture and sexuality* (ATF Press, 2012) (for a Protestant view); James Alison, *Faith Beyond Resentment: Fragments Catholic and gay* (DLT, 2001) (a Catholic treatment); Richard Elliott Friedman and Shawna Dolansky, *The Bible Now* (Oxford University Press, 2011), pp. 1–40 (re the Old Testament).

51. Pally, 'The politics of the "new evangelicals"', paraphrasing Randall Balmer and Greg Boyd (see note 44 above).

52. Michael Kirby, 'The case for marriage equality', *Religion and Ethics,* ABC, 8 September 2012, available online at www.abc.net.au/religion/articles/2012/09/08/3585826.htm; Brennan, 'Why the Church needs to rethink same-sex marriage' (note 47 above).

53. Michael Kirby, 'Religion and sexuality: Uncomfortable bedfellows', *Religion and Ethics*, ABC, 8 September 2012, available online at www.abc.net.au/religion/ articles/2012/09/19/3593803.htm.

54. Wayne Errington, 'Same-sex marriage – what is really at issue?', *Religion and Ethics*, ABC, 30 April 2013, available online at www.abc.net.au/religion/ articles/2013/04/30/3747877.htm.

55. Jim Reed, 'The tides have turned on same-sex marriage', *The Drum*, 31 July 2014, available online at www.abc.net.au/news/2014-07-31/reed-the-tides-have-turned-on-same-sex-marriage/5637770.

56. See note 50 above. The relevant snippets in Paul's letters are Romans 1:26–27; 1 Corinthians 6:9–10; 1 Timothy 1:10; Jude 1:7.

57. Milbank, 'Gay marriage and the future of human sexuality' (note 49 above).

58. David Novak, 'Same-sex couples have no right to marry', *Religion and Ethics*, ABC, 30 November 2011, available online at www.abc.net.au/religion/ articles/2011/11/30/3115445.htm.

59. Quoted in Francis X. Rocca, 'Why not women priests? The papal theologian explains', *Catholic News Service*, 31 January 2013, available online at www.catholicnews.com/data/ stories/cns/1300417.htm.

60. Ibid.

61. See Madeleine Collins, 'Sydney speaks on women's ordination', *Sydney Anglicans*, 23 October 2006, available online at sydneyanglicans.net/news/sydney_speaks_on_ womens_ordination/; cf. Porter, *The New Puritans*, pp. 87–116.

62. Assembly of the Uniting Church in Australia, *Why Does the Uniting Church Ordain Women to the Ministry of the Word?* (adopted 1990), pp. 570 (Kiek), 572 (Sanders), available online at ctm.uca.edu.au/layeducation/files/2012/08/Why-Does-the-Uniting-Church-in-Australia-Ordain-Women-to-the-Ministry-of-the-Word.pdf.

63. At the time of writing there are five women Anglican bishops in Australia: the Rt Rev Kay Goldsworthy (Assistant Bishop, Diocese of Perth); the Rt Rev Barbara Dowling (Assistant Bishop, Diocese of Melbourne); the Rt Rev Genieve Blackwell (Regional Bishop of Wagga Wagga, Diocese of Canberra and Goulburn), the Rt Rev Alison Taylor

(Bishop of the Southern Region, Diocese of Brisbane); and the Rt Rev Dr Sarah Macneil (Bishop of the Diocese of Grafton).

64. See, for example, Julia Baird, 'Going backwards into the future', *Sydney Morning Herald*, 1 December 2012, available online at www.smh.com.au/federal-politics/political-opinion/going-backwards-into-the-future-20121130-2am0e.html.

65. John Dickson, *Hearing Her Voice: A case for women giving sermons* (Zondervan, 2012; revised edition, 2014).

66. *Why Does the Uniting Church Ordain Women?*, p. 564.

67. Quoted in Graham Downie, 'Getting on with the work of God', *Sydney Morning Herald*, 12 May 2012, available online at www.smh.com.au/federal-politics/getting-on-with-the-work-of-god-20120511-1yhsi.html. On the biggest question of all – does God exist? – Bartholomew has written this: 'I have always been fascinated by the world around me. The fact that there are no snowflakes the same, even though they are all based on a hexagonal template. The wonder of metamorphism; the change from a caterpillar to a pupa and then a moth or butterfly. Why tadpoles change into frogs. How birds migrate great distances and end up in the same places that their parents, grandparents came from seasons before. All these things seem for me to indicate a Master Designer ... God. The "God who made the earth, the air, the sky, the sea ... who cares for me."'

68. Mol, *The Faith of Australians*, p. 62.

69. Bruce, *God Is Dead*, p. 158.

70. Ibid., pp. 20–21.

71. Ibid., p. 61.

72. Donald Horne, *The Lucky Country: Australia in the sixties* (Penguin Books, 1964), p. 55. Horne was mocking a prevalent, ill-informed Protestant attitude to Catholicism.

73. In Italy, for example, the 'home' of the Vatican, a 2010 survey by Eurispes found that Catholics made up 76.5 per cent of the population, but that only 24.4 per cent were observant. Just four years earlier, in the 2006 survey, the figures had been 87.8 per cent and 36.8 per cent respectively.

74. See generally Gideon Goosen, *Australian Theologies* (see note 4 to Chapter 1).

75. Fletcher, 'Anglicanism and the Shaping of Australian Society', p. 308 (see note 66 to Chapter 1).

76. Quoted in McKernan, *Australian Churches at War*, p. 11 (see note 45 to the Introduction).

77. McKernan, *Australian Churches at War*, p. 20.

78. See Campion, *Australian Catholics*, passim.

## Chapter 9: Two more belief-killers: scientism and prosperity

1. At the outset of this chapter, it is as well to acknowledge the pioneering work done in this area by other researchers. Leading international experts in the field include David Martin, Robin Gill and Steve Bruce in Britain, and – the guru – Charles Taylor in Canada. Taylor's *A Secular Age* (2007) is generally regarded as a masterwork, though not all of his conclusions are beyond argument. As regards Australia specifically, Tom Frame's *Losing My Religion* (2007) is a most valuable text, though I get the sense that Frame, like many an earnest Australian cleric before him, has become disillusioned by a self-perceived lack of success in evangelism. This colours his thinking. For instance, he surely overreaches (at p. 298) in concluding that the majority of Australians are unwilling to invest significant effort and energy into '*any* organisation or objective' and 'are completely disinterested in matters of belief and unbelief'. I am more optimistic.

2. Bruce, *God Is Dead*, pp. 9–13 (see note 33 to the Introduction).

3. Ibid., p. 35.

4.  Fletcher, 'Anglicanism and the shaping of Australian society', p. 311 (see note 66 to Chapter 1).

5.  Roger Finke and Rodney Stark, 'Religious economies and sacred canopies: Religious mobilization in American cities, 1906', *American Sociological Review*, vol. 53, no. 1, February 1988, pp. 41–49, available online at web.ics.purdue.edu/~hoganr/SOC%20 602/Spring%202014/Finke%20and%20Stark%201988.pdf.

6.  Bruce, *God Is Dead*, p. 230.

7.  Arnold J. Toynbee, *A Study of History*, Volume V (Oxford University Press, 1961; first published 1939), p. 43.

8.  James Franklin, *What Science Knows, and How It Knows It* (Encounter Books, 2009), p. 41.

9.  As paraphrased in Franklin, *What Science Knows*, p. 46.

10. See A. Sokal and J. Bricmont, *Intellectual Impostures: Postmodern philosophers' abuse of science* (Economist Books, 1998).

11. D. Lyon, quoted in Bruce, *God Is Dead*, p. 231.

12. See Bruce, *God Is Dead*, p. 229ff.

13. Conway, *The Great Australian Stupor*, p. 207.

14. Frame, *Losing My Religion*, p. 264. If you doubt Frame's assertion, view online any of the 'debates' conducted in Australia in 2014 between two visiting Americans, Professor Laurence Krauss (a sceptic) and Dr William Lane Craig (a Christian apologist). Then read the comments thread, or any blog in which atheists and believers interact.

15. Quoted in Frame, *Losing My Religion*, p. 49.

16. Frame, *Losing My Religion*, p. 272.

17. F.B. Smith, 'Symes, Joseph (1841–1906)', *Australian Dictionary of Biography* (Melbourne University Press, 1976), accessed online at adb.anu.edu.au/biography/symes-joseph-4681/text7745. See generally Frame, *Losing My Religion*, pp. 27–36.

18. Frame, *Losing My Religion*, p. 292.

19. Michael Jensen, 'Take this Sabbath day', *Eternity*, December 2014, p. 16.

20. See Mark 2:27; Colossians 2:16–17.

21. Rupert Sheldrake, *The Science Delusion: Freeing the spirit of enquiry* (Coronet, 2012), p. 7. Sheldrake, I hasten to say, is not an advocate but a critic of these assumptions. He argues powerfully that they inhibit the advancement of science.

22. Adams, *Adams vs. God*, pp. viii, 199.

23. Quoted in Mol, *The Faith of Australians*, p. 96 (see note 41 to the Introduction).

24. Charles Lyell believed in a 'Supreme Intelligence' and thought it probable that this Being directed the course of biological evolution (*Life, Letters and Journals of Sir Charles Lyell, Bart* [Cambridge University Press, 2010; first published 1881], p. 442). Charles Darwin's religious beliefs have been the subject of much debate, yet the essential position seems clear. His faith waxed and waned appreciably, and he cannot be described as having been an orthodox Christian. He was shattered by the death of his daughter at the age of ten, an event that seems to have had a greater effect on his faith than his work on evolution. Nonetheless, towards the end of his life, in his autobiography, Darwin affirmed his belief in a Deity. His reasoning process was fairly straightforward. He thought it impossible to conclude that 'blind chance or necessity' could account for 'this immense and wonderful universe, including man'. He conceived of God as 'having an intelligent mind in some degree analogous to that of man'.

25. For a convenient summary, see Terry Mortensen, 'Young-Earth Creationist view summarised and defended', available online at answersingenesis.org/creationism/young-earth/young-earth-creationist-view-summarised-and-defended/.

26. Quoted in Bruce, *God Is Dead*, p. 29. Emphasis in original.

27. Quoted in Bruce, *God Is Dead*, p. 29.

28. Bruce, *God Is Dead*, p. 107.

29. Adams, *Adams vs. God*, p. xxv.

30. See Bruce, *God Is Dead*, pp. 106–17; Dawkins, *The God Delusion*, pp. 97–103.

31. Rawson, 'Why and how Christianity changed humanity', pp. 5–6 (see note 38 to Chapter 2).

32. Quoted in Rawson, 'Why and How Christianity Changed Humanity', p. 1.

33. See Bruce, *God Is Dead*, pp. 18, 106–07, 117.

34. Ibid., p. 106.

35. Frame, *Losing My Religion*, pp. 173–74.

36. See my article 'The best arguments for God are purely scientific', first published in *The Punch* in 2011, now available online at www.perthnow.com.au/the-best-arguments-for-god-are-purely-scientific/story-fn6mhct1-1226097084420. To say the least, it did not impress some bloggers connected with the Atheist Foundation of Australia: see www.facebook.com/atheistfoundation/posts/143553122391372. For those who may be interested in my full arguments based on natural theology, see Chapters 1 and 4 of *God, Actually*.

37. Caro et al., *For God's Sake*, p. 169.

38. See R.J. Berry and T.A. Noble (eds.), *Darwin, Creation and the Fall: Theological challenges* (Apollos, 2009), passim, esp. p. 11.

39. See, for example, Kim Sterelny, *Dawkins vs Gould: Survival of the fittest* (Icon Books, 2007).

40. Baker, *Days of Wrath*, p. 445 (see note 68 to Chapter 6).

41. Quoted in Frame, *Losing My Religion*, p. 63.

42. See Franklin, *What Science Knows*, pp. 237–51.

43. See Wells, 'Why I am not an atheist' (see note 39 to the Introduction).

44. 'Nossal, Sir Gustav Joseph Victor', Faculty of Medicine Online Museum and Archive, at sydney.edu.au/medicine/museum/mwmuseum/index.php/Nossal,_Sir_Gustav_Joseph_Victor.

45. Edward Grimaux, *Lavoisier: 1743–1794 (The development of science)* (Felix Alcan, 1888), p. 53.

46. Hart, *The 100*, p. 103 (see note 29 to Chapter 2).

47. Grimaux, *Lavoisier*, p. 53.

48. Other highly eminent Australian scientists who were steeped in religion include physician and Sydney University chancellor Henry Normand MacLaurin (1835–1914); biologist Joseph James Fletcher (1850–1926); physician and conchologist Joseph Verco (1851–1933); biologist Arthur Henry Lucas (1853–1936); botanist Joseph Maiden (1859–1925) – the founder of Wattle Day!; engineer/dam- and bridge-builder Ernest de Burgh (1863–1929); and the long-time head of the CSIRO William Ian Clunies-Ross (1899–1959). Fletcher and Lucas were the sons of Methodist clergymen. MacLaurin's only brother was a Presbyterian minister. Verco's nickname was 'Holy Joe'.

49. Arthur Jose, 'Alexander Macleay: Father of Australian zoology: An indefatigable collector', *Courier-Mail*, 7 October 1933, p. 18.

50. James Jervis, *Rev. W.B. Clarke, M.A., F.R.S., F.G.S., F.R.G.S.: The father of Australian geology* (Royal Australian Historical Society, 1944); Elena Grainger, *The Remarkable Reverend Clarke: The life and times of the father of Australian geology* (Oxford University Press, 1982).

51. J.M. Barker and D.R. Stranks, 'Rennie, Edward Henry (1852–1927)', *Australian Dictionary of Biography* (Melbourne University Press, 1988), accessed online at adb.anu.edu.au/biography/rennie-edward-henry-8182/text14307.

52. Peter Spearritt, 'Bradfield, John Job Crew (1867–1943)', *Australian Dictionary of Biography* (Melbourne University Press, 1979), accessed online at adb.anu.edu.au/biography/bradfield-john-job-crew-5331/text9011.

53. D.F. Branagan and K.A. Townley, 'Selwyn, Alfred Richard Cecil (1824–1902)', *Australian Dictionary of Biography* (Melbourne University Press, 1976), accessed online at adb.anu.edu.au/biography/selwyn-alfred-richard-cecil-4556/text7473.

54. Deirdre Morris, 'Mueller, Sir Ferdinand Jakob Heinrich von (1825–1896)', *Australian Dictionary of Biography* (Melbourne University Press, 1974), accessed online at adb.anu.edu.au/biography/mueller-sir-ferdinand-jakob-heinrich-von-4266/text6893. See also interview with F.E.H.W Kritchauff, *South Australian Register*, 12 October 1896, p. 7.

55. Harley Wood, 'Tebbutt, John (1834–1916)', *Australian Dictionary of Biography* (Melbourne University Press, 1976), accessed online at adb.anu.edu.au/biography/tebbutt-john-4696/text7779.

56. L.A. Drake, 'Pigot, Edward Francis (1858–1929)', *Australian Dictionary of Biography* (Melbourne University Press, 1988), accessed online at adb.anu.edu.au/biography/pigot-edward-francis-8048/text14037.

57. D.F. Branagan and T.G. Vallance, 'David, Sir Tannatt William Edgeworth (1858–1934)', *Australian Dictionary of Biography* (Melbourne University Press, 1981), accessed online at adb.anu.edu.au/biography/david-sir-tannatt-william-edgeworth-5894/text10033. See also the piece on Edgeworth David by Pamela Smith at springwoodhistorians.blogspot.com.au/2011/01/sir-tannatt-william-edgeworth-david.html ('The Davids were community minded and sociable and members of the local Woodford Anglican Church.').

58. J.J. Cross, 'McLaren, Samuel Bruce (1876-1916)', *Australian Dictionary of Biography* (Melbourne University Press, 1986), accessed online at adb.anu.au/biography/mclaren/samuel -bruce-7409/text12887.

59. See the entry on Eccles at www.newworldencyclopedia.org/entry/John_Carew_Eccles.

60. See interview of Bickel at www.abc.net.au/radionational/programs/healthreport/howard-florey-part-one/3552906#transcript.

61. Gwyn Macfarlane, *Howard Florey: The making of a great scientist* (Oxford University Press, 1979), p. 257.

62. Trevor Illtyd Williams, *Howard Florey, Penicillin and After* (Oxford University Press, 1984), p. 363.

63. Macfarlane, *Howard Florey*, pp. 34-36.

64. Ibid., p. 63.

65. Pat Stretton, 'Lord Florey, OM', SA History Hub, sahistoryhub.com.au/people/lord-florey-om.

66. Macfarlane, *Howard Florey*, p. 380.

67. From the order of service for the memorial service for Florey, held on 28 March 1968 in Westminster Abbey, hard copy accessible at the State Library of New South Wales.

68. Clive Hamilton and Richard Denniss, *Affluenza: When too much is never enough* (Allen & Unwin, 2005), p. 4.

69. Ibid., p. 8.

70. Patrick Commina, 'Property makes Australians the world's richest, says Credit Suisse', *Sydney Morning Herald*, 14 October 2014, available online at www.smh.com.au/business/the-economy/property-makes-australians-the-world8217s-richest-says-credit-suisse-20141014-1163ip.html#ixzz3N4TOqSB6.

71. Hamilton and Denniss, *Affluenza*, p. 113

72. Ibid.

73. Davis, *Land of Plenty* (see note 124 to Chapter 4).
74. Matthew 6:24; 1 Timothy 6:10.
75. Quoted in Frame, *Losing My Religion*, p. 9.
76. Bruce, *God Is Dead*, pp. 25–26.
77. Mol, *The Faith of Australians*, p. 220.
78. Thompson, *Religion in Australia*, p. 111 (see note 29 to the Introduction).
79. There are various ways in which the American religious experience might be differentiated from Australia's. For a start, the early American colonies were founded for religious reasons. The original settlers in 1620 (the Pilgrims) were fleeing from persecution in England: the very first thing they did at New Plymouth was conduct a Christian ceremony. More generally, the history of the United States, even more so than the history of Australia, has been one of multicultural immigration. For centuries, the Churches were the critical entry point for immigrants into their new society. Another factor in the United States is the weaker role of the State; there remains a larger role for the Churches in the provision of charity and other community-based activities. But the best explanation for the apparent exception of the US to the 'secularisation paradigm' is that it is not really an exception at all. Religion is losing power and prestige there just as it is across the West, and increased material affluence is a substantial factor. The overall effects are masked somewhat by the US's uniquely diverse federal structure: some pockets of the country are much more intensely religious than others. (See generally Bruce, *God Is Dead*, pp. 204–28.)
80. For a concerted argument that Australians have always been obsessed with money, see Donald Horne, *Money Made Us* (Penguin Books, 1976).
81. McQueen, *A New Britannia*, p. 17 (see note 135 to Chapter 1).
82. Ibid., p. 127.
83. Quoted in Martin, *Henry Parkes*, p. 31 (see note 65 to Chapter 4).
84. Quoted in Shaw, *The Story of Australia*, p. 302 (see note 158 to Chapter 1).
85. Conway, *The Great Australian Stupor*, p. 203.
86. Ibid., p. 232.
87. Tony Abbott, 'Philosopher of hope and truth', *Weekend Australian*, 21–22 March 2009, p. 20.
88. Rick Morton, 'Crunch time for Apple Isle in doldrums', *Weekend Australian*, 16 August 2014, p. 17.
89. For an argument that the worship of money adversely affected religious belief and observance even in the mid-nineteenth century, see Jackson, *Australians and the Christian God*, p. 71 (see note 27 to the Introduction).
90. See Hirst, *Sense and Nonsense in Australian History*, pp. 136ff (see note 143 to Chapter 1).
91. See generally Bruce, *God Is Dead*, p. 27.
92. Ibid., p. 8. See also Mol, *The Faith of Australians*, p. 220; Fletcher, 'Anglicanism and the shaping of Australian society', p. 304; Rawson, 'Why and how Christianity changed humanity', p. 16.
93. See the website of the Australian Institute of Health and Welfare, at www.aihw.gov.au/deaths/life-expectancy/.
94. Blainey, *A Shorter History of Australia*, pp. 54–55.
95. Grimshaw et al., *Creating a Nation*, pp. 118–20 (see note 121 to Chapter 1).
96. Quoted in Grimshaw et al., *Creating a Nation*, p. 120.
97. Allison, *The Cruelty of Heresy*, p. 163 (see note 47 to the Introduction).
98. Frame, *Losing My Religion*, p. 66; Judd and Cable, *Sydney Anglicans*, p. 295 (see note 44 to Chapter 1).
99. See Elizabeth Drescher, *Tweet If You {heart} Jesus: practicing Church in the digital reformation* (Morehouse, 2011).

100. Thompson, *Religion in Australia*, p. 111.

101. Davis, *Land of Plenty*, pp. 257–58 (re gambling).

102. Hogan, *The Sectarian Strand*, p. 234 (see note 55 to the Introduction).

103. See Pope Benedict XVI's encyclical *Caritas in Veritate* (2009).

104. The seminal text is Arnold's *Philistinism in England and America*, published as Volume X of *The Complete Prose Works of Matthew Arnold*. See also, in an Australian context, Horne, *Money Made Us*, p. 210.

105. Jackson, *Australians and the Christian God*, pp. 70–71 (referring to the Rev. Ralph Mansfield, a Wesleyan Methodist in New South Wales, and the Rev. John Wollaston, an Anglican in Western Australia).

106. Conway, *The Great Australian Stupor*, p. 254.

107. Adams, *Adams vs. God*, p. xxii.

108. Bruce, *God Is Dead*, p. 25.

109. See the Australian Psychological Society's *Stress and Wellbeing in Australia Survey 2014*, available online at www.psychology.org.au/Assets/Files/2014-NPW-Key-findings-survey.pdf. A key finding was that just over seven in ten Australians (72 per cent) reported that current stress was having at least some impact on physical health, with almost one in five (17 per cent) reporting that current stress was having a strong to very strong impact on physical health. Financial issues were the leading cause of stress for Australians, with nearly half of all participants (49 per cent) citing it as a cause of stress.

110. Davis, *Land of Plenty*, p. 113.

111. See Conway, *The Great Australian Stupor*, p. 50 ('The [1930s] Depression warped the psychological attitudes of a whole generation … The worst possible disaster was the loss of material security').

112. In *Affluenza*, Clive Hamilton and Richard Denniss cited a 2002 survey which found that an amazing 62 per cent of Australians believed they could not afford to buy everything they 'really needed'. This included almost half of the richest 20 per cent of households (p. 59).

113. Hamilton and Denniss, *Affluenza*, p. 5.

114. See Jackson, *Australians and the Christian God*, pp. 28–29.

## Chapter 10: What is at stake?

1. Bently Hart, *Atheist Delusions*, p. 6 (see note 26, Chapter 2).

2. Ibid., p. 185.

3. Physicist Stephen Hawking's declaration in 1995 on a US television programme called *Reality on the Rocks: Beyond Our Ken*.

4. Personally I believe that there will be both punishment and (eventual) reward for everyone in the afterlife. In other words, punishment will be neither eternal nor retributive, but purgatorial. This, of course, has long been a hotly contested area of Christian theology. My own position is closer to the Eastern Orthodox tradition, and is very much a minority view among Australian Protestants. For a stimulating discussion of these issues, with which I substantially agree, see Kevin Hart, 'Who, then, shall be saved? The Lord's Prayer and religious pluralism', *Religion and Ethics*, ABC, 18 February 2014, available online at www.abc.net.au/religion/articles/2014/02/18/3947419.htm.

5. Hart, *Atheist Delusions*, p. 221.

6. Ibid., p. 226.

7. Waleed Aly, 'If sport is to be our uncritically loved parallel world, it must prove itself worthy', *Sydney Morning Herald*, 19 September 2014.

8. Alain de Botton, 'Why religion is too important to be left to the religious', *Religion and Ethics*, ABC, 16 February 2012, available online at www.abc.net.au/religion/

articles/2012/02/16/3432328.htm. De Botton has written a whole book on this subject, *Religion for Atheists: A non-believer's guide to the uses of religion* (Penguin, 2012).

9. Hart, *Atheist Delusions*, p. 227.

10. Ibid., p. 228.

11. See Peter Singer, *Practical Ethics* (Cambridge University Press, 3rd edition, 2011), esp. chapters 6 and 7.

12. Rachel Woodlock, 'Proselytising for humanism: Just how irreligious are these atheists?', *Religion and Ethics*, ABC, 3 August 2012, available online at www.abc.net.au/religion/articles/2012/08/03/3560142.htm. Woodlock is a Muslim.

13. Consider Thomas John Ley (1880–1947), a big-name conservative politician in New South Wales in the 1920s who campaigned for years on issues of 'Protestant values' and 'law and order' (as well as blatant anti-Catholicism). At one stage he was minister of justice. In the 1940s, by which time he was living in England, Ley was convicted of killing his mistress's lover. The 'Chalkpit Murderer', as he was dubbed, spent the rest of his life in Broadmoor Prison. See Baiba Berzins, 'Ley, Thomas John (1880–1947)', *Australian Dictionary of Biography* (Melbourne University Press, 1986), accessed online at adb.anu.edu.au/biography/ley-thomas-john-7191/text12435, p.

14. Henri Blocher, *Evil and the Cross: An analytical look at the problem of pain* (Kregel, 1994).

15. Mark Coleridge, 'Seeing Christ amid the mess: Reflections on the Pope, the Church and the Australian situation', *Religion and Ethics*, ABC, 8 March 2013, available online at www.abc.net.au/religion/articles/2013/03/08/3711447.htm.

16. See the exchange on this issue between Jane Caro (atheist) and Simon Smart (Christian) in Caro et al., *For God's Sake*, pp. 98–107 (see note 12 to Chapter 7).

17. Faith without deeds too often morphs into what the contemporary American Protestant theologian Jim Wallis has called 'Christian narcissism' or 'Christian triumphalism'. Many Protestants believe that faith alone – a gift conferred by the grace of God – is the key to salvation. But as St Paul asked rhetorically, 'Shall we continue in sin, that grace may abound?' (Romans 6:1). Avoiding this trap has been a recurring preoccupation of the Catholic Church since the Council of Trent, convened in 1545–63 during the Counter Reformation. It was also a dominant concern of John Wesley, the great English Methodist whose ideas had such a strong influence on nineteenth-century Australia (see Chapter 3). Wesley and his followers scorned shrill and hollow forms of religious observance, unconnected with any 'motivating spirit of love' or 'personal demonstration of holiness'. See Alister McGrath, *Christian Theology: An introduction* (4th edition, Blackwell Publishing, 2007), pp. 49–50, 52–53, 59, 352–53, 377–80.

18. Peter Barnes, 'Two types of righteousness', *The Pulse*, October–November 2014, p. 28.

19. Hughes, *The Fatal Shore*, p. 29. See generally on the rule of law, Vines, *Law and Justice in Australia*, pp. 111–12 (note 8 to Chapter 1).

20. The most influential legal positivists in English history were Jeremy Bentham (1748–1832), John Austin (1790–1859), and H.L.A. Hart (1907–92). In Australia, positivism's most eminent judicial champion was Sir Owen Dixon (1886–1972), who used the phrase 'strict and complete legalism' in his address upon taking the oath of office in Sydney as chief justice of the High Court of Australia on 21 April 1952. See generally on positivism, Vines, *Law and Justice in Australia*, pp. 337ff. See also Ayres, *Owen Dixon*, pp. 23–33.

21. See the Report of the Law Reform Commission of Ireland on Oaths and Affirmations (LRC 34–1990), available online at www.lawreform.ie/_fileupload/Reports/rOaths.htm.

22. Bruce, *God Is Dead*, p. 55.

23. Hugh MacKay, *Reinventing Australia: The mind and mood of Australia in the 90s* (Angus & Robertson, 1993), p. 86.

24. Thomas Halik, 'Europe after secularisation: What future has Christianity on the Continent?', *Religion and Ethics*, ABC, 16 September 2014, p. 4, available online at www.abc.net.au/religion/articles/2014/09/16/4088574.htm.

25. The phrase is John Milbank's. See 'Christian vision of society puts economics and politics in their place', *Religion and Ethics*, ABC, 8 December 2011, p. 2, available online at www.abc.net.au/religion/articles/2011/12/08/3386474.htm.

26. See, for example Phillip Hudson, 'Backbenchers feel jilted as Coalition woos the cross bench', *The Australian*, 8 September 2014.

27. Quoted in John Murdoch, *Sir Joe: A biographical sketch of Sir Joseph Cook* (Silverdale Historical Production, 1972), p. 6.

28. See, for example, on the treatment of the federal Liberal Party dissidents on the issue of asylum seekers, Margot O'Neill, *Blind Conscience* (New South, 2008).

29. Quoted in full at press-pubs.uchicago.edu/founders/documents/v1ch13s7.html.

30. Quoted in Cochrane, *Colonial Ambition*, p. 300 (see note 61 to Chapter 4).

31. See Philip Luker, *Phillip Adams: The ideas man: A life revealed* (Jojo Publishing, 2011), pp. 137–38. Adams came up with the idea in discussion with Bill Kelty. See also Brennan, *Acting on Conscience*, p. 86.

32. See Murray Goot, 'Public opinion and the democratic deficit: Australia and the war against Iraq', *Australian Humanities Review*, May 2003, available online at www.australianhumanitiesreview.org/archive/Issue-May-2003/goot.html.

33. David Marr, *Political Animal: The making of Tony Abbott* (Black Inc., 2013), pp. 63–64.

34. Ibid., p. 62.

35. Ibid., pp. 119–20.

36. Crossbencher Tony Windsor (the former federal MHR for New England) reported that Abbott had used words to this effect during negotiations with him after the deadlocked 2010 election.

37. Sheldrake, *The Science Delusion*, passim, esp. pp. 127–28 (see note 21 to Chapter 9).

38. Conor Cunningham, 'Theology must save science from naturalism', *Religion and Ethics*, ABC, 22 May 2012, p. 3, available online at www.abc.net.au/religion/articles/2012/05/22/3508607.htm.

39. Quoted in Cunningham, 'Theology must save science from naturalism', p. 3.

40. Francis Spufford, *Unapologetic: Why, despite everything, Christianity can still make surprising emotional sense* (HarperOne, 2013), p. 32.

41. See A.M. Smith, C.E. Rissel, J. Richters, A.E. Grulich and R.O. De Visser, 'Sex in Australia: Sexual identity, sexual attraction and sexual experience among a representative sample of adults', *Australian and New Zealand Journal of Public Health*, vol. 27, no. 2, pp. 138–45 (2003) (as to the figure of around 2 per cent of the population in Australia being gay); Dan Harrison, '40% of gay couples Christian', *Sydney Morning Herald*, 29 June 2012, available online at www.smh.com.au/national/40-of-gay-couples-christian-20120628-2157d.html (as to the likelihood of gay couples being Christian, a conclusion based on an analysis of answers to the 2011 census).

42. See, for a range of views on Francis, Scott Stephens, 'The Francis phenomenon, or media infatuation? Reflections on the anniversary of a pontificate', *Religion and Ethics*, ABC, 13 March 2014.

43. I mean 'visible unity' in the sense ultimately endorsed by the great American Episcopalian William Reed Huntington, in his famous lecture 'The four theories of visible Church unity' (1909): 'a simple creed, a varied worship, a generous polity'. I do

*not* mean the term in the Donatist or even Augustinian sense. See McGrath, *Christian Theology*, pp. 395–96.

44. See note 4 above.

45. See John Dickson, 'Letting go of the Lord's Prayer in parliament', *Religion and Ethics*, ABC, 17 January 2014, available online at www.abc.net.au/news/2014-01-17/dickson-parliament-prayer/5203930.

46. Frame, *Losing My Religion*, p. 19.

47. Quoted in Martin, *Henry Parkes*, p. 352 (see note 65 to Chapter 4).

48. As to foreign aid: Australian Christians do not merely talk about helping the poor overseas. Since the nineteenth century, countless individuals from all denominations have actively done so – either in person or by the donation of money to Christian humanitarian organisations. There are far too many organisations to list, but two worthy contemporary examples are Caritas Australia (the Australian arm of the worldwide Catholic Agency for Aid and Development) and Micah Challenge, a self-described 'global movement of Christian agencies, Churches, groups and individuals which aims to deepen people's engagement with the poor and to help reduce poverty as an integral part of our Christian faith'. Its Australian head office is in Sydney. Moreover, as regards foreign aid proper, some of the loudest and most heartfelt criticisms of the recent cuts made by the Abbott Government to our foreign aid budget have come from the Churches – the Australian Catholic Bishops Conference, for example, and leading Baptists such as the Revs Tim Costello and Keith Jobberns. As to asylum seekers and refugees: it is far too often overlooked, by both the Right and the Left of politics, that since the *Tampa* and 'children overboard' episodes of August–November 2001 the Australian Churches have been conspicuously outspoken in their criticism of many aspects of Federal Government policy. Countless sermons have been preached, media releases issued, books and articles written – and not merely by 'liberal' Christians. Otherwise conservative Evangelicals have also been vocal and eloquent. As recently as 24 January 2015, the president of the Australian Christian Lobby, Lyle Shelton, called for a big increase in Australia's intake of refugees.

49. See the website of the Lowy Institute, which has an excellent section devoted to Australian foreign-aid policy, www.lowyinstitute.org/issues/australian-foreign-aid.

50. Article 1.A.2 of the UN Convention Relating to the Status of Refugees (1951), as amended by the 1967 Protocol.

51. As things stand, most asylum seekers who make it to Australia by boat are found by the relevant legal authorities to be genuine refugees – in the period 2010–13 around 90 per cent of applications were successful. Sadly, for many Australians, this is the true 'problem'. See Bianca Hall, 'Overwhelming majority of boat arrivals deemed to be refugees', *Sydney Morning Herald*, 20 May 2013, available online at www.smh.com.au/federal-politics/political-news/overwhelming-majority-of-boat-arrivals-deemed-to-be-refugees-20130519-2juty.html.

52. On August 2013, during the federal election campaign, the Liberal and National Parties released a policy document entitled 'The Coalition's policy for a regional *deterrence* framework to combat people smuggling'.

53. Paul Brown, 'OECD: Australia worst greenhouse gas emitter per person', *Climate News Network*, 15 January 2014, available online at https://independentaustralia.net/environment/environment-display/australia-worst-greenhouse-gas-emissions-in-oecd-per-person,6064.

54. Interview of Tim Winton by Dr Rachael Kohn, ABC RN, 26 December 2004, transcript available online at www.abc.net.au/radionational/programs/spiritofthings/tim-wintons-faith/3429900.

55. Consider, for example, this excruciating exchange on the ABC's *Q & A* programme of 5 April 2010:

AUDIENCE MEMBER: When it comes to asylum seekers, what would Jesus do?

TONY ABBOTT: Well, Jesus wouldn't have put his hand up to lead the Liberal Party, I suspect.

TONY JONES: Okay. But someone who believed in principles [that Jesus] espoused did do that, so it's a legitimate question.

ABBOTT: Yeah, don't forget Jesus drove the traders from the Temple as well.

TONY JONES: What's the point of that? What's the analogy?

ABBOTT: The point is Jesus didn't say yes to everyone. I mean Jesus knew that there was a place for everything and it is not necessarily everyone's place to come to Australia.

It would be hard to think of a less apt Biblical analogy than the one Abbott advanced. Jesus objected to commercial activity being carried on within the surrounds of the Jews' sacred Temple in Jerusalem because it was selfish and blasphemous behaviour contrary to any number of His teachings: see Luke 19:45–46; John 2:12–17. If Abbott wanted to grapple with a relevant section of the Gospels, he should have gone straight to the Parable of the Good Samaritan or the passages about welcoming aliens and strangers. On another occasion Abbott proffered a different line, one justly described by David Marr as 'almost too embarrassing to put down in black and white'. Responding to the observation that Christ's own parents were refugees in Egypt (they fled there shortly after Jesus' birth to escape the murderous Herod: Luke 2:13–18), Abbott's retort was that the Holy Family had fled to the *nearest* sanctuary. His point presumably was that most asylum seekers bypass countries which are closer to their place of origin than Australia. They are thus sneaky forum shoppers rather than genuine refugees. A variation on this theme is that it is 'un-Christian' for asylum seekers to enter Australia by 'the back door'. All these 'arguments', and others like them, have been refuted by theologians both Catholic and Protestant.

56. 'Refugees: A challenge to solidarity' (1992), available online at www.vatican.va/roman_curia/pontifical_councils/corunum/documents/rc_pc_corunum_doc_25061992_refugees_en.html. There are equivalent statements from Protestant sources: see, for example, the statement issued by the Archbishop of Canterbury on World Refugee Day in 2013, available online at www.archbishopofcanterbury.org/articles.php/5080/archbishop-justin-on-world-refugee-day.

57. See the transcript of the Cardinal's statement to the UN reproduced at en.radiovaticana.va/news/2014/09/24/vatican_address_to_2014_un_climate_change_summit/1107182.

58. See generally, Tony Kevin, *A Certain Maritime Incident – the Sinking of SIEV X* (Scribe, 2004).

59. See note 49 above.

60. Quoted in Luker, *Phillip Adams*, p. 170.

# ACKNOWLEDGMENTS

I have several people to thank in connection with *Post-God Nation?*
Early in 2012, Greg Clarke and John Sandeman at the Bible Society of Australia commissioned me to write a book about the religious beliefs of Australia's prime ministers; it was published the following year as *In God They Trust?* That assignment boosted my confidence as a writer and whetted my appetite for knowledge about the role of religious faith in the shaping of Australian history and society. Both Greg and John are founts of wisdom and good humour.

My commissioning editor at ABC Books/HarperCollins, Amruta Slee, saw the potential for a book about the decline of faith in modern-day Australia. She gave me a precious opportunity, and, throughout the writing process, steered me in the right direction, whenever I had wandered from the track. My other editors, Mary Rennie, Sally Collings and Emma Dowden, struck a lovely balance between friendly encouragement and rigorous constructive criticism. Their intelligent attention to detail was much appreciated.

Professor Edwin Judge, of Macquarie University, provided generous assistance in relation to Chapter 2.

Along the way, throughout the whole process of research, writing and editing, I drew strength from my family, especially my beautiful wife Sally (to whom the book is dedicated) and my father Evan Williams, still the best wordsmith I know. My wonderful daughters are a constant source of inspiration, as well as keenly delivered advice, both sought and unsought.

I am also extremely grateful to my church family at Chatswood Presbyterian in Sydney, not least the Reverend Jeff Read and Carmelina

Read; our weekly Bible-study convenors, Bay and Emma Warburton; and our dear friends Jacqui Dawson and David Jury.

I hasten to add that (along with all errors and omissions) the opinions in the book are entirely my own. Literally no one will agree with me on everything. Indeed, any Christian writer nowadays must expect to evoke cries of dissent, not only from the loud secular voices in society but – on contestable points of theology – from passionate fellow believers. It is right that this be so. I believe very strongly that God deliberately left an element of uncertainty in the world. There is nothing wrong with vigorous debate provided it is conducted respectfully, and with an open mind. The search for God's Truth is the ultimate goal.

**Roy Williams**
**1 March 2015**